MW00532852

CONTESTING POWER
Resistance and Everyday Social Relations in South Asia

CONTESTING POWER

Resistance and Everyday Social Relations in South Asia

Edited by

DOUGLAS HAYNES
and
GYAN PRAKASH

UNIVERSITY OF CALIFORNIA PRESS
Berkeley · Los Angeles

University of California Press
Berkeley and Los Angeles, California

© 1991 by Oxford University Press
First University of California Press edition published 1992 by arrangement with
Oxford University Press

Library of Congress Cataloging-in-Publication Data

Contesting power : resistance and everyday social relations in South Asia /
  edited by Douglas Haynes and Gyan Prakash. - 1st University of California
  Press ed.
      p.   cm.
      ISBN 0-520-07585-4 (alk. paper)
      1. Social movements-India, South. 2. Social structure-India, South. 3.
Government, Resistance to-India. 4. Power (Social sciences) I. Haynes,
Douglas E. II. Prakash, Gyan.
  HN690.S67C66 1992
  303.48'4'09548-dc20
  91-38867

Printed in the United States of America

9 8 7 6 5 4 3 2 1

Contents

Preface

This volume of essays emerged initially from two panels on 'Modes of Protest in South Asia', organized by the co-editors at the Annual Conference on South Asia at the University of Wisconsin and at the meetings of the American Historical Association. Originally these panels were prompted by certain dissatisfactions we had, on the one hand, with the tendency in much of traditional historiography to relegate resistance to a rather secondary place in scholarship, and, on the other, with the rather single-stranded emphasis on dramatic, violent, and confrontational struggles in recent literature which had taken up the study of resistance in earnest. We organized the two panels around the theme of 'non-confrontational' forms of struggle in order to explore a middle ground between violent struggle and mere submission to authority. When we set out the proposal for this volume the theme of resistance outside the dramatic and confrontational was again the central focus. Though we wished to dictate no common theoretical perspective to the contributors, we did suggest to them that the themes of 'everyday resistance' formulated by James Scott and of 'avoidance protest' developed by Michael Adas might provide useful starting points for their analyses.

As the contributors, including the co-editors, worked on their individual essays, however, the initial problematic set out for the volume proved to be just that—a starting point. Those authors who found the concepts of everyday resistance and avoidance protest still useful to their studies employed these notions in ways that Scott and Adas could hardly have anticipated. Some authors, by the mere act of placing these notions in novel contexts, introduced analytic perspectives not present in the original concepts. Others felt that the theories needed to be modified in rather serious ways; still others found the concepts of rather limited value to their own approaches to 'non-confrontational' resistance. These varied reflections have enabled the volume to develop a number of different perspectives on the original theme of 'everyday resistance' and offer a richer understanding of the place of resistance in social practice.

The introduction to this volume represents the co-editors' view of how the essays collectively enrich and advance the analysis of resistance. Specifically, we suggest there that power and resistance be understood as phenomena which constantly condition each other in everyday life. But in developing this portrait of the collective significance of these essays, we by no means wish to implicate the other contributors in our perspective. The introduction draws upon individual essays only to elaborate and illustrate our views on power and resistance; it seeks neither to interpret individual essays nor to impose a common perspective on all the contributors. An alternative overview, written by Michael Adas, comes in the concluding essay of the volume.

We would like to thank many people who have stimulated our thinking as this project has unfolded. We would first of all like to acknowledge all of the participants in the two panels. Besides most of the authors included here, these included Anand Yang, Eugene Irschick, Robert Frykenberg, Geraldine Forbes, Nita Kumar, Stewart Gordon, and David Ludden. David Ludden's spirited comments at the American Historical Association panels were especially invaluable. We would also like to express our gratitude toward others not directly involved with the project who took time to make useful comments on parts of the manuscript or who contributed in other ways, including Cynthia Holton, Ramachandra Guha, David Hardiman, and Susanna B. C. Devalle. Finally, we would particularly like to acknowledge James Scott and Michael Adas, whose work has obviously been a major source of stimulation, and who generously gave their support to the volume in various stages of its development.

Another version of Veena Talwar Oldenburg's 'Lifestyle as Resistance' appeared in *Feminist Studies*, xvi, no. 2 (Summer 1990), pp. 259–88; we thank the journal.

Notes on the Contributors

MICHAEL ADAS is Professor of History at Rutgers University at New Brunswick. He has written several books, including *The Burma Delta: Economic Development and Social Change on an Asian Rice Frontier*, *Prophets of Rebellion: Millenarian Protest Movements against the European Colonial Order* and *Machines as the Measure of Men: Science, Technology, and Ideologies of Western Dominance*.

RAJNARAYAN CHANDAVARKAR is Assistant Director of Research, History, at Cambridge University, and Fellow of Trinity College, Cambridge. He is the author of *The Origins of Industrial Capitalism in India: Business Strategies and the Working Classes in Bombay, 1900–1940* (Cambridge: forthcoming), and of several articles on the working class and capitalism in colonial India.

NICHOLAS B. DIRKS is Professor of History and Anthropology at the University of Michigan. He is author of *The Hollow Crown: Ethnohistory of an Indian Kingdom* (Cambridge: 1987), and of many articles on South Indian history and anthropology.

DOUGLAS HAYNES is Associate Professor of History at Dartmouth College in New Hampshire. He is the author of *Rhetoric and Ritual in Colonial India: The Shaping of a Public Culture in Surat City* (forthcoming from the University of California Press in the USA, and Oxford University Press in India).

ROSALIND O'HANLON is Fellow of Clare College, Cambridge University. She has written many essays on modern Indian history, and is the author of *Caste, Conflict, and Ideology: Mahatma Jotirao Phule and Low Caste Protest in Nineteenth-Century Western India* (Cambridge: 1985).

VEENA TALWAR OLDENBURG is Assistant Professor of History at Baruch College, City University of New York. She is the author of *The Making of Colonial Lucknow, 1856–1877* (Princeton: 1984; rpt. Oxford India Paperbacks, 1989), and is now working on a major study of dowry in colonial Punjab.

GYAN PRAKASH is Assistant Professor of History at Princeton University. He is the author of *Bonded Histories: Genealogies of Labor Servitude in Colonial India* (Cambridge: 1990).

JOHN D. ROGERS is a Research Fellow at the Center of South Asian and Indian Ocean Studies, Tufts University. He is the author of *Crime, Justice and Society in Colonial Sri Lanka* (London and Riverdale: 1987), and numerous articles on the modern history of Sri Lanka.

I

Introduction: The Entanglement of Power and Resistance

DOUGLAS HAYNES and GYAN PRAKASH

Dramatic confrontations between the dominant and the dominated—manifest in riots, rebellions, revolutions and organized political movements—have always constituted a major source of attention for social historians, sociologists and political scientists, particularly those keen to find among the oppressed the universal urge toward liberation. But the tendency to focus on periods when confrontational protest and organized struggle directly and consciously challenge the social order has frequently allowed two assumptions to reassert themselves: first, that relations of power enjoy a rather uncomplicated and unchallenged life until moments of societal upheaval; and second, that, in 'normal' times, the cultural practices and identities of the dominated remain firmly grounded in a terrain mapped by the dominant. In recent years scholars operating within a variety of disciplines and studying a variety of areas have begun to question such assumptions by shifting their focus away from extraordinary moments of collective protest. Work done within the traditional field of social movement theory, most notably in the writings of James Scott, has increasingly turned its gaze toward the examination of more enduring, 'everyday' forms of resistance constantly present in the behaviours, traditions and consciousness of the subordinate. On a very different front, emerging research on the construction of class, gender, race, and colonial relations, often inspired by 'post-structuralist' literary criticism, projects power as always tenuous, and portrays the cultural practices of subordinate groups as ever-ready to tear through the fabric of hegemonic forms.

This volume aims at extending and re-examining the perspectives of these approaches through eight essays that explore the place of resistance in South Asian society and history. Covering groups from peasants to urban labourers, from women to merchants, and sometimes employing unconventional sources and methods to supplement traditional archival research, the essays collectively depict a rich variety of non-confrontational resistances and contestatory behaviours previously neglected in the study of the region's history. But at the same time, these essays taken together suggest that the notion of resistance be rethought so that it can be applied to a much wider range of socio-cultural practices and take into account the ways in which the subjectivity of the dominated is constrained, modified and conditioned by power relations.

This introductory essay seeks to draw out some of the implications that we, the authors of this introduction, feel are suggested by the essays as a whole. Collectively, the essays highlight the 'everydayness' of resistance in social life. At the most obvious level, this means that many of the individual contributors look at what James Scott calls 'everyday forms of resistance', i.e. at forms of struggle present in the behaviours and cultural practices of subordinated peoples at times other than those of overt revolt. We do not wish to claim, however, that everyday life constitutes an especially privileged site for studying resistance; moments of collective insurrection, we recognize, do indeed occur with some frequency in most societies and they often have extraordinary implications and effects. Rather than insist that one form of resistance is more significant than the other, these essays establish the 'everydayness' of struggle in yet another sense: by placing all forms of resistance within the ordinary life of power. Such an approach has two quite different implications. On the one hand, it means that the authors study the ways in which the social relations of daily existence are enmeshed in, and transfigured by, resistance, both extraordinary and 'everyday'. Power is depicted in these pages as constantly being fractured by the struggles of the subordinate. Social structure, rather than being a monolithic, autonomous entity, unchallenged except during dramatic instances of revolt, appears more commonly as a constellation of contradictory and contestatory processes. But many of the essays also indicate that episodes of resistance themselves rarely mark pure forms of escape from domination; struggle is constantly being conditioned by the structures of social and political power. In sum, neither domination nor resistance is autonomous; the two are so entangled that it becomes difficult to analyse one without discussing the other.

Such a perspective involves a departure from one common approach in social movement literature: the tendency to depict resistance as a response to radical dislocation in the nature of the social order, often from some idealized social past of harmonious relations. If resistance is an everyday phenomenon, then it need not always be seen as a product of extraordinary transformations in material and social conditions. Furthermore, even in the most commonplace of circumstances, resistance has important consequences for power. Power must be produced through social processes where it is ranged against struggle, and this consistently alters its form; domination, rather than being solid and stable under 'normal' circumstances, must be secured. If these essays sometimes first map out the objectives of dominant groups before proceeding to discuss the efforts of subordinate peoples to contest these objectives, it is often only as a strategy of explanation; the same essays also demonstrate how social structures were profoundly shaped by struggles that stopped short of confrontation and violence. Other essays, such as Veena Talwar Oldenburg's piece on the courtesans of Lucknow, tend to renounce this form of explanation altogether, showing how struggle was embedded in attitudes and lifestyles that exist under ordinary circumstances when no unusual threat is present.

Many of the essays also suggest a departure from conventional understandings of resistance as always overt and conscious. Resistance, we would argue, should be defined as those behaviours and cultural practices by subordinate groups that contest hegemonic social formations, that threaten to unravel the strategies of domination; 'consciousness' need not be essential to its constitution. Seemingly innocuous behaviours can have unintended yet profound consequences for the objectives of the dominant or the shape of a social order. Some of the essays in this volume demonstrate how rather commonplace actions, often within the bounds of legality or legitimate expression, could undercut hegemonic projects and ideological presumptions. In John Rogers' essay, ordinary Sri Lankans, resorting to the legal procedures of the colonial court system during the nineteenth century, for decades thwarted state efforts to control public gambling and to produce more disciplined subjects. In Raj Chandavarkar's study, rather unexceptional acts by mill-workers in Bombay, such as absenteeism and foot-dragging, effectively short-circuited much of the employers' effort to 'rationalize' the processes of production in the textile industry. Even relatively privileged groups can participate in resistance when engaged with the state. Haynes's essay, for instance, shows how small-scale struggles of wealthy merchants, often lodged in the rulers' own principles of justice, effectively deflated colonial attempts to 'modernize' the city of Surat. Thus, people in a great variety of class positions taking a wide range of steps can contribute to the disruption of the agendas of power. In short, it is the context and the consequences that render certain actions contestatory. Obviously, we rule out as resistance those actions of dominant groups that only further their domination. Nor can factional conflicts between vertically aligned sets of people over the spoils of power and privilege be included within this category. But the struggles of subordinated peoples need not be dramatic or informed by conscious ideologies of opposition to seriously affect relations of domination. To use resistance in its more traditional sense would mean not to consider the very processes by which power is often tested and eroded by the actions of the subordinate, and by which it reconstitutes itself in response. Prevailing approaches to resistance often also impede a fuller understanding of the ways in which struggles in everyday life can grow into large-scale and conscious challenges to the political or social order.

I

Given, on the one hand, little record of large-scale, violent revolutions or rebellions, and on the other, a strong legacy of more modest means of struggle, South Asia might seem an excellent ground for illuminating the place of non-confronta-

tional forms of struggle in ordinary social and political relations. It is now a commonplace that India's movement for
independence, led by the apostle of civil disobedience Mahatma
Gandhi, drew upon traditions of non-violent resistance that
had deep roots in the past.[1] Groups and individuals in South
Asia have often demonstrated their dissatisfactions with the
social order through acts of avoidance, most dramatically by
fleeing their plantations, villages, or cities *en masse*, but also
through smaller, everyday actions such as foot-dragging, sitting
outside an enemy's door until he relents in his behaviour,
neglecting to pay rents or taxes until a grievance is settled, and
simply ignoring intrusive laws and edicts. Yet, as Michael
Adas argues in the concluding essay of this volume, it is precisely the contestatory character of South Asian social relations and cultural life that eluded most scholars who have
worked on the subcontinent's history or social protest more
generally. The overwhelming image of India's subordinate
peoples—women, peasants, industrial workers and low-caste
labourers—produced in historical and anthropological scholarship has been that of passivity. Specialists and non-specialists
alike have presumed Hinduism, patriarchy, social dependency,
and especially caste, to be obstacles to the development of a
capacity for resistance on the part of South Asia's underclasses.
Stereotypes of Indians as 'feminine', dependent, quiescent and
consensus-oriented abound, not only in the writings of colonial
administrators but also in those of contemporary social scientists. Perhaps it should not surprise us that Lord Lytton, Viceroy
of India, could write in 1876: 'Politically speaking, the Indian
peasantry is an inert mass. If it moves at all, it will move in
obedience not to its British benefactors, but to its native
chiefs and princes, however tyrannical they may be.'[2] But
these representations have been regularly reproduced in more
contemporary writing, even among scholars who have strongly
identified with the subordinate and the cause of social justice.
Barrington Moore, a distinguished sociologist concerned with
the comparative study of dictatorship and democracy, concluded that there was a 'willing acceptance of social degradation' among Indians that stemmed from the oppressive character of the caste system and of Hindu cultural norms.[3] Such
an attitude obviously prevented any understanding of how

caste and Hinduism could themselves be grounds of serious contestation within South Asian society.[4]

To a great extent, these understandings had their historical roots in Orientalism, i.e. in the long-lived scholarly tradition, originating with late-eighteenth-century British administrators. This tradition insisted that the essence of India existed in a number of key Hindu classical scriptures such as the Vedas, the Codes of Manu and the Shastras, texts that often did prescribe hierarchical ideals.[5] The selection and canonization of Brahmanical texts that validated hierarchy received support and elaboration from Indian interpreters—always male, usually Brahman, and often upper class—who further reinforced the image of Indian society as static and consensual. The key assumptions of nineteenth-century Orientalist scholarship—that Indian society stands in opposition to a dynamic and historical West and that the way to study India is through certain core texts rather than through the experienced social life of its peoples—made their way into subsequent generations of anthropological and historical literature. Many of the more particular perceptions and judgements of early Orientalist thought also retained their authority as truth, penetrating studies that did not depend on textual analysis, such as the work of anthropologists who had spent lengthy periods of fieldwork in Indian villages.[6] For historians, the problem was perhaps compounded by the fact that the chief sources of their research materials were either the British civil servants or the 'educated Indians', who themselves often unconsciously appropriated colonial understandings and prejudices. The considerable literature on movements led by the Indian National Congress did little to dismantle the orthodox conception of South Asian society since nationalist protest was seen as having its origins in contact with the West. Even Marxist scholars sometimes found the development of alternative social paradigms resting upon struggle and conflict, rather than upon consensus and hierarchy, difficult to conceive when they discussed the 'traditional' social order, i.e. society before the intrusion of capitalist institutions and western ideologies from Europe.

This book constitutes part of a larger effort by contemporary historians to 'unlearn' the traditional models that derive from

Orientalist understandings and to construct new approaches that stress the place of resistance in the construction of everyday social relations in South Asia.

The process of questioning older paradigms about South Asian society has been taken up in much recent writing, but nowhere so insistently as in the work of a group of historians known to specialists in the field as the subalternists, largely because of their contributions to the *Subaltern Studies* series edited by Ranajit Guha.[7] This set of scholars has been instrumental in bringing the study of resistance on the subcontinent to centre-stage in historical work. Its members have explored a wide range of collective actions hitherto neglected as forms of popular protest: communal disturbances, grain riots, uprisings of hills-people, and small-scale peasant insurgencies. They have re-examined peasant participation in nationalist struggles, emphasizing that associated with Congress movements were a host of more particular resistances of underclass peoples operating with goals, commitments, and understandings that clashed with those of the elite leadership. Taken together, the subalternists' work has suggested that South Asia's underclasses have regularly generated their own forms of social action and, at least in some cases, have possessed an insurgent consciousness.

In challenging older stereotypes of popular passivity and acquiescence to elite manipulation, the subalternists at first focused largely on moments in Indian history when subordinate groups engaged in direct, violent, often very conscious challenges to colonial or elite power. Such moments dramatized the tensions between the dominated and the dominant, and highlighted the ability of the subaltern to formulate an insurgent and autonomous self-consciousness. But such a focus generally precluded a complete appreciation of the everydayness of struggle. Since we know that episodes of 'pure' resistance are not always characteristic of South Asian society, it was theoretically still possible to assume that at other times—in 'ordinary' life—the subalterns lapsed back into a ruling-ideology based slumber; that when they did not challenge power directly, they essentially accepted its dictates; that when they did not articulate an autonomous culture, they fell under the spell of hegemonic rituals and ideologies. We might even have concluded that those subordinate groupings with no history of conscious, organized protest have always succumbed completely to domination, a conclusion far from what the subalternists would wish us to make. The most noticeable gap in their scholarship—the exclusion, until volume five, of women and struggles over gender relations from its consideration— seems on closer examination a consequence of the privileging of the dramatic and confrontational.

The subalternists themselves acknowledged this shortcoming in their earlier work. David Arnold, for instance, says:

In focusing upon peasant movements and rebellions, the contributors [to *Subaltern Studies*] have given these episodes undue prominence and paid inadequate attention to the 99 per cent of the time when peasants are not insurgent or assertive. The investigation of other subaltern themes than rebellion will, no doubt, in time illustrate other sorts of elite–subaltern relations and other forms of subaltern initiative and expression.[8]

Sumit Sarkar, another contributor to the series, has echoed these comments:

a serious problem in some 'subaltern' writing has been the tendency to concentrate on moments of conflict as opposed to the relative exclusion of much longer times of subordination or collaboration . . . Subaltern groups normally enter the world of conventional historical sources at moments of explosion, consequently breeding an assumption of total passivity or an opposite stereotype of heroic revolt. What one needs to keep in mind is a vast and complex continuum of intermediate attitudes of which total subordination and open revolt are only the extreme poles.[9]

In recent writings, a number of the subalternists have in fact begun to explore this 'continuum of intermediate attitudes' between subordination and revolt. Their studies of popular *mentalités*, gender relations, and the less visible struggles of dominated groups have extended the consideration of resistance into everyday life.[10]

Yet even as they have moved from their initial preoccupation with dramatic revolts, the subalternists' examinations seem to maintain a claim for underclass autonomy, of which the initial purpose was to counter an elite historiography that saw the liberal intelligentsia and other nationalists leading and acting on behalf of the masses. Rosalind O'Hanlon has argued that, in the work of the subalternists, 'the self-originating, self-determining individual, who is at once a subject in his possession of a sovereign consciousness whose defining characteristic is reason, an agent in his power of freedom—is admitted through the backdoor in the figure of the subaltern himself.'[11] The figure of such an autonomous subject casts a shadow over the attempt to understand how subaltern subjectivity is actually constituted in the field of power relations. The subalternists have not sought to establish the everydayness of resistance in the sense it is meant in this volume, i.e. by demonstrating how an 'insurgent consciousness' is simultaneously conditioned by, and conditions, the structures of domination.

The search for theoretical insights that could inform a consideration of the ordinariness of resistance in social life would initially seem to lead us to recent work, particularly among South East Asianists, that has focused on non-confrontational forms of resistance. This research has revealed that the organized political movements of the twentieth century belonged to a much richer and more varied history of struggle that both preceded and followed the epoch of anti-colonial revolution. Michael Adas, whose earlier scholarship has primarily concentrated on Burma and Indonesia, was most responsible for highlighting the role of *avoidance protest*, in which, as he puts it, 'dissatisfied groups seek to attenuate their hardships and express their discontent through flight, sectarian withdrawal, or other activities that minimize challenges to or clashes with those whom they view as their oppressors.'[12] He has found these forms of resistance to be particularly characteristic of the period before European rule, when indigenous states existed with only a limited capacity for repression. James Scott's study of smallholders and landless labourers in a Malaysian village during the late 1970s has brought to light the importance of *everyday resistance*, the 'prosaic but constant struggle between the peasantry and those who seek to extract labour, food, taxes, rents and interest from them'. As Scott describes it, everyday resistance consists of

the ordinary weapons of relatively powerless groups: footdragging, dissimulation, false compliance, pilfering, feigned ignorance, slander, arson, sabotage and so forth. These Brechtian forms of class struggle have certain features in common. They require little or no co-ordination or planning; they often represent a form of individual self-help; and they typically avoid any direct symbolic confrontation with authority or with elite norms. To understand these commonplace forms of resistance is to understand what much of the peasantry does 'between revolts' to defend its interests as best it can.[13]

Scott has argued that while these more modest forms of struggle are often undertaken without explicit statements of intention, they serve as evidence of a larger folk culture among the peasantry that implicitly sanctioned and celebrated evasion and dissimulation.[14] Everyday resistance places serious limits on the capacity to extract resources from the oppressed, even in circumstances when the dominant classes enjoy an overwhelming advantage in coercive power. But Scott goes even further, insisting that the presence of such struggles in day-to-day life is proof that ruling groups in most societies are unable to exert any form of cultural domination over the subordinate. The subordinate are, in his view, able to 'penetrate' the ideology of the dominant and 'demystify' it, effectively exposing it as a sham. In the conclusion of his major work on the subject, *Weapons of the Weak*, Scott explicitly takes Gramsci and his more contemporary followers to task for their insistence upon the notion of a hegemony impressed upon the subordinate by dominant groups.[15]

The concepts of avoidance and everyday resistance have highlighted how processes of struggle invade the periods of 'normality' between rebellions and revolutions. But this shift in focus has come without significant questioning of the assumption of the autonomous subject, which is as pervasive here as in work stressing more confrontational forms of resistance. One might have expected an approach that concentrated on everyday life to have been an ideal context for highlighting precisely the intersection of power and struggle. But Scott sees the effects of domination primarily in the constraints imposed by the coercive capabilities and the material controls that the ruling groups are able to muster; these effects do not extend into the spheres of culture and ideology. He thus creates the impression that in these latter domains—and in struggle itself—the oppressed are able to escape domination fully.[16] The ability of the subordinate to penetrate the ruling-class ideology and achieve a consciousness free from determination from above is, in Scott's view, most clearly present in 'hidden transcripts', i.e. in the conscious statements and activities of the lower classes away from the gaze of the dominant. By contrast, when the Malay peasants act deferentially in the presence of their landlords and employers, they are engaging in a submission of behaviour but not of spirit, meaning a very conscious ruse to trick and deceive. As Timothy Mitchell points out, the material–mental dichotomy that this invokes, and the privileged place that the notion of the 'hidden transcript' assigns to the mental, create two serious limitations.[17] First, by insisting that behaviour such as social deference to landlords is deliberate and calculating, representing inauthentic acts of accommodation to material realities, Scott ignores how such acts are necessarily conditioned by hegemony. At the very least, for instance, these acts are influenced by a logic that accepts the larger structures of landholding and political power as unalterable facts. Second, Scott suggests that contestatory practice is to be found, above all, in an autonomous consciousness, thus resurrecting the concept of the self-determining subject, now in the arena of everyday life.

Scott's critique of Gramsci is also problematic. It depends upon a limited conception of Gramscian theoretical notions which insist that hegemony can exist only when the ruling ideology determines all consciousness. This conception then becomes a rather easy target for dismissal. But increasingly sophisticated interpretations of the concept have emerged in other recent work. They emphasize that conflict may be constantly present within any given hegemony, and 'contradictory consciousnesses' may coexist in the outlooks both of single individuals and of groups, with some elements supporting the social order, but others uniting—in Gramsci's terms—'the-man-in-the-mass . . . with all his fellow workers'.[18] Appreciation of this complex reality could potentially inform a reformulation of the concept of everyday resistance so that it recognizes how such struggles commonly occur not outside but inside the field of power.

II

This collection of essays locates itself largely along the continuum of attitudes and forms of behaviour that constitute attempts to contest social reality but that nevertheless stop short of confrontation. Resistance, the essays collectively suggest, is and has always been a regular feature of the region's history; struggle has consistently resided in the interstices of South Asian society, invading and resisting all deployment of power relations. Most of the contributions examine forms of struggle that exist within relations that have generally been considered those of domination, submission and consensus; a few point out conversely the continued mark of power in the midst of even overt statements of dissent. Some essays look at phenomena as diverse as collective migrations, the use of the law to frustrate state objectives, and the non-performance of expected roles. Others take us into the realms of literature, ritual, lifestyle, and oral tradition. Several of the studies combine evidence collected through ethnographic fieldwork with material drawn from archival research. The contributions probe the boundaries of conventional conceptions of resistance in South Asia, exploring non-archival materials for evidence of contestatory behaviour, and analysing forms of struggle undertaken by groups which have often been excluded from the study of social protest in the past.

Theoretically, many of the contributors address the emerging literature on avoidance protest and everyday resistance. The authors apply these concepts to social groups—such as women, merchants and industrial workers—which have only rarely been included in the existing literature on resistance, and to cultural phenomena such as ritual, lifestyles, and oral traditions that have only recently come to be considered as arenas of struggle. This breadth in coverage brings to light the importance of contestation and conflict in the constitution of South Asian social and political structure for Indianists, and enriches the comparative study of resistance among subordinate peoples. A number of the contributors to the volume explicitly apply notions developed by Scott, Adas and their colleagues in South East Asian field.

At the same time, many of these studies implicitly offer a critique of the assumption of subaltern autonomy so often present in the literature on social protest and resistance. A number of the essays explore forms of social contestation that often confirm or accept inequality, even as they contend the terms of domination for specific groups. Power and struggle appear here not as polar opposites but as phenomena which often coexist and shape each other.[19] By delving into non-confrontational struggles, we highlight the omnipresent tension and contradictions between hegemony and autonomy in consciousness, between submission and resistance in practice. Perhaps precisely because South Asia lacks a past of violent revolution, because confrontational forms of protest on the continent were generally occasional and short-lived, the study of its society may be particularly well-suited to examining these tensions.

Collectively, the essays shed light on a number of important themes of current interest, both in the study of South Asian society and in comparative social history more generally.

GENDER AND RESISTANCE

Until recently, most historians of South Asia eschewed a consideration of gender in their analyses, in part perhaps as a result of the traditional emphasis on forms of violent struggle in which men have taken a leading part. Historical work written by feminist scholars, of course, has been concerned with the role of women in South Asia much more consistently. But much of this work has unfortunately presumed passivity and total acquiescence to patriarchy until the 'position of women' came under the scrutiny of social-reform movements, or when women became involved in the nationalist struggles of the late-colonial period. Consideration of the everydayness of resistance compels historians to give struggles over gender a central place in the understanding of power instead of relegating these as issues supplementary to those of tradition and nationhood.

The essays by Veena Talwar Oldenburg and Rosalind O'Hanlon examine the contestatory relations between gendered subjects and patriarchal authority by drawing upon quite different perspectives in the literature on women and gender. Adopting and extending the objective of making women visible historical and social actors, Oldenburg's evocative study of the courtesans of Lucknow depicts a subculture of women who have created lifestyles and who have forged distinctive modes of sexuality that mock and invert hegemonic South Asian con-

structions of gendered identities. She argues that these courtesans have formed a solidarity of opposition to male domination in the midst of an arena that would initially appear to be
a special bastion of the patriarchal order. The essay thus
effectively questions orthodox understandings of prostitution
both in India and the West. If Oldenburg makes women
visible by bringing their struggles to the forefront, O'Hanlon's
essay analyses gender as a site of power and emphasizes the
conditioning effects of domination upon resistance. In her
study of a late-nineteenth-century text written by a Maharash-
trian woman, Tarabai Shinde, she first traces the role of gender
in the discourses of both colonial rulers and colonized men.
Placing the text within this larger context, she then shows how
Tarabai, responding to discussions and debates occasioned by
the issue of widow remarriage, forged a passionate critique of
patriarchal constructions of the feminine and thus challenged
the essentializing systems of male public discourse. At the same
time, however, Tarabai projected on to men many of the nega-
tively valued qualities—selfishness, inconsistency, dependency
and enfeeblement—that had been used in characterizing
women, thus reproducing colonial representations of gender
in inverted form. O'Hanlon's study thus illustrates the ways in
which structures of power can persist and be reinforced even in
the midst of bitter attacks on male behaviour. Interestingly
also, Tarabai's writings, in disputing male-imposed idealiza-
tions of the feminine, suggest the constant presence of resistance
by South Asian women within their households and families
that are quite analogous to everyday struggles found among
other subaltern groupings.

For scholars working on the history of gender outside the
bounds of formal feminist organizations, these essays indicate
important and fascinating lines for comparative inquiry. Both
of course deal with rather extraordinary women. But by exposing cracks in the seemingly formidable walls of patriarchy,
they caution historians and anthropologists against too readily
presuming male domination to be a solid, stable structure of
society except when it comes under conscious questioning
during the twentieth century. And they both suggest that it
may be wiser to view male power as always dependent upon
the domestication of gender-based resistances as, for instance,

when the courtesan is isolated to social realms that do not threaten the family. Oldenburg and O'Hanlon attribute very different degrees of autonomy to women's struggles: ironically, while Oldenburg finds a realm of freedom inside a structure that has been seen as one purely of power, O'Hanlon finds the discourse of power present in a most direct attack on men. But these apparently contradictory approaches, it would seem to us, only serve to accentuate how resistance and domination become intertwined with each other in constituting gender relations.

PRODUCTION RELATIONS

The study of labour relations in India's industries, too, has been handicapped by a preoccupation with the dramatic: strikes, trade unions and the Communist-led labour movements. Such movements have often been judged by the teleology of revolution, a tendency that sometimes results in expressions of disappointment at the weakness of 'organized' activity among workers. In his article, Rajnarayan Chandavarkar highlights the role of everyday resistance among factory labourers in Bombay, though he shows at the same time that these struggles existed alongside and supplemented more dramatic, organized, and sometimes violent, means of protest. The workers' various forms of struggle had a powerful effect on circumscribing the actions of industrialists; indeed workers' resistance effectively undercut the employers' efforts to apply work practices informed by Taylorism during the 1920s and 1930s. But he also warns against any attempt to assume that some pure form of class consciousness necessarily flows from an industrial structure. Government policies, economic vagaries, employers' practices, and competition between mill-owners could accentuate divisions among workers as much as foster new solidarities. His contribution suggests that the concept of everyday struggle is more useful in challenging rather than confirming 'the characterization of a simply adversarial, or consistently oppositional relationship' between 'exploiters' and 'resisters'.

While focused primarily on the specific process of rationalization, this study has much broader implications for the understanding of production relations, both in industry and agriculture. Capitalist relations more generally, we might suggest, should not be seen merely as social relations determined by some abstract process of development or as an outgrowth produced simply by the intentions of capitalists. Instead capitalist relations are created as the labour of human beings is converted into commodities that can be bought and sold, and this requires controlling and disciplining labour in ways that ensure profit. And since the reproduction of capitalist domination requires turning concrete labour into abstract labour, it may involve the constant taming of workers' resistances, even when labour militancy and organization are not obvious.

POPULAR CULTURE AND RESISTANCE

Popular culture, referring to those activities that texture people's daily lives, provides an especially important arena for studying the 'everydayness' of resistance. For it is in such cultural forms as work, ritual, speech, gossip, oral tradition, lifestyle and behavioural codes, dress, and entertainment that domination is constantly being forged and fissured. Anthropologists, who normally study the cultural dimensions of everyday life, rarely look for signs of contestation; when they do— as, for example, in examinations of 'role-reversal' rituals— they treat these signs as expressions of a structural logic that stages tensions only to enact their resolution. The literature on everyday resistance, on the other hand, suffers from an economistic tendency in so far as it confines itself to such 'material' questions as land, rent, wages, and work. This prevents the exploration of how resistance shapes the subject-positions of people—peasants, labourers and industrial workers—who engage in such 'material' struggles.

Two of the participants in this volume explicitly explore the role of popular culture in South Asia in the process of contending social reality and in reconstituting subaltern identity, and thus extend the notion of everyday resistance into spheres of cultural life other than the 'economic'. Gyan Prakash explores the oral traditions of the Bhuinyas, a low-caste group of landless labourers in the eastern Indian region of Bihar. He finds implicit in these traditions historical explanations of how the Bhuinyas came to acquire their lowly place in society, explanations that contested upper-caste insistence on the 'natural' inferiority of the group. The Bhuinya stories, nonetheless, reproduced power relations by acknowledging the caste hierarchy and the polluted state of the Bhuinyas within that hierarchy. Veena Talwar Oldenburg's study, mentioned above, suggests that lifestyle itself can be a form of resistance. She finds among the courtesans of Lucknow a whole range of attitudes and behaviour that clashes with the dominant constructions of gender in South Asian society.

Two other essays establish the everydayness of resistance in another sense, by examining popular culture less as a form of struggle in itself than as the site for contestatory actions. John Rogers' essay, for instance, analyses the efforts of peasants and townspeople in Sri Lanka to defend forms of popular leisure such as gambling against British and Sinhalese elite efforts to control these activities in the name of promoting 'thrift', law and order, and 'public decency'. He discusses a host of defensive techniques used by Sri Lankans, from occasional acts of violence against law-enforcement agents to the employment of the British legal system in 'ways that turned the colonial courts themselves into sites of resistance'. Rogers' essay thus challenges the notion that law should be seen merely as an instrument of social control. Its appropriation by ordinary Sri Lankans temporarily defeated state efforts to produce 'useful', 'disciplined' subjects, and preserved cultural practices that provided a major source of satisfaction and companionship for Sinhalese men. But he also shows how colonial policy-makers responded to these effective forms of subaltern struggle by tightening legal loopholes and intensifying efforts at enforcement. Nicholas Dirks's study of religious festivals in the south Indian countryside shows that even ritual events could occasion serious conflict, so much so that it was common for performances to spawn violent dispute, provoke the holding of multiple and rival celebrations, or simply not take place at all. The essay seriously questions much of the anthropological work done on ritual, which has emphasized the role of ritual in strengthening hierarchical relations and in ensuring social stability. The implication, as in Prakash's piece, is that agrarian social relations are inherently fractured and tenuous.

Together, then, these essays question a view of culture as a

mere cognitive system or as a system of values that every
society requires in order for people to understand each other
and function as a collective unit. Instead, they see popular
culture as a realm invaded both by power and by resistance.
And, as Dirks's essay suggests, this process can at times be
more dysfunctional than functional.

RESISTANCE AND THE STATE

There is nothing new, of course, in examining resistance in the
context of relations between the state and society. But often in
this literature the state is depicted merely as a formidable,
autonomous force impressing itself on subordinate groups.
Resistance is formulated only after the state is already constituted and begins to threaten local communities (which in
turn are often defined by stable moral economies until this
threat appears). The essays in this volume suggest that the
state and its agendas are often themselves shaped and altered
by rather ordinary forms of struggle. John Rogers' study, as
already mentioned, shows how the resistance of Sri Lankans
forced the state to alter its strategy to control gambling in
public places. Covering resistance by merchants in Surat from
the seventeenth century to the twentieth, Douglas Haynes
depicts how a variety of forms of struggle by merchants in
Surat, ranging from everyday resistance to mass flight, served
to check the agendas of the alien overlords who ruled the city.
At some moments in history, most notably the consolidation of
British power during the late eighteenth century and the rise
of the Congress Raj during the early twentieth century, merchant protest against old state structures could contribute to
the construction of new ones. Haynes's study, like that of
Rogers, shows colonialism to be something less than it claimed
to be; in practice its agenda of reform and modernization was
constantly being tempered and altered by everyday struggles
of colonial subjects. Haynes's essay also adds another dimension to recent research that has attributed a central role to
merchant activity in the construction of South Asian states, but
which has neglected the place of merchant resistance in affect-
ing the nature of state–locality relations.

At the same time, these essays also suggest how state struc-

tures contribute to the shape of resistance. Rogers brings out
some of the influence of the colonial legal system on the struggles
of ordinary folk; O'Hanlon similarly evokes the effects of
colonial understandings and judicial discourse on the writings
of Tarabai Shinde. Perhaps most explicitly, Haynes's study
sees merchant resistance constantly reshaping itself in adaptation to the principles of political justice espoused by the ruling
group. He rejects the assumption, present in some literature
that has examined social protest over long periods of time, that
resistance necessarily becomes more conscious, confrontational,
and liberation-oriented with 'modernity', capitalism, and the
development of the colonial state. Strategies of avoidance,
usually bearing the stamp of hegemonic political discourses,
continued to play as important a role in checking British
imperial power as they did in thwarting Mughal objectives.
All the essays in the volume implicitly challenge teleological
approaches to change in the forms and consciousness of protest that have often characterized the literature on social
protest.

Collectively, then, these essays focus on the intersection of
power and resistance, and on the complex processes in which
the two are constantly intermeshed. The authors do not arrive
at a single mode of describing these processes; instead there is
an internal dialogue and debate going on within the volume.
While Oldenburg posits the existence of distinctive sub-cultures
within the larger structure of patriarchy that nonetheless invert
patriarchal values, O'Hanlon suggests how forms of domination sustain and reproduce themselves in struggles over gender.
Haynes argues for merchant 'contests within hegemony';
Prakash speaks of Bhuinya traditions as 'practices that incorporated and displaced the structures of hierarchy and dependence which conditioned everyday existence'. But as a whole the
studies problematize a view of both power and resistance as
occupying autonomous spaces until they collide in dramatic
confrontations. The essays counter the notion that subaltern
consciousness is either a completely independent product or
that it is a mere reflection of a totalizing hegemony from above.

Such an approach might seem a purely academic exercise
when it is placed next to the literature on resistance, either
everyday or extraordinary, which has celebrated the ability of

subaltern groups to generate forms of culture and behaviour undetermined from above. But, as O'Hanlon argues, it is informed by much the same concern with emancipation. In our view, a shortcoming in the effort to recover lost histories of subordinated peoples lies not so much in the attempt itself as in the fact that these recoveries have obscured the processes by which new forms of power and domination are produced. If we are to assume that 'consciousness' is achieved in most acts of resistance and hold that the 'recovery' gives the subaltern a voice, then the critical edge provided by the notion of subalternity may be lost. For we then may fail to understand the structures that have conditioned the subaltern in the past and which continue to shape our own discourse in the present. To challenge these structures it may still be important to commend struggle, but it is equally important to understand that which enables and disables resistance, i.e. to use subaltern challenges to power as a springboard for inquiring into the conditions under which struggles are conceived, mounted and contained.

NOTES

This introductory essay has benefited greatly from the comments by the contributors to the volume, and by comments from David Ludden, Anand Yang, Geraldine Forbes, Nick Dirks, Eugene Irschick, David Hardiman and Susanna B. C. Devalle.

1. Howard Spodek, 'On the Origins of Gandhi's Methodology: The Heritage of Kathiawad and Gujarat', *Journal of Asian Studies*, xxx (1971), pp. 361–72; Richard Heitler, 'The Varanasi House Tax Hartal of 1810–11', *Indian Economic and Social History Review*, ix (1972), pp. 239–57; Dharampal, *Civil Disobedience and Indian Tradition, with Some Early Nineteenth Century Documents* (Varanasi: Sarva Seva Sangh Prakashan, 1971); Eugene F. Irschick, 'Gandhian Non-Violent Protest: Rituals of Avoidance or Rituals of Confrontation?', *Economic and Political Weekly*, xxi (1986), pp. 1276–85.
2. Lytton to Salisbury, 11 May 1876, India Office Library Records, E 218, 518 1, p. 149, cited in Bernard S. Cohn, 'Representing Authority in Victorian India', in *The Invention of Tradition*, ed. Eric Hobsbawm and Terence Ranger (Cambridge: Cambridge University Press, 1983), p. 191.
3. Barrington Moore, Jr. *The Social Origins of Dictatorship and Democracy: Lord and Peasant in the Making of the Modern World* (Boston: Beacon Press, 1967), paperback edition, chapter vi.

4. There have been major exceptions to this general pattern, even in the study of ancient and medieval India. See, most relevantly, the essays in *Dissent, Protest and Reform in Indian Civilization*, ed. S. C. Malik (Simla: Indian Institute of Advanced Study, 1977).

5. This process is examined, for instance, in Bernard S. Cohn, 'The Command of Language and the Language of Command', *Subaltern Studies IV: Writings on South Asian History and Society*, ed. Ranajit Guha (Delhi: Oxford University Press, 1985), pp. 276–330.

6. A classic example of such an approach is Louis Dumont, *Homo Hierarchicus: The Caste System and Its Implications* (Chicago: University of Chicago Press, 1970).

7. The key works in this approach are the six volumes in the *Subaltern Studies* series edited by Ranajit Guha (Delhi: Oxford University Press, 1982–6); and Guha's own book, *Elementary Aspects of Peasant Insurgency* (Delhi: Oxford University Press, 1983). We do not wish to suggest that only members of the Subaltern Studies series have been involved in this reassessment. Also involved have been Anand Yang, Majid Siddiqi, Sandria Freitag, Rudrangshu Mukherjee and a number of other scholars.

8. 'Gramsci and Peasant Subalternity in India', *Journal of Peasant Studies*, XI (1984), p. 169.

9. 'The Conditions and Nature of Subaltern Militancy: Bengal from Swadeshi to Non-cooperation, c. 1905–1922', *Subaltern Studies III*, pp. 273–4.

10. One thinks here especially of David Arnold's excellent pieces, 'Bureaucratic Recruitment and Subordination in Colonial India: The Madras Constabulary, 1859–1947', in *Subaltern Studies IV*, pp. 1–53; and 'Touching the Body: Perspectives on the Indian Plague', in *Subaltern Studies V*, pp. 55–90; and Ranajit Guha, 'Chandra's Death', in *Subaltern Studies V*, pp. 135–61.

11. 'Recovering the Subject: Subaltern Studies and the Histories of Resistance in Colonial South Asia', *Modern Asian Studies*, XXII (1988), p. 191.

12. Michael Adas, 'From Avoidance to Confrontation: Peasant Protest in Precolonial and Colonial Southeast Asia', *Comparative Studies in Society and History*, XXIII (1981), p. 217.

13. James Scott, *Weapons of the Weak: Everyday Forms of Peasant Resistance* (New Haven: Yale University Press, 1985), p. 29. Besides this book, there is an important collection of articles on the subject of everyday resistance: *Everyday Forms of Peasant Resistance in South-east Asia*, ed. James C. Scott and Benedict J. Tria Kerkvliet. Special Issue of the *Journal of Peasant Studies*, XIII (1986), pp. 1–150.

14. Scott, 'Resistance without Protest and without Organization: Peasant Opposition in the Islamic Zakat and the Christian Tithe', *Comparative Studies in Society and History*, XXIX (1987), pp. 451–2.

15. Scott, *Weapons of the Weak*, chapter VIII.

16. Timothy Mitchell, 'Everyday Metaphors of Power', unpublished paper, forthcoming in *Theory and Society*. This criticism is perhaps less true in

some of Scott's work that does not deal explicitly with everyday resistance. See 'Protest and Profanation: Agrarian Revolt and the Little Tradition', *Theory and Society*, IV (1977), pp. 1–38 and 211–46.

17. Mitchell, 'Everyday Metaphors of Power'.

18. See Gramsci, *Il materialismo storico e la filosofia di Benedetto Croce*, quoted in Joseph Femia, 'Hegemony and Consciousness in the Thought of Antonio Gramsci', *Political Studies*, XXIII (1975), p. 33. See also David D. Laitin, *Hegemony and Culture: Politics and Religious Change among the Yoruba* (Chicago: University of Chicago Press); T. J. Jackson Lears, 'The Concept of Cultural Hegemony: Problems and Possibilities', *American Historical Review*, XC (1985), pp. 567–93. This also seems to be the understanding of hegemony implicit in O'Hanlon's critique, cited above. Scott acknowledges the existence of 'contests within hegemony', but then curiously goes on to see this as evidence that the notion of hegemony should be rejected.

19. Michel Foucault, especially *The History of Sexuality, Vol. I: An Introduction*, trans. Robert Hurley (New York: Vintage Books, 1980), pp. 92–7.

2

Lifestyle as Resistance: The Case of the Courtesans of Lucknow

VEENA TALWAR OLDENBURG

It is only in the last decade that the word 'gender', with its expanded meaning connoting the social organization of the sexes in society, has been hospitably received in American academia. It still unnerves mainstream historians of South Asia, although women populate the pages of Indian history thickly enough as subjects of the social and political reform issues in the nineteenth and twentieth centuries, and 'women's issues' continue to be energetically explored. I was quite uneasy myself about the research I unwittingly found myself doing on the courtesans of Lucknow beyond the boundaries of time and 'relevance' that I had set for myself. I found myself engaged in garnering their self-perceptions as powerful, independent, even subversive women, while I observed and learned about their way of life, rituals, and celebration of womanhood in the privacy of the *kotha* (upper-storied apartments) and their liberation from the rules of the patriarchal world beyond their own walls. Romila Thapar's essay on the ascetic lifestyle as dissent provided the analytical framework for the unconventional data I had collected.[1] The several detailed interviews with the courtesans of Lucknow about their changing profession and about their worldview were, in sum, stories of self-consciously elaborated, subtle, and covert forms of resistance against patriarchal culture. Equally remarkable was the realization that this form of feminist resistance was as old as the profession itself, and had not found its inspiration in western liberalism or the women's movement, or Gandhian modes of protest. *Their style of non-confrontational resistance is not a part-time or sporadic activity, but a way of life.*[2]

The moral condemnation of prostitution, subscribed to even by those who endorse women's rights, had added to the reluctance I felt in acknowledging that it was important to document the voices and self-perceptions of these women. Gradually my own stereotypical views of prostitution, of its exploitation of women and collusion with patriarchy, of the 'normal' woman in the 'normal' world, were slowly stood on their head. I decided to write about the courtesans of Lucknow, in the full and frank spirit of my informants, only after I was admitted to their inner circle. I mulled over my data for several years and presented them orally at various academic fora in order to arrive at a fuller understanding of their implications for gender relations in South Asia. From time to time, over several years (1976–84), I revisited many of my informants with the questions that scholars, including American feminist colleagues, had raised. The courtesans received these questions with amusement and tolerance, and answered them with candour. But their rebuttals led to even rougher terrain. The issue of homosexuality (which is central to understanding the worldview of the courtesan) has not been part of the discourse on South Asian history, and this, too, made me nervous. But it also made it clear to me that the deference to 'mainstream' historians had gone too far. Instead of tiptoeing around (in our blue stockings, of course!) what the scholarly South Asian establishment will *not* accept, it is time that feminist historians took an active part in widening and deepening the social history research agenda.

There is also a larger historiographical issue that this paper explicitly addresses. South Asian historiography has had its share of acrimonious debates, with Marxist, imperialist, nationalist, Namierites of the Cambridge School, etc., having held their ground with scholarly zeal. A new generation of historians, who call themselves 'the subalternists', in the recent influential volumes emerging from the Oxford University Press in Delhi, have not only parried the chief ideological thrust of the Cambridge-wallahs but also expanded the scope of the field and enriched it greatly with their path-breaking work on the often violent activism of hitherto ignored subaltern (as opposed to elite or dominant) groups. But they have failed to take into adequate account women, the largest, ubiquitous, and most obvious 'subaltern' group of all. Their task has been to rescue the history of sporadic violent protest of subaltern groups in South Asia from obscurity. They have commendably documented violent revolts of peasants, factory and plantation workers, untouchables and minority groups, among others. Yet they have ignored the invisible activism in the domestic arena where women invent and use covert strategies to resist and undermine the oppression and drudgery of the average patriarchal household. Social historians can no longer exclude gender relations as a legitimate theme from the discourse on power relations in South Asia.

This exclusion is possibly the oldest and most serious shortcoming that informs the research and writing of South Asian history. If we push this 'blame' further we find that it lies in the conventional written sources on which historians depend, which naturally also reflect the prejudice against perceiving women as actors responsible for shaping the history of societies as much as men; and in this infinitely regressive mode we come back to the behaviour of the women 'actors' in a male-dominated society. They are inaccessible to male researchers because of the enforced rules of modesty. This forces women, who are 'properly' socialized, to contribute to their own lack of recognition as actors in shaping history. So the historiographical problem is exacerbated by methodological limitations: male historians have no direct access to women either in the conventional sources or in the field; women's activities and influence remain 'invisible' and the *effect* of the cultural construction of gender is mistaken for its *cause*. It is, therefore, hardly surprising that modes of protest invented and used by women against male oppression in the home have not received scholarly attention, except, of course, the brief notice they earn in discussions of Gandhian revolutionary techniques.[3]

If the genius of women has received only inadequate credit for authoring or inspiring these non-militaristic means to undermine hegemony, gender relations within the home have gone unacknowledged as the testing ground for many covert, non-confrontational, even devious ways in which women survive, influence decisions on the allocation of resources, and affect the politics of the world from which they are often, quite literally, veiled. This is where the courtesans with their private ideology stand out as a group that has historically existed in a patriarchal society without suffering from its worst constraints and repression by avoiding the inevitability and challenging the 'respectability' of the central patriarchal institution— marriage.

I do not wish to go into the history of the institution of the courtesan in India, nor the familiar tale of how it was a synthesis of the finest in Hindu and Muslim traditions, like much of Hindustani music and the fine arts.[4] My object is to re-examine the changing lifestyle of the courtesans of Lucknow from the time of the Awadh court, through the colonial period to the present day, to extract the ideology which informs their covert subversion of gender roles. The courtesan is more readily seen as a product and a perpetuator of patriarchy; her rather more subtle and self-interested rebellion against social constraints imposed on women has attracted little attention. This attitude stems from either a concern about the sufferings and risks women endure as street prostitutes or a cultural faith in the 'innate' purity of women. The concern, valid though it is in other settings, does not apply to the courtesans of Lucknow, who were historically entitled to the protection and patronage of the royal court. Later, under the British, government regulations spared them the dependence on pimps or middlemen. The second view, which is really a part of a larger debate, has been cogently and carefully rebutted by Judith R. Walkowitz in her work on the politics of prostitution in Britain. Discussing the early historical links between feminism and repressive crusades against prostitution, pornography, and homosexuality, Walkowitz concludes that the criticism of these was a 'hydra-headed assault on nonmarital, nonreproductive sexuality' and in 'their defence of prostitutes and concern to protect women from male sexual aggression, feminists were limited by their own class bias and by their continued adherence to a "separate sphere" ideology that stressed women's purity, moral supremacy, and domestic virtues.'[5]

Although the situation of the courtesans of Lucknow has undergone enormous changes in the last century and a half, since the onset of colonial rule, their beliefs emerge best by interweaving their past with their present. Hence, the account which follows is thematically rather than chronologically organized. In 1976, my first meeting with a group of courtesans

in the flesh, so to speak, coincided with my discovery of information about their predecessors in the local colonial records
of 1858–78. Both were chance encounters, and it might be
best to explain how these occurred because they are an important part of the evidence I offer, along with my analysis of
the ethnographic material gathered from several group and
individual interviews with thirty courtesans over eight years
(1976–84), to support my argument that the underlying philosophy that shapes their way of life resists the repressive intrusion of society in their own lives.

In 1976, when I was doing the research for my study on the
social consequences of colonial urbanization, I came across
the city's famous courtesans for the first time in the civic tax
ledgers of 1858–77 and in the related official correspondence
preserved in the Municipal Corporation record room in
Lucknow.[6] They were subsumed under the occupational category of 'dancing and singing girls', and to compound the
surprise of finding women in the tax records was the even more
remarkable fact that they were in the highest tax bracket, with
the largest individual incomes of any in the city. Their names
were also on lists of property (houses, orchards, manufacturing
and retail establishments for food and luxury items) con-
fiscated by British officials for their proven involvement in the
siege of Lucknow and the rebellion against colonial rule in 1857.
These women, though patently non-combatants, were penal-
ized for their alleged instigation of and pecuniary assistance
to the rebels. On yet another list, some twenty pages long,
were recorded the spoils of war seized from one set of 'female
apartments' in Kaisar Bagh, where some of the deposed ex-
king Wajid Ali Shah's three hundred or more consorts resided
when the complex was seized by the British.[7] It is a remarkable
list and eloquently evocative of a very privileged existence:
gold and silver ornaments studded with precious stones,
embroidered cashmere wool and brocade shawls, bejewelled
caps and shoes, silver, gold, jade and amber-handled fly whisks,
silver cutlery, jade goblets, plates, spittoons, hookahs, and silver
utensils for serving and storing food and drink, and valuable
furnishings. The value of this part of the booty of war was
estimated at nearly four million rupees (there were approximately ten rupees to the pound in 1857).

Courtesans appeared in other colonial records as well. They were the subject of frequent official memoranda written in connection with a grave medical crisis that engulfed the military establishment in Lucknow, and in all the major cantonments of British India. When European casualties during the mutiny and rebellion of 1857 were reckoned, it was discovered that more soldiers had died of disease than in combat. The shock of this discovery was compounded by the embarrassing fact that one in every four European soldiers was afflicted with a venereal disease. It became clear that the battle to reduce European mortality rates would now be joined on the hygienic front, to ensure a healthy European army for the strategic needs of the Empire. It became imperative that the courtesans and prostitutes of Lucknow, along with those in the other 110 cantonments in India where European soldiers were stationed, be regulated, inspected, and controlled. The provisions of Britain's Contagious Diseases Act of 1864 were incorporated into a comprehensive piece of legislation, Act XXII of 1864; it required the registration and periodic medical examination of prostitutes in all cantonment cities of the Indian empire.[8] The collective impact of these regulations, the loss of court patronage, and the material penalties extracted from them for their role in the rebellion, were a severe blow to the courtesans and signalled the gradual debasement of an esteemed cultural institution into common prostitution.

These new challenges provoked these women to intensify their struggle to keep out an intrusive civic authority that taxed their incomes and inspected their bodies. Characteristically they responded by keeping two sets of books on their income, bribing the local *dai*, or nurse, to avoid bodily inspections, keeping the local policemen 'happy' with sex and money to avoid arrests for selling liquor to the soldiers, or publicly refusing to pay taxes even when threatened with imprisonment. The tactics were new but the spirit behind them was veteran. These methods were imaginative extensions of the ancient and subtle ways the courtesans had cultivated to escape patriarchy, and add up to a spirited defence of their own rights and privileges by a group traditionally mistaken for merely perpetuating patriarchal values.[9]

Yet another set of documents finally led me to a group of

courtesans living in Lucknow in 1976, proud descendants of those who had survived first the pressures of a century of systematic harassment by the colonial authorities, and then the ban placed on their activities by the government of independent India. These documents were the intercepted letters written by the ex-king, Wajid Ali Shah, to some of the wives he had been forced to abandon in Lucknow after the British annexed Awadh in 1856 and forced him into exile. I engaged a young Persian scholar, Chhote Mian,[10] to help me decipher these Persian letters. He not only provided the entrée required to visit this group of courtesans, but also, quite fortuitously, the key to comprehending their world. He explained why he had only been given a pet name (roughly, Mr Small) instead of a serious Muslim family name. He was the son of a courtesan and she had never revealed to him who his father was. Ironically, his sad life-story had all the elements of the socialization and upbringing accorded to a girl in a 'normal' household:

While I love and respect my mother and all my 'aunts' [other courtesans] and my grandmother [a *chaudharayan*], my misfortune is that I was born a son and not a daughter in their house. When a boy is born in the *kotha*, the day is without moment, even one of quiet sadness. When my sister was born there was a joyous celebration that was unforgettable. Everyone received new clothes, there was singing, dancing, and feasting. My aunts went from door to door distributing *laddus* [a sweet traditionally distributed to mark an auspicious event]. The musicians were drunk and received expensive gifts.

My sister is, today, a beautiful, educated, propertied woman. She will also inherit what my mother and grandmother own. She will have a large income from rents; she doesn't even have to work as a courtesan, if she so chooses. I am educated, but I have no money or property. Jobs are very hard to come by, so I live in a room and subsist on a small allowance that my mother gives in exchange for running errands for her and helping her deal with her lawyers. [She was trying to evict a tenant from a house she owned.] She paid for my education but a degree is pretty worthless these days. My only hope is that I may marry a good woman who has money and who gives me sons so they can look after me in my old age, or find a way of getting a job in Dubai, as my cousin did. Otherwise my chances in life are pretty dim. Funny isn't it, how these women have made life so topsy-turvy?

In order to appreciate this rather remarkable inversion in a society that blatantly favours males over females, a brief sketch of the historical background of the courtesans of Lucknow is in order.[11] At all Hindu and Muslim courts in the many kingdoms that made up the subcontinent before the British began to displace the rulers, the courtesans were an influential female elite. The courtesans of Lucknow established themselves as a notable group of women in the eighty-odd years that the Awadh dynasty had Lucknow as its capital city, under the lavish patronage of the chief noblemen, merchants, and the official elite. Abdul Halim Sharar, a novelist and journalist who chronicled the history of the nawabs of Awadh and their cultural innovations, writes that

> in Lucknow, association with the courtesans started with the reign of Shuja ud Daula [reigned: 1753–74]. It became fashionable for the noblemen to associate with some bazaar beauty, either for pleasure or for social distinction. A cultivated man like Hakim Mahdi, who later became Vazir [prime minister of Awadh], owed his initial success to a courtesan named Piyaro, who advanced her own money to enable him to make an offering to the ruler on his first appointment as Governor of a Province of Awadh. These absurdities went so far that it is said that until a person had association with courtesans he was not a polished man. . . . At the present time [*c.* 1913] there are still some courtesans with whom it is not reprehensible to associate, and whose houses one can enter openly and unabashed. Although these practices may have a deteriorating effect on the morals, at the same time manners and social finesse improved.[12]

Ensconced in equally lavish apartments in the bazaars of Chowk, and in the Kaisar Bagh, they were not only recognized as preservers and performers of the high culture of the court, but actively shaped the developments in Hindustani music and Kathak dance styles.[13] Their style of entertainment was widely imitated in other Indian court cities, and their more recent influence on the Hindi film is all too patent.[14] They commanded great respect in the court and in society, and association with them bestowed prestige on those who were invited to their salons for cultural soirées. It was not uncommon for the young sons of the nobility to be sent to the best-known salons for instruction in etiquette, the art of conversation and polite manners, and the appreciation of Urdu literature.

The world of the *tawaif* of Lucknow was as complex and hierarchical as the society of which it was part. Courtesans were and still are usually a part of a larger establishment run by a chaudharayan, or chief courtesan, an older woman who has retired to the position of manager after a successful career as a tawaif. Having acquired wealth and fame, such women were able to recruit and train women who came to them, along with the more talented daughters of the household. Typically, a wealthy courtier, often the king himself,[15] began his direct association with a kotha by bidding for a virgin whose patron he became with the full privileges and obligations of that position. He was obliged to make regular contributions in cash and jewellery, and privileged to invite his friends to soirées and to enjoy an exclusive sexual relationship with a tawaif. His guests were expected to impress the management with their civilities and substance so that they would qualify as patrons of the women who were still unattached, or at least as 'regulars' of the kotha. The chaudharayan always received a fixed proportion (approximately a third) of the earnings to maintain the apartments, pay to hire and train other dancing girls, and attract the musicians, chefs, and special servants that such establishments employed. Many of the musicians belonged to famous lineages and much of late-nineteenth-century Hindustani music was invented and transformed in these salons, to accommodate the new urban elite who filled the patronage vacuum in the colonial period.

The household had other functionaries beyond the core group of daughters or nieces of the senior tawaif. These women, called *thakahi* and *randi*, were affiliates of a kotha but were ranked lower. Their less remarkable appearance and talent restricted them to providing chiefly sexual services in rather more austere quarters downstairs. Another very interesting group of women secretly associated with the establishment were *khangi*, or women who were married and observed strict purdah, but who for financial or other reasons came to the kotha for clandestine liaisons; the chaudharayan collected a fee from them for her hospitality. Doormen, watchmen, errand boys, tailors, palanquin-carriers and others—who lived in the lower floors of the house or in detached servants' quarters and were also often kinsmen—screened suspicious characters at the door, acted as protectors of the house, and spied on the activities of the police and medical departments. Pimps or other male agents simply did not exist, then or later.

The idea that the chaudharayan's recruitment practices were and are shady and unscrupulous has gained wide currency over time. It is popularly believed that the most common mode of recruitment was/is kidnapping; that the tawaif were linked to a large underground network of male criminals who abducted very young girls from villages and small towns and sold them to the kothas or *nishatkhanas* (literally, pleasure houses). This belief was romantically fuelled, if not actually generated, by Lucknow's famous poet and litterateur, Mirza Hadi Ruswa, in his *Umrao Jan Ada*. The novel first appeared in 1905 and was 'an immediate and thunderous success. Critics acclaimed it as the best narrative on the life and culture of Lucknow and praised Ruswa's mastery of Urdu prose. Several editions of the novel were sold out.'[16] It was translated into English in 1961 under the aegis of UNESCO, and it has been reissued on demand several times since it was reincarnated as a film in 1981, by the Lucknow Shi'i nawab turned film director, Muzaffar Ali.

The influence this novel has exerted on the popular imagination is enormous. It is the single most important source of information on the courtesans of Lucknow, and by extension, the entire profession as it was practised in the nineteenth century in northern India. Set in the second half of the nineteenth century, it is a melodramatic story of a tawaif, Umrao Jan, who as a beautiful child of five is kidnapped and sold to a tawaif in Lucknow, where she trains and becomes, after a few complicated twists and turns in the plot, a renowned and much-sought-after courtesan. Ruswa uses the classic ploy of writing an introduction wherein he explains that he is merely recording the true story of Umrao Jan, told to him by the protagonist herself. His use of the first person in the 'memoir', in which the courtesan frequently addresses him by name, makes it all the more convincing.

The glimpses Ruswa provides of the rigorous training and worldview of the courtesan are very true to life. But Ruswa also had a keen interest in crime, and several of his translations and adaptations were of contemporary Victorian and Urdu pot-boilers. He published a then-popular series of *khuni* (literally, bloody killer) novels some of whose titles, such as *Khuni Shahzada* (The Killer Prince), *Khuni Joru* (The Killer Wife),

Khuni Ashiq (The Killer Lover), betray his predilection for the sensational. One of the older women who knew the author when he was alive gave the book a mixed review: she commended Ruswa for understanding the mentality of the courtesan, but blamed him for inventing characters such as the 'evil kidnapper' and the exploitative madame who became the stuff of later stereotypes.[17]

The greatest harm was done to the reputation of the kothas by British political propaganda. The older tawaif, who spoke keenly about contemporary politics, the law, and had connections among the local power elite, were equally well informed about the history of their city. In their view the British had deliberately muddied the truth about their kothas in order to denigrate nawabi culture, and to thus justify annexing the kingdom of Awadh in 1856 as well as exiling the beloved king, Wajid Ali Shah. After quelling the mutiny and rebellion of 1857, the British turned their fury against the powerful elite of Lucknow. The tawaif were perceived as an integral part of the elite. In a campaign waged against them to reduce their influence, the new government resumed control over much of the prime real estate given to them by the nawabs, and discredited the nobility who associated with them as dissolute and immoral. Yet, when it came to matters such as using these women as prostitutes for the European garrison, or collecting income tax, the eminently pragmatic British set aside their high moral dudgeon, and decreed rules to make this possible. It became official policy to select the healthy and beautiful 'specimens' from among the kotha women, and arbitrarily relocate them in the cantonment for the convenience and health of the European soldiers. This not only dehumanized the profession, stripping it of its cultural function, but made sex cheap and easy for the men, while exposing the women to venereal infection from the soldiers.[18]

Kidnapping may be one of the methods by which girls find their way into the tawaif households, but it is certainly not the most common. In my interviews with the thirty women, whose ages ranged from thirty-five to seventy-eight, a very different picture emerged. In recording the life-stories of these women, the compelling circumstance that brought the majority of them to the various tawaif households in Lucknow was the misery they endured in either their natal or their conjugal homes. Four of these women were widowed in their early teens, two of whom hailed from the same district and had lost their husbands in a cholera epidemic; three were sold by their parents when famine conditions made feeding these girls impossible. Seven were victims of physical abuse, two of whom were sisters who were regularly beaten by their alcoholic father for not obliging him by making themselves sexually available to the toddy-seller. Three were known victims of rape and therefore deemed ineligible for marriage; two had left their ill-paid jobs as municipal sweeper-women, because they were tired of 'collecting other people's dirt', two were battered wives, one had left her husband because he had a mistress, and one admitted no particular hardship—only a love for singing and dancing that was not countenanced in her orthodox Brahmin home. Three said they had left their marriages without much ado; they saw the advantage of earning their own living and being at liberty to use their resources as they wished, and did not want to have children; and the remaining four were daughters of other tawaif. Not one claimed that kidnapping had been her experience, although they had heard of such cases. This assortment of refugees from the *sharif*, or respectable, world gave a completely ironic slant to the notion of respectability.

The problem, according to Saira Jan, a plump woman in her early forties who recounted her escape from a violent and alcoholic husband at length and with humour, was that there were no obliging kidnappers in her *muhalla* (neighbourhood). 'Had there had been such *farishte* [angels] in Hasanganj I would not have had to plot and plan my own escape at great peril to my life and my friend's, who helped me.'[19]

This catalogue reflects the wide range of unfavourable, even dangerous, circumstances from which these women had escaped. Desertion has been traditionally resorted to by those trapped in situations they had no other effective means of fighting or changing. To the list of fugitives from oppression—which includes Black slaves in the *ante bellum* United States, bonded labourers on colonial plantations, and drafted soldiers —can be added women fleeing the quotidian suffering they encountered as daughters, sisters, or wives.[20] Gulbadan, who was a chaudharayan from her late thirties (she claims she was born in 1900 and initiated when she was thirteen years old), had been the niece of a tawaif and was raised in the household she now managed. She spoke of the kotha as a sanctuary for both men and women; men escaped the boredom of their domestic lives and women found in it a greater peace and freedom than in the normal world. She reminded Saira that she was a miserable, underweight, frightened wretch when she had first appeared at her doorstep. 'She was thin as a stick, her complexion was blotchy, her eyes sunk in black holes, and she had less than two rupees tied to the end of her sari. Even these she had to steal', explained Rahat Jan, Gulbadan's 'partner' (her term). 'Now look at her, we call her our *hathini* [female elephant], who eats milk and *jalebi* [syrup-filled, deep fried sweets] to keep herself occupied between meals, although she argues it is to keep her voice melodious.'

Most women told their stories of their prior lives with enthusiasm. They had wanted to escape 'hell' (the word *jahannum*, the Islamic hell, was frequently used to describe their earlier homes) at any cost. The rigours of learning professional skills and earning their own money helped them develop self-esteem and value the relative independence they encountered in Rahat Jan's kotha. It may well be that some of the women exaggerated the past, but the kernels of their stories were embedded in the reality of the gender bias in society. Here they could be women first, and Hindus and Muslims in a more mutually tolerant way, since the culture of the kotha represented elements of both, and was acknowledged as a truly synthetic tradition. The story of one of the Hindu child widows, Rasulan Bai, 35, is especially compelling because it exposes the ineffectiveness of the social-reform legislation passed in the last 150 years and the lack of options for young childless widows even today. While it is the story of a habitual but covert rebel, it also explains why a courtesan is not willing to engage in questioning her status as a collaborator in perpetuating patriarchal values that keep other women in powerless positions:

I was married when I was ten. My natal family was Rajput, my father and uncles owned fifty acres of irrigated land; my mother did not have to work too hard because we had two servants who did most of the household work. I had attended three years of school but I barely knew how to recognize the letters that spell my name. My *gauna* ceremony occurred just three months after menarche. I remember being taken to my husband's house with my dowry, and plenty of gifts for my in-laws. My father sent several sacks of wheat, sugar, lentils, and other produce from the farm because I was married to a young Rajput boy whose father had gambled away most of their wealth. That summer [1960] there was a very big flood, which washed away the mud huts in the village, the livestock and our food reserves. While my husband was out with his brothers trying to salvage some of the food stored in earthenware jars, he slipped and fell into the water and three days later was dead after a severe bout of cholera. I survived but I often wished I were dead. The local Brahmin said that my ill-starred presence had brought flood and death to the village. My jewels, clothes, and the few silver coins which I had hidden away, were all forcibly taken away from me, and I became a widow in white who did all the nasty, heavy chores for the household. I was fed scraps when I cried out in hunger. You talk about the laws that were passed by the British to prevent child marriage, you talk of the rights we won when the Hindu Civil Code [1956] was passed but I sneer at all that. I had no recourse to the laws, or to lawyers, only to my wits sharpened by adversity. I first tried to get back at them with sly acts of sabotage. I did the washing-up indifferently, leaving a dull film on the metal platters and the pots. For this my mother-in-law thrashed me. I would sneak into the kitchen when my sister-in-law had finished cooking and add a heavy dose of salt to the lentils and vegetables. I would hide my smile when I heard the yells and abuse heaped on her by the men folk. She caught me one day and thrashed me soundly until I howled with pain. Her husband came home and gave me another hiding. Life was unbearable but I was trapped; there was nowhere that I could go. My parents, who had come for the funeral to our village, were distressed but they did not offer to take me back because they still had my younger sisters to marry. Fights, violence erupted all the time. My sister-in-law kept wishing me dead. Finally, when they found out that I stole money, to buy snacks from the vendor, they threatened to burn me alive. I wanted to run away but didn't know where I would go, except to the river to drown myself. Finally when an itinerant troupe of entertainers was encamped in our village I saw the performance and thought I would secretly apply to work for them, just do their housework or something. They agreed to shelter me after I told them my troubles and showed them the bruises on my body. They smuggled me out of that hell, gave me bit parts in their dramas, and finally brought me to the lap of Bibi Khanum [another tawaif] in Lucknow, and I have never looked back. I had no option but to run away. Tell me, sister, what would you have done in my place?[21]

There were many stories, each with its own flavour of horror, and of courage, and none that did not have a happy ending. Comparable employment opportunities for women simply did not exist. Gulbadan explained that not all women in need can make the kotha their refuge. Some were not talented enough to become professionals, and some were too anxious about their moral standing. Women, particularly from the higher strata of Hindu and Muslim society, feared violent reprisals if discovered by their families, or shrank from exposure to strange men.

Many women flee their homes in the villages and come to the anonymity of the city to work as domestic servants, as *ayahs* or maids, or cooks. Some join road gangs run by government or private building contractors only to break bricks into small pieces with a hammer, all day in the sun, and earn in a month what we make in a few hours of passing the time in civilized company.[22] To make ends meet they have to sleep with their employers and the *dalal* or middlemen, who found them their jobs, and get beaten up by their husbands when they find out. A woman compromises her dignity twenty-four hours of the day when she has no control over her body or her money.[23]

This response was peppered by the concern of the others for the fact that women are always vulnerable to the exploitative demands of men in the outside world.

The women who said that their own parents had sold them when they were unable to feed them, let alone set aside money to pay for a wedding and a dowry, felt that their parents were forced by circumstances to take such a hard decision. They sent money home every month to take care of their impoverished families, which was gratefully received, and whatever resentment they may have felt for being abandoned as children had dissipated through understanding the limits imposed on women in this world. Gulbadan, who spoke more aphoristically than the others, explained that even fifty years ago there was very little scope for women to change the lives they grumblingly led.

What they couldn't change they called their *kismat*, their fate. Here, in our world, even though things are not as good as they were before the Birtish [British] came, women change their kismat. Even philosophers and poets will tell you that no one can change their kismat.

Ask these women, who have lived and worked together for more than twenty years, whether or not they think that I taught them how to mould their own fate like clay with their own hands.

I did, and they agreed, with laughing nods, while they celebrated Janma Ashtami (birthday of the Hindu god Krishna, the patron of their dance) and the Muslim festival of Id on the third floor of Gulbadan's impressively large building. And this was the very essence of their worldview.

Gulbadan had tossed this off as she sat on the large platform covered with an old Persian rug and velvet-and-brocade bolsters that propped her up. Watching her deft fingers prepare a *paan*, or betel leaf, with its half dozen nut-and-spice fixings, I felt I was in the presence of an alchemist who had transformed base fortunes into gold. She, along with her septuagenarian friends, had inherited a way of life and struggled to preserve it, quite selfishly, in the face of an increasingly hostile future. Their business was neither to exploit women, nor to transform the lot of the generality of womankind, but to liberate and empower those with whom they were associated. The high level of camaraderie, wit, teasing, and affectionate interaction that I observed and participated in on several visits to their apartments over eight years affirmed this impression repeatedly.

The process of 'changing one's fate' (*kismat badalna*) is, under closer scrutiny, a psycho-social process through which the social construction of gender (and sexuality, as we shall see) is stripped bare. The chaudharayan acts in several capacities, the most challenging being to inspire, in the women who come to them, a confidence in their own ability and worth, restore shattered nerves and set about undoing the socialization they had received in their natal homes. This delicate and difficult task, at one level, is not unlike the task modern psychotherapy purports to perform in western society:

The problem was to forget the meaning of the word *aurat* [woman] that had been dinned into my mind and had shaped my behaviour from the day I was born. Fortunately I was still a child [thirteen or or fourteen] so forgetting was not as difficult as it might have been even a few years later. I forgot my misery upon arriving in a house where a different meaning for that word was already in place, where

Amina Ba'i and Zehra Jan [Gulbadan's granddaughters] were acting out those meanings for us all.

They did not fear men because they were admired and praised by men; nor had they ever been nagged by their mother and grandmother about not doing this or that or they would not be able to get married, nor slapped by a father for being 'immodest'. They had never been upset at being a burden to their parents since the shadow of *dahej* [dowry] has never darkened their lives. I resented them to begin with, thought them spoilt and selfish, but slowly I began to realize that they were of a different mould. I would have to break my own mental mould and recast myself. I got a lot of love from Gulbadan, Rahat Jan, and Amiran. They would listen to me, and I would regurgitate all the sorrow, pain, and poison I had swallowed, again and again. Now when I tell you my story, it is as if I am telling you another's tale. Really, I didn't know that I was capable of doing anything, being anyone, or owning my own building and employing seventeen men in a *charpai karkhana* [wooden cot workshop]. I had the mentality of a timid and ugly mouse; now I am accused of being too arrogant, and am envied for the property I own.[24]

The process of rehabilitation for these women is vastly quickened since they arrive young and are plunged into a welcoming environment. The self-affirming ethos of the kotha makes it possible for them to assimilate their newly revised perceptions and behaviour patterns. They unanimously agreed that living among a host of nurturing and supportive women without the fear of men, and freedom from the pressure of the 'marriage market' where grooms were 'for sale', gave them the inner courage to develop their skills and treat men as equals, or even inferiors.

There are other therapeutic devices invented over the ages that are still in use in these salons. The novices are introduced to a secret repertoire of satirical and bawdy songs, dances, informal miming and dramatic representations, aimed at the institution of marriage and heterosexual relations, that are privately performed only among women. These 'matinée shows', as they call them, are not only crucial for the solidarity and well-being of the group, but also help the newcomers to discard the old and internalize the new meaning of being an *aurat*. I recognized this, when in answer to one of my early (and very naïve) questions I was treated to a vignette on the 'joys' of marriage:

VTO: Gulbadan, since you are a handsome woman, so well educated, with all this money and property and jewels, why didn't you marry a *sharif* (respectable) nawab (there are several descendants of noble families in Lucknow who use this honorific) and settle down to a life of respectability?

Gulbadan (first frowned in thought, and then laughingly said): We first thought you were a *jasus* (spy) for the government or for the Christian missionaries; Chhote Mian tells me you visit their offices all the time with your notebook. But, you are very naïve because you ask strangely ignorant questions, which you call doing Amriki [American] research. Is marriage 'respectable' in Amrika? Are women not abused there? Are you married? No? Yes? Don't know? Well let us show you what marriage is before you wish it on an old and respectable woman like myself, or any of us here. Let us dispel the darkness in your mind about the nature of marriage.[25]

Of what they then played out for me, I can only offer an inadequate summary, because it is difficult to capture the visual details of the half-hour-long satirical medley of song, dance, dialogue and mime that followed: Rasulan immediately took her *dupatta* (long scarf) and wound it around her head as a turban to play the husband. Elfin Hasina Jan took her cue as the wife, others became children and members of the extended family, while Gulbadan remained on her settee amid the bolsters, taking occasional drags from the hookah, presiding, as a particularly obnoxious mother-in-law, on a scene of domestic disharmony. The wife/mother first surveys the multifarious demands on her energy and time: the children squall, ask for food and drink, and want to be picked up; the mother-in-law orders that her legs, which have wearied from sitting, be pressed; the husband demands his food and undivided attention; the father-in-law asks for his hookah to be refilled, and a sister-in-law announces that she cannot finish doing the laundry, nor knead the chapati dough because she is not feeling too well. Hasina is defeated, harried, and on the brink of a nervous breakdown. While muttering choice obscenities under her breath she begins, in a frenzied way, to do the job of a wife.[26] She lights the coal stove, dusts and tidies the room, cooks, presses the legs of the mother-in-law who emits pleasurable grunts, carries live coals to replenish the hookah, tries to soothe baby who is now wailing, puts plates of food in front of the demanding husband while she is dragged down by another child. She finally collapses, her hands striking her own brow as she croaks a '*hai tobah*' ('never more'). A little later the din subsides and she, choked with sobs, says that her kismat is terrible, that she would do anything not to have to be the *bahu* (daughter-in-law) in this or any household, if only she had the choice. She is chained to this frightful life, all for the sake of money to fill her stomach and for shelter. The rest of the household snores noisily while her husband, who is belching and hiccupping after his food and drink, makes a lunge at her for some quick sex. She succumbs, and after thirty agitated seconds of his clumsy effort she asks him for money for household expenses. He grudgingly parts with twenty rupees and reminds her that he finished off the bottle of the local brew. She complains that the money is just not enough even for the groceries, for which she receives a slap, weepingly renders an accounting of the money she spent last week, cries some more and finally falls asleep, wretched and hungry.

Apart from the cathartic and didactic value of such a representation, it transmuted grim reality into mordant comment, marked with its own special brand of mockery. The women pointed out the several 'morals' embedded in the story: Those who dare to hold 'moral' objections to the life of a tawaif should first examine the thankless toil of an average housewife, including her obligation to satisfy a sometimes faithless, or alcoholic, or violent, husband, for the sake of a very meagre living. Such an existence is without dignity, and was not the situation of the housewife tantamount to that of a common prostitute, giving her body for money?[27] 'It is we who are brought up to live in *sharafat* [genteel respectability] with control over our bodies and our money and they who suffer the degradation reserved for lowly [*neech*] women.'[28]

Such vivid reversals of social perception and logic are stock idioms in their speech and song. Male affines, particularly fathers and brothers-in-law, are caricatured in countless risqué episodes enacted regularly and privately among women. They mock the repressive relationships and male sexuality in the conjugal home, even as they amuse, educate, and edify the denizens of the kotha.[29] These routines, studded with subversive and irreverent jokes and obscene gestures, are performed like secret anti-rites,[30] which have been carefully distilled and historically transmitted from generation to generation, to form the core of their private consciousness and oral heritage.

I had also seriously questioned the courtesans' use of the *burqa*, which is a long over-cloak that Muslim women in purdah wear for extended seclusion outside the home. This cloak, usually black or white, is worn over regular clothes and covers the wearer from head to foot. It has a small rectangular piece of netting that fits over the eyes and enables the wearers to see, while they cannot be seen at all. It is certainly an artefact of a male-dominated society, where men could dictate that women keep themselves covered so as not to provoke male lust.[31] It was, at first, inexplicable why tawaif not only used the burqa to move around when they went visiting or shopping, but actually insisted that I too should wear one as they led me to other kothas in the vicinity, since injunctions about female modesty did not apply to them. It was precisely because they were not expected to be in purdah, they reasoned (in another classic reversal of patriarchal logic), that they chose to block the gaze of men. It was an extension of the autonomy they enjoyed in their living space and their *jism* (bodies), unlike 'normal' women whose bodies were the property of their husbands and who were secluded but lacked privacy in their own homes. The latter were kept in purdah to maintain (and increase) *khaan-daani izzat*, or family honour; for them to show their faces in public would bring disgrace to their families. 'Ah, but our case is just the opposite', said Saira,

men long to see our faces. If they could brag among their friends that they had seen Gulbadan or Amiran in the bazaar without a covering, they would go up in the esteem in which their friends hold them. We are not in the business of giving them cheap thrills. While we walk freely and anonymously in public places, looking at the world through our nets, they are deprived because we have blinkered *them*. We do not, as you know, bestow anything on men without extracting its price.[32]

I would have disputed this had I not experienced the freedom the burqa gave *me* to walk along the winding alleys in a very old-fashioned and gossip-filled city, where I formerly never passed without being accosted with vulgar taunts from the idle youths who mill on the streets. These women had appropriated the power of the gaze while eluding the leer of sexually frustrated men. Playing by the rules of strict segregation practised in this patriarchal society to restrict female sexuality among 'respectable women', the tawaif find the burqa liberating instead of restrictive, and are aggressively invisible to all those who wish to behold their faces. They know they can discard the burqa at will, as some of the younger women in the outer world are doing in defiance more and more, but they *choose* to use it as a perforated barrier between the world and them. Yet its use remains an indictment of male behaviour and culture.

A great deal has been said and is known about the rigorous training and education courtesans undergo to ultimately please and entertain their patrons.[33] What has never received discursive treatment is a very significant part of their secret skill—the art of *nakhra* or pretence that courtesans have to master in order to spare no opportunity of coaxing money out of their patron and his friends. Their avowed and unabashed purpose is to amass a tidy fortune as early in their careers as possible, so that they can invest the surplus in income-producing properties or enterprises, and retire comfortably at the age of thirty-five or so. To achieve their material ambitions they use, in addition to their exorbitant rates, an arsenal of devious 'routines' that make up the buried text of an evening's entertainment. These are subtly deployed to bargain, cajole, and extort extra cash or kind from their unsuspecting clients.[34] Some of these are learnt, some invented, some even improvised, but nuances are refigured with care to suit the temperament of a client or the mood of the moment to feel 'spontaneous'. They are repeatedly rehearsed between the chief courtesan and the trainee, and evaluated by the adept tawaif, until no trace of the pretence is discernible.

These well-practised ploys—the feigned headache that interrupts a dance or a song, feigned anger for having been neglected, a sprained ankle, tears, a jealous rage—have beguiled generations of men to lose thousands of extra rupees or gold coins to these women. The tawaif's refusal, at a critical juncture, to complete a sexual interlude with a favourite patron is a particularly profitable device, because feigned coital injuries or painful menstrual cramps involve expensive and patient waiting on the part of the patron. Gulbadan said she often carried the game a step further by 'allying' herself with the patron against the 'offending' courtesan to set the seal of authenticity on the scene. She would scold and even slap her till the patron begged her not to be so harsh. Gulbadan was the privately acclaimed champion of these more serious confidence tricks, and others cheerfully confessed to having blackmailed, stolen, lied and cheated for material gain as soon as they acquired competence in this art. This may sound more like self-enrichment than resistance, but because society has virtually denied women control over wealth or property, it is essential to establishing a counter-cultural way of life.

The formula, Gulbadan confided, is to win the complete trust of the man. This they do by first mastering all the information about the man—his public reputation, his finances, his foibles and vanities, his domestic life, and the skeletons in his closet:

Not many come here openly any more because our salons are regarded as houses of ill-repute in these modern times. Most come to drink and for sexual titillation. We know how to get a man drunk and pliant, so that we can extort whatever we want from him: money, even property, apologies, jewels, perfume, or other lavish gifts. Industrialists, government officers, other businessmen come here now; they have a lot of black money [undeclared cash] that they bring with them, sometimes without even counting it. We make sure that they leave with very little, if any. We know those who will pay large sums to ensure secrecy, so we threaten them with careless gossip in the bazaar or with an anonymous note addressed to their fathers or their wives.

We do not act collectively as a rule but sometimes it may become necessary to do so. We once did a drama, against a moneylender who came and would not pay us the money he had promised for holding an exclusive soirée for him. So when a police officer, who had fallen in love with me, came by, we all told him tales of how the wretched man would not return jewels some of us had pawned with him. We filed a police report, he was arrested, and some of the pawned items (which the jeweller had taken from some of our recently straitened noble patrons) were made over to us by the love-lorn officer; others of his debtors sent us sweets and thanks for bringing the hated Ram Swarup to justice.

But our biggest nakhra of all is the game of love that makes these men come back again and again, some until they are financially ruined.

They return every evening, like the flocks of homing pigeons, in the vain belief that it is *we* who are in love with *them*.[35]

In *Umrao Jan Ada* this particular nakhra is described with insight:

I am but a courtesan in whose profession love is a current coin. Whenever we want to ensnare anyone we pretend to fall in love with him. No one knows how to love more than we do: to heave deep sighs; to burst into tears at the slightest pretext; to go without food for days on end; to sit dangling our legs on the parapets of wells ready to jump into them; to threaten to take arsenic. All these are parts of our game of love. *But I tell you truthfully, no man ever really loved me nor did I love any man.*[36]

A discussion of this last nakhra, which occurred only after several visits, brought perhaps the most startling 'hidden' text to light. It was difficult to imagine that these women, even though they were economically independent, educated, and in control of their lives, would spurn the opportunity for real intimacy and emotional stability. Everyone agreed that emotional needs do not disappear with success, fame, or independence; on the contrary, they often intensify. Almost every one of the women I interviewed during these many visits claimed that their closest emotional relationships were among themselves, and eight of them admitted, when I pressed them, that their most satisfying physical involvements were with other *women*. They referred to themselves as *chapat baz* or lesbians, and to *chapti*, or *chipti*, or *chapat bazi*, or lesbianism.[37] They seemed to attach little importance to labels, and made no verbal distinctions between homosexual and heterosexual relations. There was no other 'serious' or poetic term for lesbianism, so I settled for their colloquialisms. Their explanation for this was that emotions and acts of love are gender free. 'Serious' words such as *mohabbat* (Urdu) or *prem* (Hindi), or love (English) are versatile and can be used to describe many kinds of love, such as the love of man or woman, the love for country, for siblings, parents of either sex, so there was no need to have a special term for love between two women, nor was there a need to flaunt it in any way. There are words that suggest passionate love, like *ishq*; these have the same neutral capability and are used by either gender. Although their lesbianism was a strictly private matter for them, the absence of a specialized vocabulary reduced it to a simple fact of life, like heterosexual love, or the less denied male homosexual love. The lack of terminology may be interpreted as the ultimate disguise for it; if something cannot be named it is easy to deny its existence. Urdu poetry, too, is often ambiguous about gender, and homosexual love often passes for heterosexual love.[38] Many poems really express homosexual love, of the persona of the poem for a young boy, who is described in the idioms for feminine beauty.

The frank discussions on the subject of their private sexuality left some of my informants uneasy. I had probed enough into their personal affairs, they insisted, and they were not going to satisfy my curiosity any further; they were uncomfortable with my insistence on stripping their strategic camouflage, by which they also preserved their emotional integrity. Their very diffidence to talk about their lesbianism underscores the thesis that they believe in a quiet but profound subversion of patriarchal values. It became clear that for many of them heterosexuality itself is the ultimate nakhra, and feigned passion an occupational hallmark. My ardour for precise statistics faded as the real and theoretical implications of their silences and their disguises began to emerge.[39]

What do all these stories signify? Does the courtesans' presentation of their lifestyle add up to a subversion of existing gender relations in heterosexual marriage? Can their beliefs and behaviour be seen as 'feminist' by standards of modern scholarship, or are they just another example of that widespread affliction, 'false consciousness'? How do we reconcile the horizontal stratifications of class with the vertical divide of gender, and their anomalous position in either group? Do they qualify as a subaltern group as women, and as an elite group by virtue of their power and connections? Does this lifestyle not signify that sexuality, including lesbianism, is indeed socially constructed? Let me begin to hack at this thicket by citing Romila Thapar again. In taking ascetics (an equally unlikely-seeming group of rebels) both as individuals or in organized groups, as dissenters, she sees in their rejection of the *grahasta-ashrama*— the householder stage in a prescribed four-stage cycle of an upper-caste Hindu male's life—the essence of their rebellion:

The Brahmanical theory of the four ashramas, first propounded in full in the Jabala Upanishad, brought asceticism into conventional custom by making it the last stage of a man's curriculum and access-ible to the upper castes. By implication however the grahasta-ashrama was a necessary prior requirement. Thus only those who moved directly from *brahmacharya* [celibate student stage] to *sam-nyasa* [ascetic stage] could be called dissenters. An ageing grahasta taking to samnyasa was merely conforming to the ideal *vita*. . . . The negation of the family as a basic unit of society is evident from the opposition to the grahasta status and specially the insistence on celibacy.[40]

Thapar goes on to say that inherent in the act

of opting out of the existing lifestyle and substituting it with a dis-tinctively different one . . . [is that] the characteristics of the new lifestyle be seen as a protest against the existing one. To this extent such movements may be regarded as movements of dissent. But the element of protest was muted by the wish, not to change society radically, but to stand aside and create an alternative system.[41]

The lifestyle of female ascetics could not be reckoned as a true counterpart because, as Thapar points out, even among as-cetics, females, with few exceptions, were always subordinate to the authority of males. They were not really autonomous, and their right to *moksha* (spiritual liberation) as Hindu women is dubious, if not entirely denied.

I would argue that the true female counterpart of the re-bellious ascetic, and perhaps the more daring, is the tawaif. By listening carefully to the stories the courtesans tell, it be-comes undeniable that they, too, are rebelling, all the more explicitly, against the housewifely stage, since this is the *only* 'stage of life' implicitly mandated for all women in both Hindu and Islamic cultural systems. It is in this stage that she must achieve total fulfilment because she does not graduate, as the men do, to a maturer level. The informal 'student stage' for a girl used to be, and still is for the majority, the acquisition of practical experience in house work and child care. Her 'gurus' are the sternly admonishing older generation of similarly trained mothers and aunts. Modesty, obedience, and other subordinate behaviour patterns are drilled into her until she comes to hold the single-minded belief that her eligibility for marriage is the only index of her worth. This domestic curriculum is the bedrock on which women's social roles are founded, and it stands in sharp contrast to the cultural education and sense of self-esteem generated in women in the kotha, who consciously but cautiously flout the normative expectations of gendered behaviour. It is the 'normal' woman's social and sexual regimen that courtesans-in-the-making must unlearn and supplant by undergoing a radically different socialization process, and by adopting the lifestyle that gives them the liberation they desire, without jerking the reflexive muscle of a repressive system.

While lifestyles of the male ascetic and the female courtesan are both modes of social dissent, the sexual differences, and the social prescriptions on which they are predicated, produce interestingly contrasted strategies and ideologies. The former emerges from a religious interpretation of grahasta, with the *denial* of sexuality, lineage, and property ownership as its strategic thrust to gain spiritual liberation. The latter, on the other hand, emerges from a secular and domestic context in which women's lives are enmeshed. The courtesans seek material and social liberation by reversing the constraints imposed on women's chastity and economic rights, and establishing a female lineage of selected and ascriptive members who make up their *gharana*. It is in this interpretive light that their lifestyle can be seen, not as one of willing exploitation by patriarchy but as a necessary compromise to escape from its stifling power. The male becomes celibate, renounces property and the privileges of his gender in this world for 'other-worldly' rewards; the female becomes sexually active and aggressively acquisitive, prefers autonomy to 'virtue', and seeks this-worldly 'women's liberation'.

Yet some consequences of these divergent paths are strikingly similar. Both lifestyles subvert the hierarchies of caste and class since in both groups lower-caste and economically disadvantaged persons find refuge. The tawaif have created a secular meritocracy based on talent and education, accepting Hindus and Muslims alike. They too, like the ascetics, are respected by the society at large, and both counter-cultures exist by maintaining vital links to the overarching patriarchal culture, while consciously inverting or rejecting its values. While neither group has the pretension of changing the entrenched notions of grahasta-ashrama, both serve their own personal ends by elaborate strategies of avoidance. By opting for the institutional security of a monastery or a brothel, both groups wielded political power: through the powerful heads of sects in ancient Hindu kingdoms in the subcontinent or through the chaudharayan in nawabi Lucknow and in several other court cities, such as Hyderabad, Rampur, Banaras, Bijapur, and Golkonda. In unfavourable historical circumstances both groups lost political power, but their patented lifestyles still remain viable modes for men and women to elude the shackles of patriarchy and seek their own brands of liberation.

During the reign of the nawabs of Awadh, while these women could manipulate powerful courtiers and the nawabs themselves, even the most powerful patron did not have any authority over their lives. The executive authority and managerial functions were the exclusive preserve of the chaudharayan and her appointees. An angered patron had few options because he had made material investment in a kotha, and there were no refunds or exchanges; his izzat, too, would be on the line since gossip about him would quickly and freely circulate in the bazaar. It is, therefore, not the patron who is ultimately significant, but the matron, who creates the ethos, reputation, and the quality of life and services in her gharana.

If the battle had been against marital oppression and economic powerlessness, then that battle was indeed won through these covert strategies. The courtesan's position is much diminished by the events and reconfigurations of equations of power in the colonial and post-colonial periods. Fully aware of this history, these women find hope in other educational and employment opportunities that have also opened up for women. Their basic goal is to free themselves from an economic dependence on men, even though it is achieved through their patronage. They already had daughters or nieces competing for and obtaining posts in the banking system, or as pleaders in the local courts, but these professions were not, as Amiran pointed out, a way of life. Women might become financially independent but without the refuge of the kotha they would again be forced to marry and suffer the degradation to which the average husbands subject their wives. Amiran's daughter is a

banker who married and had a daughter. 'We were wary of
this alliance, and sure enough her husband took up with
another woman and my daughter and granddaughter are back
with us. She looks after our investments and bank work, so
that she does really contribute to the household with her
labour just as we all do.' In other words, they shrewdly recognized that while financial independence was important, it
did not solve the central problem of the gender inequality
inherent within marriage in a patriarchal society.

Some of the covert strategies of courtesans that I have described earlier defy analysis since they do not fit the scholarly
definitions of 'protest' and 'resistance'. The defections of abused
daughters, child widows, or unhappy wives, are indeed unorganized, sporadic, individual attempts prompted by thoughts
of self-preservation or self-interest; their *nakhre* (plural of
nakhra)—which include blackmail, theft, confidence games,
and even feigned heterosexuality—smack more of a sleazy
underworld than of the acts of determined rebels, particularly
since the consequences of such acts neither threaten nor change
the overall power relations against which they are aimed. Most
of my analytical and definitional qualms have been eradicated
in the masterly analysis presented by James C. Scott in his
path-breaking study on everyday forms of peasant resistance in
his book, *Weapons of the Weak*. He cuts his way through the
tangle of theoretical objections with such incisive and insightful arguments that I find it pertinent to quote him at some
length:

Real resistance, it is argued, is (*a*) organized, systematic, and co-
operative, (*b*) principled or selfless, (*c*) has revolutionary consequences, and/or (*d*) embodies ideas or intentions that negate the basis
of domination itself. Token, incidental, or epiphenomenal activities,
by contrast, are (*a*) unorganized, unsystematic, and individual,
(*b*) opportunistic and self-indulgent, (*c*) have no revolutionary consequences, and/or (*d*) imply, in their intention or meaning, an accommodation with the system of domination. These distinctions are
important for any analysis . . . [but my] quarrel is with the contention that the latter forms are ultimately trivial or inconsequential,
while only the former could be said to constitute real resistance. This
position, in my view, fundamentally misconstrues the very basis of
economic and political struggle conducted daily by subordinate
classes—not only slaves, but peasants and workers [and, I would add,

women] as well—in repressive settings. It is based on an ironic combination of both Leninist and bourgeois assumptions of what constitutes political action.... [T]he problem lies in what is a misleading, sterile, and sociologically naïve insistence upon distinguishing 'self-indulgent', individual acts, on the one hand, from presumably 'principled', selfless, collective actions, on the other, and excluding the former from the category of real resistance. To insist on such distinctions as a means of comparing forms of resistance and their consequences is one thing, but to use them as the basic criteria to determine what constitutes resistance is to miss the very wellsprings of peasant politics.[42]

If traditional constructs of class and class struggle are not directly relevant to the clandestine and unorganized struggles of the peasants in Malaysia, they are even further removed from the arena of *gender relations* and the courtesans' style of reversing an oppressive order. The concern has been to compare the options open to women, married or unmarried, rich and poor, who escape or ameliorate male oppression and gain a significant measure of material and emotional autonomy by embracing a profession that affords an alternative lifestyle. It is futile to use conventional analytical tools and look for a full-blown 'class struggle' or a women's movement in progress. One does not use a hammer to prune a rose bush. Their struggle obviously cannot be a collective, revolutionary 'class struggle', for the gender divisions are vertical, not horizontal, and cut through class lines. The validity of their struggle cannot be refuted on the grounds that it is engaged in at a private, unobtrusive level. Their will to resist existing gender relations and reproduce the radically reordered social relations within their ambit is as self-conscious and intractable as it is undeniable. The *struggle* is, indeed, the process whereby these women, *qua* women, discover new meanings and new possibilities informed by not a false but a realistic consciousness about their place in society. Their object is limited to improving things for themselves, and not to lead a revolution for all women against patriarchy.

The courtesans have uniquely combined the elements of struggle for material *needs* with those of an ideological struggle against patriarchal *values*, by creating and living behind their many masks. They live in outward harmony with male power and male sexuality, for the struggle can only be effective if their subterfuges are mistaken for compliance and their true intentions as collusion with men against *other women*. Their co-operation with some women outside the kotha, such as the *khangi*, or the married women to whom they rent space, so that they too can earn (undisclosed) extra money, is also little known, and it would be no longer politic or possible if it were uncovered. It is true that without a basic redefinition of social roles, women will remain the subaltern minority, for their weapons are indeed the weapons of the weak, effective only within the limits pre-scribed by men, whether they be the nawabs of Awadh, power-ful local patrons, a colonial bureaucracy, or the Government of India.

The various other nakhre of the courtesans are legitimate strategies invented to meet the exigencies of power relations in the repressive, often brutal setting of patriarchal society, used more and more intensively as the nature and quality of the patronage changed over time. In 1854, for example, in the kingdom of Wajid Ali Shah the courtesan was truly as 'free' as any courtier and practised her skills just as much as, say, a lawyer did to enhance his wealth and reputation; in 1856 with the British takeover even the king became a powerless prisoner in exile along with his influential courtiers. The largest and most impressive rebellion in the history of the Indian empire to date occurred shortly thereafter, in 1857, and the courtesans' role in that rebellion is documented as covert but generous finan-ciers of the action. Stripped of their privileged status under the control of the colonial army, they fought against the assaults on their persons, their property, and their 'immorality'; in other words, from then on down to the present day they struggle to retain their validity and some of the tangible benefits of a professional group. Even western feminists see women breaking into the ranks of various professions in society as a key political strategy; tawaif have believed in the same strategy and be-longed not only to the oldest profession but to the *only* profes-sion open to women in those times; they certainly think that today their own daughters must seek other available profes-sional alternatives. Their fear is that this can hardly be done without acquiring the baggage of middle-class family morality and the loss of the relative autonomy they have as unmarried women with only 'illegitimate' children.

It is for these reasons that courtesans have had to resort to outward conformity and the 'partial transcript', as Scott calls the offstage behaviour of Sedaka peasants:

> That the poor should dissemble in the face of power is hardly an occasion for surprise. Dissimulation is the characteristic and necessary pose of subordinate classes everywhere most of the time. . . . No close account of the life of subordinate classes can fail to distinguish between what is said 'backstage' and what may be safely declared openly.[43]

If it can still be argued that no matter what the tawaif's self-perceptions, actions, goals, and ideology are, they were and are still complicitous in perpetuating patriarchal relations in society, it is to insist on the ideal instead of the possible in a struggle for power. It is also to deny that history has fabricated their consciousness, and that this has actively manipulated an institution created for male pleasure into an arena for gaining privileges at par with men.

> I know we are blamed for enabling men to perpetuate their double moral standards and dominate women. Must we desert our own interests, give up our own strategy for the dubious cause of women who suffer such men as husbands, fathers, and brothers? Today we are silent, we are despised and the law has cracked down on us; has that helped the cause of women or only made life harder for us?[44]

In fact their silence is so well held that, for all official intents and purposes (such as taxation), this category of women is no longer acknowledged in post-colonial India. This for them is a mixed outcome: it is a small triumph, because their professional incomes are no longer taxed, yet among their 'patrons' are a large number of public officials; it is a larger defeat because officialdom can piously claim that it has banned female sexual exploitation while converting their once proud profession into a species of 'vice'.

And finally I return to the question of sexuality, as reality and as a nakhra, because there is the larger question of the social construction of sexuality that may well be illumined by analysing the worldview of the courtesans of Lucknow. It is obvious that hegemonic gender relations are effectively perpetuated and sexuality itself constructed through the process of differential socialization of men and women. I would (tentatively) argue further that by systematically reversing the socialization process for females, in order to combat the disabilities inherent in women's existing social and sexual roles, the courtesans have logically 'constructed' lesbian existence as a legitimate alternative, just as much as Indian society at large constructs and enforces, through the institution of compulsory marriage, heterosexuality as 'normative' behaviour. Heterosexual relations for most of the courtesans was work, not pleasure. Right from birth, if we recall the testimony of Chhote Mian, the female is celebrated, empowered, cherished; those who arrive as adolescents in the kotha are methodically re-educated within the context of this parallel and exclusive society of women, and its radical vision of power relations. Their relationships with men in the kotha are congenial but business-like; except for kin, only very few ever become emotional bondsmen. Men play diverse roles: not only are they servants, cooks, watchmen, and musicians, but also they are wealthy, generous, powerful patrons. The latter relate on equal terms with the courtesans precisely because power is genuinely shared in that cultural setting. It is therefore not preposterous to suggest that it is in the kotha, rather than in the 'normal' world where power relationships tend to be more skewed, that female sexuality has the chance of being more fairly and fearlessly constructed by women.

If I had the space to explore the subject cross-culturally, I would offer, in support of this contention, the growing evidence of lesbianism in brothels, salons, geisha houses, and apartments of call girls in international capitals, which is a universal common denominator across time and space.[45] That sexuality competes with economics for priority in the struggle against gender inequality is not surprising; that male sexual control and aggression are neutralized in a setting where the heterosexual sex act is mere routine, and passion and pleasure are simulated or distanced, is perhaps an essential mechanism that women have universally used to preserve their emotional integrity and dignity. All the courtesan's nakhre, particularly the sexual pretences, are brilliantly echoed in the following interview Studs Terkel conducted with a hooker, Roberta Victor:

Of course we faked it. . . . The ethic was: . . . You always fake it.
You're putting something over on him and he is paying for something he really didn't get. That's the only way you keep any sense of
self-respect. The call-girl ethic is very strong. You were the lowest
of the low if you allowed yourself to feel anything. . . . The way you
maintain your integrity is by acting all the way through. It's not too
far removed from what most American women do—which is to put
on a big smile and act. . . . Here I was doing absolutely nothing,
feeling nothing, and in twenty minutes I was going to walk out with
fifty dollars in my pocket. . . . How many people could make fifty
dollars for twenty minutes' work? [and] no taxes, nothing. . . .
*She speaks of her profound love for a woman who she'd met in prison; her nurs-
ing her lover when the woman had become blind.* [Terkel's words inter-
spersed with Roberta's are in italics in the original.] I was in control
of every one of their relationships. You're vulnerable if you allow
yourself to be involved sexually. I wasn't. They were. I called it.
Being able to manipulate someone sexually, I could determine when
I wanted that particular transaction to end. 'Cause I could make the
guy come. I could play all kinds of games. See? It was a tremendous
sense of power. . . . Here's all these guys slobbering all over you all
night long. I'm lying there, doing math or conjugations or Spanish
poetry in my head. (Laughs.) . . .

The overt hustling society is the microcosm of the rest of society.
The power relations are the same and the games are the same. Only
this one I was in control of. The greater one I wasn't. In the outside
society, if I tried to be me I wasn't in control of anything. As a bright
assertive woman, I had no power. As a cold manipulative hustler I
had a lot. I knew I was playing a role. Most women are taught to
become what they act. All I did was act out the reality of American
womanhood.[46]

Roberta's philosophy of life and her indictment of contemporary American society matches, in startling detail, that of the
courtesans of Lucknow, and this 'coincidence' gives their
stories a compelling ring of truth. In quest of a room of their
own and considerably more than five hundred pounds a year,
these women had taken control of their lives by reversing not
only the rules, but even the sexual fantasy of patriarchy.

NOTES

The research for this paper was unwittingly funded by the American Institute for Indian Studies (1975–6) and the American Council for Learned Societies (1980–1), and the Social Science Research Council (1985–6), for which I am very grateful. I thank Douglas Haynes, Philip Oldenburg, Frances Pritchett, Ellen Ross, Katherine R. Stimpson, Romila Thapar, Judy Walkowitz, Judy Walsh, and Gauri Vishwanathan for their prompt and insightful comments.

1. Romila Thapar, *Ancient Indian Social History* (New Delhi: Orient Longman Ltd, 1978), pp. 63–104. The essay I refer to, 'Renunciation: The Making of a Counter-culture?', is a brilliant discussion of samnyasis, the inherent notion of dissent in their way of life, and their attempt to create a parallel society without trying to radically alter society at large.

2. This line of analysis was also helped by observing and reading about the U.S. in the nineteen-sixties and early seventies, when university campuses were stirring not only with demonstrations and protest marches but also with a variety of 'counter-cultural' lifestyles that were invented or imitated to resist the overarching capitalistic and militaristic values of those who had mired the nation in the Vietnam war.

3. Lloyd I. and Susanne H. Rudolph have an excellent discussion on this point in *Gandhi: The Traditional Roots of Charisma* (Chicago: University of Chicago Press, 1983); and so does Madhu Kishwar, 'Gandhi on Women', in *Economic and Political Weekly*, vols xx and xxi, 5 and 12 October 1985.

4. There are several books on the subject, a fairly solid account from Mohenjodaro to medieval times being Moti Chandra's *The World of the Courtesan* (Delhi: Vikas Publishing House, 1973). Courtesans are mentioned in great detail in several classic sources that describe Indian society: Kautilya's *Arthashastra*, Vatsyayana's *Kamasutra*, and Bharata's *Natyashastra*.

5. Judith R. Walkowitz, 'Male Vice and Female Virtue: Feminism and the Politics of Prostitution in Nineteenth Century Britain', *History Workshop Journal* (Spring 1982), p. 93. This passing mention of a significant debate should not be viewed as a dismissal of it; this only signifies my own position on it and my essential agreement with Walkowitz's argument.

6. For a detailed account of these sources, taxation policies, and the subtle and overt forms of resistance and evasion adopted by the citizens of Lucknow, see my *The Making of Colonial Lucknow, 1856–1877* (Princeton: Princeton University Press, 1984), chapter 5. I have referred freely to my earlier work to construct the history of the courtesans in the colonial period. A full analysis of earlier interviews, specially those conducted in 1980–1, 1983, and 1984, is presented here for the first time.

7. The last Shi'i nawab or king of Awadh, Wajid Ali Shah, acquired a large harem of singers and dancers by using a Shi'i variant of Islamic

marriage called *mutah*. This allows a man to contract a limitless number of alliances with women, which automatically cease when the stipulated time elapses. It saves men and women from the accusation of adultery, and in Wajid Ali Shah's case gave him the opportunity to be a true patron of these talented women by bestowing on them some of the best real estate in the capital of the Muslim state of Awadh, Lucknow. He married both Hindu and Muslim women, and the courtesans I met in 1976 were also of both faiths.

8. Oldenburg, *passim*. For a detailed account of British reaction to the mortality statistics in the colonial army and their control of prostitutes, see Kenneth A. Ballhatchet, *Race, Sex and Class under the Raj* (London: Weidenfield and Nicolson, 1980).

9. Oldenburg, pp. 131–42.

10. This scholar also requested that his name, address and relationship to the courtesans not be revealed, so I have referred to him as Chhote Mian. The interview took place in January 1976.

11. This section is summarized from Oldenburg, pp. 131–42. Corroborative evidence from other sources will appear in the notes. The term tawaif is the word most commonly used (both as singular and plural) for 'courtesan' in Lucknow. Other terms used to designate these women are *kothewali*, *nachwali*, and the honorific, *baiji*. I will use the first term, and this will distinguish the courtesans from common prostitutes, whose main service was to provide sexual services to their clients.

12. Abdul Halim Sharar, *Lucknow: The Last Phase of an Oriental Culture*, trans. and ed. E. S. Harcourt and Fakhir Hussain (London: Paul Elek, 1975), p. 192.

13. Peter Manuel, 'Courtesans and Hindustani Music', *Asian Review* (Spring 1987), pp. 12–17. In this brief piece Manuel sketches the role of courtesans in enriching the musical traditions of India, and describes the development of *thumri* and *gazal*, semi-classical genres of singing, by the courtesans of Lucknow in their bid to adapt to the taste of their new patrons, the *taluqdars* of Awadh, after Wajid Ali Shah and his chief courtiers were exiled in 1856. I have discussed the role of rural taluqdars and their transformation into an urban elite in great detail in my *Making of Colonial Lucknow*, pp. 215–30.

14. Most Hindi films, called *masala* or formula films, are popular because of the songs and dances in them. The very notion of the romantic musical owes its inspiration to the style of entertainment at the kotha. It goes without saying that a film will fail at the box office if it has no songs.

15. The romantic and generous patronage of Wajid Ali Shah, who 'fell in love' with a large assortment of 'female palanquin bearers, courtesans, domestic servants, and women who came in and out of the palace, in short with hundreds of . . . beautiful and dissolute women', is legendary and retold by Sharar. He goes on to say that 'soon dancers and singers became the pillars of state and favourites of the realm.' (page 63)

16. Mirza Mohammad Hadi Ruswa, *Umrao Jan Ada*, trans. Khushwant Singh and M. A. Husaini (Madras, India: Sangam Books, 1982), p. ix. This is cited from Khushwant Singh's preface.

Veena Talwar Oldenburg

58 *Veena Talwar Oldenburg*

17. Interview with Gulbadan, aged 83, in August 1980, after the release of the film *Umrao Jan Ada*. Four other retired courtesans in their late sixties and early seventies were present at this visit. They had not seen the film but had read the novel; two of them claimed to have known Ruswa personally in their youth. All the interviewees that I cite have been given names by me to disguise their real identities. I have translated into English the substance of the unstructured interviews I conducted; these were mostly in the form of conversations in Urdu with these women. The paragraph which follows is constructed out of the conversation we had on this occasion.

18. See Oldenburg, pp. 138–41, for a detailed account of this. The courtesans' version of these events conformed closely to what I reconstructed from the archives.

19. Saira spoke to me for two hours on 2 November 1976. She never failed to add her opinion to those being voiced on countless other occasions if she was within earshot.

20. An extremely interesting article by Raymond A. and Alice H. Bauer, 'Day to Day Resistance to Slavery', *The Journal of Negro History*, vol. XXVII (4 October 1942), presages much of the literature on what they call 'less spectacular' and 'indirect retaliation for their enslavement'. It was very useful in formulating the argument that I present here, and I thank Geraldine Forbes for the reference.

21. This story is the story of the courtesan I call Rasulan Bai, although it echoes the tone and substance of the lives of the other widows that I interviewed. They are all from the same clan of Rajput Hindus from western Uttar Pradesh. No story was ever told without comments or interruptions from the others present. This life-story was related to me in November 1980.

22. In the 1860s in Lucknow 'a randi . . . charged a nightly rate of five rupees and often more; tawaif insisted on a hundred rupees a night and also received lavish gifts of jewellery and property. A male labourer was only paid two to four annas [one rupee = 16 annas] and a female labourer only half that' (Oldenburg, p. 138). A century later, with the number of generous patrons on the wane, the disparities in income were only slightly less ridiculous. A contractor paid women labourers between seven and ten rupees a day, and a well-known tawaif charged three thousand rupees for a musical evening. Most had regular income besides, from investments, rents, and sale of produce from orchards or shops.

23. Interview with Gulbadan, November 1980.

24. Interview with Rasulan, 35, Amina Bai, 42, and Zehra Jan, 48, in December 1980. Rasulan is the speaker here.

25. I was not allowed to take notes or record this performance, play-cum-mime, nor any of my conversations with these women, since this is a part of kotha life that is not shared with male patrons or outsiders. What I present here is a prosaic version of what I saw, reconstructed from memory and the notes I wrote after the meeting. This event occurred in September 1976, and was repeated in a slighly modified

version (since an oral tradition is not bound by a text), at my request in July 1984.

26. These, it is useful to point out, are not the run-of-the-mill obscenities heard in the bazaar; they are special *gaaliyan*, poetic, funny, stylized terms and phrases of abuse. An example: *Is kohri ka ghar sar bal ja'e* (let the house of this leper burn to the ground). Many wish impotence or boils on male genitals.

27. Similar sentiments are expressed about the bourgeois housewife in Karl Marx's *Communist Manifesto*.

28. Rasulan Bai, November 1980. Elsewhere prostitutes also express a strong aversion to marriage. Geraldine Forbes brought to my attention a late-nineteenth-century account of the profession in Bombay that reiterates these sentiments: 'No *Bhavin* [very degraded category of prostitute] would consent to contract matrimony with a person of her own caste, or remain in his keeping, as prostitution, in their view, is more honourable; it enriches and makes them sole mistresses of their liberty and property, and their protectors are ever ready to be at their command', in K. Raghunathji, 'Bombay Dancing Girls', *Indian Antiquary*, vol. 13, June 1884, pp. 165–78. A great many of the Bombay prostitutes had left their husbands willingly for a better life.

29. Ruswa has Umrao Jan flatly deny the existence of these 'obscene' routines performed privately among the courtesans, but informs her that there are eye-witness reports to the contrary; she finally concedes that such things do go on but refuses to explicate any further. (Ruswa, p. 32.) Less risqué versions of such songs form the repertoire of village women, and they are sung at weddings or as women go about doing their daily chores.

30. Mary Douglas, in a very interesting analysis of joking rites, in her essay entitled 'Jokes', in *Implicit Meanings* (London: Routledge & Kegan Paul, 1975), pp. 90–114, writes: 'The message of a standard rite is that the ordained patterns of social life are inescapable. The message of the joke is that they are escapable. A joke is by nature an anti-rite. . . . Recall that a joke connects and disorganizes. It attacks sense and hierarchy. The joke rite then must express a comparable situation. If it devalues social structure, perhaps it celebrates something else instead. It could be saying something about the value of individuals as against the value of social relations in which they are organized' (pp. 103–4).

31. The most comprehensive treatment of the subject of purdah is to be found in Hannah Papanek and Gail Minault (eds), *Separate Worlds: Studies of Purdah in South Asia* (Delhi: Chanakya Publications, 1982).

32. Interview with Saira Bai, July 1984.

33. The Kamasutra describes the sixty-four arts the courtesan was supposed to master as a skilled practitioner of her profession (pp. 69 ff.). Ruswa describes in great detail the musical and formal education of Umrao Jan Ada (pp. 19–23) and, throughout the book, comments on her mastery of Urdu poetry and the styles of the leading poets, her ability to write poems, and converse with wit and wisdom.

34. Only after I was accepted as a friend and confidante among them were

they willing to apprise me of their many stylized nakhre or feigning games. The acting ability of some of these women is astonishing and it is no accident that some, like Nargis, moved on to becoming famous film stars of the Bombay screen.

35. Interview with Gulbadan, November 1980.

36. Ruswa, *Umrao Jan Ada*, p. 71. Emphasis added to make clear the discussion that follows.

37. I am grateful to Katherine R. Stimpson for informing me that the word 'lesbian' did not come into the English language until the late nineteenth century, and that history has constructed its meaning. I was unable to find another Hindi or Urdu equivalent. Platt's *Urdu, Classical Hindi and English Dictionary* does not give a root or even an English definition of these terms. It only defines them with customary bashfulness in Latin: '*capat*, s.f. [feminine] = *capti* (used in comp.):– *capat baz*, s.f. Femina libidini sapphicae indulgens:– *capat-bazi*, Congressus libidinosus duarum mulierum.' *The Kamasutra of Vatsyayana*, trans. Sir Richard F. Burton (New York: E. P. Dutton, 1962), refers to this practice being rampant among courtesans but does not give it a name (p. 198). No term is in common usage and an organization of Indian lesbians in the U.S. tellingly calls itself Anamika, i.e. nameless.

38. This is discussed in C. M. Naim, 'The Theme of Homosexual (Pederastic) Love in Pre-Modern Urdu Poetry', in Muhammad Umar Memon (ed.), *Studies in the Urdu Gazal and Prose Fiction*, South Asian Studies Series, no. 5 (Madison: University of Wisconsin, 1979), pp. 120–42. Shaikh Qalandar Bakhsh Jur'at, an Urdu poet from Lucknow (1749–1809), wrote a poem, *Chapti Namah*, in which he describes the sexual intimacies shared by two married women lovers, who elude their husbands every afternoon and speak wistfully of frequent gatherings with other married women of the same persuasion. I am grateful to C. M. Naim for the reference.

39. I have to confess that I wanted a precise head-count of the lesbians, because I wanted to bolster these facts with figures, but they refused to oblige, for it militates against their interest to have me as a credible witness who might want to 'testify' in writing one day. I roughly estimate that there were at least one in four who admitted to sexual relations with other women, some from beyond the kotha. Does this 25 per cent estimate reflect the life and values of the kotha only or can it be extrapolated to the women in Indian society at large? This will remain a rhetorical question until women agree to talk about their sexuality, not as a matter of duty bounded by normative rules, but as a matter of truth. Even though my sample of thirty women is a somewhat self-selected sample of women from that society, this finding has interesting implications about female sexuality in general, since that is the truly hidden text, which defies investigation even by women scholars of South Asia. It would bring to light the many ways that 'normal' women use *their* sexuality, by denying it, by making it available, or by disguising it entirely, to gain varying measures of autonomy in a world dominated by men.

40. Thapar, pp. 73–4 and 86.
41. Ibid., p. 84.
42. James C. Scott, *Weapons of the Weak* (New Haven: Yale University Press, 1985), pp. 292–3 and 295. The theoretical implications of his analysis of everyday forms of peasant resistance are contained in the two final chapters of this exceptionally lucid and compelling work.
43. Scott, p. 284.
44. Interview with Rahat Jan in July 1984.
45. While there is no room here to cite the literature on courtesans in other areas of the world, work done on geishas in Japan, women in the brothels of Czarist Russia, and call girls in the United States—as well as films such as *Mona Lisa* and *Working Girls*—suggest that lesbianism is found among such groups cross-culturally.
46. Studs Terkel, *Working* (New York: Ballantine Books, 1974), pp. 94–103.

3

Issues of Widowhood: Gender and Resistance in Colonial Western India

ROSALIND O'HANLON

I. INTRODUCTION

One of the most striking features of the recent surge of interest in the history of subordinated classes in South Asia has been its indifference to issues of gender. This has deprived us of an extremely valuable perspective with which to rework key concepts for the study of power and protest, identity and community, resistance and autonomy. It has also hindered our understanding of how gender systems themselves were both shaped by, and profoundly shaped, other forms of power in the wider world of colonial social relations. In the case of *Subaltern Studies*, of course, critics have stressed that this exclusion is not accidental, and is the consequence of looking at resistance largely in terms of violence and rebellion.[1] Just as importantly, however, it is the product of what has sometimes been an uncritical and romanticized notion of 'community'. Interpreting resistance simply in terms of the 'autonomous' struggles of communities, of poor peasants, landless labour, mill-hands, tribals and the like, poses severe problems for the study of women's subordination. It disguises the extent to which these 'communities' may themselves be fractured by relations of power, with gender prominent among them.

Responding to these problems, historians of women have developed a number of very different strategies. One of these is represented by Oldenburg's study of Lucknow's courtesans in this volume. This emphasizes the extent to which women themselves were able to develop enclaves of autonomy and resistance against Indian forms of patriarchy. In her conclusion, for example, Oldenburg argues that a courtesan's ability to simulate sexual pleasure as a means of manipulating her clients is evidence that 'women had taken control of their lives by reversing not only the rules, but even the sexual fantasy of patriarchy'.[2] In their forms of social organization, in their means of livelihood and the values they created, these courtesans managed to create a neutral space that 'resists the repressive intrusion of society'.[3]

I find this approach deeply problematic. For it appears that the Lucknow courtesans, while not the inert victims of patriarchy, have found their means of resistance in reversing or inverting its structures. In their contempt for male clients, and in their manipulation of male sexuality, they seem to me to have reproduced in their own practice something very similar to patriarchy's own hatred of women. This is hardly evidence of autonomy, of a space for women that enables them to escape and detach themselves from patriarchal values. It points rather to the informing role which patriarchy has for their own attitudes towards gender, and thus to a very much more complex set of relations. Here, women's resistance did not insulate them from broader struggles over social meanings and resources;—rather, it brought them into new relationships with these. In them, the reproduction and strengthening of hierarchy in one area was often the heavy price of its subversion in others.

There is a strong, if unstated, parallel here with the way in which historians of peasant or tribal insurrections have claimed to see spheres of autonomy and self-generated resistance for their participants. Working within a historiography so dominated by the idea of community, by the themes of cultural autonomy and indomitable resistance, it is tremendously tempting to seize the same polemical tools to stake out a place for women. In the long term, however, such a strategy does little to make women in general more visible as historical subjects, or make clearer the links between gender and wider forms and relations of power. These tasks are not best approached by finding enclaves of women's autonomy or women's resistance to match those of other subordinate groups. Rather, we need to uncover how gender relations intersected with, and profoundly shaped, wider social and political relations in colonial India, in ways which historians have hardly begun to appre-

ciate. This represents a much more powerful strategy for a
feminist history than seeking to accommodate women within
prevailing frameworks of interpretation, whose concepts of
community will always inhibit the study of gender relations.

I propose to explore these themes in a somewhat different
context, through the issue of widow remarriage in late-nineteenth-century India. On this, as on other issues of Hindu
social reform, colonial administrators and liberals, nationalists
and Hindu conservatives conducted voluminous and protracted discussions from very early in the nineteenth century.
Focusing on the 1880s, I shall examine arguments and assumptions put forward by male observers from a variety of different
political perspectives, and compare these with one of the very
few detailed and systematic Marathi commentaries on the
same issues which we have for this period written by a woman,
Tarabai Shinde. Tarabai was the daughter of a prominent
Maratha family in the town of Buldhana in the Central Provinces. Her father was active in non-Brahman politics, and her
single venture into authorship was in part occasioned by the
controversy surrounding the prosecution in Surat, in the early
months of 1881, of a young Brahman widow, Vijayalaksmi,
for having murdered her illegitimate child. Yet her critique,
entitled *Stri-purusha-tulana*, 'A comparison between women and
men', and written in the most bitter and forceful terms,
ranged far beyond the immediate circumstances of the trial
and the predicament of widows, exposing and denouncing the
systematic forms of oppression which men had practised in the
history of the tradition, and continued to practise on their
womenfolk.

My purpose in setting up this comparison is twofold. First, it
is to explore how gender categories and relations were significant for the recruitment of men as agents of colonial power. We
cannot advance our understanding of histories of women in
colonial India without addressing this question. Here, then, I
examine the very different implications for men and for women
of changing constructions of Hindu tradition: not only in the
realm of public debate and representation, but in the administration of textual Hindu law and its longer-term consequences
for social practice in areas such as women's rights to remarriage.

Second, I use Tarabai's commentary to reconstruct something of the way in which women themselves might have perceived, experienced and protested at the consequences for them of changes in the relations between men and women under colonial rule.

2. GENDER RELATIONS AND DOMINANCE IN COLONIAL INDIA

The freedom of widowed women to remarry is actually a very good point of reference from which to discuss the implication of gender categories and relations in colonial structures of authority. Its prohibition, at least in the earlier part of the nineteenth century, was a feature of high-caste and particularly of Brahman social practice. This was a point heavily emphasized in early British attempts to compile digests of Hindu textual law and custom in the Bombay presidency, and to determine which areas of the sastric law presumed to govern high-caste arrangements were applicable to all Hindus, and which were actually at variance with the established practice of lower-caste communities. Assembling his digest for the Bombay Deccan in 1826, which sought to establish a comprehensive ranking of all castes in the region, Arthur Steele noted that 'The custom of a second and inferior marriage, allowed to wives and widows in many castes', formed one of the chief points of difference between custom and Hindu law as it could be ascertained from the various authorities of the Dharmasastra: 'The second marriage of a wife or widow (called Pat by the Mahrattas and Natra in Goozerat) is forbidden in the present age at least, and to twice-born castes. But it is not forbidden to Soodrus.' The prohibition of widow remarriage, Steele reported, served also to mark a ranking within caste groupings, distinguishing Maratha families claiming a Rajput descent and Kshatriya status from ordinary Kunbi communities of agriculturalists: 'Such of them as are high Mahratta (as the families of the Sattara Raja, and other houses of pure Mahratta descent) do not allow their widows to form Pat.'[4] In the absence of any sort of statistical evidence, it is hard to know how accurate Steele's report was. By mid century, however, it was certainly an administrative commonplace that the higher castes disallowed remarriage, while lower castes permitted it.[5]

In spite of these apparently extensive limitations on its social application, the proscription of widow remarriage was a constant preoccupation for male reformers from the earliest decades of the nineteenth century. One of the targets of Rammohan Roy's criticism during the 1820s, the issue was taken up strongly in western India in mid century by the group of Bombay liberals who formed around the deist reform society, the Paramahansa Sabha. M. G. Ranade, the prolific Marathi polemicist Gopal Hari Deshmukh, and the reformer Vishnushastri Pandit combined together in 1862 to set up the reformist newspaper *Induprakash* to campaign on this and other social-reform issues.[6] In 1865 Vishnushastri Pandit also brought out a Marathi translation of Ishvarchandra Vidyasagar's *Remarriage of Hindu Widows*, which had sought to establish that the weight of sastric authority was actually in favour of allowing remarriage. Pressure for legislative intervention in the form of statute, most intense with Vidyasagar's campaign in Bengal, arose because Hindu textual law, as expounded by the Anglo-Indian courts and embodied in a progressive accretion of case law, proscribed widow remarriage for higher castes and held the children of such marriages to be illegitimate.

The passing of the Hindu Widows' Remarriage Act of 1856 did not, of course, result in any substantial liberalization in high-caste practice. Rather, as Lucy Carroll has argued, the act contained an important ambiguity with very material consequences, not for the high-caste communities for whose use it had been intended, but for those amongst whom widow remarriage was already established under customary law.[7] It was not clear whether the act was intended to apply to the whole Hindu population, superseding all previous law, both textual and customary, or whether its purpose was simply an enabling one, applicable to particular communities that wished to take advantage of it. This was a crucial issue. If the remarriage of a widow was deemed to have taken place under the act, its second section disinherited her, in accordance with British interpretations of Hindu textual law, from all rights which she might have had in her first husband's estate. If, on the other hand, the marriage was held to have taken place under customary law, she retained her rights in the estate, unless customary law demanded forfeiture. With their more immediate proximity to local communities, subordinate courts in the three presidencies showed a greater sensitivity to the varied realities of local customary practice, and tended towards the latter interpretation. The High Courts of Calcutta, Madras and Bombay, on the other hand, preferred the fixity of textual law over the mutability and variety of custom. Their predominantly Indian Brahman and patrician Victorian judges—the latter with their own views as to the proper sphere of women's rights and independence—argued that the act applied to all Hindu widows remarrying, and that no widow taking a second husband should be able to retain property inherited from the first. In subsequent contests over widows' inheritance rights in the provinces subject to their authority after 1856, therefore, customary law tended to be pushed out and replaced by a statutory law based, as Carroll notes, on 'Brahminical values which held widow remarriage in disrepute and insisted on some penalty (in this case forfeiture of inheritance rights) being imposed for a breach of the preferred norm of the chaste, prayerful widow.'[8]

These longer-term implications for lower-caste practice notwithstanding, elite reformers in the Bombay presidency continued their campaigns, with Vishnushastri Pandit's establishment of a society for the promotion of widow remarriage in 1866, and the public celebration in 1869 of the high-caste reformer Moraba Kanhoba's marriage to a widow. Conservatives in the presidency responded with a society of their own, the Hindudharma Vyavasthapak Sabha, and the two engaged in a series of public contests, culminating in Pune in 1870 with a formal public debate, over which the Shankaracharya of Karvir Math near Kolhapur presided, to determine the question of sastric authority. Vishnushastri's party were declared in error, and most of them accepted the rituals of penance and purification prescribed by the Shankaracharya.[9] With this defeat, reformist efforts and the hostility of the orthodox subsided for a decade. The issue emerged again amid renewed acrimony early in the 1880s, when the Parsi reformer, Behramji Malabari, published a series of essays in the *Indian Spectator*, with lurid descriptions of the suffering caused by infant marriage and the hidden epidemic of sanguinary crime associated

with 'enforced widowhood'. Pressing for legislative intervention, Malabari submitted two Notes to the government of
India, and the latter instituted in 1884 a broad process of public
consultation through presidency and local governments to
elicit further information and opinion from 'such official or
non-official persons as were considered to be well-acquainted
with native feeling on the question'.[10] The weight of these was
against legislation on either issue, but the question of widow
remarriage remained a constant focus of reformist concern,
periodically intensified by particular cases of widows brought
to trial, and very highly publicized throughout the decade in
the work and writing of Pandita Ramabai.[11]

Ironically, amid this preoccupation with the plight of high-
caste widows, the impression of many contemporary observers
from the 1870s seems to have been that the proscription of
widow remarriage was actually spreading as a feature of lower-
caste social practice. Many of the male respondents to the
government of India's enquiries in 1884 argued this to be the
case. Shantaram Narayen, a pleader in the High Court of
Bombay, pointed out this apparent assimilation of elite social
practice:

Widow remarriage being disallowed among the latter as sinful, the
lower classes, though exempted from the ban, intuitively, as it were,
learn to look upon it with some prejudice: and, in illustration of this,
one could mention non-Brahman communities among whom widow
remarriage was allowed, and prevailed formerly, but who have, within living memory, declared themselves against the custom.[12]

Venkut Rango Katti, a translator in the Education Department
from Dharwar, reported having seen similar instances:

Shaved widows wearing red cloth can be seen in numbers among the
Komties, the Kasars, the Sonars and the Gingars. I have read a long
letter in the last month written by a Lingayet priest of Hoobli to one
of the Canarese priests of Dharwar, in which the writer condemned
widows remarried, freely availed of by his sect, as a stepping stone to
the hell, and invited his castemen to adopt widow celibacy which he
praised in the most alluring terms.[13]

Tarabai Shinde was driven into writing about the state of relations between men and women, she said, because the practice of

prohibiting widow remarriage 'has spread through many places and many jatis, like a terrible disease':

It's just not true these days that only the Brahman castes stop their widows from getting married again. Lots of other castes and families do the same: Prabhus, Shenvis, Gujaratis, Bhatias, Marwadis, Marathas, Desais, Deshmukhs, Inamdars; and Marathas with names like Shirke, Mahadik, Jadhav, Bhosle and Mane, families from places like Sholapur, Satara, Pune, Gwalior and Indore, the very families who died for the Maratha power. You can see an even harsher rule than the Brahmans in their families against the remarriage of widows.[14]

The Bombay non-Brahman activist N. M. Lokhande likewise reproached some of his Mali and Maratha-Kunbi caste fellows 'among whom there was the custom of widow marriage, and now, imitating what the Brahmans say, do not remarry young widows'. In fact, he urged, it was quite untrue that the sastras forbade widow remarriage, in spite of the recent defeat of the reformist party in Pune: 'The real fruits of this prohibition are the widow's unhappiness, the sin of adultery, stain on the family and stigma on the caste.'[15]

As in the case of sati earlier in the nineteenth century, it is very difficult to find precise statistical evidence, either for the presumed liberality of lower-caste practice in the early decades of the century, or for a subsequent spread of prohibition, linked or not with its overt public and judicial association with elite social practice.[16] However, the figures for female widowhood in the Bombay presidency given in the Imperial Census of 1818 (which included statistics on marriage, divorce and widowhood for the first time) indicate a pattern which diverges quite sharply from the official commonplace about the liberality of middle- and low-caste practice. The table on page 70 gives figures for male and female widowhood in the Deccan region of the presidency within a range of caste groups. The first three represent 'high castes', the next two the Deccan's major agriculturalist communities, the next five its most prominent castes of craftsmen, and the last two its most numerous 'untouchables'. The total number of male and female widows for the Deccan was given as 124,705 and 439,032 respectively; for the whole presidency 443,917 and 1,424,739.

What is striking about the figures in the table is their sug-

Male and Female Widowhood per thousand
in the Deccan, 1881[17]

	Under 15		15 and over	
	(M)	(F)	(M)	(F)
Deshasta Brahman	2	12	130	371
Konkanastha Brahman	1	7	103	338
Prabhu	3	3	85	317
Maratha-Kunbi	2	8	73	288
Mali	2	7	70	257
Sonar	12	19	101	286
Sutar	3	9	72	233
Kasar	4	10	101	277
Kumbhar	5	11	82	257
Lohar	3	7	72	234
Mahar	3	8	62	259
Mang	3	9	73	234

gestion that if the numbers of widowed women relative to men are any guide, middle- and lower-caste practice by the 1880s did not actually differ fundamentally from that of the first three high-caste groups in the table. The report itself repeated the usual view that 'the remarriage of widows is a practice confined to the lower and middle classes', but almost in the same breath pointed out that 'the large proportion of the widowed females is one of the main characteristics of the returns for the whole indigenous community'.[18] It gave no overall explanation for the very large numbers of widowed Hindu women, merely noting that these were diffused over the whole age range, rather than being concentrated at the end of life as amongst Muslims;[19] and that although the famine in the southern part of the presidency in 1876–7 had pushed up the numbers of widows there, their ratio for the Deccan and Gujarat was actually very similar.[20]

If these figures can be taken to indicate a real curtailment in the numbers of middle- and lower-caste women remarrying, many different explanations might be possible. However, it may very well have been that these communities had held up to their women a model of womanly chastity not only identified very firmly in social-reform debate, as well as in judicial discourse, with elite social practice, but one which offered to men themselves a new and very material source of control over their womenfolk: in this instance, a means to prevent property from moving outside the family unit established by a woman's first husband. For the very broad range of Maratha and lower-caste communities associated with non-Brahman political organizing, moreover, these processes were compounded in two ways. As I have described elsewhere, non-Brahman politics was itself an outcome of and a protest against the privileging of Brahmanic religious authority associated with colonial rule.[21] Yet the redrawn model of the history, identity and social practice of the Bahujan Samaj, the 'community of the majority' which formed the basis of non-Brahman political organization, was itself torn between emulating Brahmanic religious values and rejecting them, emphasizing the Kshatriya and twice-born ritual status of a backward-classes community brought into new forms of unity and solidarity.

Secondly, most non-Brahman radicals took as their main concern the general educational, occupational and religious disabilities of lower-caste communities, whose 'backwardness' placed them at an acute political disadvantage in their contests with the upper-caste and western-educated. Their campaigns here placed a heavy emphasis upon the health, social discipline and education of families. This was to be brought about in part through the discouragement of drinking, heavy expenditure on marriage and other ritual occasions, and needless factional disputes within caste communities; but also through controlling sexual relations. All of these were to be enforced through a properly constituted and authoritative *panch* of the senior men in the community. N. M. Lokhande's text, referred to above, was typical in its preoccupation with women's adultery, marital disputes and desertions, illegitimate pregnancies, young widows and infanticide, the damage to domestic life and the stain on the community's reputation which these produced:

Women boldly commit adultery and bring a stain on the caste, because although it is carried on secretly, all of the local people know about the affair. So other new wives do not fear at all to follow the example. The reasons for these things happening is that the panch does not do its duty properly, and so the crime is not punished as it should be; it spreads more widely, and from this much harm results, disgracing the caste: abortions, the ruin of honour, quarrels between caste members, and so on.[22]

While for Lokhande the remarriage of young widows seemed one means of limiting these forms of immorality, it is clear that the general model of sexual relations which he proposed, with its concern for public respectability and its emphasis on regulation by male seniors in the community, entailed a very much greater degree of masculine control over women and over their social and sexual behaviour. With the emphasis on twice-born ritual status in non-Brahman ideology, and with the material control over widows' property implicit in a public declaration against the custom of widow remarriage, other and more conservative caste leaders may have felt that these same concerns would be equally well served through a more rigid interdiction on remarriage. Paradoxically, then, it seems likely that these efforts at ideological and economic reconstruction served actually to reinforce rather than to undermine the administrative and judicial dissemination of Brahmanic or sastric models for social practice.

This perspective touches on central issues in the current debate concerning the nature of Hindu cultural reconstruction during the nineteenth century. Here, recent research has moved away from the emphasis upon 'sanskritization' as a process simply intrinsic in all Hindu societies. Drawing on the insights of Edward Said and, less directly, of Michel Foucault, it suggests that what has until very recently been presented to us as an inert and caste-bound Hindu tradition, was in peculiar and complex senses the creation of nineteenth-century colonialism itself.[23] These new approaches in turn raise the question of how elites amongst the colonized themselves could have been prepared to recognize as their own—and as the very essence of Hindu tradition and social relations—discursive and institutional constructs which historians now suggest were the novel and alien impositions of colonial rule. As a part of the effort to answer this question, a growing number of historians and cultural critics have explored the many-layered connections between gender categories and relations and the discursive and institutional structures of colonial power.

The approaches which have been developed here seem to me to fall roughly into three groups. In the first, critics have investigated the ways in which gender categories and images appeared in colonial ideology, so that the masculinity of Anglo-Saxon imperial culture stood juxtaposed to a Hindu tradition embodying peculiarly feminine qualities.[24] For colonial rulers, this provided a means of representing colonial authority in the image of a natural right. What is harder to explain, however, is why so many articulate men at elite levels of Hindu society should also have been willing to understand and depict the tradition in the same terms. For the use of such gendered images of cultural inferiority during the nineteenth century was not restricted to reformist colonial administrators and missionaries. As several of the critics referred to above have noted, they formed a central idiom in the social commentaries not only of Indian liberals and reformers, but, in an inverted form, of those who sought to defend Hindu social organization and what they took to be its central values. In their public exchanges, particular themes emerge with extraordinary regularity: regret at the passivity of the mass of ordinary Hindus, their helplessness before the rigid prescriptions of caste and their vulnerability to priestly influence; or, as a contrary view, the celebration of their pious adherence to unchanging values of duty, purity and self-sacrifice. In the same masculine debates, Hindu women themselves appeared most often as the epitome and embodiment of these ascribed qualities: either, in their ignorance and passivity, their uncritical religiosity and their moral vulnerability, as the personification of an unchanging tradition of Hinduism's caste- and custom-bound masses, or, in their honoured and virtuous contentment, as the supreme testimony to its enduring solidarities and real moral worth. These apparently contrary characterizations actually derived from the same basic set of qualities and priorities, which women were presumed most concretely to embody, observed and interpreted from different male perspectives. These priorities, the outgrowth of an essential Hindu religiosity, placed community and solidarity over the individual, stability over change, domestic and social pursuits over the public spheres of politics and administration.

With slightly different emphases the same principle of feminization, with its implicit juxtaposition to the openness and dynamism of the colonial masculine, made its appearance in the field of non-Brahman politics. As Maratha polemicists— and the same is almost certainly true of the non-Brahman movement in the south—denounced the inflation of Brahmanic religious authority and the elevation of Brahmanical texts as the ruling principle of Hindu social life, they tapped a vein of colonial ideology in which antinomies of gender appeared with particular clarity. Colonial racial theory arose, of course, in part through the efforts of military historians and administrators to distinguish martial races in India, who might be more suitable material for the Indian army than the general type of the mild Hindu. Sikhs and Rajputs most closely fitted the ideals of the colonial masculine, but, with their own claims to Rajput ancestry and their history of martial valour, Marathas assimilated themselves and were in turn assimilated into the same category. By the end of the nineteenth century, this argument of martial qualities had become a staple of Maratha political ideology, used to produce that classic pair of opposed figures which is ubiquitous in non-Brahman polemic: that of the weak, effeminate but guileful Brahman, at once the apex and essence of an unreformed Hindu tradition, and his straightforward and soldierly Maratha antagonist, defrauded of his inheritance through the artifices of priests and pandits.[25]

The second group of historians has examined an issue closely connected with these processes of feminization. This is the constitution of women as a sign for Hindu tradition. In her path-breaking work on sati, for example, Lata Mani has described how male discussion about the condition of Hindu women proliferated during the nineteenth century: in the first decades, in arguments over sati and female infanticide, and later in exchanges about issues such as child marriage and the problem of early consummation, the effects of women's seclusion, the condition of widows and the state of women's education. For all their overt concern with women, however, these debates neither offered women any voice as subjects themselves, nor admitted that they possessed any power of agency. Rather, they stressed the weakness and ignorance which made women easy victims, either for domineering male relatives or for a manipulative priesthood. This, Mani argues, was because the real concern and point of contest in these debates was not women at all. Rather, they were arguments about the status of Hindu tradition and the legitimacy of colonial power, which male colonial administrators, missionaries, Hindu liberals and reformers, conservatives, and ultimately nationalists, conducted among themselves. 'In this process women came to represent "tradition" for all participants: whether viewed as the weak, deluded creatures who must be reformed through legislation and education, or the valiant keepers of tradition who must be protected from the first.'[26] As figures, Mani contends, women were peculiarly suited thus to be signs for a tradition in need of salvation through their own wide cultural association with submission, weakness and purity.

The third approach has been to trace the more concrete transformations brought about in the structure of power relations between men and women themselves in colonial society. During the nineteenth century, of course, the colonial regime enacted a range of specific measures to liberalize the legal position of women.[27] However, historians such as Lucy Carroll, Alice Clark, Madhu Kishwar and Maria Mies have argued that the same period also saw a more subtle but much more important erosion of women's rights and powers. This occurred through the displacement of local, customary or lower-caste forms of family organization by the prescriptions of Anglo-Hindu law. These, the combined ideological product of male Brahman lawyers and Victorian judges, brought about an extension of the power of men over women in a number of crucial fields: in inheritance and property rights, in rights to divorce and remarriage, in access to land and in the control of women's numbers.[28]

As we might expect in a relatively novel and complex field for argument, however, a number of issues remain open and problems unresolved. First, it is not clear how the processes described in these three approaches, each of them crucial to our understanding of gender relations in colonial India, were connected to each other. Two questions stand out here in particular. How were literate and articulate Hindu men brought to accept the recasting of tradition in the image of a particular kind of femininity, whether interpreted in positive or negative terms? And if women were constituted as the sign for this tra-

dition, what were the implications for the powers and rights
of different classes of men and women during the nineteenth
century?

Second, much of our discussion still tends to remain within
the dichotomies of masculine and feminine themselves. Having
noted that the imposition of these categories was a way of
naturalizing colonial authority, our most fruitful strategy, as
Gyan Prakash has argued, is to get outside and disassemble
them.[29] We can best do this by reminding ourselves that in their
content they are not universal categories at all. This is the
difficulty with Mani's idea that women lent themselves to their
role as representatives of a tradition in need of redemption
through their own wide association with qualities of passivity,
helplessness and purity. Yet women may have, and in the
South Asian context certainly did have, a very much wider
and more varied set of presumed implicit qualities and powers:
in some contexts, those which Mani mentions certainly, but in
others of danger, pollution, cosmic strength, prosperity, fertility
and so on.[30] Why should colonial rulers and elite Hindu men
have concurred in depicting Hindu women in these particular
terms? Clearly, these apparently natural categories were constructed out of, and imposed on to, sets of power relations which
were actually quite heterogeneous in character. But how are we
to understand this as a process, and its implications for the forms
of power available to different classes of men and women in
colonial society?

To answer these questions, we need to explore two processes
which were implicit in public debate and colonial law-making
as they applied to Hindu social organization. One of these is
the constitution of woman as the sign for a tradition which was
disempowered and objectified in very real ways. The second
is the simultaneous re-empowering of different groups of elite
men as the transcendent social critics of that tradition.

Neither for colonial observers nor for the elite men amongst the
colonized—who likewise made the tradition the target of their
scrutiny and concern—was their particular adoption made at
random, or from some universal or contextless association between femininity and weakness or inferiority. At least some of
the forms of femininity which both sides employed to characterize the tradition in broad terms—its durability, its primarily

domestic and religious rather than political significance, its communitarian spirit and the interdependence among its members—had a quite specific social derivation. These particular characterizations took their shape precisely as constructs placed upon and built around some of the actual legislative and institutional consequences of British rule for Hindu social relations, now selected and reflected back as the image of tradition in colonialism's distorting mirror.

The presumption that passivity, inertia, mutual dependence and extreme religiosity were qualities innate within Hindus themselves was, of course, an essentialist fiction. What was true, however, was that the colonial state had, from very early in the nineteenth century, pursued a series of institutional and legislative means to sever the sphere of Hindu social relations and ritual practice from their pre-colonial incorporation within the realm of politics and state structure, and to designate them as matters of purely 'social' concern for Hinduism's primarily domestic and religious collectivities of caste, family and local community themselves. Colonial officials couched this disintegrative and depoliticizing process in terms at once of a version of contemporary Western distinctions between domains of public and private, and, very overtly after 1858, of the state's assurance of non-interference in what were essentially the private religious concerns of its subjects. In western political contexts, of course, distinctions between private and public were employed ideologically to emphasize the personal freedoms of the individual. In their redrawn colonial form, these distinctions juxtaposed the realm of the state's competence not to that of individuals, but of Hindu communities. Within this ideological framework the colonial state had, in a variety of ways, worked to enforce a far greater degree of collective responsibility and interdependence in the management of Hindu social relations: through its very withdrawal from the adjudication of caste and religious disputes, and its insistence that these were matters for adjudication by the communities concerned, for example, or in its institution of a separate domain of Hindu personal law, which, as David Washbrook has argued, 'entrenched ascriptive (caste, religious and familial) status as the basis of individual right'.[31] It was also the case that the same colonial strategies implied, and in some respects succeeded in realizing, a fixity in this sphere of Hindu social relations: most obviously in their drive to define the original and essential in Hindu textual tradition as the basis for law. Lastly and perhaps most importantly, the colonial state had, by its very disarming and disempowering presence, decreed men in many contexts and at many levels of colonial society incapable of the superior exercise of public political authority, effectively disqualifying them from access to the main instruments of state power.

Out of this general disenfranchisement, however, British rulers found, in the very structuring of social-reform debate and in their judicial redefining of Hindu law and tradition, a variety of means through which to re-empower groups of men at many different levels of colonial society. For the literate and articulate regional elites who took part in social-reform debate, these were implicit wherever the state, in its legitimizing moral concern and its reifying drive to construct a unitary legal and religious tradition for its Hindu subjects, induced them to appoint themselves as the privileged spokesmen for a tradition which colonial officials themselves nevertheless constantly identified with the feminine. Constituted in this way, otherwise quite divergent groups of elite men were placed in a common and peculiar relation with the tradition, at once of authoritative identity and of dissociation. This relation carried in turn a colonial invitation to the exercise of new kinds of power. It offered public participation in the moral and judicial discourses, many of the most intensely contested of which concerned women, through which a generalized Hindu tradition was defined, represented and made the basis not only of colonial legislation, but, in different forms, of contemporary nationalists' own efforts to construct a cultural equivalent for India as a political entity. The employment of woman as a sign thus instituted a strong naturalizing parallelism in this particular form of detached authority: authority over a tradition whose essential qualities were characterized in terms of a feminine, and authority to pronounce upon and sometimes to determine in very real ways what should be the proper status and forms of freedom allowed to Hindu women. For men in other areas of colonial society who were never privileged in this way, such as the lower-caste communities which identified themselves with non-Brahman politics in the Bombay presidency, the same reconstructions of tradition offered other novel and more immediately material means of power over women, to affect social practice in areas such as widow remarriage. In so far as colonial officials, with their own notions of the proper status of women, did not routinely invite women themselves at any level of society to participate in the very public discourses which most crucially concerned them, these same processes operated correspondingly at once to disqualify them from these means to a public voice and competence, and to render them subject in new ways to the views and judgements both of elite men, and of those within their own families and communities.

It is in these complex processes, then, at once of dispossession, signification and re-empowerment, that gender difference may be seen most effectively recruited to solicit different groups of men into colonialism's enterprise of objectification and its depoliticizing strategies. Such a perspective enables us to get outside colonialism's naturalized binaries of feminine and masculine, by noting their construction around forms of dominance themselves many-sided in character, and at the same time to take account of its often contrary implications for men and women themselves.

3. FEMINIZING TRADITION: WOMEN AND WIDOW'S CHASTITY IN MALE DISCOURSE

With this broad framework for analysis, I should like to turn now to examine these processes as they appeared in public debate around the particular issue of Hindu widow remarriage itself in the Bombay presidency in the mid 1880s, around the time that Tarabai Shinde wrote. I should like to focus here on the large collection of written replies to Malabari's papers on the subject, collected by the presidency governments and passed on to the government of India between 1884 and 1886. These commentaries are useful most obviously because they contain a mass of very detailed information and opinion on the issue, written from very varied perspectives. More fundamentally, they formed part of an important all-India initiative by the state, in which colonial officials invited large numbers of prominent local men (no women were asked) to characterize the saliences of a generalized Hindu tradition, the proper status of women within it, and its relation to politics and the state, as the basis for the latter's own judicial stance. At this level, what is striking is not so much the overt divergences of opinion concerning the true state of sastric opinion on second marriages for women, or the accuracy of Malabari's descriptions of the prevalence and moral iniquities of enforced widowhood; it is rather their common constitution, at once authoritative and self-dissociating, of woman as the sign for a tradition reified and feminized in the ways suggested above. This relation underlay the positions both of those who took a sanctified widowhood as the ultimate expression of the tradition's moral strength, and of those who regarded such restrictions to be a particularly regrettable instance, most often actually perpetuated by the women themselves, of the ordinary Hindu's blind susceptibility to the inflexible demands of priest and caste. As against these objectifying representations, respondents did, of course, often stress that Hindu social relations were also characterized by variety and change. What they tended to focus on here, however, was not regional diversity in the availability of remarriage to women, or the possibility that local custom rather than scriptural authority should determine practice, or indeed that the colonial state itself had already been the source of a fundamental change in the larger relationship between politics and Hindu social organization. Rather, they singled out caste itself as the basis of all difference. The issue of remarriage was thus one that applied largely to the higher castes who tended most often to proscribe it, although, as a number of critics pointed out, many lower-caste communities had in recent years attempted to institute such proscriptions themselves.

As Lata Mani has described, colonial knowledge about sati in the early years of the century was built up largely through the questioning of pandits attached to local courts, the pandits themselves being asked to base their replies on what officials assumed to be the ultimate authority of sastric texts.[32] By the 1880s, the question of sastric derivation still appeared unfailingly in social-reform debate, but these processes of interpolation had been broadened to include very much wider constituencies of elite men, who brought in their own views and presumptions about Hindu womanhood. Many of those asked for their views in 1884 were government servants: deputy collectors, district judges, pleaders, education inspectors, headmasters and a variety of lower-ranking administrative assistants and clerks. Others, where their interests and occupations appear, were prominent social reformers, philanthropists, eminent pandits, surgeons and leaders of local political associations. What almost all of these agreed upon, at least in the Bombay presidency, was that Hindu social relations themselves should be seen as wholly religious and domestic matters, and their survival for centuries in a relatively unchanged form as a lesson against sudden or drastic interference. Urging the more gradual means to progress in education and public discussion, Hariparsad Suntokram Desai of Bhavnagar in Gujarat warned that 'No one in the world is more attached to his ideas and customs than the usually conservative Hindu.'[33] Another respondent, Nanabhai Haridas, argued in a similar vein:

Government cannot, consistently with its avowed policy, and ought not to, interfere in purely social and religious matters. However unreasonable certain usages and customs in India may appear to foreigners, it must not be forgotten that to the people at large, among whom they obtain, they appear in another light, and that the fact of their having existed for centuries is in itself some evidence of their being adapted to the circumstances of the people.[34]

The prominent Pune reformers Bhaskarrao Pitale and Nana Moroba warned against state interference in the same terms: 'The political effect on the country would very likely be that the large Hindu subject population will feel hurt and dissatisfied, nay oppressed, considering it to be an attack on their cherished religious institution.'[35] Considerably more hostile to any extensive liberalization on the grounds that it would violate scriptural authority, 'the ordinances of the Hindu law which the upper classes among the Hindus are bound by religion to observe', Gavarishanker Udeyshanker of Bhavnagar emphasized the essentially religious character of Hindu social relations: 'No observer of Hindu life can afford to ignore the fact that religion is the basis upon which the whole fabric of society is built.'[36]

Within this general framework of objectification, the readings of tradition which male respondents produced differed
widely. Yet it is possible to see in them a similar construction
around colonialism's own implied gender categories and the
institution of woman as sign, and a common presumption at
once of identity and transcendence. For reformers and those
hostile to what they took to be the tradition's archaic immobility, this reading viewed Hindus in general as the passive
and timid creatures of caste, custom and priest. Decrying 'the
tyranny of custom and the bigotry of priesthood', Pandurang
Balibhadra, a Prabhu liberal, regretted that

For want of firm resolution and patient perseverance, people have
fallen off by dozens from the side of their leaders and withdrawn their
support from a cause which they had at first heartily espoused. The
majority, again, rather than sacrifice their ease, comfort and convenience, outwardly conform to existing usages even when they believe them to be wrong in principle and mischievous in practice.[37]

Writing from Ahmedabad, Rao Bahadur Bholanath Sarabhai described how 'Custom, which is the paramount power
among the Hindus, has become law and religion. The abomin-
able institution, known as caste, which is the greatest stumbling
block in the way of all kinds of reforms, exercises its binding
force equally on the educated and the uneducated.' What was
most regrettable was that neither caste nor current marriage
practices were actually in conformity with the sastras, for 'all
those noble precepts which have been inculcated for us by the
far-sighted Rishis and law-givers, in clear and unmistakable
terms, have been abused by the Hindu society'.[38] Many respondents writing from this perspective viewed caste in this way,
as the animating principle of Hindu social relations and the
source of their enfeeblement. Lalshankar Umiashankar, a
sub-judge from Ahmadnagar and member of the reformist
Prarthana Samaj, who had with M. G. Ranade set up a home
for widows and their children at Pandharpur, took this view:
'Caste, assisted by priests and heads of sects, is the chief cause
of enforced widowhood. Many there are who admit the
necessity and legality of widow remarriage, but they have no
moral courage to go against custom and caste.'[39]

If the mass of ordinary Hindus displayed these regrettable

qualities, they appeared most exaggerated in women themselves. Narayan Bhikaji, a deputy collector from Nasik, warned that 'The religious belief is still *very very* strong among the people, particularly among women. They attribute all calamities to sins committed by them in former lives and look to happiness in future ones by conducting themselves piously.'[40] Uttamram N. Metha saw the obstacles to reform in similar terms:

There are many difficulties to eradicate the custom at once, and they arise from the following facts:

    I. That it has become a custom of long standing.

    II. That the Hindus are conservative in their character, and they would look upon any reform as an innovation, the acceptance of which would degrade them.

    III. That the masses of people, and particularly the females, are ignorant. This makes them stick to what has descended to them from their ancestors.[41]

Motilal Lalbhai, a first class sub-judge from Ahmedabad, drew attention to the particular credulity of women in religious matters: 'It is through them that the priest chiefly exercises his influence.'[42] This identification of women themselves as the ultimate embodiments and carriers of a tradition debilitated in these ways led many respondents to urge the education of women themselves as the best long-term strategy for change. Rao Saheb Vishram Ramji Ghollay, an assistant surgeon of Pune and one-time non-Brahman activist, recommended this solution: 'The obstacles to any kind of reform amongst us arise chiefly from our women owing to their being uneducated, but now that education has begun to permeate the female society, the obstacles to reform will melt away, and many superstitious customs, including child marriage, will disappear.' Ghollay upbraided Malabari for singling out Hindu widows in particular as women whose moral vulnerability led them into immorality and crime: this evil was 'not peculiar only to the Brahmin or Brahminized widow, but prevails more or less in communities who practise and allow widow remarriage'.[43] Significantly, however, neither Ghollay nor any of the other liberal and reformist respondents drew attention to the men who actually consorted with such women as themselves a source of criminality. It was always the scandal of the immoral lives of women which preoccupied them as the symptom of a deeper social malaise.

As a prominent local politician, with a strong history of concern for the education of women and the plight of Hindu widows, Jotirao Phule was also enlisted by the government of Bombay as a representative of native opinion. His description of 'the miserable state of the deluded people of this country' employed colonialism's feminizing categories in an even more sharply stated manner. Characteristically, Phule placed particular emphasis on the priestly manipulation of scriptural authority, and his account makes clear how these categories formed an important non-Brahman resource not only for written denunciations of Brahman power, but at the level of street challenges to the local Brahman community. After a lurid account of the promiscuous sexual indulgence which their sastras permitted to Brahman men, he recounted the story of a chaste but ignorant Brahman widow, Kashibai, who had worked some years previously as a cook in the house of one of his Brahman friends. Her seduction at the hands of 'a shrewd and cunning Shastriboova of a Brahmin caste', and her subsequent trial and sentence to transportation for infanticide, had compelled him, he said, 'to establish a foundling house, in my own compound at Poona, for the Brahmin community immediately after the trial was over'. The move was evidently a highly publicized one, and intended not least to advertise the moral failings of local Brahmans themselves:

The enclosed copy of printed notices were [sic] then pasted on the walls of the corners of streets, where the Brahmins reside. From its commencement up to the present time, thirty-five pregnant widows came to this house and were delivered of children, of whom five are living and thirty died by the injuries done to them while in the womb by the poisonous drugs which the mothers must have taken with a view to conceal their pregnancy.

The institution of enforced widowhood, which Phule represented here as a purely Brahman problem, was the work of 'selfish and wicked lawgivers', who 'must have added such unjust and nonsensical clauses into their shastras with malice towards the female sex'. He concluded with a plea that barbers should be forbidden to shave widows' heads, and the latter given as much freedom to remarry as Brahman men.[44]

In this outright hostility to all religious texts, Phule stood very much as the exception amongst moderate liberal and reformist respondents. Most commonly, the latter pointed out that the social norms laid down in the sastras contained much that was sensible and good. Difficulties arose rather when the norms themselves varied from one text to another, and when the gradual introduction of a rigid caste structure led Hindus to desert them altogether. A number of respondents pointed out the confusions which resulted in the minds of many ordinary Hindus, which the innovations of Anglo-Hindu law had only compounded. Interestingly, these liberal observers recommended not the reintroduction of localized custom as the basis for social practice, but rather a further rationalization of sastric texts themselves to form an authoritative guide in disputed matters such as that of widow remarriage. Tirmal Rao Venkatesh, an *inamdar* of Dharwar, for example, referred to this confusion and urged that 'If the Legislature were to collect all Hindu law books, examine them, and declare which of them are to be acted upon, which modified and which rejected, it would be conferring a great benefit to the country, and there would then be no disputes of this nature. Many native pleaders are of this opinion.'[45]

Not all of those whom local governments asked for their views, of course, saw themselves as liberals or reformers. Many male respondents affirmed rather that the presumed immobility and essentially religious imperatives of the tradition represented its greatest virtues. The source of these qualities lay neither in priestly manipulation, nor in the imposition of rigid caste distinctions upon a reluctant or misguided population. These qualities were instead the emanation of a much older spiritual identity in which the whole Hindu community of the country participated, and which provided a continuity and moral discipline which formed their greatest strength. What is striking, however, is that these apparently quite contrary representations of the tradition similarly institute the figure of woman as its sign, at once icon and index. Kalianrao Desai of Broach, who identified himself as 'an orthodox Hindu', defended the celibacy of Hindu widows in precisely these terms. It was not, he said, priestly influence or caste oppression which led the people to dislike the idea of women remarrying, but rather 'a deeper philosophy of human nature, and nobler ideas of womanly honour and integrity'. Hindus placed great value on the control of 'the debasing and degrading influence which passions exercise on the nature of man, which, on the other hand, rises higher and higher and attains to a nobler perfection in proportion to the control he is able to put on them'. These high ideals, most perfectly realized in the chastity of women, made the idea of their marrying a second time quite repellent to the Hindu community:

Now a widow remarrying is evidently a woman with whom a healthy control over her passions is altogether an impossibility. To espouse the bed of a second husband after she has become the wedded wife of a previous one is, in the opinion of the public, the highest degradation to which a woman can stoop.[46]

Pandit Panchnadi Guttalal Ghanashyamji of Bombay, consulted as 'one of the spiritual heads of the Vallabhacharya sect of the Hindus' and 'a distinguished Sanskrit scholar', put this argument of woman as a gift between male givers in an even sharper form. Arguments for the equality of men and women in marriage were fundamentally misguided, for, as he asserted, the real truth here was that 'the male is the enjoyer and the female a thing to be enjoyed. The bride is given by her father, etc., to the bridegroom with a (solemn) declaration, and not the bridegroom to the bride.' Once bestowed in this fashion, woman could not then be possessed by other men:

The thing called woman is the crowning piece of all the objects of enjoyment in this world, and, being subject to the special power of the husband, is not, like a house, etc., capable of being enjoyed by the husband's relations. How much more incapable must she then be of being fit for remarriage and enjoyment by a stranger. Like a dining leaf used [previously by another person] she is unfit to be enjoyed by another person.[47]

A number of conservatives pointed out, of course, that some Hindu women did actually live immodest and degraded lives, as Malabari had described. These, however, were the few deviant exceptions, where the state's intervention, otherwise quite inappropriate and illegitimate, would be very welcome. Manmohandas Dyaldas, editor of the *Vartoka Sadhodha Rasraj,* a Bombay Gujarati monthly, drew attention to this exception to the rule against legislative interference with religious matters: 'As Government have made abortion punishable by law, so should they also make the pregnancy of a widow punishable by law. This will put an end to all incontinence on her part.' Prostitution, of course, formed the greatest social evil arising from this kind of incontinence: 'If it be desired to preserve public health, then the best course is to drive away all prostitutes from cities. They are a source of immense mischief.'[48] Ganpatram Shastri of Kaswa likewise regretted that amongst the great majority of chaste and devout widows there were a few 'persons of questionable moral character who transgress the path of virtue devised for them by the Shastras and society, and who by their detestable example now and then convulse the peace of society'.[49]

Many respondents not only employed these evocations of womanly chastity in this way to construct the image of an integrated cultural tradition with a clear basis in scriptural authority, but put these forward as the natural basis for a Hindu community of a much more overtly political kind. In these terms, the same Ganpatram Shastri defended the 'patient and single life' of the Hindu widow as 'the result of a system based upon philosophical resignation, upon moral discipline which the humanity in India has undergone through thousands of generations, and upon the national instincts created and kept up by traditions, precedents and usages coming down from ancient times'. If there were restrictions on widows, the intention was not to oppress them, 'but to raise their lives to a lofty pitch of moral training and human refinement based upon mental resignation which alone is the true source of happiness according to oriental notions'. Pandit Ghanashyamji affirmed that 'The non-performance of widow-marriage is based upon Shrutis and Smritis, and is not devised by priests.' Any attempt to institute its practice would be 'opposed to Dharmashastra of the whole country'.[50]

What is also striking, within this general framework of feminization, is the frequency with which respondents of all shades of opinion refer to the effects of India's warm climate on the sexual development of Hindus themselves. These effects, at once inflammatory and debilitating, meant that Hindus in general stood in greater need of the moral restraint of early marriage. The prominent Bombay reformer, Sakharam Arjun, cautioned against too sudden a change in the practice of early marriage in these terms:

Taking human nature as it is, bearing in mind the climatic influences on the native physique and the enervating effect of social customs, recognizing the fact that the mental culture—the basis of self-restraint —of our community, particularly the female part of it, is at best only partially developed, and must continue to be so for years to come— all these facts considered, I am fully persuaded that our system of marriage is most wholesome under present circumstances.[51]

Venkut Rango Katti of Dharwar, a Kanarese translator in the Education Department who viewed the tradition and its roots in the Dharmasastra in much more positive terms, likewise drew attention to the fact that 'girls in India arrive at maturity much earlier, generally in the twelfth year, than those in Europe or any other temperate climate'. Delaying marriage after the onset of puberty, Katti warned, 'leads to looseness of character and disease'.[52] Manmohandas Dyaldas made the confident assertion that, in contrast to a 'warm country' like India, 'women in Europe attain puberty between the 15th and 20th years', and this, he said, on the authority of European doctors.[53] The surgeon and non-Brahman activist Vishram Ramji Ghollay referred to the 'early development of sexual proclivities' brought on by the climate in India. Marriage before puberty was necessary so 'that the male youths may be saved from the pernicious effects of masturbation', an evil, he said pointedly, 'which exists to a great extent amongst the boys of the higher castes'. This sort of incontinence had arisen among the Hindus, he asserted, 'owing to the peaceful times which they enjoy'.[54]

Set out in very schematic form, then, these seem to me to be the dominant frameworks within which an otherwise quite divergent body of elite men viewed the significance of Hindu women within the tradition, and found themselves constituted as the authoritative spokesmen for colonialism's own gendered idioms. With the great weight of their opinion against legislative action, in commentaries received from Bombay and other local governments alike, the government of India ruled out legislative intervention as a possibility for the time being. Ironically from the point of view of lower-caste communities in the Bombay presidency at least, the liberalization of the position of widows was to be left 'to the improving influences of time, and to the gradual operation of the mental and moral development of the people by the spread of education'.[55]

4. TEXTS CONTESTED: 'A COMPARISON BETWEEN WOMEN AND MEN'

I should like to turn now to some of the implications for women themselves of these masculine representations, seen from the particular perspective of Tarabai Shinde's critique. I have rather little information about her personal life.[56] She lived in the small provincial town of Buldhana between about 1850 and 1910. The family owned some land outside the town, but her father, Bapuji Hari Shinde, worked as a head clerk in the office of the deputy commissioner's office in Buldhana. Shinde had himself been asked for his views in the 1884 official survey, and had replied with a short note in which he did not mention his daughter's recent venture into polemic, but simply urged legislative means to protect widows who wished to remarry.[57] He was also an early member of Jotirao Phule's Satyashodhak Samaj, the precursor of organized non-Brahman politics in western India, for which he was reportedly considerably harassed by his Brahman fellow employees.[58] Very likely as an effect of her father's reformist and non-Brahman commitments, Tarabai herself learned to read and write, not only in Marathi, but to some extent in English and Sanskrit also. She married, although she was reputed not to have wanted to, and the arrangement was that her husband, who came from a poorer and less educated family, should come to live in her maternal home. The marriage may also have been a result of her father's reputedly immense affection for her. Tarabai outlived her husband, although it is not clear when she was left a widow. The pair had no children, and she did not marry again.

Two specific personal memories of her have been preserved. The prominent Vidharba Maratha leader Barrister Ramarao Deshmukh, who was at school in Buldhana between 1901 and 1907, remembered how terrified he and his childhood friends

were each time they had to pass the Shinde house, partly because of its pair of large guard dogs, but much more for the
'harsh grey figure' of Tarabai herself.[59] Gadadhar Govind
Pathak, a vakil of the town, recalled having seen Tarabai at
about the same time:

She was a short and dumpy woman, with thick glass spectacles on her
eyes. There was always a stick in her hand. She had her fields where
the T.B. sanatorium now stands in Buldhana. She used to go off to her
fields very spiritedly on foot; I never saw her ride a horse. Her face was
very cruel looking. She had a very fiery temper. Whenever she saw
small children, she would chase after them, hitting at them with her
stick. We children used to be very much afraid of her. We never saw
her husband.[60]

Such accounts of shared childhood terrors, mediated no doubt
through an adult male knowledge of Tarabai's outspoken
venture into print, give us an insight into some of the images
which she had acquired for herself towards the end of her life.
These were of isolation and singularity, of deviation from the
gentle public maternality more properly associated with a respectable Maratha woman, explicable only in terms of a de-
ficiency in temperament, and, perhaps, of the adverse effects
on a woman of too much reading.

As the deliberately educated daughter of a non-Brahman
activist, it seems likely that Tarabai would have been fairly
familiar with the central themes in contemporary male social-
reform debate, particularly as these concerned women. The
trial of the widow Vijayalaksmi, which had goaded Tarabai
into her attempt at public intervention, had actually taken
place in 1881, two years before Malabari's initiative and the
government of India's recruitment of local opinion. Very much
the same themes, however, and more exaggerated by the very
extremity of Vijayalaksmi's circumstances as a young widow,
her crime and her trial, were identifiable in the public discussion surrounding the case. In the first hearing of the case in the
district court at Surat, the sessions judge sentenced her to hang
on the grounds that moral depravity, not social deprivation, explained her crime. At the higher levels of the judiciary and
colonial administration, however, there was a strong sense that
a lenient view should be taken of crimes such as Vijayalaksmi's,
so long as women remained unprotected, either through an act

of direct legislation by the state, or through the private efforts of Hindu social reformers, from the impossible demands placed upon them by the tradition. The sentence was commuted in the High Court to transportation for life, and this in turn reduced to five years as an act of clemency by the Government of Bombay.

Public discussion of the case in the English and vernacular press revealed a broad spectrum of opinion, from sympathy for Vijayalaksmi in view of the temptations to which the miserable lot of Hindu widows made them vulnerable, to outraged demands that her unchaste life and monstrous crime receive the extreme penalty. The reformist *Subodha Patrika*, for example, pointed out these temptations to vice and crime, and urged that widows be educated as a means of inculcating moral restraint.[61] The *Bombay Samachar* agreed that the crime of infanticide was indeed a horrible one, but that account should be taken of widows' peculiar circumstances, and a period of imprisonment instead of outright execution used to deter women from wickedness.[62] The *Yajdan Parast* emphasized that it was this refusal of remarriage which led hapless young widows into a life of indecency and the crimes of abortion and murder.[63] In very much more hostile tones, a correspondent to the *Shivaji* demanded to know why any mercy should be shown to this inhuman mother: widows, he said, ought to refrain from immoral lives, and if they abandoned themselves to vice they must take the consequences.[64] For the editor of the *Pune Vaibhav*, a virulent opponent of contemporary efforts in Pune to establish a high school for girls, efforts to give widows greater freedom endangered the virtues of all Hindu women, and produced just the kind of delinquency into which Vijayalaksmi had fallen.[65] What these different male perspectives shared in common, however, was the focus upon women's immorality, rather than that of the men willing to consort with them, and upon women's conduct in general as the central and sensitive barometer of the moral health of the tradition.

For a woman like Tarabai observing these debates, their constitution of woman as sign had a number of pressing consequences. Most obviously, they implied new and intensified forms of sensitivity in the public scrutiny of women's own conduct. These, however, were directed not at discovering the real pressures and contingencies which shaped women's lives, but at searching out the grounds on which women could be drawn into an equivalence with tradition according to the perspectives of different male interpreters. Where the latter celebrated the personification of its purity and moral strength in women, this suggested novel and extremely confining models of behaviour for women themselves, and an especial revilement—such as that which the *Pune Vaibhav* had reserved for the widow Vijayalaksmi—for women seen publicly to have transgressed these. Reformist or liberal representations, on the other hand, evoked Hindu women's passivity, ignorance and moral weakness as the embodiment of all of the tradition's failings. In slightly different ways, both perspectives created a position for women in public discourse at once of acute responsibility and of powerlessness, confined within an essentialized nature and deprived of any recognized presence or power of agency on their own account. It is against this background, of simultaneous denigration and confinement, that we can best understand Tarabai's outrage, and the particular forms which her protest took. In examining these as an effort at critique, my purpose will be to illustrate how it was possible for her to employ categories and images from a range of contemporary discourses: in some areas only to reproduce them again, in others reproducing but inverting them, and, in others still, beginning to question and break down the categories themselves. This enables us to view her project as protest or resistance, rather than simply a denial or rejection of contemporary constructions of feminine nature.

At the core of this project lay an acute concern with the representation of women in texts: not only in newspaper reports or the discussion of cases such as that of Vijayalaksmi, but in contemporary plays and short stories, and in the texts of classical and puranic Hinduism and their Marathi popularizations from the sixteenth century. What drove Tarabai in particular here, as it did her male contemporaries active in non-Brahman politics, was a sense of the divergence between these texts and the social realities whose legal and moral basis they were presumed to describe. For Marathas and others, of course, this conflation most importantly distorted and exaggerated the religious authority of Brahmans. The most striking incongruity for Tarabai lay in these texts' simultaneous celebration of the *pativrata*, the virtuous and dutiful wife, and abhorrence of women themselves as the source of all worldly temptation, and what she herself observed to be the realities of men's and women's lives in contemporary society.

She began by explaining how public criticism of the widow Vijayalaksmi, together with a more general intensification of women's maltreatment at the hands of men, had filled her with indignation. 'Every day now we have to look at some new and more horrible example of men's reckless violence and their shameless lying tricks. And not one single person says anything about it. Instead people go pointing the blame at women all the time, as if everything bad was their fault.'[66] Since no man came forward to protect women from this kind of defamation, or to fight the cause of widows by attacking the prohibitions on their remarriage, she had felt compelled to assume the role of protector herself: 'When I saw this, my whole mind began just churning and shaking out of feeling for the honour of woman-kind. So I lost all my fear, I just couldn't stop myself from writing about it in this very biting language.'[67] The best means of defence lay in looking at men and women simply as universals, and making comparisons of their real natures and social conduct:

So is it true that only women's bodies are home to all the different kinds of recklessness and vice? Or have men got just the same faults as we find in women? I wanted this to be shown absolutely clearly, and that's the reason I've written this small book, to defend the honour of all my sister countrywomen. I'm not looking at particular castes or families here. It's just a comparison between women and men.[68]

Her remarks, she made clear with a strong note of defensive irony, were addressed to the men themselves who were the source of misrepresentation. She intended to expose their natures and conduct as the real source of social degeneration:

You men are all the same, all cunning and devious. But I come from the weaker side of nature, so you'll see all sorts of faults in the book. With powerful intelligence like yours you'll find all types of criticisms to make of it, and all different ways to sing the praises of your own kind instead. Still, all I've done here is write down what I could see with my eyes.[69]

She opened her attack on the divergence between text and reality with a contrast between the model of pativrata enjoined on women in the puranic story of Savitri, and her own vigorous observations of how a real wife would speak to her husband about the home. The former recommended a wife to smile and beg the husband, who kicked her, to stop lest he hurt his foot; not to cry if he cuffed her with his fist, but to run and fetch fresh butter to rub on his hand to soothe it.

Who'd do any of this nowadays? Far from stroking his hand she'd more likely tell him to shove it in the stove. If he dislikes some food she's meant to avoid it too. It's just the opposite, though—he throws it down and she picks it up straight, so much the sweeter! . . . If the husband asks for water she's not standing ready with a clean brass vessel. Instead the lady tells him, 'Oh yes, I'm dying for some water, there's some in that pot over there, get yourself some and get me some while you're at it. What am I supposed to do? This child here just won't let me get up.' The husband's only got to mention his bath and she's meant to lay out the stool, get a bucket of hot water and stand ready to scrub his feet. But actually she just calls out, 'Anyone out there? Come in here Ramya boy, he wants his bath, fetch him water and fold his dhoti for him. If he asks for me tell him I'm having my tea.'

This, Tarabai asserted, 'is what pativrata means these days. If I was to tell you all of it from start to finish it would take up a whole separate book. Who on earth really follows the sastras to the letter?'[70]

While stories such as that of Savitri would almost certainly have been available at the level of oral culture to a woman of Tarabai's class, she made it plain that it was not so much the stories themselves that she objected to, but their inclusion by men in religious texts which were held up as authoritative models for women's behaviour. In many cases, she argued, the sastras themselves actually held up very bad examples for women to follow: that of Dropadi, who already had five husbands, even as she cherished desires towards Karna; of Satyavati and Kunti, who gave birth to Vyas himself and Karna outside marriage, and of Ravana's wife, Mandodari, who attempted to

persuade Sita into her husband's bed: 'All your big talk—you
make it all up on the basis of the sastras. But in fact the people
who write all these books ought to be ashamed of themselves.'[71]

Tarabai's main narrative device in elaborating the comparison between women and men was to select two passages
which she felt represented in an authoritative way the real
misogynism of Indian masculine culture, and to refute them
point by point. She did not identify the passages in any way,
but simply laid them out and then launched into her own
furious rebuttal. The first verse actually comes from the
Ramavijaya, a sixteenth-century Marathi celebration, after the
Mahabharata, of the exploits of the Pandavas, by the prolific
pandit of Pandharpur, Shridhar. The second is taken from the
Sanskrit *sataka-trayam*, or 'three centuries of verse', of the poet
Bhartrihari:

ovi

Woman is only the axe, who cuts down trees of virtue
Hindrance to creatures through thousands of births
Know her to be the temptress, embodiment of pains in this world.

sloka

A whirlpool of whims, a house of vice, a city of shamelessness
A mine of faults, a region of deceit, a field of distrust
Obstacle at heaven's door, mouth of hell's city, well of evil magic
Who made this woman-device, sweet poison and trap of all creatures?

Thus, Tarabai accused her male readership, 'you heap up all
your contempt on women's heads, and so it's you who become
the very images of virtue!'[72]

Her strategy, conducted in the same rhetorical style, was
then to take these representations of female nature by men
based on parts of vernacular and Sanskrit literary canons and
what she felt to be their echoes in contemporary debate about
women, and to argue that each of them was actually more
appropriately applicable to masculine nature and to the
realities of the conduct of men rather than of women: 'It's true
women are whirled about by many whims. But it's because
they're uneducated that every kind of whim makes its home
in their minds.' In reality, it was men's own minds which were

'constantly churned up with all sorts of cunning schemes, to do with things native and foreign, imaginary and practical'.[73] In terms of causing suffering, the main culprits were men who married their little daughters to old men out of greed for money, men who gave their daughters as second, third or fourth wives or to husbands who were vicious and violent, or who, out of excessive love for a daughter, arranged for her to marry a poor and uneducated boy in order to be able to keep her at home.[74] When women committed the ultimate sin of running away with another man, therefore, the responsibility lay very largely with their fathers for having neglected to make a happy and suitable choice of husband for them. It was also men, in reality, who were responsible for the sufferings of widows:

Once a woman's husband has died, not even a dog would swallow what she's got to. What's in store for her? The barber comes to shave all the curls and hair off her head, just to cool your eyes. All her ornaments are taken away. Her beauty vanishes. She's stripped and exposed in all sorts of ways as if she belonged to no-one.[75]

As far as sexual enticement was concerned, this too should be laid at men's door:

You men are just like bees, you like to move on from one flower to the next. Womankind is different—work it out for yourselves. With one woman there loving you with all her heart and mind, there you are eying up a second, then when you've had enough coming and going with the third off you go after number four.

This random sensuality was quite alien to female nature: 'Does a wife ever treat people like this? Doesn't she just try to obey you and please you, whether times are good or bad? Does a wife ever say to herself, "He's got no money and he's ugly too, I think I'll go off with someone else"? Whose crimes are worst then, women's or men's?'[76] The faithlessness of men derived frequently from vanity as well as from sexual licence. Some men, she said, started out poor and were quite happy with the clumsy girls their parents found for them, 'girls which seem to you at the time like heavenly nymphs'. But then, later in life, 'you get the force of offices and money behind you, and people call you Appasahib this, Babasahib that. So you get the idea you should have a new wife to go with it and start looking forward impatiently to your wedding day.'[77]

If men's selfishness and sensuality made them morally weak, they compensated for this with the depth of their cunning. No field had presented them with greater opportunities for its exercise than that of the Hindu religion, for here women's credulous belief in its divine origin and powers made them most vulnerable. It was clear, she argued, that the authors of the sastras had been men, and that this was why they permitted men to marry almost limitless numbers of women, while enjoining women themselves to isolation and celibacy after the death of their partner.[78] The same sastras enjoined a dharma of women, which meant that no matter how cruel and violent a man might be, his wife should worship and wait on him with a smiling face, as if he were a god.[79] Exactly the same masculine cunning might be seen in the numbers of false holy men who preyed on women in contemporary society. Holy men came in all shapes and sizes and outward forms of self-mortification, yet, 'if anyone could see in, they'd just see two scorching flames of desire, for women and wealth'.[80] The worst thing about these false sadhu was their manipulation of credulous female devotees:

There are all kinds of these tricksters, josis, kanphotas, bairagis, who lead women on and deceive them with promises that they'll be able to win all their husbands' love for themselves and keep them how they want forever. 'You'll get a boy if you look at a house where there are children on a Saturday night when there's a full moon then light a fire.' 'Choose a Saturday night when there's no moon, wash your hair, put a broken pot on your head, then come out without any clothes on and take a darsan at eleven temples of Maruti.' Women listen to these false promises and put instant faith in them.[81]

Tarabai addressed herself particularly to the most notorious kind of infamy for which women attracted male condemnation, that of prostitution. Here too, the effect of her rhetoric was to dismantle the essentializing systems of signification in male public discourse, by drawing attention to the real material circumstances and contingencies of women's lives and the active collusion of men in creating them:

There's not a nest somewhere, that all prostitutes come out of. It's you who start it, speaking so sweetly to her, making her eager, luring her out over the doorstep and making her a stranger to her own house.

You get along with her somehow so long as she's in the full flush of youth; then when she's stripped and spoiled you desert her along with her fate. So she takes up the evil trade quite openly.[82]

Men's efforts to conceal their own complicity, by depicting prostitutes as a special evil species of women created apart, should thus be understood as an insult to all women, including the mothers, sisters, daughters and wives for whom most men professed at least public respect:

These are all women too, aren't they? Or are they all different, all from a different species of women? If you talk about women, you have to talk about them all. You say women are like axes, vessels of all cunning, marketplaces for wickedness, wreckers of the path to heaven? But if you hand out names like that to women, what names should we call you? Mother-haters? Slanderers of your own mothers?[83]

At these levels, then, Tarabai's text reveals what seems to me an extraordinarily accurate identification of the essentializing strategies and textual biases in contemporary male discourse, and a ferociously sharp awareness of the moral dilemmas and material pressures which these strategies often entailed in women's own lives. With its emphasis upon the insubstantiality of sastric texts, and the very material agency of men as well as women in creating a difficult and painful social world, her critique forms a remarkable contrast to the detached and moralizing commentaries of elite male observers such as those examined above. Evidently, theirs was a form of authority and a reading of tradition from which Tarabai felt women to be not so much excluded on the basis of their sex, but brought in and held to account as the tokens of exchange between discourses in which they themselves never appeared as speaking agents.

Tarabai's exposé of contemporary relations between men and women and their representation in male texts did not limit itself to domestic, sexual and religious matters. It extended very firmly into the sphere of politics itself, to provide a novel and, in contemporary terms, extremely adventurous critique of Indian men's desertion of their own social and material heritage and their consequent complicity with the culture of alien rulers:

What's happened now to all those places that once made silk brocade, costumes of silver and gold, aigrettes of jewels for turbans and turbans embroidered with gold, lengths of cloth from Chanderi, nine yard saris from Paithan, gold-bordered headdresses, woven dhotis from Nagpur, soft red leather slippers?[84]

Even women had been affected by men's craving for the supposed superiority of English dress: 'When women's husbands take up new manners and habits, women start trying to do just the same themselves. They haven't got the fashion yet of wearing full-length gowns like English women. But they've already started putting on coats, jackets with fancy pleats and long sleeves and shoes and stockings on their feet.'[85] These pretensions, Tarabai affirmed derisively, only made men a general laughing-stock: 'These people are just better than you a thousand times over. Do they copy a single one of our people's customs on these sorts of worthless whims? Just the opposite, they look at these get-ups of yours and laugh.'[86]

Yet these same men, even as they embraced alien manners, forms of consumption, education, employment and travel for themselves, had the effrontery to put themselves forward as the champions of an inviolate religious tradition at home:

I quite agree with the old proverb that says, 'A stranger steps in and harm comes to the house', and I would have followed it in what I did if you hadn't taken on a single one of these peoples' habits, if you'd followed your own dharma to the letter. Even the poor widows would have realized their fortunes were never going to get better and would have kept quiet. But all that Manu, it's changed and gone now. What's left of it?[87]

It was not, therefore, the supposed failings of women which produced suffering and decline in contemporary society. Instead, Tarabai expostulated, it was actually the puerile efforts of men to affect the manners and habits of their colonial masters:

So it's you men and these wretched fads and fancies of yours that have wrecked all our own native ways of making a living, so our tradesmen and skilled craft people are all perishing of hunger. Our glory has all been driven away and Lakshmi, whom all of you press to make her home in yours, she's seen these fads, these dirty defiling habits of yours and she's taken herself away now, on the road to a far distant country.[88]

Men's enfeeblement and impotence derived not only from their eager participation in the culture of colonial rule, but

from their pursuit of employment and rewards within its
bureaucratic structures:

> In the old days of the Maratha raj, there really were heroes of the
> sword, those men who harassed the ancient throne of Delhi. But now,
> under the rule of the English all your success and prosperity have
> vanished . . . Call yourselves heroes, then, but only at pushing pens!
> Who's going to deny it? Or better still with the way things are now,
> it should be 'heroes in the cause of your own bread and butter!'[89]

Political emasculation takes on almost sexual overtones as Tarabai ridicules men's efforts at public and political organization:

> Oh, all your superiority and courage—it never gets outside the house!
> It's just like when there's a blind old mother sitting in the middle with
> five or six little boys playing round her, and one of them says, 'I
> wanna be the king!' and the second one says, 'Mummy, I'm the
> minister', and the third says, 'I'm the general of the army! Now, let's
> make a kingdom! This is the army! This is the king's court!' This is
> how you go on, all just floods of water in a mirage. In fact, there's
> not one of you can lift up your hero's *vida* to do anything.[90]

This same craven inertia explained why no substantial
progress had ever been made on the issue of widow remarriage
itself, in spite of the great shows of public energy and eloquence
indulged in by male reformers:

> Your mouths are full of talk about reform but who actually does any-
> thing? You hold these great meetings, you turn up to them in your
> fancy shawls and embroidered turbans, you go through a whole ton of
> *supari* nut, cartloads of betel, you hand out all sorts of garlands, you
> use up a tank full of rosewater, then you come home. And that's it.
> That's all you do. These phoney reform societies of yours have been
> going now for thirty, thirty-five years. What's the use of them?
> You're all there patting yourselves on the back, but if we look
> closely, they're about as much use as a spare tit on a goat.[91]

Women's own means of entry into these new spheres of
public organization, employment, education and consumption,
with their offer of substantial rewards as well as the empty
forms of power, took a very different and much more sharply
limited form. It was certainly true that they now had some
access to formal education, which gave them a much broader
understanding of right and wrong as it applied to themselves,
of the best means to conduct their domestic lives, and particularly of male recommendations that they should adhere to

the virtues of *svadharma* and pativrata. Even here, however, the transformation in men's opportunities served only to underline the relative confinement of most women's lives:

With you, you don't use the knowledge you have in your own bodies. You roam around from one place to the next, looking through all sorts of books. You get so full of learning you can play any part you please, get yourself out of difficulty—it all comes so easy to you. But these poor women, always shut in the house—what knowledge can they have, except of what's between the stove and the doorstep?[92]

At these levels then, Tarabai mounted a remarkably telling and perceptive assault on male systems of representation, on the dignity of sastric texts which underpinned male authority, and on men's practical ability to use social change to strengthen their power over their womenfolk. But this moment of opposition, and whatever of its spirit Tarabai was able to live in her day-to-day life, are not best understood simply in terms of choice, self-determination, an intellectual space secured against the intrusions of male power. What is striking about her critique at other levels is its similarity to the strategies employed by the courtesans of Lucknow. Like them, Tarabai works in part by inversion, so that what were originally masculine forms of hostility and contempt for women are turned around and directed back at men. As I noted above, Tarabai utilized well-worked-out techniques for mockery whose effectiveness was already established in non-Brahman polemic. Her critique drew on another set of categories from non-Brahman argument. In her transfer to male nature of the weaknesses which Indian men past and present had laid at the door of women, Tarabai invoked a whole dictionary. What is most marked about her language here is its reproduction and deployment of colonial officials' own gendered representations of Hindus themselves: of facilitating moral weakness and unmanly dependence on outward social convention, of sexual appetites at once inflamed and enfeebling, of a strength and power of agency present only in the form of devious manipulation and petty cunning. Assimilated and transferred to women in elite male discourse and, with slightly different emphases, to Brahmans in Maratha polemic, the same dictionary reappeared in her own critique, now applied to Hindu men in general.

The effect of this inversion was actually to limit her perceptions in important ways. She had a very sharp sense of the essentialization of feminine nature in public debate. But she did not, any more than her male contemporaries, see this as a reproduction from the gendered idioms which colonial officials employed in the naturalization of their authority, reappearing in different fields of discourse among Indian men themselves. Colonial rule appeared in her argument actually as the consequence of Indian men's degeneracy, rather than as the primary agent of that representation. She saw women's sufferings in general as the result of men's deliberate viciousness, rather than as a product of complex structures of power that transcended individual intention. This is not to dismiss her achievement. It is only to note that it was won as she engaged with the world of masculine discourse and endeavoured to turn its resources to her own account. As with many kinds of resistance, this engagement exacted a price.

Despite her relative youth, when *A Comparison Between Women and Men* appeared in 1882, as well as her own evident powers of rhetoric and invective, Tarabai never published again. In this she was unlike the great majority of her male contemporaries active in the production of Maratha polemic, for whom authorship and publication usually represented ongoing activities engaged in over a number of years. Part of the reason for this may have been that her book was received with contempt and ridicule in one of the two major non-Brahman newspapers of the period. This was the *Shetakarayanca Kaivari*, edited by Krshanarao Bhalekar, himself the author of numerous anti-Brahmanical texts. The original of this newspaper has not survived, but there is a short reference to it in one of Jotirao Phule's works, an attempted periodical entitled *Satsar*, 'The essence of truth'. It was certainly true, Phule said, that Tarabai's opinions had been rather forcibly stated.

But one stupid newspaper editor at least did not like what she wrote, probably because he feared that the burden of all her accusations would fall around his own neck. So in order to denigrate Tarabai's book, he poured scorn on all the advice given in it and threw it down amongst the rubbish, and thus with great disdain repaid Tarabai's efforts by abusing her instead.[93]

This kind of public hostility may in part explain Tarabai's reticence in later life. What E. Fox-Genovese notes of pre-twentieth-century European women writers, moreover, was probably also true for Tarabai. Very few women, even those of the most privileged classes, 'managed to acquire educations equal to those of the most learned men, or managed to produce as much high-level work as those men. A disproportionate number of aspiring women intellectuals ended their lives in silence or illness'.[94]

Confronted with overt and deliberate challenges to authority, historians concerned with the marginal and dispossessed have often found it tempting to celebrate their sheer defiance and their apparent autonomy. I have sought to emphasize equally the ways in which resistances also enter into the processes by which structures of domination persist or renew themselves. Like the courtesans of Lucknow, Tarabai refused to conform to the ideal of submissive Hindu womanhood. Like theirs, her refusal brought her a means of self-expression and dignity, an opportunity, as she said, 'to defend the honour of all my sister countrywomen'. But in neither case did these means to dignity and self-expression represent some neutral space of freedom from Hindu forms of patriarchy. For a part of their cost was precisely the reproduction, in an inverted form, of some of patriarchy's own forms of sexual essentialism, belittlement and contempt.

In making this emphasis, my intention is not to dismiss these efforts at critique and contest. But as Ranajit Guha has remarked, one of our concerns in studying protest must surely be to explore possibilities for emancipation.[95] Our aim must therefore be not only to mark and celebrate the strengths of particular projects of resistance. It must also be to understand how forms of domination are themselves sustained and reproduced. As Prakash and Haynes have suggested in the introduction to this volume, this process of renewal does not occur automatically or by some force of habit. Rather, power must be secured continually: in part through extraordinary and violent struggles, in part through familiar and mundane practices. But power may be secured also through the struggles of those who refuse to conform, when they take up its strategies or seek to invert its logics on their own account.

This is not to say that such struggles made no difference, that resistance and power are locked here in some eternal cycle where nothing ever changes. They did make a difference. They helped in some cases to provide alternative values and visions for social life. They demonstrated where power was weak, where its claims to dignity could be ridiculed and its material structure circumvented. Yet this very engagement meant that there could be no neutral spaces from which women could defy and hold themselves apart from Indian forms of patriarchy. Indeed, the mere celebration of what look like autonomous defiances may do grave disservice to those who refuse to conform themselves, in underestimating the actual weight and harsh social cost entailed in contesting authority. The recognition of such a weight and cost does not return subordinate classes to the kind of insensible submissiveness to which elite-centred historiographies have often assigned them. Rather, in making clearer the real social terms and possibilities within which they conduct their struggles, it underscores their capacity for challenge and sacrifice.

NOTES

The research on which this article is based was made possible with grants from the Cambridge University Smuts Memorial Fund, the Nuffield Foundation, and Clare College, for whose support I am most grateful. I should also like to thank Crispin Bates, Vidyut Bhagvat, Nick Dirks, Doug Haynes, Tanya Luhrman, John Smith, Gyan Prakash, Bob Scribner, Dorothy and Burton Stein, and David Washbrook for their assistance in working out many of the arguments on which this paper is based.

1. Ranajit Guha (ed.), *Subaltern Studies: Writings on South Asian History and Society* (Delhi: Oxford University Press, 1982–7), 5 vols. For a more extended critique of the series, see R. O'Hanlon, 'Recovering the Subject: *Subaltern Studies* and Histories of Resistance in Colonial South Asia', in *Modern Asian Studies*, 22, 1 (1988).
2. Veena Oldenburg, 'Lifestyle as Resistance: The Case of the Courtesans Lucknow', in this volume, p. 55.
3. Ibid., p. 27.
4. See, for example, the definition of *pat* given in James Molesworth's *Marathi–English Dictionary*, compiled in Pune with the assistance of seven Brahman pandits and first published in 1831: 'a second and inferior sort of marriage, esp. among the widows of the lower classes'. J. T. Molesworth, *A Dictionary, Marathi and English* (Bombay: Education Society's Press, 1857), p. 501. In similar terms, the legal theorist Sir William Hay Macnaghten reported that 'Second marriages, after the death of the husband first espoused, are wholly unknown to the Hindu law; though in practice, among the inferior castes, nothing is so common'. *Principles of Hindu and Mohammadan Law* (London: 1862),

quoted in Lucy Carroll, 'Law, Custom and Statutory Social Reform: The Hindu Widow's Remarriage Act of 1856', in *The Indian Economic and Social History Review*, 20, 4 (1983), p. 363.

5. Arthur Steele, *The Law and Custom of Hindoo Castes within the Dekhun Provinces subject to the Presidency of Bombay* (London: W. H. Allen and Co., 1868), pp. xvii, 26, and 101. The Report was originally submitted in 1826.

6. For a general but conventional overview of social-reform movements in the nineteenth century, see C. H. Heimsath, *Indian Nationalism and Hindu Social Reform* (Bombay: 1964).

7. See Carroll, 'Law, Custom'.

8. Ibid., p. 379.

9. The debate and the textual evidence adduced by both sides were re-printed in a number of contemporary Marathi pamphlets, many of them celebrating the victory of the orthodox party as embodied in the decision of the Shankaracharya: see, for example, Raghuvira Viththala Daptardar and Antaji Dinkar Bedarkar, *Vidhavahavivaha khandanacha sadyanta itihasa* [A complete history of the refutation of widow re-marriage]: *An account of the discussion amongst pandits at Poona on the question of Hindu widow remarriage, with quotations and translations of Sanskrit texts bearing on the subject* (Pune: Jagadhitecchu Press, 1870).

10. These commentaries were collected and published by the government of India in 1886: see *Selections from the Records of the Government of India in Home Department, No. CCXXIII: Papers relating to Infant Marriage and Enforced Widowhood* (Calcutta: Government Printing Press, 1886), p. 1.

11. Pandita Ramabai Sarasvati's most publicized critique of women's subordination was *The High Caste Hindu Woman*, first published in 1887. An account of her campaigns for Hindu widows' emancipation and women's education, and of the controversy surrounding her conversion to Christianity in 1883, is in Padmini Sengupta, *Pandita Ramabai Saraswati: Her Life and Work* (Bombay: Asia Publishing House, 1970).

12. *Papers relating to Infant Marriage and Enforced Widowhood*, p. 195.

13. Ibid. p. 97.

14. Tarabai Shinde, *Stri-purusha-tulana* (Pune: Sri Shivaji Press, 1882), Introduction and p. 1. A copy of this work is in the Marathi collection in the British Library. References hereafter are to the original 1882 edition. A reprinted edition, with a short biographical introduction, was published in 1975: S. G. Malshe, *Kai. Tarabai Shindekrt Stri-purusha-tulana* (Bombay: Mumbai Marathi Granthasangrahalaya, 1975). I have prepared a translation of Tarabai's text for publication (forthcoming, Delhi: OUP, 1991).

15. N. M. Lokhande, *Panch Darpan: Useful regulations of all the castes* (Bombay: Anglo-Vernacular Press, 1876), p. 25 (Marathi).

16. Although it was certainly the assumption of colonial officials during the 1820s, both in Bengal and in Bombay, that their efforts to discourage sati by specifying a very narrow 'sastric' model for its legal performance, tended actually to popularize the ritual: see *Parliamentary Papers: Papers relating to East India Affairs: Hindoo Widows and Voluntary Immola-*

tions, House of Commons, 10 July 1821, vol. XVIII, p. 253, for Bengal, and in the same series, *Communications and Correspondence relative to Hindoo Widows*, House of Commons, 17 May 1927, vol. xx, pp. 147–8, for Bombay.

17. *Imperial Census of 1881: Operations and Results in the Presidency of Bombay*, Central Government Press, Bombay, 1882, vol. II, pp. xli–xlvii.

18. Ibid., vol. I, p. 83.

19. Ibid., p. 89.

20. Ibid., p. 85.

21. R. O'Hanlon, *Caste, Conflict and Ideology: Mahatma Jotirao Phule and Low Caste Protest in Nineteenth-century Western India* (Cambridge: Cambridge University Press, 1985).

22. N. M. Lokhande, *Panch Darpan*, p. 1.

23. See especially Nicholas B. Dirks, *The Hollow Crown: Ethnohistory of a Little Kingdom in South India* (Cambridge: Cambridge University Press, 1988).

24. See, for example, Ashis Nandy, *At the Edge of Psychology: Essays in Politics and Culture* (Delhi: Oxford University Press, 1980); *The Intimate Enemy: Loss and Recovery of Self under Colonialism* (Delhi: Oxford University Press, 1983); K. A. Ballhatchet, *Race, Sex and Class under the Raj: Imperial Attitudes and Policies and their Critics, 1793–1905* (London: 1980); Dagmar Engels, 'The Age of Consent Act of 1891: Colonial Ideology in Bengal', in *South Asia Research*, vol. 3, no. 2 (November 1983). See also Edward Said, *Orientalism* (London: Peregrin Books, 1985). Said does not make this point about feminization overtly, but it runs as a constant theme through his analysis of the Oriental constructed for western consumption: its irrationality and capricious violences, its outward submissiveness and inner guile, its inflamed sexual appetites, juxtaposed to the openness and self-mastery of the Anglo-Saxon masculine. Much more sharply aware of the centrality of gender categories in Orientalist representation is Malek Alloula, *The Colonial Harem* (Manchester and Minnesota: Manchester University Press, 1987).

25. R. O'Hanlon, *Caste, Conflict and Ideology*, part 4.

26. Lata Mani, 'Contentious Traditions: The Debate on *Sati* in Colonial India', *Cultural Critique*, Fall 1987, p. 153. See also Veena Das, 'Gender Studies, Cross-Cultural Comparison and the Colonial Organization of Knowledge', in *Berkshire Review* (1986).

27. For useful summaries, see J. Liddle and Rama Joshi, *Daughters of Independence: Gender, Caste and Class in India* (London: Zed Books, 1986), chs 3–4.

28. Lucy Carroll, 'Law, Custom and Statutory Social Reform: The Hindu Widow's Remarriage Act of 1856', *Indian Economic and Social History Review*, 20, 4 (1983); Alice Clark, 'Limitations on Female Life Chances in Rural Central Gujarat', in *Indian Economic and Social Review*, 20, 4 (1983), p. 31; Madhu Kishwar, 'Toiling without Rights: Ho Women of Singhbhum', in *Economic and Political Weekly*, vol. XXII, no. 3 (17 January 1987); Maria Mies, *Indian Women and Patriarchy: Conflicts and Dilemmas of Students and Working Women* (New Delhi: Concept Publishing Company, 1980), pp. 83–90.

29. Gyan Prakash, 'Comments on Das', in Veena Das, 'Gender Studies', p. 79.
30. See, for example, F. A. Marglin, *Wives of the God-King: The Rituals of the Devadasis of Puri* (Delhi: Oxford University Press, 1985), or J. S. Hawley and D. M. Wulff, *The Divine Consort: Radha and the Goddesses of of India* (Berkeley: University of California Press, 1982).
31. D. A. Washbrook, 'Law, State and Agrarian Society in Colonial India', in *Modern Asian Studies*, 15, 3 (1981), p. 654.
32. Lata Mani, 'Contentious Traditions', pp. 130–5.
33. *Papers relating to Infant Marriage and Enforced Widowhood*, p. 65.
34. Ibid., p. 89.
35. Ibid., p. 79.
36. Ibid., p. 137.
37. Ibid., p. 143.
38. Ibid., p. 103.
39. Ibid., p. 146.
40. Ibid., p. 49.
41. Ibid., p. 156.
42. Ibid., p. 100.
43. Ibid., pp. 132–3.
44. Ibid., pp. 45–7.
45. Ibid., p. 61.
46. Ibid., p. 77.
47. Ibid., p. 175.
48. Ibid., p. 165.
49. Ibid., p. 128.
50. Ibid., p. 173.
51. Ibid., p. 107.
52. Ibid., p. 94.
53. Ibid., p. 163.
54. Ibid., p. 131.
55. Ibid., p. 2.
56. See the short biographical introduction to S. G. Malshe's *Kai. Tarabai Shindekrt Stri-purusha-tulana*, pp. 1–3.
57. *Papers relating to Infant Marriage and Enforced Widowhood*, pp. 268–9.
58. There is a short reference to Shinde's difficulties in P. S. Patil's early Marathi biography of Jotirao Phule: *Mahatma Jotirao Phule yance charitra* (Chikhali: 1927), p. 67.
59. Barrister Ramarao Deshmukh to S. G. Malshe, 12 March 1975, quoted in S. G. Malshe, *Tarabai Shinde*, pp. 2–3.
60. Gajanan Gadadhar Pathak to S. G. Malshe, 24 March 1975, ibid., p. 3.
61. *Subhodha Patrika*, 29 May 1881, quoted in *Reports on Native Newspapers for the Bombay Presidency*, week ending 4 June 1881.
62. *Bombay Samachar*, 15 June 1881, ibid., week ending 18 June 1881.
63. *Yajdan Parast*, 26 June 1881, ibid., week ending 2 July 1881.
64. *Shivaji*, 1 July 1881, ibid., week ending 9 July 1881.
65. See the reference in P. J. Jagirdar, *Mahadeo Govind Ranade* (Government of India, Publications Division, 1971), p. 110. Tarabai herself also re-

ferred in passing to the *Pune Vaibhav* as one of the strongest opponents of women's education and the remarriage of widows: *Stri-purusha-tulana*, pp. 15 and 19.

66. Tarabai Shinde, *Stri-purusha-tulana*, Introduction, pp. 2–3.
67. Ibid., p. 3.
68. Ibid., Introduction, p. 1.
69. Ibid., p. 3.
70. Ibid., pp. 2–3.
71. Ibid., pp. 3–6.
72. Ibid., p. 22.
73. Ibid., p. 23.
74. Ibid., pp. 27–31.
75. Ibid., p. 12.
76. Ibid., p. 46.
77. Ibid., p. 31.
78. Ibid., pp. 12–13.
79. Ibid., p. 1.
80. Ibid., p. 31.
81. Ibid., pp. 34–5; *josi* is a general Marathi term for a priest; a *kanphota* is a religious mendicant with heavily pierced and ornamented ears; *bairagi* is an ascetic in general.
82. Ibid., p. 36.
83. Ibid., pp. 44–5.
84. Ibid., Introduction, p. 1.
85. Ibid.
86. Ibid., p. 17.
87. Ibid., pp. 16–17. Tarabai plays on the double meaning of the term 'Manu' here. Manu is the author of the Institutes of Manu, most authoritative of orthodox Hindu law-books, but the name is also generic: each age has its Manu, and the passing of ages is measured by each one.
88. Ibid., Introduction, p. 2.
89. Ibid., p. 11.
90. Ibid., p. 7. *jahamardica vida*, 'the hero's vida'. *Vida* is betel leaf rolled up, ready for chewing. The phrase 'lifting up the *vida*' means simply 'to accept a challenge', but I think Tarabai intended her taunts to have a sexual dimension here as well.
91. Ibid.
92. Ibid., p. 44.
93. Jotirao Phule, *Satsar: The Essence of Truth*, no. 2. In D. Keer and S. G. Malshe (eds), *Mahatma Phule: Samagra Vadmaya* (Bombay: 1969), in Marathi.
94. Elizabeth Fox-Genovese, 'Culture and Consciousness in the Intellectual History of European Women', in *Signs*, vol. 12, no. 3 (1987), pp. 534–5.
95. Ranajit Guha, *Elementary Aspects of Peasant Insurgency in Colonial India* (Delhi: Oxford University Press, 1983), pp. 336–7.

4

Workers' Resistance and the Rationalization of Work in Bombay between the Wars

RAJNARAYAN CHANDAVARKAR

In the 1920s and 1930s, the spirit of Frederick Winslow Taylor stalked the subcontinent. 'Rationalization' became a buzz-word, rather like 'popular culture' or 'everyday forms of resistance' within a more circumscribed world. In particular, rationalization and scientific management became, in public discourse, the panacea for the crisis of the cotton textile industry and, above all, the remedy for what came to be perceived as its 'labour problem'. It was advocated by a wide range of interests, but offered most solicitously by colonial officials, as the alternative to tariff protection which, they feared, might damage further the failing competitiveness of British exports in the Indian market. At least nine committees of enquiry discussed and commented upon the question and monitored the progress of its implementation by the mill-owners.[1] At least three of the longest and most fiercely contested general strikes in Bombay, in 1928, 1929 and 1934, took shape in direct response to the rationalization schemes.[2] This essay examines the interplay between workers' resistance and the attempt by mill-owners to rationalize work practices in the Bombay cotton textile industry in the 1920s and 1930s.

The prominence which rationalization acquired in public discourse has facilitated the assumption that fundamental changes flowed from its formulation. The late 1920s have become, for some historians, a watershed in the history of the industry, when mill-owners adopted modern techniques and methods of management, or when workers and capitalists became increasingly conscious of their class interests, and the lines of antagonism were more sharply drawn.[3] Yet, despite its scientific pretensions and transformative claims, the striking fact about rationalization is not how much it changed but how little. It did not represent a uniform and consistent attempt by the mill-owners to introduce the newest and best technology, to implement more modern methods of labour control, or to effect a more consistently rational deployment of labour. While it led to the diversification of output and the use of some new machinery in a few mills, it meant, for the most part, little more than lower wages, higher workloads and, until the late 1930s, falling employment.[4]

For their potential as instruments with which to break workers' resistance, the rationalization schemes, once formulated, must have appeared attractive, in principle, to most mill-owners. This is readily comprehensible in the light of the scale and intensity of industrial action witnessed in the late 1910s and 1920s. Yet it would be misleading to suppose that the mill-owners joined unanimously in the concert. Among them, mutual suspicion and jealousy, strife and division, arising from the bewildering diversity of interests in the industry, clouded any simple, collective view of its future. For the mill-owners, as a body, nothing was more difficult to achieve or more likely to expose their internal schisms than the formulation of a coherent, long-term strategy towards labour. Nothing was more hazardous than to embark, simply in the name of some higher ideal of efficiency, on a course of hostilities with labour, whose outcome was impossible to predict. On the other hand, if their aim had been to undermine workers' resistance, rationalization only appeared to intensify its determination. Indeed, the threat of working-class action sometimes severely circumscribed the mill-owners' options. However, collective action by the working classes did not necessarily signal the entrenchment of a permanent sense of common interests. Solidarities negotiated between diverse groups of workers for limited objectives within specific political conjunctures remained, for this very reason and by their nature, fragile, and indeed highly vulnerable.

This essay attempts to situate workers' resistance in Bombay firmly within the context of capitalist strategies. Its intention is, thereby, to bring the work people do nearer the centre of a discussion of workers' politics. Its focus rests upon the daily social relations of the workplace and the quotidian dimension of resistance. But in addressing 'everyday forms of resistance', and extending its consideration from the peasantry, to whom it was believed to be particularly relevant, to industrial workers, I do not intend to invest the term with a novel theoretical meaning or a transcendent analytical significance.[5] Rather, it takes for granted the commonplace that where power is unevenly distributed in 'everyday life', attempts to exercise it are liable to provoke resistance in a variety of forms. As such, it calls for no special explanation. It cannot be assumed to reflect a 'venerable popular culture of resistance' or the peculiar sociology of the peasantry. As this essay attempts to show, resistance may take everyday forms under conditions in which open confrontation is possible; conversely, there is no reason to assume that concealed and anonymous acts of resistance flourish solely or even primarily when the possibilities of collective action are obstructed.

The first section of this essay sets out the economic and industrial context within which the discourse of rationalization emerged in Bombay, and then examines the response of the mill-workers to it. While rationalization did not, in practice, signify fundamental change, the daily processes of negotiation, tension and conflict at the workplace were marked by important continuities. The second section of the essay, therefore, elaborates the constraints within which workers' resistance was forged and investigates the relationship between quotidian resistance and large-scale confrontation, between workplace conflicts in the individual mill and general strikes across the whole industry. Finally, peering through the dust of the carding room and the weaving shed, it offers a critical perspective upon the conceptual armoury of 'everyday forms of resistance' and the assumptions upon which its theoretical canons are mounted.

I

Rationalization was primarily a discourse of industrial management whose principles were nowhere comprehensively applied in practice, not even in the USA and Europe where its doctrines were first enunciated and discussed most intensively, and where it became intricately intertwined with the wider intellectual and political currents of the day.[6] Indeed, in the West, its significance began to shift in the 1920s from Taylor's more limited notions about managerial efforts to maximize labour efficiency to a broader and more radical vision, inspired by Ford, of the fundamental reorganization of production, not only in relation to labour but also in its wider commercial and financial aspects.

In India, too, in the 1920s and 1930s, the distinction between these two levels of rationalization was sometimes made in public discourse. In India, as elsewhere, rationalization was liable to an infinitely elastic set of meanings, leading the Textile Labour Inquiry Committee to complain in 1940 that 'a discussion about it tends to result in confusion'.[7] We may sympathize with the Committee's sentiment. Neither rationalization nor the programmatic declarations which accompanied its enunciation should be interpreted too literally. Contemporaries were wary of defining it at all. When they were asked to explain the scientific basis of their methods, the representatives of the scientific management consultants, the Eastern Bedaux Company, confessed: 'We have gradually brought up efficiency more by guess work than by any other method.' Invited to reveal the secret of the Bedaux system, J. M. Moore dilated on its sophistication of Taylorism: 'Taylor said, "It takes ten seconds for a man to walk from A to B." Bedaux said, "All right, put a hundred pound sack on that man's back and he will still walk from A to B in ten seconds." '[8] Moreover, if, as the Textile Labour Inquiry Committee observed, rationalization 'has a wider and a narrower meaning', and 'improvements in labour productivity and efficiency' constituted only 'one aspect of the latter sense', then the Bombay mill-owners limited themselves to the partial and uneven application of this narrow construction of its scope.[9] In Bombay, rationalization did not signify the application of systematic reasoning to financial and labour management, or indeed the introduction of the newest technology, but primarily the diversification of output into higher counts of yarn and finer varieties of cloth, increased workloads and lower wages. These objectives were intimately related, for the production of finer varieties often required fewer workers and enabled them to operate a larger number of machines. Yet, even in this minimalist interpretation of the term—'efficiency schemes' as they were called—little was

achieved. Less than 10,000 workers were employed on 'efficiency schemes' in 1939, which in any case meant little more
than the allocation of a larger number of machines to each of
them in certain specific processes.[10] These schemes did not
necessarily require major technological change or large in-
novation. Moreover, it is important to stress that the diversification of output and the cheapening of labour dovetailed
conveniently with the imperatives imposed upon the mill-
owners by the competitive pressures which they faced as they
entered the slump of the 1920s.

The Bombay textile industry had developed largely as a
spinning industry, exporting yarn to China in the late nineteenth century.[11] During the First World War and in its immediate aftermath, the Bombay mills enjoyed 'unprecedented
and unparalleled prosperity',[12] producing cloth to satisfy an
insatiable military demand; and, accordingly, they turned their
back on the China trade. As the post-war boom sputtered to a
halt in 1922, the Bombay mills found themselves effectively excluded from the Chinese market by Japanese competition,
which had already posed a growing threat since the 1890s.[13]
Bombay would now have to rely upon the production of
piecegoods for the domestic market. But the domestic market
was saturated with coarse goods produced by up-country mills,
which had proliferated over the two preceding decades and
which enjoyed the considerable advantages of an abundant
supply of cheap labour and proximity to the cotton tracts and
local markets.[14] But if the domestic market was thus saturated
in what were Bombay's staple lines of production, diversification into higher counts and finer varieties brought it into direct
confrontation with the rival Ahmedabad industry, the growing
volume of Japanese imports and, of course, the competition of
Lancashire. The Japanese mills, it seemed, could import raw
cotton from India, produce yarn and piecegoods in the middle
ranges, of a superior quality to the comparable Indian product,
and place it on the Indian market at less than the manufacturing costs of an average Bombay mill.[15]

Although the most obvious response in a depression was to
cut wages, the Bombay mills found this far more difficult to
effect than either Ahmedabad or their up-country rivals. Their
attempt to remove the industry-wide bonuses of a month's

wages in 1924 resulted in a month-long general strike, and a reduction of 11.5 per cent in 1925 led to another general strike from which the mill-owners had to withdraw gracefully after three and a half months.[16] Then another option began to close upon them. The mill-owners sought tariff protection, primarily, they argued, from Japanese competition. But keeping the Indian market open for Lancashire had been one of the main principles of colonial policy. Not surprisingly, the Indian Tariff Board, appointed to investigate the case for protection, preferred to stress the inefficiency of the Bombay industry, and especially its high labour costs. Wagging its finger at the mill-owners, the Tariff Board argued that the 'true line of advance' lay in the adoption of rationalization and the introduction of efficiency schemes.[17] Faced with intense competition within contracting markets, it was unrealistic to expect the Bombay mill-owners to risk their capital in revamping the structure and methods of their industry. So they could only follow the 'true line of advance' along the very narrow front of squeezing wages. The discourse of rationalization allowed the mill-owners to dress up the old expedients of reducing wages, retrenching workers and increasing workloads, in the guise of 'efficiency schemes'. But it also exposed a fundamental contradiction at the heart of the industry's predicament. To escalate out of the constraints they faced, the only course open to the mill-owners was to exploit labour more intensively; yet they had been placed in this situation partly because of the severity, indeed tenacity, of workers' resistance.

From the late 1920s onwards, the mill-owners' case for tariffs would be appraised according to the progress they had made in the implementation of rationalization schemes. It would be facile, however, to conclude that the limitations of rationalization were exclusively the result of the unfavourable policies of the colonial state. The constraints imposed upon the industry, whether in terms of the colonial tariff, monetary and budgetary policies, or its impoverished markets, or its fractious labour force, interacted with prevalent business strategies, which had in part developed in response to these constraints and whose pursuit sometimes only narrowed the mill-owners' freedom of manoeuvre.

It was a widespread practice in the cotton textile industry to regulate production according to the short-term fluctuations of demand, and thereby avoid accumulating stocks.[18] Falling prices reinforced this tendency. 'There are many mills', one mill-owner observed in the 1930s, 'which either through their financial position or for reasons of general policy do not make heavily to stock. They do not subordinate their selling to their production. They make what they sell.'[19] Seasonal fluctuations in the supply and price of various types of raw cotton, and in the demand for varieties of yarn and piecegoods, necessitated a greater sensitivity and alertness to the market. These factors were afforced by the scarcity of capital and its tendency to rush to proven and reputable enterprises. To attract capital, in some cases to meet high interest charges, it was necessary to maintain a rapid turnover, show quick profits and pay high dividends. As a consequence, another mill-owner admitted, 'if a certain line is moving profitably, I am afraid we all pounce down on it. People will sell only these profitable styles, there is over-production, the price comes down and there is a setback.'[20] Moreover, the Indian market was highly fragmented and the mill-owners competed across the whole spectrum of its products. The diversification of output in the name of rationalization only accentuated the range of their production. In 1934, it was reported, the mills 'produce the lowest as well as the highest qualities and weave a bewildering variety of cloth'.[21] It may conceivably have been possible for mill-owners to overcome these structural weaknesses in relation to the market through collusion. But the Indian market was, in this period, reputed to be the most open in the world. Attempts to control output or fix prices in Bombay would only have strengthened the position of Indian rivals and, above all, would have been devastated by foreign, especially Japanese, competition.[22]

These business strategies necessitated considerable flexibility in the organization of production. Materials and machine settings suitable for a particular quality and variety of product might have to be switched to another. The flow of orders could require the use of wide looms for narrower widths of cloth. Workloads could be increased at short notice in one process and labour rendered idle in another. Since machinery had to be imported and was expensive, mill-owners often bought equipment which had been scrapped or simply maintained and improvised upon machines which had been fully depreciated.[23] Invariably, machines were run above the speeds prescribed by the manufacturer, commonly employed elsewhere in the world or warranted by the quality of the material running through them.[24] This method of utilization often required a larger complement of workers and increased the intensity of effort demanded of them. It was not an uncommon sight, recalled 'a retired mill manager', to come across a spinning frame 'with many a broken end and the floor underneath covered with fluff . . . and piecers sweating and struggling to piece up the broken ends'.[25]

The diversity of conditions and working practices in the industry opened up major differences between the mill-owners and rendered it virtually impossible for their Association to formulate general policies acceptable to its members. Its instructions and circulars were, according to the Government Labour Officer, 'never read or understood' by mill managers and the attempt to impose its will simply led to the resignation of its members.[26] Frequently, this anarchy embarrassed the mill-owners. Thus, Fred Stones, the managing director of the Sassoon group, sought to justify competitive wage-cutting by individual mills in the early 1930s as 'definitely a concerted action . . . It was a concerted decision that each mill should tackle it [wage-cuts] separately', and then when pressed harder that, perhaps 'it may not have been concerted action, but it was a concerted agreement that concerted action did not pay'.[27] It is scarcely surprising, therefore, that when the Mill-owners' Association was required to formulate a comprehensive blueprint for rationalization by the Fawcett Committee in 1928, their committee consulted only as narrowly and informally as possible.[28] In 1939, asked to repeat the exercise by the Textile Labour Inquiry Committee, the mill-owners put forward for discussion a scheme only as detailed and accurate as it was possible to devise in six hours, despite the fact that a scheme 'which should be taken seriously', as Maloney, the secretary, remarked, 'would take months' to prepare;[29] they then proceeded to take care to conceal its details from the bulk of their members. 'This scheme', Maloney told the Committee, 'is not known to all members of the Association. It has not been endorsed by them.'[30]

If the business strategies of the mill-owners required considerable improvisation in the use of machinery, raw materials and the deployment of labour to achieve changing production targets, it also served to heighten their dependence on the skill and resourcefulness of the workers. Not only did this generate wage competition between rival mill-owners to procure the best workers, it also reinforced the workers' bargaining strength and sometimes made managers and employers appear particularly vulnerable.[31]

At the same time, this degree of improvisation exposed an opposite, contradictory, tendency in the politics of the workplace. Short-term changes in production and the composition of output had diverse consequences for different groups of workers within the same mill, even within the same department of a single mill.[32] The effects of employer policies or indeed trade fluctuations fell differentially upon the workforce. It would be misleading to assume that the aggregation of large masses of industrial workers forged solidarities among them, imparted a homogeneity to their interests and provided a common base for industrial and political action.

The introduction of rationalization and efficiency schemes in this context of diverse and individual practice was always liable to exacerbate existing differences between mills as well as between workers. The crux of rationalization was simply how far workloads could be increased without damaging the quality of output. To achieve this, it was essential to fulfil a number of basic conditions to ensure that optimal mixings of cotton passed through the machines, that the machinery was kept in good repair and set appropriately for the task, that spinners and weavers had an adequate complement of helpers, that the buildings and machines were laid out to facilitate easy and quick movement between them, that the preparatory departments were able to sustain the flow of work to the subsequent processes, and that long runs of production were sustained. Yet each of these conditions was open to definition and liable to conflicting interpretation. They provided, as we shall see, the stuffing of the daily politics of the workplace. The fulfilment of these conditions could have serious effects on earnings as well as workloads, reducing the former or increasing the latter beyond the workers' willingness to bear. In the late 1920s, the rejection of tariffs, the stickiness of wages and the grudging recovery of their markets led to the competitive introduction by the mill-owners of hastily assembled and gimcrack efficiency schemes. Mill-owners used the opportunity of changes in the composition of output to effect, what one of them called, 'the surreptitious cutting of wages'. Moreover, 'without making any preparations', they 'began to reduce the number of workers. The result was that a man was asked to do something it was impossible to do.'[33] This spiral of wage-cutting and labour retrenchment culminated in the general strikes of 1928 and 1929. Rationalization introduced in this arbitrary, competitive and inevitably piecemeal fashion widened disparities in wages and conditions. Yet these wage disparities had, since the earliest days of the industry, ranked among the prominent causes of strikes.[34] If wage disparities promoted industrial action, individual mill-owners also sometimes perceived efficiency schemes as a means of breaking workers' resistance. They could, for instance, increase workloads and use the threat of retrenchment to discipline the most truculent workers. Alternatively, they could manipulate the efficiency schemes to upset wage differentials and to breach privileges which protected the more skilled workers. But it should not be supposed that the mill-owners' efforts to reduce skill and break workers' resistance met with unqualified success.

On the one hand, then, business strategies and the managerial practice of the industry created a substantial area in which workers and managers could define and negotiate the daily conditions of work and indeed relations of production in constantly changing circumstances. On the other hand, mill-owners and mill managers tried to use rationalization as an instrument for extending their control over the workforce. It is not surprising, therefore, that the daily social relations of the workplace came to be deeply imbued with tension and antagonism. Indeed the threat of resistance sometimes proved sufficient to frustrate the intentions of the mill-owners and inhibit the implementation of their policies. It is to this resistance in its quotidian dimension that this essay will turn.

Disputes over wages, especially over changes in piece rates, like the larger question of wage disparities, constituted another common cause of strikes. Fixing piece rates had always been a fractious process. The most favoured method of procedure was trial and error. When a new variety of cloth was introduced, for instance, piece rates were tested against output and then adjusted according to earnings. But, as S. D. Saklatvala explained, 'In the beginning it is very difficult to fix up a rate . . . The weaver himself adopts an indifferent attitude and does not turn out the production which later on he does.' Once the rate was fixed, it might be that 'in the first month, the weaver does not work to his fullest efficiency'. But subsequently, Saklatvala complained, he would raise the pace and take home earnings far beyond the expectations of the employer, who would then be left with having to try and cut the piece rate.[35] Conversely, inferior mixings of cotton, machinery in poor repair, or a rush of orders which required cloth to be woven on a wider loom, could each reduce the weaver's wage. Interruptions in the flow of work or an inadequate complement of helpers could further damage his earnings.[36] Because the weaver's wage was 'based on a very complicated system of working out rates for different kinds of work', the Commissioner of Labour, who arbitrated in wage disputes, observed, it was 'liable to give rise to a certain amount of suspicion in the mind of the worker . . . that he has been wrongly paid'.[37] But such complexities, arising out of the type of cloth, the count of yarn, the mixing of cotton, the speed and width of loom, the heaviness of construction, and so on, also enabled employers to manipulate rates, for when a bewildering variety of cloth was woven, 'workers sometimes do not notice these cuts'.[38] In fact, most disputes over wage rates occurred 'on the weaving side . . . where you arrive at wages by intricate calculations of perhaps 200 different sorts in the course of a month'.[39]

The wide disparities in earnings and conditions between mills induced considerable labour mobility and wage competition.[40] Not only did they intensify competition between employers for the best workers but they also led siders and piecers, doffers and carders, to make what the Government Labour Officer described as 'odious comparisons'.[41] The demand among spinners in the Textile Mill that they should be given the same allowance as their fellows in the neighbouring Century Mill set in motion the events which culminated in the general strike of 1919.[42] The Labour Officer reported in the mid 1930s, 'there

are always cases cited in which one mill is said to be paying say
12 pies per pound for a particular kind of cloth as against $13\frac{1}{2}$
pies paid by a certain other mill for the same kind of cloth
because weavers get together in their chawls and they discuss
rates, etc.'[43] Similarly, when managers switched lines of production and altered the quality of materials passing through the
machines at short notice, disputes occurred within the jobber's
or foreman's gang or at the level of departmental heads, and
carding, spinning or weaving masters about the distribution of
the best raw material and the allocation of the most efficient
machinery, the best paying varieties and the least arduous
tasks.

   Workers also contested the conditions in which they operated.
In the late 1930s, it was reported, the age of the machinery was
a less frequent grievance among piece workers than 'complaints that the jobbers do not attend to the machinery properly
when it requires attention', which could result in a loss of
earnings.[44] Underlying these complaints was a perennial
source of conflict in the weaving shed. Line jobbers were paid
according to the production of the weavers they supervised.
Since it was in their interests to keep the machines running as
long as possible, they stopped the looms for repairs or other
necessary adjustments as rarely as they could manage. When
cloth was damaged as a consequence, they could attempt to
recover lost wages by levying fines on their team of weavers.[45]
Conversely, absenteeism, the spoiling of cloth and the deliberate slowing down of production by weavers could also act
as effective checks on the arbitrary exercise of the jobber's
power.[46] At the same time, it was said in 1929, 'weavers who
sustain losses owing to defective machinery and yarn are always on the look-out for better jobs'.[47] In the 1930s, as unemployment grew, the weavers' mobility declined. Since the
cloth trade had become increasingly the dynamic sector of the
industry, however, the weaver was always more assured of
finding a demand for his services than spinners or carders.

   Similarly, weavers sought to retain control over the looms
which they worked. It was widely observed that weavers often
preferred to stay with the same mill and after being laid off
sought to return to the loom upon which they had worked before. To Fred Stones this demonstrated that Indian workers

were peculiarly conservative.[48] Behind this apparent conservatism, however, lay sound material calculation, for the weaver having used a particular loom over the years had 'thoroughly mastered it . . . learnt to understand his machine's many and odd eccentricities and knew how to get the most and the best work out of it'.[49] Put onto a new loom, the weaver was also liable to find his earnings reduced. The special relationship between man and machine took many years to nurture and it was only too easily discarded.

Weavers were, of course, among the most skilled workers in the industry and they were able to appropriate for themselves important areas of control over their own labour. Weavers alone gained the right to appoint their substitutes when they stayed away from work. Moreover, their earnings were calculated according to the production of the looms allotted to them and they paid the substitutes themselves out of their own wages.[50] Julahi Muslims and other hereditary weaving castes laid claims to a skilled status. Muslim weavers of Jacob Circle, mill-owners repeatedly complained, refused to work on night shifts;[51] 'do not ordinarily work in mills except in higher paid occupations',[52] took away higher earnings than their Hindu counterparts and sometimes appeared to 'have a lien on their post'.[53] Weavers, in general, and Julahis, in particular, registered the highest rates of absenteeism in the industry.[54] They were skilled, permanently and not casually employed, and among the most urbanized in the labour force. No simple correlation is to be found between the migrant character of the workforce and their attitudes to work or their level of commitment to the industrial setting.

The diversity of conditions within the industry meant that the number of workers required for particular lines of output varied from mill to mill, while changing lines of output ensured that labour needs varied not only from day to day but also within the same mill on a single day. These conditions of production called for flexibility in the deployment of labour and resulted in the ambiguous definition of duties. It is not surprising, therefore, that the attempts to increase workloads prompted disputes about the specific nature of an occupation. The ambiguous definition of duties intensified rivalries between workers as they attempted to stake out and protect their own occupational territories. When the employers required siders to clean their machines, S. A. Dange, the trade union leader, explained, 'the operatives said it was not their duty and there was a strike. It is in fact in your interests that the duties are defined.'[55] But the mill-owners for their part argued that the definition of duties foreclosed their options and provoked trouble. The secretary of the Mill-Owners' Association regarded it

practically impossible to set out a definition of the duties which each particular workman in a mill should perform. In fact, today they will vary from mill to mill, and the danger of putting down the duties that you think will cover the general case is that they do not cover a particular case. Then you have labour troubles, because some fellow reads a definition of duties, and if he has to do a little bit of unspecified work, he will say 'I will not do this unless I get more money.'[56]

But, as workers complained, the refusal to define duties enabled employers to increase workloads or the intensity of effort demanded of the workers without warning or negotiation.

If labour needs varied from hour to hour, there were often workers to be found at any time of day who were, as one mill-owner put it, 'somewhat redundant in the mill'.[57] The mill-owners liked to argue that the retrenchment of labour only dispensed with these surplus workers. Some historians have concluded that the mill-owners, following the Tariff Board's recommendations, effected a tighter and more disciplined system of labour management.[58] But the evidence suggests that the continuities were striking and the changes deceptive. In 1939, the Government Labour Officer estimated that 25 per cent of the workforce could be found 'sitting outside the mill' at any one time.[59] Factory discipline was not simply determined by the pattern of production; it was also negotiated, albeit on unequal terms, between managers, jobbers and workers. Loitering at the workplace or slowing down production need not be construed simply as the negative responses of rural migrants to the industrial setting. They also signified the attempt by workers, faced with uncertain and fluctuating flows of production, to control the pace of work and the intensity of effort which employers demanded of them. 'The workers in Bombay', opined the loquacious Fred Stones, 'seem to favour the idea of half-work for everybody rather than full work for a few.'[60] Women employed as reelers and winders adopted effective work-sharing practices in order to limit the retrenchment of workers.[61]

Finally, workers' resistance also played upon business strategies in the industry, and sometimes served thereby not only to inhibit attempts to introduce new technology but also to define the limits of rationalization. This is illustrated by the case of the automatic loom. The Northrop loom required a greater capital outlay, a higher rate of depreciation and more expensive spare parts than the ordinary Lancashire loom. Its use would also have required technical adaptations in winding and other preceding processes, the use of improved mixings and preparation of cotton, and the steady supply of higher counts of yarn and longer production runs, which in turn would have required changes in the deployment of labour at every stage. Since prices were tending to fall, and the demand for the finer varieties was, following an initial spurt of growth, more or less stagnant, and in the 1930s even contracting, the viability of the automatic loom came to turn increasingly upon labour costs, or in other words, the number of looms allocated to each weaver. However, as the Tariff Board observed in 1927, 'it would be difficult to get weavers in Bombay to look after more than four looms'. Yet, according to their calculations, even if weavers agreed to mind six automatic looms, the ordinary Lancashire loom would still be more economical.[62] The Thackersey mills were wise to leave their automatic loom in its packing case for twelve years.[63] It was not so much 'the lack of capital' as the 'opposition of the workers', the mill-owners repeatedly argued, which proved to be 'the main cause of slow progress' in the implementation of rationalization.[64] This frequently appeared to frustrate and annoy the mill-owners. Thus, in 1939, the mill-owner, S. D. Saklatvala, thundered: 'If a Lancashire girl could manage six looms—and you know what type of girls you have in Lancashire—and a Japanese girl perhaps with an even weaker constitution manages eight plain looms, how could the hefty, strong Indian . . . claim that he cannot manage more than two looms?'[65]

II

Although workers' resistance may have deterred mill-owners from embarking upon a radical programme for the restructuring and reorganization of the industry, it was not the sole explanation for the slow advance of rationalization. Indeed, it would be misleading to exaggerate its efficacy. The very fact that the lowest common denominator of rationalization signified fewer workers minding more machines, sometimes with greater intensity of effort accompanied by a reduction in the general level of wages, scarcely suggests that workers' resistance was invincible.[66] On the other hand, as the mill-owners were fully, even painfully, aware, it was by no means negligible. After all, industrial action had forced the mill-owners to raise wages by up to 80 per cent in the post-war boom and then ferociously obstructed their attempts to cut wages back in the slump which followed.[67] By the late 1920s, Bombay's mill-workers had aquired an awesome reputation for militancy and the working-class districts of the city had come to be perceived as the bastion of communism.[68]

There was an underlying economy to the daily social relations of the workplace and the efficacy of workers' resistance may be measured by its parameters. Business strategies in the industry, determined by the inescapable constraints which the mill-owners faced, made it very difficult for them to combine to influence, let alone discipline, their markets. On the other hand, their insistence on flexible production strategies and emphasis on improvisation in the use of machines, raw materials and labour, sometimes weakened their position in relation to the workforce. Mill-owners recognized that to follow the more radical remedies which the numerous diagnosticians of their crisis prescribed with enthusiasm would lead inevitably to serious conflict with labour. Strikes might allow them to dispose of stocks in times of slump, but they could also tie up capital, increase fixed charges, discourage investors and severely damage the mills' position in the domestic market, leaving the field open to up-country and Japanese rivals.[69] In an industry which relied so heavily upon a rapid turnover to meet interest charges, pay off debts and attract capital, such unpredictable interruptions of work were rarely to be welcomed. Rather than adopt the newest and best technology or attempt to restructure their workforce according to some higher ideal of efficiency, many mill-owners preferred to keep production going and maximize profits within the constraints of the existing situation.

The introduction of rationalization schemes did not initiate everyday forms of resistance in the cotton mills. Where every aspect of workplace relations had always been open to negotiation, everyday resistance had necessarily become an integral part of everyday life. However, through the uneven introduction of new machines, the diversification and changing composition of output, the numerous adjustments of wage rates and repeated changes in conditions of work, rationalization heightened the uncertainty felt by workers and increased the scope for negotiation and conflict in the daily social relations of the workplace. By exacerbating differences between workers as well as mills, it also imparted a fresh intensity to everyday resistance. In these conditions of insecurity and uncertainty, however, resistance could not simply be mounted at will or regarded as a readily available option for the workers. The sanctions against truculent workers were powerful and employers were prepared to wield them ruthlessly.

These conditions of uncertainty arose from, and indeed were functional to, the flexible production strategies which the mill-owners had adopted throughout the history of the industry. Frequently, they widened the employers' options in disciplining their workforce. Until 1891, mills did not even specify their opening or closing times, or their periods of rest through the working day, and their hours of work varied through the year, sometimes in the same season, not only across the industry as a whole but also in individual mills.[70] This informality was not an attempt by the mill-owners to facilitate the adjustment of rural migrants to the rhythms of industrial work and metropolitan life. On the contrary, anxious to 'avoid being late' for the varying times at which the mill gates were opened, workers, it was said, 'often find themselves arriving at the mill long before it begins work. The operatives who are too early may . . . be found lying about the approaches to the mill sleeping.'[71] The demand for legislation to stipulate a fixed time of opening came not from employers seeking to reform the peasant mentalities of a migrant labour force, but from the workers who, while they were expected to be averse to factory discipline, were in fact seeking a clearer definition of their conditions of work.

From the earliest days of the industry, the demand for labour was liable to fluctuate, even through the course of a single day within the same mill. In the 1890s, about one-third of the workers were hired on a daily and casual basis; estimates for the 1930s do not suggest an appreciable decline in this proportion.[72] The methods of recruitment and discipline, which depended largely on the jobber system, sometimes heightened the insecurity and uncertainties which marked the experience of work. The jobbers' position, and indeed livelihood, depended upon their ability to maintain a regular supply of labour in the face of fluctuating demand. To achieve this, and indeed to discipline workers effectively, jobbers tried to attract larger numbers of workers to their team than the average number of workers they were likely to hire each day. But it was easier under these circumstances to attract workers than to retain their loyalty. So jobbers had to distribute enough employment between their recruits to prevent them taking their custom elsewhere, without necessarily ensuring regular work for each. Consequently, they held, within the industry's pool of labour, a supply of workers considerably in excess of its needs. The greater the number of recruiting agents, who in hiring relatively small complements could not accurately predict the demand, the wider would be the margin of surplus labour held on the fringes of the industry's workforce.[73] To hedge against the uncertainties of the labour market, workers sought to exercise leverage, wherever it was to be found, upon the jobber. To blunt the dominance of the jobber, they might draw upon their connections of kin and caste, village and neighbourhood, and less frequently, when it proved possible, upon the solidarity of fellow workers.[74]

Mills depended upon highly intricate, personalized and individual arrangements for the management of labour. They were often also intimately connected with networks of power and control in the neighbourhood. Not surprisingly, mills remained averse to exposing these alliances to the meddling and supervision of the Mill-owners' Association or mixing them in with the arrangements of their rivals. Each mill management, therefore, jealously guarded its autonomy from central direction in matters of labour discipline and control. Rules and regulations governing the conditions of work, drafted for the industry as a whole for the first time in the early 1890s, largely remained a dead letter;[75] individual mills kept their own counsel and doggedly followed their own usage. Characteristically, muster rolls were poorly maintained, absenteeism often recorded erratically and leave procedures followed only arbitrarily.[76] What appeared to constitute inefficient administrative practice served to increase the discretionary powers of mill managements and to widen the arena within which workers had to negotiate with their bosses to limit the arbitrary exercise of power.

Methods of wage payment also narrowed the workers' freedom of manoeuvre and served as a powerful instrument of managerial coercion. It was customary for mills to pay their workers at monthly intervals and to hold at least two weeks' wages in hand. New workers were, therefore, paid only six weeks after they were employed. Methods of wage payment varied enormously and some mills held large arrears of pay.[77] Wages in arrears enabled managers to fine workers more readily for irregular attendance, indiscipline, or what they considered poor workmanship. It deterred strikes. It also inhibited workers from leaving their employment without notice, served to subordinate them more firmly to the structure of authority in the mill and exposed them to the capricious decisions of jobbers, clerks and the serried ranks of managers.

Mills formally demanded a month's notice from their workers both when they sought temporary leave and when they wished to quit their job. In practice, however, mill managers did not always or regularly insist upon the fulfilment of these conditions and sometimes left themselves free to decide when and to whom to apply them. Nor were workers always made aware of these requirements. 'Many ignorant new hands', one observer reported in the early 1920s, 'leave without notice and consequently forfeit their pay.'[78] Nonetheless, this formal requirement remained a powerful sanction against workers. Absence without adequate notice could result in a fine of double wages for the period of absence.[79] Absence during the currency of the notice might render it invalid. Workers who quit or remained absent for more than five consecutive days without notice, it was said, were 'liable to the wholesale forfeiture of wages'.[80] According to the code of regulations formulated by the Mill-Owners' Association in 1892, on the basis of the prevailing conventions, workers could forfeit wages for participating in strikes or trade union activity.[81] It is by no means clear that managers invariably insisted on the provision of written notice, although pleaders' touts were often active in the quest for such business in the mill districts.[82] In any case, it is likely that this rule, as many others, was in practice permissive and applied with flexibility. Whether a worker's absence from work constituted permissible temporary leave or delinquent absenteeism often depended upon the discretion of his supervisors and managers.[83] In some cases, workers might be allowed to return to their old jobs even if they had absented themselves without notice; in others, 'the notices are not accepted although legally served'.[84] The business strategies of the mill-owners and especially their willingness to manipulate the wage relationship and deploy its sanctions to discipline labour meant that most workers held only the most tenuous grip on their jobs. The means of coercion which employers commanded at the point of production imposed severe constraints upon resistance, obstructed combination and placed seemingly insuperable difficulties in the way of strikes across departments and mills.

Despite the fact that mill-workers were 'operating . . . at a structural disadvantage and subject to repression',[85] perhaps precisely because of this, their struggles could not be limited to everyday forms. Indeed, if these were to constitute 'the only option available',[86] they would soon have been left without any option at all. In the face of 'the duress of the quotidian',[87] workers in Bombay intermittently formed trade unions or combined to mount large-scale compaigns in defence of their own interests. Of course, the 'duress of the quotidian' shaped in important ways both the nature of trade-union organization and the patterns of industrial action. At one level, it forced workers to establish connections with publicists and agents outside the mill to represent their grievances and to organize and conduct their strikes. The sometimes vociferous presence of the latter in the politics of the industry came to be regarded by officials, and especially mill-owners, as 'the outsider problem'. But their presence was, for workers, a necessary consequence of the repression to which combinations were subjected at the workplace. Workers who were active in organizing or effecting resistance were liable to be dismissed.[88] Moreover, the dismissal of some workers could be used as a threat to others and as a means of dividing and destroying trade-union organization within the individual mill. By establishing effective linkages across the industry, workers could try to restore in their favour the delicate balances upon which labour control rested within the single mill.

As a result of these quotidian compulsions, trade unions were forced to operate at a level removed from the workplace. Employers could thus strive to break the connections between workers and 'the outsiders' who sought to represent them, sometimes by dismissing those who forged and maintained such connections and, more usually, simply by consistently refusing to countenance the intermediaries who spoke on behalf of their employees. Publicists and representatives of labour's cause had broadly two types of responses to these constraints. Some attempted to establish their credentials with the employers and the state as respectable and responsible spokesmen. But it was usually difficult to satisfy the exacting definitions of their role which employers, and to a lesser extent officials, imposed upon them without compromising workers' interests or being seen by them as so doing. Others tried to defy the hostility of individual mill-owners, collect grievances as widely as possible, and or-chestrate widespread support as well as, if necessary, large-scale action. Denied access to the workplace, trade unions sought to establish their connections in the neighbourhood. They might seek to establish linkages through confrontation across the industry and thereby bring the employers to the negotiating table or even extract concessions from them. Of course, the confrontational response tended, by its very nature, to gener-alize the limited disputes of a team of workers or a department to an entire mill, the neighbourhood and the industry as a whole. Industrial disputes thus rapidly acquired an explicitly political dimension.[89] Significantly, the conditions which necessitated the use of everyday forms of resistance also served to escalate them into open, collective strategies of confrontation.

Conversely, collective acts of open defiance and dramatic confrontations between workers and employers contained an important quotidian dimension which often shaped their course. Industrial action placed jobs in jeopardy. For those who were allowed to return to work, participation in strikes could de-cisively alter their position and status within the mill in more

peaceful times. They could be overlooked for promotion, subjected to discrimination in the allocation of raw materials and
machinery, and placed high on the list of candidates for
retrenchment when markets slumped. Indeed, there is some
force in the trade union leaders' characterization that employers
frequently treated strikes as a breach of contract.[90] Consequently, when strikes occurred, employers might, if they could,
simply dismiss those who refused to work; if the strike was too
widespread, they might lock out the workers until they were
starved into submission, or wait until such time as they were able
to recruit a new set of jobbers and men to replace the strikers.[91]
Employers, seeking urgently to break a strike, would try and
keep production going by recruiting blacklegs, shepherding
them into the workplace, under guard if necessary, and working
as many machines, departments and even mills as possible. By
raising the temper of the confrontation, and thus also the threat
to jobs, employers hoped to encourage their men to drift back
to work. As workers began to return, it became easier to break a
strike. As soon as some workers returned, the danger of losing
their jobs brought several others back to the workplace. The
effect of this reaction, once set in motion, could overcome a
sizeable section of the workforce. Employers could then dictate
the terms on which the workers returned. Significantly, they
could choose which of the workers they would re-employ,
giving them an opportunity to replace the most militant sections of the workforce.

Jobs were particularly threatened when a strike was partial.
In situations of widespread solidarity, it was difficult for employers or their jobbers to recruit strike-breakers. For workers
and their leaders, it was always difficult to estimate, at the out-
set, how complete a strike would be. Yet the strength of the
strike was likely to play an important part in the decision of
workers and jobbers to join it. For this reason the beginning
as well as the end of strikes were marked by hesitancy and va-
cillation. Workers would appear at the mill gates on the morning of the strike to check whether the general tendency
favoured a stoppage. Workers, thus collected, might join the
stampede to cross thinly manned pickets, or alternatively turn
upon those who were trying to go to work. At every stage of a
strike, the commitment to industrial action imposed complex

calculations upon the workers. They had to consider not only their immediate chances of success but also the extent to which their urban as well as rural resources would enable them to bear the costs of industrial action. They had to measure the possible gains which collective action might bring against the price which they often had to pay on the shopfloor individually upon their return to work. Collective action could only be effected in the face of these severe, even crippling, pressures, and was sometimes undermined by them. Yet workers could scarcely escape the fact that if they were to retain their jobs and force their employers to listen or negotiate, let alone obtain redress and concessions, it was imperative that the strike was total and complete.

Subjected to these powerful constraints, trade unions appeared to take rather unconventional forms. Most trade unions were short-lived. They often operated as little more than strike committees. Frequently, they formed during strikes and collapsed when they ended.[92] In periods between strikes, they tried to provide substance and coherence to the diverse interests which had coalesced around them. But the task of presiding over the heterogeneous and fragmented elements which made up their coalition, in itself extremely complex, was often rendered impossible by the hostility of employers and indeed their refusal even to accredit or negotiate with them. The Bombay Textile Labour Union, which emerged out of the successful, three-month general strike of 1925, was precisely such a coalition of disparate interests. In the years which followed, it sought to build upon the linkages forged during that strike. In its representation to the Royal Commission in 1929, the Union pointed out that it had 'been able to redress a number of workers' grievances', and indeed in mills where it had retained some influence after the strike, 'some mill managers and other officers had admitted the usefulness and utility of this Union'. Ruminating upon their decline and fall in the late 1920s, its representatives continued:

Had the mill-owners been a little sympathetic towards the Union, the success it had achieved would have been more substantial and the Union would not have required to go through the agonies it went through after the 1928 strike . . . Thanks to the short-sighted policy of a majority of the mill-owners and their born hatred of trade unions, the activities of the Union had to be curtailed for the present and it could not continue in the manner in which it did function before the 1928 strikes!!⁹³

The representatives of the Union expressed irony as well as outrage in their exclamation marks. For their eclipse during the 1928 strike, a consequence, as they saw it, of the mill-owners' policies, had entrenched the young communist leaders of the strike committee in the politics of the industry. The Girni Kamgar Union experienced repression of a severity which had never been visited upon the Bombay Textile Labour Union, and the mill-owners' attempt to exclude it from the mills received significant official support in the 1930s.⁹⁴

Although the colonial state was anxious to avoid being seen as the political arm of the Mill-Owners' Association, it nonetheless found it difficult to sustain sympathy for the communists. While it enlisted in the counter-revolution against them, official pronouncements also began to revive old arguments about the need to encourage the growth of 'healthy' and 'responsible' trade unions. Legislation formulated repeatedly since the Trade Disputes Act of 1929 was intended to work towards this end. By June 1934, arguing against New Delhi's suggestion that they 'start some propaganda' to further 'our campaign against communism',⁹⁵ Home Department officials in Bombay took the view that 'The real way of countering communist activity among the mill-hands is to set up a sound organization to deal with industrial grievances so that the worker need not fall an easy prey to the agitators.'⁹⁶ The Trade Disputes Conciliation Act passed after the 1934 strike was intended to serve precisely this purpose: it was, the Government of Bombay declared, 'an open effort on the part of Government to prevent Communists and extremists from interfering in the textile affairs of Bombay City'.⁹⁷ While the Mill-Owners' Association had refused, since 1929, to recognize the Girni Kamgar Union as a bargaining agent on behalf of the workers, the new legislation compounded the Union's difficulties by assigning to the Labour Officer the task of receiving and redressing workers' complaints and, further, when they could not be readily resolved, both referring them to conciliation and, if no acceptable alternative was to be found, representing the workers' interests in these proceedings. In short, the Labour Officer was to replace the trade union in the daily politics of the workplace. In 1938, under the aegis of the provincial Congress ministry, a further round of legislation elaborated these conditions. The Industrial Disputes Act of 1938 required the provision of a notice to strike, and laid down procedures for conciliation and arbitration before a strike was declared. It also stipulated that only trade unions which could claim a membership of at least a quarter of the workforce were to be deemed truly 'representative' of labour and thus allowed to act on its behalf both in negotiations at the workplace and before the arbitration tribunals. Its primary purpose, as the faithful old lady of Bori Bundar triumphantly explained, was 'to prevent Communists and troublemakers from holding a pistol to the head of industry'.[98]

In practice, these provisions served not only to undermine malignant trade unions but also to enfeeble the healthy varieties they were intended to encourage. For workers to give notice of their intention to strike was simply to allow employers the time and the means to pick them off. With the exception of a brief period in 1928–9, when the Girni Kamgar Union claimed the membership of almost half the workforce, no trade union in Bombay came close to enlisting a quarter. The Girni Kamgar Union remained, in the face of repression, the most popular and powerful trade union in the city, but it was effectively excluded from the daily affairs of the workplace. Indeed, these matters had become, since 1934, the special preserve of the labour officer. Since trade unions seemed incapable of obtaining redress in the mills, workers saw little purpose in joining them. Indeed, the risks of membership swiftly appeared to exceed its possible rewards. The connections between the workers and the union became increasingly tenuous. On the other hand, the increasingly stringent conditions which had to be satisfied before a strike could be called—the provision of notice and the conciliation and arbitration procedures—allowed employers time to threaten, dissuade, cajole and bully the workers into acquiescence and certainly to magnify the uncertainties and intricate political calculations which had always attended the launching of large-scale industrial action.

In the 1930s, officials as well as mill-owners attributed the failure of rationalization to the lack of effective trade unions or alternatively, to the irresponsibility of those which existed. 'The

absence of any organized representation of labour', the Tariff
Board explained in 1932, 'has prevented further discussion of
the schemes' for rationalization and standardization, drafted in
1928–9, which, in its opinion, could 'probably be adopted with
little or no modification as soon as proper representatives of
labour can be organized to discuss it'.[99] Towards the end of the
decade, the Mill-Owners' Association found in the 'unwilling-
ness of labour to co-operate' the real reason for the slow advance
of rationalization.[100] Yet, as mill-owners themselves readily
admitted, referring to the communist leaders of the Girni
Kamgar Union, 'our attitude definitely was, if the workers
changed these men we would meet them' and since 'they did not
do so . . . we had to refuse recognition of these unions'.[101] Thus
excluded from the shopfloor, the Girni Kamgar Union, the
only effective labour organization in the industry, could have
no knowledge, as its leaders admitted, of the 'day to day working of the processes in the mills'.[102] Under these conditions when
trade unions could not readily establish themselves and those
which did were repressed, they could scarcely become the
effective bargaining agents which the mill-owners claimed so
loudly and longingly to desire.

III

In the period between the wars, the Bombay mill-owners tried
to make their labour force bear the brunt of their industry's
problems. Labour, it appeared to them, was the only element in
their situation which lay within their ambit of control. They
could neither collude with other Indian textile centres to fix
prices nor compete effectively in the finer varieties with Japan
and Lancashire. They could not command the banking and
financial services they required, and their influence over the
financial, tariff and monetary policies of the colonial state
appeared frustratingly weak. Cotton prices seemed to be determined by the volume of supply from the United States and,
like demand in the domestic market, by the monsoon and the
harvest.[103] Yet, even in relation to labour, their strengths were
often more apparent than real. If they tried to exploit labour
more intensively to postpone their moment of truth, they
found their initiatives stubbornly resisted, often subverted,

and in any case, frequently culminating in widespread strikes, sometimes for seriously damaging periods of time. The rhetoric of rationalization may, in the context of India's agrarian, colonial and dependent economy, appear to have been nothing more than a mummery, a shadow play of movements whose real place lay in the USA or Germany. In fact, it was a function of, and indeed, proved integral to, the mill-owners' desperate attempts to survive the successive crises of the 1920s and 1930s. But the mill-owners, and the powerful capitalist interest they represented, sometimes in alliance with the colonial state, could not easily impose their intentions upon a migrant labour force, in an overstocked market, divided by caste and religion, and largely lacking the protection of trade unions. Workers' resistance, however divided and enfeebled, often thwarted their initiatives and opened up and exposed serious divisions within their own ranks.

In his fascinating study of Sedaka, James Scott drew attention to 'everyday forms of resistance' as the particular characteristic of peasant society. Individual, anonymous and covert acts of resistance, avoidance strategies and non-confrontational forms of protest were, according to Scott, 'eminently suited to the sociology of the class from which it arises'.[104] They followed from the peasant's 'lack of discipline and leadership that would encourage opposition of a more organized sort'. By contrast, and for these very reasons, factory workers are expected to manifest an inherent propensity to collective action. In the Bombay textile industry, however, 'everyday forms of resistance', including foot-dragging, absenteeism, loitering, damaging cloth or indeed more occasionally arson and sabotage, were an integral part of workers' resistance and occurred alongside, rather than in place of, the more spectacular confrontations which they staged. But this quotidian resistance cannot simply be attributed to the peasant character of Bombay's workers. For workers with village connections were among the most determined defenders of their collective interests and often deployed their rural base to sustain strikes for extensive periods.[105] The peasant character in this case stimulated and facilitated open defiance and large-scale confrontation, just as proletarians resorted to forms of foot-dragging, absenteeism and insubordination.

On the other hand, the evidence of Indian industrialization suggests that we should not take it for granted that natural solidarities flowed from the concentration of workers in large factories. Rather, the conditions of production ensured that government policies, economic fluctuations and managerial decisions often exacerbated the divisions within the workforce. These divisions did not simply derive from their caste and kinship ties or village and neighbourhood connections but were developed and elaborated at the point of production. But industrialization did not only divide the workers. By shifting the focus away from dramatic confrontations between the big battalions of capital and labour, to what Scott called 'the quiet, unremitting guerilla warfare that took place day-in and day-out',[106] it is possible to challenge rather than confirm the characterization of a simply adversarial, or consistently oppositional relationship between 'exploiters' and 'resisters'. Competition and conflict between the mill-owners, and indeed between them and the colonial state, weakened their control and limited their ability to exploit. The exploiters were themselves divided by the processes which sharpened antagonisms among the resisters.

At the same time, the specific issues at dispute in this 'constant process of testing and re-negotiation of production relations between classes'[107] would also be familiar to the historian of collective bargaining in the context of advanced industrial societies. Conflicts over the nibbling of piece rates and increase in workloads, the demarcation of duties and the disparities and differentials in wages, the allocation of materials and machinery and the defence and status of skill, have riddled the history of work, workers and trade unions in Britain, Western Europe and the USA. In Bombay, these disputes occurred in the absence of trade unions. Yet the weakness of trade unions was neither a function of backwardness nor the expression of workers' consciousness in the 'early stages of industrialization'. Industrial action in Bombay represented neither a case of collective bargaining by riot nor the sullen resistance often expected of peasants and migrant workers. The defence of their interests drew workers into calculated and strategic campaigns, not simply spontaneous and spasmodic actions. Labour history in the advanced capitalistic societies has sometimes elided the growth of trade unions into the social history of the working class and assumed that the development of the former faithfully reflected the level of consciousness of the latter. Yet only a small minority of workers in Britain, France or Germany belonged to trade unions or labour parties in the early twentieth century.[108] At the same time, the central issue in British labour history, we are told, is whether industrial relations were shaped more 'by informal groups or spontaneous social and economic processes than by institutional forces', such as trade unions or the arenas of collective bargaining.[109] But this dichotomy, sustained by explanatory frameworks which have proceeded largely by generalizing from limited cases, appears rather meaningless when it is measured against a context where trade unions have no more than an ephemeral and evanescent existence, and where their absence does not preclude negotiation and collective bargaining between workers and employers. Indeed, to emphasize the autonomy of the role of institutions in collective bargaining is to beg the question about why employers and the state accepted workers' combinations in the first place. The vagaries and weaknesses of trade unions, as the Indian case suggests, should not be interpreted as a reflex of the values, aspirations and consciousness of the workers; rather, it is more consistently explained in terms of the hostility and the politics of employers and the state.

While the analysis of popular politics has been hindered and distorted by the teleology of revolution, it is equally misleading to assume that resistance is latent to, and a natural condition of, the subordinate classes. The lines of dominance and exploitation moved in diffuse and complex ways through society. The dominant and subordinate classes were separated not by a sharp and absolute divide but by fine gradations and complex patterns of social differentiation. Between them were to be found numerous intermediate strata who in shifting circumstances could be identified with either category and who in any case facilitated both processes of exploitation and resistance. Nor should the history of resistance in its various forms be reduced to a sliding scale from 'low' to 'high classness', on which the latter facilitates the political realization of interests which are held objectively in common. Rather, class itself should be regarded as a political construction, the product of alliances

forged between diverse elements which may, at certain times
and for specific purposes, seek to define themselves in its terms.
The politics of resistance and revolution cannot, therefore, be
deduced or derived from its social base. Just as forms of resistance may sometimes be explained in terms of the options
available, so peasants and workers may manifest the attributes
and rhetoric of class, more or less, according to the specific
political context in which they operate. As this study of
Bombay has suggested, everyday resistance could both flourish
alongside, as much as it might occur to the exclusion of, more
spectacular forms of collective action, while everyday life could
serve to define the limits of solidarity and expose fundamental
differences among the resisters. We scarcely need to recall that
the relationship between the history of revolution. and class
formation has been awkward and deeply ambiguous.

NOTES

1. The Indian Tariff Board (Cotton Textile Inquiry), 1927; the Bombay
Strike Enquiry Committee, 1928; the Court of Enquiry into a
Trade Dispute between Several Textile Mills and their Workmen,
1929; the Bombay Riots Inquiry Committee, 1929; the Royal
Commission on Labour in India, 1929–31; the Indian Tariff Board,
1932; the Special Tariff Board, 1936; the Textile Labour Inquiry
Committee's Interim and Main Inquiry, 1937–40. The proceedings of
some of these committees, especially those which inquired into the
riots and strikes of 1928–9, were reported in extensive detail in the
press.
2. For an account of the strikes in the late 1910s and 1920s, see R.
Newman, *Workers and Unions in Bombay, 1918–29: A Study of Organization in the Cotton Mills* (Canberra: 1981); on the political background
to working-class action in the inter-war period, see R. Chandavarkar,
'Workers' Politics and the Mills Districts in Bombay between the
Wars', *Modern Asian Studies* (henceforth *MAS*), xv, 3 (1981), pp. 603–
47.
3. M. D. Morris, *The Emergence of an Industrial Labour Force in India: A
Study of the Bombay Cotton Mills* (Berkeley and Los Angeles: 1965),
pp. 121–8; Newman, *Workers and Unions*, pp. 34–5, 69–84, 253;
S. Bhattacharya, 'Capital and Labour in Bombay City, 1928–29',
Economic and Political Weekly, Review of Political Economy, xvi, 42 and 43
(17–24 October 1981), pp. PE36–PE44.
4. This essay will not attempt to provide a comprehensive account of

rationalization or the political and intellectual context in which the schemes were formulated in Bombay. These issues are examined in greater detail in R. Chandavarkar, *The Origins of Industrial Capitalism in India: Business Strategies and the Working Classes in Bombay 1900–1940* (Cambridge, forthcoming), chapter 8.

5. James Scott, 'Everyday Forms of Resistance', in J. C. Scott and B. J. T. Kerkvliet (eds), *Everyday Forms of Resistance in South-East Asia* (London: 1986); J. C. Scott, *Weapons of the Weak* (Yale: 1985). The particular value of Scott's work lies in its excellent ethnography. But its theoretical ambition to produce 'an unwritten history of everyday forms of resistance' reaffirms the agenda of 'social history' as it was conceived in the 1960s and early 1970s. This agenda sought to reconstruct the 'everyday lives' of 'ordinary people' and taking this further, in the words of one of its early practitioners, 'to uncover the social meaning of lost or disappearing forms of struggle, ritual or myth, and to reconstitute their coherence'. G. Stedman Jones, 'Class Struggle and the Industrial Revolution', in *Languages of Class: Studies in English Working Class History, 1832–1982* (Cambridge: 1983), p. 25. For a more systematic programmatic statement, see Eric Hobsbawm, 'From Social History to the History of Society', in M. W. Flinn and T. C. Smout (eds), *Essays in Social History* (Oxford: 1974), pp. 1–22. It is not surprising to find prominently among Scott's 'theoretical' sources, therefore, some of the most influential 'social histo... of that generation: E. P. Thompson, Eric Hobsbawm, George Rudé, Eugene Genovese and Richard Cobb.

6. See, for instance, C. S. Maier, *In Search of Stability: Explorations in Historical Political Economy* (Cambridge: 1987), pp. 19–69, and 'Between Taylorism and Technocracy: European Ideologies and the Vision of Industrial Productivity in the 1920s', *Journal of Contemporary History*, v, 2 (1970), pp. 27–61. See also R. Brady, *The Rationalization Movement in German Industry* (Berkeley: 1933); J. A. Merkle, *Management and Ideology* (Berkeley and Los Angeles: 1980); H. Braverman, *Labour and Monopoly Capitalism: On the Degradation of Work in the Twentieth Century* (New York: 1974).

7. *Report of the Textile Labour Inquiry Committee, 1940* (henceforth *TLIC*) (Bombay: 1953), vol. II, p. 180.

8. Proceedings of the TLIC, 1937–40, Main Inquiry, Oral Evidence, Representatives of the Eastern Bedaux Company, 2 April 1939, File 77-C, pp. 4955–7, Maharashtra State Archives (henceforth MSA).

9. *Report of the TLIC*, II, p. 183.

10. Ibid., II, table XLIV, p. 187.

11. For an account of the early history of the industry, see Chandavarkar, *Origins of Industrial Capitalism*, chap. 6. See also the useful official history of the industry, S. D. Mehta, *The Cotton Mills of India, 1854–1954* (Bombay: 1954); A. K. Bagchi, *Private Investment in India, 1900–1939* (Cambridge: 1972), chapter 7; M. D. Morris, 'The Growth of Large-Scale Industry to 1947', in *The Cambridge Economic*

140   *Rajnarayan Chandavarkar*

History of India, Vol. II: c. 1757 – c. 1970, edited by Dharma Kumar, with Meghnad Desai (Cambridge: 1982), pp. 572–83.

12. *Annual Report of the Bombay Mill-Owners' Association* (henceforth BMOA), 1920, Proceedings of the AGM, Chairman's Speech, p. vii.

13. For a useful detailed analysis of the problems of the Bombay textile industry in the 1920s, see *Report of the Indian Tariff Board, 1927 (Cotton Textile Industry Enquiry)* (henceforth *ITB, 1927*), vol. 1.

14. See K. Gillion, *Ahmedabad: A Study in Indian Urban History* (Berkeley and Los Angeles: 1968); M. Mehta, *The Ahmedabad Cotton Textile Industry: Genesis and Growth* (Ahmedabad: 1982); C. J. Baker, *An Indian Rural Economy: The Tamil Nadu Countryside, 1880–1955* (Oxford: 1984), pp. 339–80.

15. *Report of the ITB, 1927,* I, pp. 39, 50.

16. For an account of these strikes, see Newman, *Workers and Unions,* pp. 138–67. On Ahmedabad, see Sujata Patel, *The Making of Industrial Relations: The Ahmedabad Textile Industry* (Delhi: 1987).

17. *Report of the ITB, 1927,* I, pp. 124–67.

18. These business strategies are examined in greater detail in Chandavarkar, *Origins,* chapters 3, 6–8.

19. Proceedings of the TLIC, Main Inquiry, Oral Evidence, Confidential Examination of the BMOA, File 78-C, p. 5338, MSA.

20. Ibid., Main Inquiry, Oral Evidence, BMOA, File 57-A, p. 101, MSA.

21. Labour Office, Bombay, *Report on Wages and Unemployment in the Bombay Cotton Textile Industry* (Bombay: 1934), pp. 43–4.

22. These issues are examined in greater detail in Chandavarkar, *Origins,* chapters 6 and 7.

23. Proceedings of the TLIC, Main Inquiry, Oral Evidence, Mr F. Stones, Director, E. D. Sassoon & Co. Ltd, File 70, pp. 3469–70, MSA.

24. Ibid., Main Inquiry, Oral Evidence, BMOA, File 57-A, pp. 194–5; Main Inquiry, Oral Evidence, Representatives of the Eastern Bedaux Company, File 77-C, p. 4978, MSA.

25. A Retired Mill Manager, *The Bombay Cotton Mills: The Spinning of 10s, 20s and 30s Counts* (Bombay: 1907), p. 5.

26. Proceedings of the TLIC, Main Inquiry, Oral Evidence, Mr A. W. Pryde, Labour Officer to Government of Bombay, File 66, p. 2479, MSA.

27. Ibid., Main Inquiry, Oral Evidence, F. Stones, Director, E. D. Sassoon & Co. Ltd, File 72, pp. 3624–5, MSA.

28. Proceedings of the Bombay Strike Enquiry Committee (henceforth BSEC), I, pp. 645–6, 650–3, MSA.

29. Proceedings of the TLIC, Main Inquiry, Oral Evidence, BMOA, File 79-A, p. 5338, MSA.

30. Ibid., Main Inquiry, Oral Evidence, BMOA, File 79-A, p. 5541, MSA.

31. Proceedings of the BSEC, I, p. 257, MSA.

32. Chandavarkar, *Origins,* chapter 7.

33. Proceedings of the TLIC, Main Inquiry, Oral Evidence, F. Stones, File 70, p. 3455, MSA.

34. *Indian Textile Journal*, III, no. 36 (22 September 1893), p. 237; *Report of the Indian Factory Labour Commission* (henceforth *IFLC*) (London: 1908), vol. I, pp. 6–8; *Annual Report of the BMOA, 1905*, p. 8; Sir George Lloyd, Governor of Bombay, to E. S. Montagu, Secretary of State for India, 20 October 1919, Montagu Papers, Mss EUR D523/24, pp. 140–1. India Office Records (henceforth IOR); *Report of the Industrial Disputes Committee, 1922* (Bombay: 1922).

35. Proceedings of the Bombay Strike Enquiry Committee, 1928–9, I, p. 118, MSA.

36. Proceedings of the TLIC, Interim Inquiry, A. W. Pryde, Labour Officer to Government of Bombay, File 42, pp. 457–8, MSA.

37. Ibid., Interim Inquiry, Oral Evidence, J. F. Gennings, Commissioner of Labour, Bombay, File 42, p. 419, MSA.

38. Ibid., Interim Inquiry, Oral Evidence, Representatives of the Girni Kamgar Union (Alwe-Kandalkar Faction), File 42, p. 109, MSA.

39. Ibid., Interim Inquiry, Oral Evidence, J. F. Gennings, Commissioner of Labour, Bombay, File 42, p. 433, MSA.

40. Proceedings of the BSEC, I, pp. 66–7, MSA; Labour Office, Bombay, *Report on Wages and Unemployment*, pp. 25–8, and *passim*; Proceedings of the TLIC, Interim Inquiry, Oral Evidence, A. W. Pryde, Labour Officer to Government of Bombay, File 42, p. 459, MSA.

41. Proceedings of the TLIC, Main Inquiry, Oral Evidence, A. W. Pryde, Labour Officer to Government of Bombay, File 66, p. 2337, MSA.

42. F. A. M. Vincent, Commissioner of Police, Bombay, to Secretary, Government of Bombay (henceforth GOB), Judicial, 29 January 1919, in GOB, Judicial Department, Bombay Confidential Proceedings, vol. 46, p. 26, IOR.

43. Proceedings of the TLIC, Interim Inquiry, Oral Evidence, A. W. Pryde, Labour Officer to Government of Bombay, File 42, p. 459, MSA.

44. Ibid., Main Inquiry, Oral Evidence, A. W. Pryde, Labour Officer to Government of Bombay, File 66, p. 2334, MSA.

45. Labour Office, Bombay, *Report on an Enquiry into the Deductions from Wages or Payments in Respect of Fines* (Bombay: 1928).

46. Proceedings of the BSEC, I, p. 494, MSA; *Royal Commission on Labour in India* (henceforth *RCLI*) (London: 1931), Evidence, Bombay Presidency, Seth Ambalal Sarabhai, I, ii, p. 14; *Annual Report of the BMOA, 1938*, p. 53.

47. *RCLI*, Evidence, Bombay Presidency, Mrs K. Wagh, Senior Investigator, Labour Office, Bombay, I, i, p. 193.

48. Proceedings of the TLIC, Main Inquiry, Oral Evidence, F. Stones, Director, E. D. Sassoon & Co. Ltd, File 70, p. 3534, MSA.

49. *RCLI*, Evidence, Bombay Presidency, Mr M. S. Bhumgara, I, i, p. 501.

50. Labour Office, Bombay, *Report on Wages, Hours of Work and Conditions of Employment in the Textile Industries (Cotton, Silk, Wool and Hosiery) in the Bombay Presidency (excluding Sind), May 1934: General Wage Census, Part I—Perennial Factories, Third Report* (Bombay: 1937), p. 19.

51. Proceedings of the TLIC, Main Inquiry, Oral Evidence, F. Stones,

Director, E. D. Sassoon & Co. Ltd, File 72, p. 3883, MSA.

52. Ibid., Main Inquiry, Oral Evidence, BMOA, File 57-A, p. 193, MSA.
53. Ibid., Main Inquiry, Oral Evidence, BMOA, File 58-A, p. 358, MSA.
54. M. M. Shah, 'Labour Recruitment and Turnover in the Textile Industry of Bombay Presidency', unpublished Ph.D. thesis, University of Bombay, 1941, p. 143.
55. Proceedings of the TLIC, Main Inquiry, Oral Evidence, Bombay Provincial Trade Union Congress, File 80-A, p. 5683, MSA.
56. Ibid., Main Inquiry, Oral Evidence, BMOA, File 79-A, pp. 5506–7, MSA.
57. Ibid., Main Inquiry, Oral Evidence, F. Stones, Director, E. D. Sassoon & Co. Ltd., File 73, p. 4097, MSA; see also Proceedings of the BSEC, I, pp. 11–12, MSA; Labour Office, Bombay, *Report on Wages ... in Textile Industries: General Wages Census, Part I, Third Report*, pp. 19–20. For similar comment in the period before 1914, see *Report of the Indian Factory Commission, appointed in September 1890, under the Orders of His Excellency, the Governor-General-in-Council, with Proceedings and Appendices* (henceforth *IFC, 1908*) (Calcutta: 1890), p. 14; and *Report of the IFLC*, I, pp. 21, 27.
58. Morris, *Industrial Labour Force*, pp. 121–2.
59. Proceedings of the TLIC, Main Inquiry, Oral Evidence, A. W. Pryde, Labour Officer, Government of Bombay, File 66, p. 2365, MSA.
60. Ibid., Main Inquiry, Oral Evidence, F. Stones, Director, E. D. Sassoon & Co. Ltd, File 70, p. 3426, MSA.
61. Ibid., pp. 3506–7, MSA.
62. *Report of the ITB, 1927*, I, pp. 143–5; *Report of the Indian Tariff Board regarding the Grant of Protection to the Cotton Textile Industry* (henceforth *Report of the ITB, 1932*) (Calcutta: 1932), pp. 65–7.
63. Mehta, *Cotton Mills*, p. 110.
64. Proceedings of the TLIC, Main Inquiry, Oral Evidence, BMOA, File 57-A, p. 63, MSA.
65. Ibid, p. 255, MSA.
66. For some, albeit ambiguous, evidence on what might be interpreted as gains in productivity, see *Report of the ITB, 1932*, pp. 11–12; *Report of the Special Tariff Board on the Enquiry regarding the level of duties necessary to afford adequate protection to the Indian Cotton Textile Industry against imports from the United Kingdom of cotton piecegoods and yarn, artificial silk fabrics and mixture fabrics of cotton and artificial silk* (Delhi: 1936), p. 17 and Table III, p. 16. For evidence on falling wage levels in the 1930s, see Labour Office, Bombay, *Report on Wages and Unemployment*; and *Report of the TLIC, 1937, Interim Report* (Bombay: 1937), vol. I.
67. *RCLI*, Evidence, Bombay Presidency, Government of Bombay, Memorandum on Conditions of Industrial Labour in Bombay Presidency, I, i, pp. 72, 116–28; see also Newman, *Workers and Unions*.
68. Chandavarkar, 'Workers' Politics'.
69. See *Report of the ITB, 1932*, p. 118.
70. *Report and Proceedings of the Commission appointed to Consider the Working of*

the Factories in the Bombay Presidency (Bombay: 1885), pp. 7–8; *Report of the IFC*, pp. 13–14; *Report of the IFLC*, pp. 6–8; Morris, *Industrial Labour Force*, pp. 101–6.

71. *Report of the IFC, 1890*, p. 13.
72. Royal Commission on Labour, Foreign Report, vol. II, *The Colonies and the Indian Empire*, Memorandum on the Labour Question in India. *Parliamentary Papers*, 1892, XXXVI, p. 129; Labour Office, Bombay, *Report on the Wages . . . in the Textile Industries: General Wage Census, Part I, Third Report*, p. 20.
73. Chandavarkar, *Origins*, chapter 3.
74. Ibid., chapter 5; Chandavarkar, 'Workers' Politics'.
75. *Annual Report of the BMOA, 1891*, pp. 15, 172–5; Morris, *Industrial Labour Force*, pp. 107 ff.
76. Shah, 'Labour Recruitment and Turnover', pp. 11–12.
77. *RCLI*, Evidence, Bombay Presidency, Government of Bombay, I, i, pp. 89–91, BMOA, I, i, pp. 400–1, E. D. Sassoon & Co. Ltd, I, i, pp. 480–1; J. H. Kelman, *Labour in India: A Study of the Conditions of Indian Women in Modern Industry* (London: 1923), pp. 118–19; Labour Office, Bombay, *Report on Wages . . . in the Textile Industries: General Wage Census, Part I, Third Report.*
78. A. R. Burnett-Hurst, *Labour and Housing in Bombay: A Study in the Economic Conditions of the Wage-Earning Classes in Bombay* (London: 1925), p. 57.
79. *Report by W. O. Meade King on the Working of the Indian Factories Act in Bombay together with Certain Suggestions and Proposals* (Bombay: 1882), p. 2; Labour Office, Bombay, *Report of an Enquiry into Deductions from Wages or Payments in Respect of Fines* (Bombay: 1928); *RCLI*, Evidence, Bombay Presidency, Government of Bombay, I, i, pp. 82, 89.
80. *Times of India*, 11 January 1917, Letter to the Editor from H. A. Talcherkar, 'Millhands and Law Touts'.
81. *Annual Report of the BMOA, 1891*, pp. 172–3; Morris, *Industrial Labour Force*, appendix VI.
82. Government of Bombay, General Department, Order no. 3253/62, Confidential, 15 May 1917, in Bombay Confidential Proceedings, 1917, vol. 25, p. 15, IOR.
83. *RCLI*, Evidence, Bombay Presidency, Bombay Textile Labour Union, I, i, p. 351; Kelman, *Labour in India*, p. 119 and n. 3.
84. Burnett-Hurst, *Labour and Housing*, p. 57.
85. Scott, 'Everyday Forms of Resistance', p. 6.
86. Ibid.
87. Ibid., p. 14.
88. *RCLI*, Evidence, Bombay Presidency, Social Service League, I, i, p. 445; Proceedings of the TLIC, Main Inquiry, Oral Evidence, A. W. Pryde, Labour Officer, Government of Bombay, File 66, pp. 2371–2, MSA.
89. Chandavarkar, 'Workers' Politics'.
90. V. B. Karnik, *Strikes in India* (Bombay: 1967).
91. The following account of the pattern of industrial action is based on

descriptions of strikes in Bombay, particularly in the press and in police reports. To some extent, it generalizes detailed evidence presented in Chandavarkar, 'Workers' Politics'.

92. The impressive fluctuations of membership which trade unions experienced can be observed in 'The Principal Trade Unions in the Bombay Presidency', *Labour Gazette, passim.*

93. *RCLI*, Evidence, Bombay Presidency, Bombay Textile Labour Union, I, i, p. 353.

94. The leaders of the Girni Kamgar Union were arrested and charged with conspiracy to overthrow the King-Emperor in 1929. They were tried at Meerut and imprisoned and began to emerge from gaol only in the mid 1930s. This was merely the tip of the iceberg. The parts beneath the water-line may be examined in the files of Government of Bombay's Home Department (Special), MSA.

95. Secretary, Home, Government of India, to Secretary, GOB, Home (Special), 23 June 1934, in GOB, Home (Special), File 543 (48) E of 1934, p. 59, MSA.

96. Departmental Note, 26 June 1934, in ibid., p. 61, MSA.

97. *Indian Textile Journal*, XLIV, 11 (August 1934), p. 380; see also, GOB, Home (Special), File 543 (48) of 1934, MSA.

98. *Times of India*, 4 August 1938; GOB, Home (Special), File 550 (24) of 1938, MSA.

99. *Report of the ITB, 1932,* p. 62.

100. *Report of the TLIC,* II, p. 100.

101. Proceedings of the TLIC, Main Inquiry, Oral Evidence, BMOA, File 57-A, p. 214, MSA.

102. Ibid., Main Inquiry, Oral Evidence, Bombay Provincial Trade Union Congress, File 58-A, pp. 503–5, MSA.

103. *Report of the ITB, 1927,* I, pp. 31–2.

104. Scott, 'Everyday Forms of Resistance', p. 28.

105. *RCLI*, Evidence, Bombay Presidency, M. S. Bhumgara, I, i, p. 499; Bombay Presidency Police, *Secret Abstracts of Intelligence, 1928,* no. 3, 21 January, para 61.

106. Scott, 'Everyday Forms of Resistance'.

107. Ibid., p. 18.

108. R. Geary, *European Labour Protest, 1848–1939* (London: 1981), p. 15.

109. J. Zeitlin, 'From Labour History to the History of Industrial Relations', *Economic History Review*, 2nd series, XL, 2 (1987), pp. 159–84.

5

Becoming a Bhuinya: Oral Traditions and Contested Domination in Eastern India

GYAN PRAKASH

It is usual to think of resistance as the negation of domination, as something conceived and mounted in opposition and external to, if not autonomous from, the prevailing forms of power. The aim of this essay is to explore the issue of resistance in other terms—as a practice which, while being internal to the field of power relations, activates slippages, disruptions, and transformations of domination. To highlight resistance that fractures the apparently solid body and career of domination, the essay interprets the oral traditions of the outcaste Bhuinyas who have traditionally worked as the *kamias* or dependent labourers of *maliks* or upper-caste landlords in the southern part of Bihar in eastern India. Inhabiting the districts to the south of the Ganges, and becoming more preponderant in the southern reaches of the region where the Gangetic plain rises up to meet the Chotanagpur plateau, the Bhuinyas' position as kamias, nineteenth-century written sources tell us, could be traced to the money, grain, and a small plot of land that they received from the maliks when marrying their sons. Called *kamiauti*, such transactions were termed 'loans', and the relationship was increasingly constituted as 'debt-bondage' during colonial rule.[1] But the kamias' ties with the maliks predated the designation of the relationship as bondage in the nineteenth century. The Bhuinya oral traditions, for instance, contain memories suggesting that their status as kamias, involved in irrigating and cultivating the maliks' lands, probably goes as far back as the fourteenth century when Hindu and Muslim warriors began to subordinate the region and its inhabitants. These memories, however, have been preserved and transmitted as 'mythic' accounts, perhaps also going as far back as the fourteenth century, narrating how they became an out-caste group of dependent labourers. So, paralleling the long history of the Bhuinyas as kamias is the equally long existence and transmission of oral traditions seeking to explain how the Bhuinyas became incorporated into the Hindu caste hierarchy as outcastes and subordinated as dependent labourers. Viewing these 'mythic' accounts as Bhuinya attempts to constitute their own subjectivity, I argue that on the one hand, the oral traditions incorporated the principles of caste hierarchy and dependent ties, but, on the other, they also inadvertently ex-ceeded and expanded the limits within which they were con-stituted as outcaste kamias by the prevailing power relations. In other words, in reproducing the Bhuinya social existence, the oral traditions did not simply replicate an 'original' scheme of hierarchy and dependence; rather, they fissured and prised open the Bhuinya position as outcaste and dependent labourers for reformulation and reconstitution. In this sense, the role of the oral tradition in the reproduction of the Bhuinya's domi-nated existence—identified in the difference between replica-tion and elimination of power relations—highlights the 'every-dayness' of resistance in the daily life of domination.[2]

If, however, we concede that the oral traditions spoke the language of hierarchy and dependence, then how could they also have contestatory effects? Furthermore, is it not necessary for the traditions to step decisively outside the discourse of hierarchy and dependent ties and speak in the language of freedom and equality if resistance was to mean anything?[3] Implicit in these objections is a proposition positing an either/ or relationship between domination and struggle, and they rest on the unstated and untenable assumption according to which a particular configuration of power relations, once established, remains fixed and exists unaltered until a counter-hegemonic discourse arrives. Until the arrival of such a moment, the reproduction of empowered social relations appears an un-problematic replication of an established domination. From this point of view, unless that moment of counter-hegemony arrives, everyday routines, religious rituals, cultural practices and 'traditions' cannot escape the designs of domination; on the contrary, they function in order to contain resistance and reinforce power. It is just such a view that surfaces at moments in the works of the 'Subaltern Studies' group of historians. Ranajit Guha writes: 'These [the traditions of insurgency] are operative in a weak and fragmentary manner even in everyday life and in individual and small-group resistance, but come into their own in the most emphatic and comprehensive fashion when those masses set about turning things upside down and the moderating rituals, cults and ideologies help no longer to maintain the contradiction between subaltern and super-ordinate at a non-antagonistic level.'[4] Of course, it is true that when pitted against the power relations mobilized and exercised by the state and the dominant classes, the resistance of the oppressed often takes concentrated and violent forms because it too assembles and consolidates struggles dispersed throughout the society. But the drama of such occurrences, when the bipolarity of the subaltern and the elite is violently asserted and contested, should not make us forget that this binary opposition is not an ontological fact but a construction that social practices attempt to institute and displace at these moments of dramatic conflict. This should also keep us open to the possibility that the struggle over the establishment of social heterogeneity and difference into an elite–subaltern opposition is not an episodic but a constant feature in the field of power relations.[5]

It is the struggle over the constitution of empowered identities—and its tenuousness—that this essay illuminates, highlighting the dominated being of the Bhuinyas as a matter of a ceaseless, rather than single, construction. It suggests that, in participating in this process, the oral traditions neither spoke from, nor envisioned, a field free of power. But while speaking the language of hierarchy and dependent relations, they made it dissonant, thus turning the subordinated existence of the Bhuinyas into something different. This notion of transformation, not from pre-cultural (natural) to cultural but of 'becoming' in history, owes something to Simone de Beauvoir's pithy formulation, 'One is not born, but rather becomes, a woman.'[6] Paraphrasing Beauvoir, one could say that one is not born, but rather becomes, a Bhuinya. Here, the verb 'become' is intended to strip the caste hierarchy and dependent ties of their garb of naturalness, and assert that the Bhuinyas were culturally constructed. In their oral traditions, this is what the Bhuinyas do by representing their position as cultural rather than natural, by providing a narrative account of how the Bhuinyas became what they were not before. These accounts of origins do not escape the language of caste hierarchy and dependent ties, but they problematize the 'naturalness' of dominance and make possible definitions of Bhuinya existence not intended by dominant ideologies.

My essay focuses on oral traditions precisely because, removed from the great drama of violent confrontations, they appear to embody just those rituals and ideologies that we consider 'mythic'. Performed with regularity, and observing predictable narrative strategies, they define the routine existence of the Bhuinyas as outcaste kamias. It is, however, this concern with the regular that makes the oral traditions extremely significant for the understanding of the reproduction of social life because they reveal how the existence of domination was rendered tenuous and fluid by the 'everydayness' of resistance. Thus, even though the Bhuinya oral epics articulate and enact dramas in terms of distant origins and legendary heroes that lend it a 'mythical' character, my essay will argue that they concerned the 'real' environment; it will treat the Bhuinya traditions as important routine practices that incorporated and displaced the hierarchy and dependence which structured their everyday existence.[7]

BHUINYAS AND THEIR ORAL TRADITIONS

Derived from the Sanskrit word for land, *bhumi*, the term 'Bhuinya' means 'of the soil'. Historically, groups of varying statuses dispersed widely over eastern India were known by this name. Thus, in the nineteenth century, Pawri Bhuinya groups in highland Orissa, chieftains in Chotanagpur plateau called *tikaits* and *ghatwals*, and kamias in the south Bihar plain who worked as dependent labourers of upper-caste maliks, were all called Bhuinyas. Confronted with the fact that there existed a variety of different groups with the same name but commanding a range of economic resources, possessing different statuses, following a multiplicity of religious and cultural practices, the colonial ethnologists speculated along evolutionary lines.[8] They

suggested that the 'primitive' Bhuinyas of highland Orissa represented the original habitat and state of the group, from
where it evolved into higher stages and dispersed in the surrounding region, reaching the stage of caste society in south
Bihar. Here, the Bhuinyas acquired the outcaste status, and, as
a mark of this degraded status, being identified as the lowly
Musahars in some areas, became dependent labourers of the
upper-caste landlords known as maliks. Now, while ideas
centring on evolution and dispersion were, of course, characteristic aspects of the nineteenth-century colonial discourse,
they command very little respect today. What survives un-
tarnished, however, is the assumption of the formulation that
after the historical change from an original pre-caste state to
caste society, hierarchy and bondage became settled facts,
beyond contests. This blindness to change characterizes even
the concept of 'Sanskritization' which, while allowing for
change, treats the lower-caste adoption of 'Sanskritic' styles as
no more than demands for juggling the pieces within the system,
and as a mechanism whereby new groups are accommodated
in the Hindu ranking system. As a result, conflicts arising from
the demands made by lower castes for high status, as David
Hardiman remarks, are underplayed, and the coincidence of
movements for ritual 'purification' by lower castes with their
demands for changing the power equation is overlooked.[9]
Consequently, it appears that the social organization is, and
has always been, animated by the drive for ritual purity. At
first glance, this stance appears to receive support from the fact
that, because the oral traditions also articulate the principle of
hierarchy, the Bhuinyas did not contest their subordination.
To determine if this was the case requires, initially, that we
look at the nature of the oral traditions and understand why the
Bhuinyas have preserved them.

Many of the Bhuinya oral traditions concern their legendary
ancestor, Tulsi Bir, and other heroic figures whose names also
end with the suffix *bir*, meaning a hero. Performed usually at
marriages, this oral poetry is known by all and identified by its
refrain, '*hijra main dekhun, ab pattara main dekhun*'. The meaning
of the refrain, which literally says, I look at the *hijra* (the Islamic
calendar), now I consult the pattara (the Hindu almanac), is
unknown to the Bhuinyas today. The refrain itself serves as a

poetic device of rhythmic value, and functions as a core image
that invokes birs as the referents of the epic. The calendrical
reference to the Islamic hijra and to the Hindu pattara, however, is significant; it suggests that even though the literal
meaning is lost today, the narrative was originally conceived as
a tale anchored in time. This explains, perhaps, why epics
bearing this refrain always speak of the past, omitting all references to the present. It is probably also because of the self-
consciously historical frame of the epics that only accomplished
narrators perform them, even though nearly every Bhuinya
knows them. These accomplished performers, accompanied by
the throbbing beat of the *mandar* drum, sing these epics into the
early hours of the morning, extolling the greatness of the
Bhuinya birs and depict how, overcoming adversity, displaying
courage and cunning, these birs performed miraculous feats and
defeated powerful enemies. These bir epics seem to be patterned after the genre of heroic oral poetry common among
the lower castes. Thus, the Bhuinyas deploy plots and sub-
plots drawn from a repertory that is common among the lower
castes of the region: wrongful imprisonment, duels with powerful human and animal adversaries, challenges to perform
miraculous feats, are plot structures that, drawn from a larger
stock of lower-caste oral traditions, provide the means by which
the narrative can demonstrate the heroic nature of the birs. For
example, the plot of wrongful imprisonment of the hero's ancestors that the Bhuinyas use in elaborating the core image of
bride-capture was also employed in a tradition (probably
recited by a member of the Dusadh caste because the story
honours its deity) recorded by a colonial official, George
Grierson, in the late nineteenth century.[10] The invocation of
gods with which these epics begin shows a common pattern.
In addition, the sub-plot used in the tradition recorded by
Grierson, according to which the boy-hero becomes aware of
his ancestors' confinement only when his playmates accuse him
of cowardice, also occurs in a Bhuinya epic wherein many of
the same names are used, although its hero is a Bhuinya. The
wide and long-standing circulation of the oral epic traditions,
of figures, plots, and sub-plots among the lower castes that these
examples suggest is confirmed by a recent study of bir shrines
and epic traditions in north India.[11] The fact that the Bhuinyas

themselves, spread over south Bihar and eastern Uttar Pradesh, have used these plots and sub-plots in different epics and performances, and that these form part of the remembered tradition, is also indicated by the following example. One sub-plot establishes the bir's disarming charm and cunning when he is shown to captivate a demon, ready to devour him, with the use of endearing terms. This episode, which occurs in a tradition concerning the ritual pollution of a Bhuinya bir that I recorded in 1982, was also used, in the late nineteenth century, by the Bhuinyas of eastern Uttar Pradesh in another narrative.[12]

From these examples, it should be clear that the lower castes possess a rich repertoire of plots and sub-plots which are available to the performer in recounting stories. Because of their usefulness to the narrative design, these plots and sub-plots form a part of the remembered tradition, and more accomplished performers string together a large number of plots and images very skilfully in heightening the dramatic impact of the oral narrative.

While recognizing that the Bhuinya oral poetry is patterned after the genre of lower-caste heroic epics, and, therefore, that oral performers invoke the available stock of images, plots, and sub-plots, it is important to note that at the heart of these epics lie what interpreters of oral traditions call clichés.[13] These are highly compressed codes that exist in the form of phrases, proverbs, and plots. In the Bhuinya epics, clichés take the form of core plots. For example, a series of events leading to the ritual pollution of Tulsi Bir, a plot culminating in a marriage described as a victory over a Dusadh chief, are core plots that present an historical account in a highly condensed form. As Joseph C. Miller argues, these clichés may even implicitly contain the memory of a succession of events that happened, not because they occurred but on account of the importance assigned to them.[14] This memory, however, survives in a stereotypical plot. The formulaic nature of the plot allows the survival and transmission of the tradition over generations. Oral performers embellish the cliché by interjecting formulaic plots and sub-plots, by evoking images available to them. This is not to say that the cliché is some sort of historical kernel and the rest is distortion. On the contrary, each telling, every performance and version, constitutes the tradition anew, and an examination

of changes over time gives an indication of how the Bhuinyas
have transformed their tradition. This will become clear from
the three versions of the pollution cliché presented later in the
essay. For now, I want to stress that the point in recognizing the
distinction between core plots that serve as clichés and the plots
and images that the performers use to elaborate the core is that
the narrative as a whole is produced in relation to the cliché.
It is this key element that provides the oral performers the
textual basis for constructing a whole narrative.

While the identification of the recurring clichés, formulaic
images, and stereotypical plots and sub-plots help us understand how they have facilitated the survival and transmission of
the oral epics, there is only sketchy explicit evidence on how long
these traditions have been in existence with the Bhuinyas. The
reference to the performance of the Lorik epic in a fourteenth-
century text indicates that the genre of lower-caste oral poetry
was in existence then, but we cannot conclude from this
that the Bhuinyas have been using the genre since that time.[15]
More recent records, however, show that the Bhuinya traditions and the lower-caste epics have used a common stock of
images, plots, and sub-plots at least since the late nineteenth
century, and there is reference to Tulsi Bir in an early-
nineteenth-century account.[16] In other words, there are scattered references suggesting that the oral epics have been in
existence with the Bhuinyas at least for the last two centuries.
The important role that these traditions play in marriages
indicates that the Bhuinya use of the epic form may be even
longer-standing, going back perhaps even to the fourteenth
century when the process of their subordination as outcaste
labourers appears to have gathered momentum.

These heroic epics were, perhaps, first composed in the tu-
multuous context of the fourteenth century and after, when
warfare and aggressive agricultural colonization pitted the
local inhabitants of scarcely populated regions—such as the
Bhuinyas in the southern reaches of the south Bihar plain—
against the local lords and migrant warriors. But how do we
explain the long-standing existence of these traditions? Have
the Bhuinyas performed these oral epics for centuries, when the
original event that they purport to record and explain was
long gone, because they want to preserve their version of

history? Accepting this explanation means that we treat the Bhuinyas as historicists: they record events and preserve a memory of them simply because they happened. To try another explanation, is it possible, as the immersion of these traditions in the caste hierarchy and dependent labour relations would seem to suggest, that the Bhuinyas have preserved and used these traditions because they reflect and legitimize power relations? The problem with this line of reasoning is its implicit assumption that the oral traditions simply reflect but do not constitute the reality; if they do anything at all, that action is bounded by the intention of legitimizing the existing power relations. To limit the meaning of oral traditions by intentionality, however, is to overlook that these epics, using language and employing images, plots, sub-plots, stereotypes, and clichés, do not mirror but represent reality: they do not reflect but reflect *upon* reality. It is this dimension of oral traditions, as social commentary and critique, as attempts to constitute history, that throws light on why the Bhuinyas have preserved and performed these traditions for centuries.

THE POLLUTION CLICHÉ AND THE CONTESTED HIERARCHY

Among the clichés that the Bhuinya oral epics contain, one occurs most frequently in the form of a plot outlining how the legendary ancestor of the Bhuinyas acquired a low ritual status in the caste hierarchy because of his contact with objects regarded as polluting by high-caste Hindus. The oral performers elaborate the formulaic plot by interjecting other formulaic images, plots and sub-plots at different points, heightening the drama by deferring the end with constant twists and turns in the plot. Of the three available versions of this elaborated cliché presented in this essay, the first two, published in 1906 and 1935, give what appear to be highly condensed summaries of the plot, perhaps leaving out the details that the authors of the published texts considered superfluous. The third version presents a written summary of a performance I recorded in 1982. Although all three are summaries, the first two are highly compressed and provide only the main plot. Conventionally, the collectors of such narratives have tended to dis-

miss the historicity of these accounts because they lack credible
'facts', and have seen them as indicators of the Bhuinyas'
'mythic' consciousness, of their lack of a sense of history. It is for
this reason that the collectors of traditions give us only a 'thin'
outline of the plot. Consequently, what the telling of these
traditions may have accomplished for the Bhuinyas, just as
the writing and reading of histories do for us, is lost from our
sight. The fuller summary of the performance I recorded, on
the other hand, retains the performative character of the
narration. Its attention to the numerous sub-plots and to the
twists and turns that the narrative takes is meant to stress that
the telling of, and listening to, the tale are creative and constitutive acts—acts that remake the Bhuinyas. Keeping this
aspect in mind, a comparison of the three versions reveals that
despite variations in the way the core plot was elaborated, all
three of them hinge upon the formulaic core plot. While
variations over time in the elaborated narratives disclose how
Bhuinyas have constantly redefined and transformed what it
means to be a Bhuinya, the interpretation of the cliché reveals
the incorporation, displacement and reformulation of the
Bhuinya-dominated existence.

The pollution cliché consists of a core plot describing how
the apical Bhuinya ancestor—called Rikhmun or Rikhiasan in
the earlier versions but equated with Tulsi Bir who is the
subject of the third version—acquired an unclean or outcaste
status. The plot begins with the ancestor performing labour
that was required of him. In two versions, this labour, consisting of repairing a breached embankment, is made the cause
of his pollution by the superior powers who trick him into eating
beef or the flesh of an unclean animal. In the remaining version,
he is asked to remove the carcass of a dead calf; later, Hindu
gods impose an unclean status on him because he had eaten
fruit from a tree that had grown on the spot where the dead
calf had lain.

Of the three versions in which I found the pollution cliché
elaborated, the first is the following, published around the turn
of this century by L. S. S. O'Malley, the author of the district
gazetteer for Gaya:

... an embankment having been breached by flood, no one was able
to repair it and save the crops from destruction, until Rikhminia

came with his four brothers and rebuilt it in a single night. This act gave him the name of Bhuiya or saviour of the land—a designation which was not regarded as disparaging until a river god managed to get the Bhuiyas to eat the flesh of an unclean beast in revenge for the repair of the embankment. Thenceforth Rikhiasan and his descendants were a despised and degraded race.[17]

The next version comes from S. C. Roy, an anthropologist who published the following account some three decades later:

Rikhmun (corruption of *Rishi Muni*), our tribal ancestor, was one and the same as *Tulsi Bir* to whom worship is still offered by us Bhuiyas. *Tulsi Bir* lived at Maner (now in Patna district). He was the youngest of seven brothers of whom Bhagwan (God) was the eldest. One day while Tulsi Bir, with his wooden sandals on, was going to bathe in the Ganges he saw a dead calf in front of the house of his brother Bhagwan. As Tulsi Bir was the youngest of the brothers he was asked by his eldest brother Bhagwan to throw away the carcass of the calf. Tulsi Bir at first declined to do so on the ground that it would mean ceremonial pollution, and social degradation. Whereupon Bhagwan said, 'No, if you take a bath after throwing away the carcass, you will be purified and we shall eat with you.' And so Tulsi Bir did as he was told to do. On his return after a bath he found that a plantain tree had shot up over the spot where the carcass had been thrown away. And before he could leave the spot the tree attained its full growth and bore fruit and the fruit ripened. Rikhmun ate the fruit and went back to his brothers and told them what happened. The brothers told him, 'You have eaten beef. So we won't eat with you.' Tulsi Bir protested and said that he had not eaten beef. Bhagwan said, 'All right; let me test you.' And Bhagwan placed five fruits on his neck. And thereupon five lumps of beef came out of Tulsi Bir's mouth. Since then nobody would eat with him . . . he became 'Rikhmun' whereas his other brothers became higher *Muns*.[18]

The third version comes from the performance that I recorded in 1982. The following is a summary of the narrative that in its original form consisted of verses sung by a Bhuinya oral narrator.[19] According to this version, once upon a time, a man of the landed Babhan caste came to Tulsi Bir's house and pleaded for his help in mending a breached embankment. Tulsi Bir was reluctant but agreed to lend a hand when his mother told him that the Babhan was none other than his father's malik. So, reminded of the gratitude he owed, Tulsi Bir set out to seek the blessings of all the gods in order to ensure success. One by one, he went to Surya Bhagwan (the Sun-god), Sultan Bir, the god who lived in the west, Hanuman (the monkey-god of the epic *Ramayana*), and Mother Ganges, the river goddess. The journey to these gods and goddesses was perilous; ferocious animals and demons threatened to devour him. But, overcoming every obstacle, he reached every god and goddess, all of whom promised assistance, gave advice, and wished him success. Thus blessed, he returned home. Soon, Lord Bramha—who, at this point of the story, became none other than the old Babhan malik of Tulsi Bir's father—was at his door to tell him that the moment to fulfil his promise had arrived. Carrying his pickaxe, Tulsi Bir set out for the breached embankment where several hundreds of thousands of men and elephants were at work, trying to fill the breach. When Lord Bramha saw that Tulsi Bir had arrived, he asked everyone to cease work immediately. Then Bramha and Vishnu wrote him grants of several hundreds of villages. The assembled kings and chiefs laughed at the sight but, thinking that Tulsi Bir would fail just as others had, they too gave away land grants. Tulsi Bir surprised them all when, remembering and invoking the assistance of gods who had blessed him, he filled the breach effortlessly. The assembled deities, kings and chiefs could do nothing but give him possession over the villages they had granted. But while they took him from village to village, showing him his lands, they secretly laughed at him. How would a destitute like him find the ploughs and labourers to cultivate the lands? Tulsi Bir, too, was aware of his predicament. So, he returned home, dejected. But his wife, using inner power born of her purity, came through with a miracle. Thousands of ploughs and bulls suddenly appeared, as did a large fort befitting Tulsi Bir's new status as lord of a large territory. Thousands of Bhuinya kamias milled about in the fort, and men of Rajput, Babhan, and Dusadh castes came bowing to Tulsi Bir to seek employment. Tulsi Bir's glory made Lord Basudev intensely jealous. Determined to destroy his power, Basudev asked him to secure the flesh of an animal that was neither dead nor alive. Once again, his wife came to his help. She suggested that he go to her friend, a Dagarin—a woman of the Chamar caste and a midwife by occupation—for advice on how to accomplish what seemed to be an impossible task.

But avaricious sentries, wild beasts, and bloodthirsty demons inhabited the roads and jungles leading to the Dagarin's town. Tulsi Bir bribed the men, appeased the beasts, and charmed the demons into letting him pass unharmed. When he finally reached the Dagarin and told her what he was looking for, she sent him to a cowherd whose cow had just given birth to a calf. When the cowherd heard Tulsi Bir's story, he pointed to the placenta and said that it was the flesh from an animal that was neither dead nor alive. Having finally found what he was looking for, Tulsi Bir at once returned with it to Basudev who, now more determined than ever to break his power, planned yet another trick. Tulsi Bir was invited to a feast where the placenta was served in his meal. Inebriated, Tulsi Bir ate it, but immediately realized what had happened. Throwing up, he uttered a curse that his vomit, which grew into a banana tree, would be used in the worship of the deceitful gods, and his caste fellows would cut down Basudev's abode—the Pipal tree. This vengeance, however, could not undo Tulsi Bir's defilement. It was thus that the Bhuinyas came to be an unclean caste.

The core plot in all three versions will ring familiar to scholars of South Asia; several studies have noted that low castes and outcastes have traditions claiming that they once possessed a high status.[20] Like other lower-caste traditions, these three narratives can be interpreted as origin myths claiming that the Bhuinya existence as outcastes originated in their ancestors' ritual pollution. The first two versions speak of the degradation of Rikhminia, a compound of two terms for renunciating sages, rishi and muni. The choice of a renunciating sage, a person who lives outside society, enables the oral traditions to represent the fall in status dramatically. The third version achieves the same effect by making Tulsi Bir an ancestral figure who signals the very beginning of Bhuinya existence, the point of absolute origin. All three, then, establish the original point before which no pollution could ever occur. Leaving the variations aside for the moment, it is clear that in all three versions the core plot describes the consequences of acculturation; the original ancestor's good deed, his participation in culture, ends with the acquisition of an outcaste status. The low status of the Bhuinyas, therefore, is interpreted not as a natural fact but as a consequence of the cultural incorporation of the natural and original state. This is in sharp contrast to the Hindu theory about the origin of castes.

According to the classical Hindu theory, the four varnas, the classificatory basis for castes or *jatis*, arose from the body of the primeval man; from his mouth arose the Brahmans; his arms gave birth to the Kshatriyas; the Vaishyas came from his thighs; and from his feet were born the lowly Shudras. As the cultural basis of the sociological entities that we know as jati, the ideology of varnas invests, marks, and brands the primeval body with hierarchy. But it regards the thus acculturated body as its natural state. With the cultural order of hierarchy corporealized and viewed as the natural state of the body, varnas, and by direct implication jatis, become natural rather than cultural. Although it is true that this attempt to establish the naturalness of hierarchy deconstructs the implicit nature–culture opposition in so far as it is culture that asserts the supremacy of nature, it is equally evident that the ideology remains imprisoned within binary thinking. McKim Marriott thinks otherwise. In an essay that has enjoyed considerable influence,[21] he argues that Hindu thought overcomes the nature–culture opposition. According to him, because Hindu thought does not distinguish between person and action, between substance and the code of transactions, it regards persons as 'dividuals' who consist of heterogeneous substances in transactional flows, rather than as the fixed and stable individuals of Western thought. Therefore, caste ranks also depend on the value of transacted substances ('substance-code') instead of an embodied essence. This schema does not, however, support the case that Marriott makes, namely that Hindu thought escapes the nature–culture opposition. For, even if we concede that the 'ranks attributed to castes are evaluations of their natures according to the donor and recipient relationships in the transactions that are believed to have formed those natures',[22] the values of transacted essences refer back to a seemingly natural differentiation of 'substance-codes' embodied in the 'original Code Man'. The perfect and harmonious mixture of energy represented in this primeval man contains within it the principle for ranking 'substance-codes',[23] for ordering and ranking the original body according to the corporeal distribution of different acculturated natures. Thus, from the vantage point of Hindu ideology, because jatis derive from naturally-ranked varnas their 'substance-codes' are also natural.

According to the pollution cliché of the oral traditions, on the other hand, the Bhuinyas became a low-status outcaste only when the natural body of the primeval Bhuinya was acculturated. Although this acculturation involved practical activities—such as touching the carcass of the dead calf and repairing the breached embankment—which brought on ritual defilement, practical activity in itself was not polluting. Nor was the Bhuinya hero forced to perform these tasks because he was already polluted. Rather, it was when his labour caused others to trick him into committing polluting acts that the Bhuinyas and their practical activities became marked with an unclean status. This interpretation of the Bhuinya identity departs sharply from that of the caste ideology. From the latter's position, the Bhuinyas' outcaste rank and their polluted 'substance-codes' appear to be inherently interlocked and are proposed as given facts of their natural being. The pollution cliché, on the other hand, contends that the Bhuinya status is historical, not natural. This contention may appear similar to Marriott's argument that caste ranks depend upon culturally-ordered transactions, but his reference to transactions had implications other than those raised by the oral tradition's invocation of 'mythic' actions. For, whereas Marriott's transaction model reads the ideology of caste into events, the cliché invents events that contest the ideology that renders the Bhuinya association with their 'substance-codes' natural; while Marriott's ethnosociology sketches the transactions that operationalize the logic of 'dividuality', the oral tradition contains a story of actions that seeks to provide an historical account for the emergence of 'dividuality'. Pulling down the ideological mantle of hierarchy, the oral traditions reconstitute the Bhuinya outcaste status by placing it in history. This reconstitution does not mean the reproduction of the same; it involves a movement from one cultural interpretation of hierarchy to another. The Bhuinya was an outcaste to begin with, but the oral tradition changed what it meant to be an outcaste Bhuinya. What is noteworthy here is that the oral narratives did not rely, at least not entirely, on a strategy of inversion.

Thus, instead of claiming that they too are, or once were, ritually pure upper castes, they historicize the caste-system itself. So, while renewing the hierarchical subordination of the Bhuinyas, the tales of pollution denied the ideological claim of the Hindu theory; rather than reaffirm the claim to the naturalness of hierarchy by inverting its application, they riddled the ideology with history. Displacing the question as to why the Bhuinyas were an outcaste with the question of how they became an outcaste, the oral traditions turned historical consciousness into a means for reconstituting the social reality. What we are inclined to consider 'mythic', what we are predisposed to interpret as cultural operations by which the Bhuinyas make sense of the world, turn out to be discursive practices that contested the language of hierarchy even as they spoke in it.

IMAGES AND SLIPPAGES OF POWER

Another telling example of how the field of power relations constituted but did not determine the social construction of the Bhuinyas comes from the cliché of marriage-by-conquest in their oral traditions. This cliché, apparently part of a larger lower-caste tradition in the region, also exists in the form of a formulaic plot describing how a Bhuinya bir seized a woman of chiefly lineage for marriage.[24] While its representation of marriage in the form of a conquest befitting groups with warrior status may explain its popularity among the lower castes, for the Bhuinyas such a marriage had an added significance.

According to the core plot, a Bhuinya bir seized a woman of chiefly lineage, and after defeating the leading warrior of her lineage, and freeing his imprisoned ancestors, he married her. When performed, the core plot was elaborated with numerous twists and turns in the narrative, and the image of Tulsi Bir as a warrior was embellished with descriptions of his control over vast areas of land, with the depiction of a large number of kamias working his lands, and with accounts of his Sanskritic practices, such as having a Brahman priest for his son's birth ceremony. What is most significant in the narrative, however, is its assertion of a warrior status for the bir through an equation of marriage with conquest. Marriage as conquest has a parallel in the term *charhui* that the Bhuinyas use even today for a form of marriage. Charhui is derived from the verb *charhna*, which means to climb, or to move up. In the context of marriage, the verb 'to climb' is used in the sense of conquest or a military expedition (the word for which is *charhai*), and refers to the form in which the groom goes to the bride's home for the wedding ceremony. This is a more valued but less commonly practised form than *karhui*, derived from the verb *karhna*, meaning to pull out, or to extract. In this form, the bride goes to the groom's home for the wedding ceremony. In view of these two contrasting forms, to claim that the bir married by conquering the bride's army amounts to asserting a warrior status for him. Any such claim by a lower caste or an outcaste amounted to an assertion of a status denied them by the caste hierarchy. In the Bhuinyas' case, such a claim was especially significant because of their position as kamias.

The heroic warrior status that the oral tradition asserts is at odds with the dependence on the maliks that, as kamias, the Bhuinyas experienced and renewed when they entered into kamiauti transactions with the maliks in getting their sons married. Although a kamia required the malik's help on numerous occasions, the money, grain, and sometimes a small plot of land that he received from the malik at the time of his son's marriage was a strategic deployment of the malik's resources.[25] This was so because the material goods that the kamia received from the malik at the time of his son's marriage was no ordinary help that the kamia was forced to solicit because of his poverty, but the enactment of an extraordinary rite of passage. Having received the blessings of the malik, expressed in the grant of money, grain, and land, the kamia's son too became a kamia. This process was repeated in the next generation when the kamia's son, who had become the malik's dependent labourer at the time of his marriage, wanted to get his son married. Marriage, therefore, was the occasion for the renewal of kamia–malik ties. The grant of material resources at this time made the Bhuinya familial reproduction dependent on the malik's munificence, and thereby transformed a rite of passage to adulthood into a rite of passage towards dependence. It is this conditioning of the Bhuinya familial reproduction on the enactment of the kamiauti transactions, the inscription of marriage with the writing of kamia–malik relations, that was contested by the bride-seizure cliché.

In suggesting that Tulsi Bir was a warrior, as the marriage-by-conquest plot did, the oral traditions challenged the nature of control that the maliks exercised over Bhuinya marriages through kamiauti transactions. As a heroic warrior, the bir did not have to subject himself to the control exercised by the maliks; he seized his bride forcibly, and fought and defeated those who opposed his marriage to a woman of chiefly lineage. The narrative does not mention, let alone elaborate, the theme of romantic love. There is not even a suggestion of a desire for the conquered bride; she was chosen for forced marriage only because she was of chiefly lineage. Her forcible possession by the hero enabled the plot to advance the claim that the Bhuinya bir was a warrior who possessed sole control over familial repro-duction. Like the pollution cliché, this, too, was an attempt to reconstitute the Bhuinya status. Suggesting that the maliks had not always exercised power over the Bhuinya marriages, it claimed that the Bhuinya ancestors had also once been malik-like warriors who had control over the reproduction of their families. To be sure, this account of their warrior origins did not prevent the kamias from making kamiauti transactions with the maliks; however, it would be hasty to dismiss the oral tradition as insignificant for this reason. For, even as the kamias renewed their dependent ties with kamiauti transactions for marriages, the performance of oral traditions during the wed-ding ceremonies attempted to recapture what they had given away. It is true that there is no evidence to suggest that the Bhuinyas themselves saw their tradition in this way, but we need not invoke their self-consciousness in seeing their oral tradition as a critique of their constitution as dependent sub-jects. All we need to do is to recognize that the transformation of the kamias into a community of warriors accomplished by the oral performance problematized the reality of kamiauti transactions. At the very least, it broke up their singular identity as dependent labourers into a heterogeneous collection of existential moments extending from warriorship to depen-dency.

If the Bhuinyas resisted domination by formulating, trans-mitting, and performing oral traditions over centuries, they also did so in terms internal to the field of power relations. This is evident from the fact that the central figure in the cliché, the warrior, was patterned after the malik who enjoyed social domination because he embodied the principles validated by power. The malik was a martial figure. He controlled land, he commanded men, and his marriage, too, was styled as conquest. Force, battle, command, control, and conquest, were all key elements that defined the malik's dominant position. The Bhuinya bir also embodied these elements: he lived a martial life; he rescued his captive ancestors, he defeated the enemy chiefs, and avenged his honour by seizing a woman from the enemy clan for marraige. In oral performances, the narrator elaborated this image by even making the bir a landed lord who commanded warriors, peasants and kamias. Thus, it was the existence of the malik's cultural style, authorized by power, that enabled the Bhuinyas to reformulate their dominated being. It is worth noting, however, that the figuration of the bir as a warrior did not replicate the malik: the bir was malik-like but he was not a warrior; he possessed the attributes of a malik but he was still a Bhuinya—the tradition did not claim a Brahmanical or upper-caste status even though the bir followed Sanskritic practices. In this context, it is also significant that the tradition did not invert the Bhuinyas' relationship with their upper-caste maliks, i.e. it did not make the Bhuinya birs into upper-caste maliks and the latter into outcaste kamias. Thus, neither replicating nor inverting the malik's figure, the Bhuinya bir was produced by mimesis; he was patterned after, but not identical with, the malik. But not only was the copy different from the 'original', the fact that the genuine could find its identity in relation to the imitation also meant the displacement of the 'original'. And so, the cliché of marriage-by-conquest took the malik's warrior status, loosened it from an upper-caste identity and reformulated it in configuring the Bhuinya bir.

CONTESTATORY NARRATIVES AND THE SOCIAL REALITY

The interpretation presented above suggests that we view oral traditions as narratives constituted in power relations but not determined by them, speaking in terms of hierarchy while also rearranging it. This obviously means that resistance did not equal autonomy. Also, the references that the Bhuinya epics make to 'Bhagwan', the 'Mother Ganges', 'Bramha', and 'Basudev' make clear that the claim for autonomy would be somewhat rash. In addition, the invocation of Hindu gods and figures who belong to what is generally called the 'Great' tradition and appear in such written epics as the *Ramayana* indicates that orality could not be the sole context for the production of these traditions; there is considerable evidence here for the interpenetration of literate and oral cultures, of 'Little' and 'Great' traditions.[26] But if this interpenetration denies an autonomous voice to the Bhuinya oral traditions, can we locate its contestatory dimension in intentionality, as a self-conscious protest?

In fact, what is remarkable about the oral traditions' resistance to hierarchy, as I have argued above, is that it occurred in practices that also reconstituted them as a subordinate caste. Performed at the end of the wedding ceremony, the singing of the traditions, preceded by a communal feast, re-created the community by enacting a 'mythic' history of the Bhuinya birs. This does not, however, mean that oral performances are rituals charged with enacting the myth contained in the oral epic.[27] In fact, the myth–ritual or theory–practice oppositions obscure the complex character of the oral traditions. Thus, while it is clear that the ritual performance of the oral traditions created a Bhuinya community among whom kin relations could be established, this very task presupposed the notion of a Bhuinya community, a caste that is separated and exists in a certain relationship with other castes. So, the very performance of the tradition, apart from the content of the epic, established a theory of social organization; the singing of epics, then, was as much theory as practice. Where it differed from the content was that whereas the performance created the Bhuinya community by taking the listeners back to their past, to their ancestors, the content of the tradition reconstituted the Bhuinyas by bringing them from their past to the present. The narrator told the story as if he were witnessing the episodes, and, as the narrative progressed, the description of events carried the

narrator and his listeners from the past to the present. In this
sense, the content of the tradition was not some ideational
statement that the ritual expressed; it was also a practice that
reformulated what it meant to be a Bhuinya by making the
participants experience the history of their birs. Consequently,
when the story ended and the participants in the performance
were brought to the present, that present became purely a
historical moment in their existence.

Hence, even though the traditions were only charged with
accomplishing the marriage by re-creating the Bhuinya community, since they accomplished this by telling a story, they
ended up historicizing, and thus contesting, the outcaste and
dependent status of the Bhuinyas. Rather than the product of a
conscious intention, it was the very act of narrativizing the
Bhuinya existence, in order that different lineages could establish kin relations, that challenged the 'natural' appearance of
hierarchy. But if narrativization questioned how caste hierarchy
constituted the Bhuinya existence, the possible grounds for such
a contestation were always given. After all, narrativization
meant determining what constituted the Bhuinya past, choosing what was to be remembered and transmitted. This determination and choice in defining the social reality, however,
could not occur from a pre-hierarchical space; power relations had already determined the grounds on which the
Bhuinyas stood as performers and transmitters of the oral
traditions. Constituted as an outcaste group of kamias, they
formulated and transmitted clichés that incorporated and
contested their status as outcaste labourers. In this sense, the
Bhuinyas were always in a state of 'becoming'. Formed as outcaste dependent servants of their masters, they were always
transforming themselves into a different status. Since hierarchy
was not a fixed and static thing but an interpretation of in-
cessant activities, of lived social life, any attempt to define what
it meant to be a Bhuinya had to reformulate, reinterpret, and
renew already established interpretations of what it meant to be
a Bhuinya. So, when the Bhuinyas performed their oral traditions during marriages to establish the Bhuinya community,
they reinterpreted the interpretations already given, transformed the identity already established. I take these re-

interpretations and transformations as tantamount to resistance because change occurred only in the wake of struggle to 'become' different from what they already were.

If the interpretation of oral traditions shows that they ceaselessly transformed the Bhuinyas from what they already were, the analysis of variations in the oral traditions over time demonstrates that the terms of transformation also changed. Even though the preservation and transmission of clichés over centuries appear to lend a certain fixity to the Bhuinya attempts at self-construction, we should note that the clichés have existed in the form of performances. Because the clichés were not sacred words or lists, the performances elaborated them with other remembered parts which included the stock of plots and images that the performers used to enhance the dramatic effect. But since the transmission of the Bhuinya narratives was not controlled, as is the case with sacred words or lists of kings, the oral performers had considerable room to innovate; they could scan the available repertoire of images and plots and string them together into an extended elaboration of the formulaic core plot. In this sense, every performance was unique, every representation of the Bhuinya past different from another. Now, because there are no records of each performance over centuries, it is difficult to delineate the content of each transformation. But a comparison of the three versions of the pollution cliché, cited earlier, illustrates the general argument that what the oral texts transformed the Bhuinyas into was itself constantly changing.

The three versions of the pollution cliché given earlier tell the story of Tulsi Bir's fall from an exalted status. Even though the abbreviated nature of the first two versions limits the scope for comparing the content of transformations involved in Bhuinya self-constructions, two important changes are still clearly evident from the way the core plot is elaborated in the three versions. The first concerns the very figure of the Bhuinya ancestor, and the second relates to the role of the others in his pollution.

On the description of the ancestor depends how the tradition represents the fall in status. In the first version, the story claims that the ancestor was a heroic figure, and the claim is elaborated by showing that he and his brothers repaired the breached embankment after everyone else had failed. The narrative emphasizes the act of repairing the embankment that gave the ancestor the name 'Bhuinya'. Since the name was a reward rather than a punishment, the Bhuinyas owed their original position to their valuable labour rather than ritual purity. This means that, according to the text, ritual pollution was the mode of incorporation of the Bhuinyas into the caste hierarchy. From being simply people capable of performing miraculous feats, they were transformed into an unclean caste. The second version, on the other hand, begins by asserting that the ancestor's original position was ritually pure. He was the younger brother of the Hindu god, and when he went to bathe he wore wooden sandals to protect himself from polluting agents. His exalted position was not due to any feats that he performed; he was ritually pure. The transformation in this version, therefore, was from ritually pure to impure. In the third version, like the first, the repair of the embankment forms the principal means for claiming that the Bhuinya ancestor, Tulsi Bir, was a heroic figure who, too, was rewarded for his miraculous feats with grants of land. But this version also uses a host of other images to exalt Tulsi Bir's status; the Babhan landlord comes to his door requesting him to repair the embankment even though his father had been a labourer on the landlord's estate; after the lords grant him villages as a reward, he cultivates them with his own kamias; priests, warriors and others flock to his estate for employment. From this position of a landed heroic figure, Tulsi Bir falls to the status of an unclean caste. This version too, like the first, represents pollution as the mode of incorporation of the Bhuinyas into the caste hierarchy, but, unlike the first, the ancestor is not simply a person with miraculous powers; he is a landed chief, with his own army of warriors and kamias. Such variations in the description of the ancestor enabled the different versions to incessantly change the meaning of the narrative. While all three versions spoke of how Bhuinyas became an unclean caste historically, the different figurations of the ancestor enable each of the three to interpret the historicity of the Bhuinya status differently.

A similar difference is also evident in the way the three versions describe the process of ritual pollution. In all three versions, the performance of labour becomes the occasion for pollution, but it is not labour itself that leads to the ancestor's unclean status. In fact, the first and the third versions exalt labour and attribute the ancestor's subsequent short-lived glory to this labour. Even in the second version, where the contact with the dead calf is considered demeaning, the pollution is not irreversible. What is significant, however, is the way in which the three describe the subsequent turn of events. The second version suggests that Tulsi Bir became unclean almost inadvertently; he realized the danger of pollution and initially declined to touch the animal carcass; his subsequent pollution was the result of a conspiracy of circumstances. Even though the unclean status was imposed by Bhagwan, Tulsi Bir himself was partially responsible for his pollution. The other two versions, on the other hand, attribute pollution quite clearly to the deliberate intentions of the others. But the first version qualifies the deliberately engineered pollution by suggesting that it was nature's retribution. The third version, on the other hand, enlists the aid of the entire organic universe in acculturating nature. For this text, pollution was a dirty trick played on Tulsi Bir by the deities revered by the upper castes. Attributing the pollution to malice enables the narrative to end with Tulsi Bir avenging himself, thus magnifying the contestatory meaning of the cliché.

These variations in the three versions of the pollution cliché show that the very elaboration of the core plot with other plots and images transformed the contestatory meaning of the tradition. While our understanding of the range and the texture of these transformations remains sketchy, even the limited collection of oral traditions suggests that the narratives and their meanings must have changed considerably over time. With these, the contestatory refashioning of the Bhuinyas' dominated position must also have taken a variety of forms.

CONCLUSION: POPULAR CULTURE AND POWER RELATIONS

In conclusion, it seems important to reconsider our customary notions about the relationship of popular culture with power relations. We tend to either celebrate popular culture as autonomous from power relations, or we deride it as derivative and legitimizing. In the first case, it appears to be contestatory, and in the second a willing servant of power relations.

It would be easy to romanticize the Bhuinya oral traditions; we could interpret their transmission and performance over centuries as evidence of that cultural resistance which, by preserving a pristine orality close to the lower classes, defied elite attempts to impose a hegemonic literate culture. This, however, would overlook the fact that oral traditions were formulated and performed in a context consisting of literate traditions and elite domination, making the construction of a purely oral and a completely popular tradition impossible. The Bhuinya oral traditions, for example, appropriated figures from written epics and styled their legendary ancestors after upper-caste maliks; they incorporated gods and goddesses mentioned in Hindu texts and attributed Sanskritic features to their caste heroes. These features of the Bhuinya oral traditions imply that popular culture cannot be considered as an autonomous domain severed from the elite culture. Of course, because oral traditions consist of lived self-interpretation of the Bhuinya social existence, they must be treated as practices specific to the Bhuinyas. After all, it is through their oral traditions that the Bhuinyas have constituted their being as outcaste dependent labourers. But in self-constituting themselves, they could never proceed from a pre-historical or pre-Bhuinya position; the oral traditions had to begin with the recognition of an existence already defined, with a status already interpreted. Consequently, to interpret the Bhuinya existence meant to reformulate, renew, contest, and transform the outcaste dependent status already given by the larger historical context.

While the complicity of oral traditions in power relations, and the consequent lack of autonomy, may not strike many as surprising, there may be questions about the significance of their contestatory role. It could be said that because oral traditions did not step outside the ground of hierarchy and bondage, they could be termed, at best, non-antagonistic challenges and, therefore, not sufficiently counter-hegemonic. Of course, they did not approach the dazzling appearance of a violent rebellion; they did not increase the kamias' wages or the size of the little plots of land that they cultivated for themselves. These and

other facts may well be cited to argue that the resistance contained in oral traditions was not particularly significant; they
may have made the burden of bondage a little easier to shoulder,
moderated the impact of hierarchy, but did little to change the
'real' condition of the Bhuinyas. To put the objection along
these lines more starkly, one may say that the oral traditions
deluded the Bhuinyas into thinking that they were reconstituting hierarchy and labour relations when, in fact, they did
nothing of the sort. What this objection assumes, however, is
that social reality is a fixed phenomenon; with non-antagonistic
challenges unable to make a dent on its solid body, it remains
intact and unchanged. By positing a life-and-death relationship
between continuity and change, between power and struggle,
this approach concedes a self-same identity to domination.[28]
In my interpretation of the Bhuinya oral traditions, on the
other hand, I have argued that power was not fixed and static;
it was a relation that was constantly altered and transformed.
If hierarchy and bondage constituted the Bhuinyas' position as
outcaste bonded labourers, the oral traditions contested the
designation of their status as natural and asserted the historicity of their being. In changing their being from natural to
historical, however, they redeployed, renewed, and regener-
ated hierarchy and bondage, thus transforming and reproducing power relations.

What is important to note about the historicization, transformation, and reproduction of the Bhuinya status in the oral
traditions is that they throw open the very question of what constitutes social reality. By representing the Bhuinya condition in
historical terms, they strike at the very heart of what is defined
as real by power relations. To term the outcaste and bonded
status of the Bhuinyas as historical, as the oral traditions do, is
to question the very constitution of their selves as natural by
power. Surely, any attempt that contests the reality authorized by power, that modifies and changes its operation, is
significant.

NOTES

1. For a history of this process, see Gyan Prakash, *Bonded Histories: Genealogies of Labour Servitude in Colonial India* (Cambridge: Cambridge University Press, 1990). Also, the present essay's interpretation of oral traditions and resistance draws from and develops the material presented in the book.

2. By 'everydayness' I do not mean the everyday resistance that James Scott isolates as a form, and privileges over the dramatic forms of resistance. See his *Weapons of the Weak: Everyday Forms of Peasant Resistance* (New Haven: Yale University Press, 1985).

3. This is precisely the assumption that underlies Michael Moffatt's position. Thus, while rightly criticizing studies that tend to separate lower-caste culture from caste ideology as a whole, he ends up questioning the contestatory significance of outcaste interpretations of their own existence. His view that those at the bottom are as deeply immersed in hierarchy as those at the top of the caste ranking, his emphasis on consensus and continuity, expressed in his finding that the caste system looks the same from the top, middle, and the bottom, and his observation that the Untouchables participate in the hierarchical system of ranking, lead to the conclusion that 'at the present state of consciousness, the Untouchables cannot even comprehend, let alone question, the forces that subordinate them'. See his *An Untouchable Community in South India* (Princeton: Princeton University Press, 1979), p. 303.

4. Ranajit Guha, *Elementary Aspects of Peasant Insurgency in Colonial India* (Delhi: Oxford University Press, 1983), p. 12. In this particular case, Guha's reliance on the anthropological concepts of Max Gluckman and Victor Turner in interpreting the rites of ritual inversions handicaps his otherwise convincing argument for the central role of resistance in Indian history. For example, in a brilliant chapter arguing that the subalterns achieved 'self-consciousness' through negativity, he treats the calendrical rituals of inversion as executions of counter-insurgency's intentions (pp. 28–37). Insurgency and counter-insurgency are thereby placed not as effects of historical practices but as ontological categories that impose their respective and antagonistic will on history. Now, it is true that the calendrical regularity of the rites of inversion attempts to normalize and sacralize the social order by defining the inversion as irregular. But equally true is the fact that the very effort to define the social order as natural admits the possibility of its historicity and contingency. But these definitions and exclusions of possibilities can only exist as effects of historical practices. This implies that rituals, even when laden with already existing meanings, have to inscribe their 'counter-insurgent' messages through ritual actions; the 'counter-insurgent' meanings cannot rest on a previous inscription but must reinscribe them. The necessity of reinscription to ensure that the rituals convey the intended meanings, that they do not go 'out of control',

also suggests that there cannot be a single and unitary meaning. In fact, a single message has to be secured by appropriating, subordinating, and effacing others. To neglect, as functionalist anthropology does, this multiplicity of possible effects that ritual practices can have, marginalizes the place of resistance in the dominated existence of the subaltern.

5. Of course, the 'Subaltern Studies' scholars have themselves argued that social life in Indian history has always been marked by resistance; Ranajit Guha's *Elementary Insurgency*, and his more recent 'Chandra's Death', in *Subaltern Studies V*, ed. Ranajit Guha (Delhi: Oxford University Press, 1987), are brilliantly insightful from this point of view, as are those of several other 'Subaltern' historians. There is a tendency, however, in this group to regard the subaltern–elite opposition as given and view the subalterns as autonomous subjects. For a critique along these lines, see Rosalind O'Hanlon, 'Recovering the Subject: *Subaltern Studies* and Histories of Resistance in Colonial South Asia', *Modern Asian Studies*, 22, 1 (1988), pp. 189–224.

6. I draw this reading of Beauvoir from Judith Butler, 'Variations on Sex and Gender: Beauvoir, Witting and Foucault', in Seyla Benhabib and Drucilla Cornell (eds), *Feminism as Cultural Critique* (Minneapolis: University of Minnesota Press, 1987). See also her *Gender Trouble* (New York and London: Routledge, 1990), pp. 8–12, 33.

7. The fact that oral traditions may have a great deal to do with the 'real' is often overlooked by the oral–written opposition. Oral traditions are frequently left to the collectors of local titbits, to amateur folklorists and the writers of district gazetteers, who record these to add colour and authenticity to their descriptions of everyday life. The written document, on the other hand, is treated as a source where 'real' history can be found: reality is imprinted in the printed word! Of course, historians who work with oral sources have often been aware that the traditions, containing such information as king-lists and tales of migration, have political functions. But because they perform these functions, they are treated as myths. Thus, Jan Vansina, one of the pioneers in using oral traditions for historical reconstruction, describes an oral testimony as 'a mirage of the reality it describes'. Jan Vansina, *Oral Tradition: A Study in Historical Methodology* (Chicago: Aldine Publishing Company, 1965), p. 76. It should be mentioned, however, that Vansina has been primarily concerned with using oral sources as evidence. But, in highlighting the specificity of oral traditions as evidence, he overlooks that the divergence of the 'mythic' oral traditions from the 'real' written records makes historical representation a contested domain. To be fair, this is not Vansina's concern. But this lack of concern is consistent with the oral–written opposition posited in his otherwise fine recent study of oral traditions. See his *Oral Tradition as History* (Madison: University of Wisconsin Press, 1985), pp. 186–96. For a somewhat different critique of the oral–written opposition, see Jonathan Parry, 'The Brahmanical Tradition and the Technology of the Intellect', in Joanna Overing (ed.), *Reason and Morality* (London: Tavistock, 1985).

8. For example, H. H. Risley, *Tribes and Castes of Bengal* (Calcutta: Bengal Secretariat Press, 1891), I, pp. 108–10.

9. David Hardiman, 'Adivasi Assertion in South Gujarat: The Devi Movement of 1922–23', *Subaltern Studies III*, ed. Ranajit Guha (Delhi: Oxford University Press, 1984), pp. 212–15.

10. George Grierson, 'Song of Bijai Mall', *Journal of Asiatic Society of Bengal*, 43, 3 & 4 (1884), pp. 95–140.

11. Diane Marjorie Coccari, 'The Bir Babas of Banaras: An Analysis of a Folk Deity in North Indian Hinduism', unpublished Ph.D. dissertation, University of Wisconsin, Madison, 1986.

12. William Crooke, 'Folktales of Hindustan', *Indian Antiquary*, 23 (March 1894), pp. 78–81.

13. Joseph C. Miller, 'Introduction: Listening for the African Past', in Joseph C. Miller (ed.), *African Past Speaks: Essays on Oral Tradition and History* (Kent, England: Dawson Archon, 1980), pp. 7–8; see also Vansina, *Oral Tradition as History*, pp. 19–20, 27–32, 137–46.

14. Miller, 'Introduction', pp. 24–8.

15. The earliest written reference to a lower-caste heroic epic, called Loriki, comes from the fourteenth century, in S. K. Chatterjee and Babua Misra (eds), *Varna-Ratnakara of Jyotisvara-Kavisekharacarya* (Calcutta: Royal Asiatic Society of Bengal, 1940), pp. xxiv–xxv.

16. Francis Buchanan, *An Account of the Districts of Bihar and Patna in 1811–12* (Patna: Bihar and Orissa Research Society, 1936), I, p. 169.

17. *Bengal District Gazetteers: Gaya* (Calcutta: Bengal Secretariat Press, 1906), p. 93.

18. S. C. Roy, *Hill Bhuiyas of Orissa* (Ranchi: Man in India Office, 1935), pp. 26–7.

19. This was performed by a locally recognized accomplished narrator. The performance occurred at the end of a Bhuinya marriage, following a communal feast. The relatives of both the bride and the bridegroom participated in the performance; they warmly appreciated the narrator's skill in constantly introducing twists and turns in the story; joined the narrator in singing at different points; uttered words of approval, admiration, and wonder when Tulsi Bir's heroic acts were recounted; expressed sorrow when he was wronged; and expressed anger and outrage against those who were hostile to him. Lasting well into the early hours of the morning, everyone was visibly moved by the performance, as if they had just witnessed and participated in events described by the epic.

20. Bernard S. Cohn, 'The Changing Status of a Depressed Caste', in McKim Marriott (ed.), *Village India* (Chicago: University of Chicago Press, 1955); William L. Rowe, 'The New Cauhans: A Caste Mobility Movement in North India', in James Silverberg (ed.), *Social Mobility in the Caste System in India* (The Hague and Paris: Mouton, 1968); David G. Mandelbaum, *Society in India*, II (Berkeley and Los Angeles: University of California Press, 1970), pp. 442–67.

21. 'Hindu Transactions: Diversity without Dualism', in Bruce Kapferer (ed.), *Transaction and Meaning* (Philadelphia: ISHI, 1976).

22. Marriott, p. 114.
23. McKim Marriott and Ronald Inden, 'Caste Systems', *Encyclopedia Britannica*, fifteenth edition (Chicago: 1974).
24. The same core plot, describing battles to free the hero's imprisoned ancestors, followed by his marriage with the slain enemy's daughter, occurs also in the tradition recorded by George Grierson. See his 'Song of Bijai Mall', pp. 146–8. The version presented in this essay was recorded in 1982 during my fieldwork.
25. Historical records strongly indicate that although the kamias received assistance in money or kind from the maliks on numerous occasions, advances given for a son's marriage were charged with special significance. Bihar State Archives: Government of Bengal Revenue Department (Agriculture) Proceedings, December 1892, nos. 41–9; Government of Bihar and Orissa, *Final Report on the Survey and Settlement Operations in the District of Gaya, 1911–18* by E. L. Tanner (Patna: Government Printing Press, 1928), p. 63.
26. Rosalind O'Hanlon, *Caste, Conflict, and Ideology* (Cambridge: Cambridge University Press, 1985), pp. 164–86, contains a fascinating treatment of such interpretation in nineteenth-century western India.
27. My argument here closely follows S. J. Tambiah's treatment of the relationship between myths and rituals in *Buddhism and Spirit Cults in North-East Thailand* (Cambridge: Cambridge University Press, 1970), pp. 304–9.
28. In this context, it is relevant to note that Ranajit Guha's brilliantly 'thick' description of the subaltern insurgency stands in stark contrast to a 'thin' depiction of inequality and domination. This assymetry between a concretely described resistance and abstractly defined relations of domination concedes, in my view, an unproblematic existence to power.

6

Cultural and Social Resistance: Gambling in Colonial Sri Lanka

JOHN D. ROGERS

Despite the disapproval of both the state and Sinhalese elites, in the nineteenth and early twentieth centuries many Sri Lankan men of modest means came together regularly to bet on the outcome of various games, most of which were played with dice or cards. This gambling gave rise to resistance at two levels. First, the very fact that it continued in the face of elite and official attempts to reshape popular culture represented resistance. Although gambling was common in pre-British times, when neither elites nor the state were terribly concerned about the recreations of poor people, by the middle of the nineteenth century both elite ideology and the law expressed disapproval of the practice. This change was part of a Victorian effort to shape the lives of the less powerful so that they reflected the dominant values of stability, predictability, thrift, and work. The poor were well aware of this project, but they did not abandon gambling, which provided them with recreation, companionship, and excitement. The peasantry and urban poor refused to accept the new vision of respectability.

Gambling also gave rise to resistance at a second level. Faced with poor people acting in a manner offensive to dominant values, the state and elites turned to the law to suppress gambling. But they found that gamblers resisted this effort in a number of ways. Some of these measures were passive, such as playing in an obscure place, in the hope that the gambling would not attract the attention of those who wanted to stop it. Others were more confrontational, and included the selective use of violence. An alternative option was to co-opt the local representatives of the state by bribery or other means. Finally, and perhaps most importantly, gamblers used the courts, the very instrument created by the state to maintain order, to defend themselves, harass their opponents, and change the rules under which prosecutions were conducted. Taken together, these strategies were effective enough to allow gambling to continue as an important aspect of lower-class male culture. It is this second level of resistance, which was directed against attempts to suppress gambling, that forms the main subject of this essay.

Analysis of the resistance of Sri Lankan gamblers has broad implications for understanding social relations in colonial South Asia. The suppression of gambling was only one of a number of attempts by the state and elites to 'improve' and make respectable the social and cultural practices of ordinary people. Some of these campaigns used propaganda and social pressure; others relied on criminal law. Issues included temperance, raising the age of consent, changing sanitary practices, curbing expenditure on marriage ceremonies and religious festivals, the abolition of dowry, and the control of 'criminal tribes'.[1] These campaigns all sought to create a stable, productive, and disciplined populace. They consumed a good deal of energy, but few were unqualified successes.

This article is a case study of the ongoing resistance to an attempt by elites and the state to 'improve' lower-class culture in order to make it compatible with a social vision that encompassed the capitalist values of work, thrift, and rationality. There was no political controversy about gambling in colonial Sri Lanka; the government and elites agreed that it was detrimental and that it should be restricted by law. The class base of the struggle over gambling was so one-sided that the conflict could not be fought in conventional political terms. Lower-class gamblers had no political representation; they had to rely on their own resources. The success of their resistance under these circumstances testifies to their ingenuity and creativity.

The choice of gambling as a topic rests with its historical significance in Sri Lanka; there is nothing inherent in the action of gambling itself that gives rise to resistance. The Federated Malay States in the late nineteenth and early twentieth centuries illustrates this point.[2] The government rented gambling monopolies, which were usually purchased by the owners of tin mines. Most gamblers were employed in these mines, and gaming houses were situated near the places where the miners received their pay. Gambling in these establishments provided miners with recreation, but it cannot be characterized as resistance. The mine-owners used their control of gambling to get back a portion of the wages that they paid their workers; and the government used the gambling rents, which accounted for nearly ten per cent of the state's revenue, as a convenient way to collect a consumption tax from the miners.

Only those forms of gambling that gave rise to resistance are treated in this essay. Consequently, several forms of gambling are excluded. Lotteries, which were illegal after 1844, were fairly common, but the few prosecutions brought under the lotteries ordinance were aimed at the organizers, not the purchasers of tickets.[3] There was also betting by British residents and wealthy Sri Lankans at horse races and over private games of cards. These activities were both legal and socially acceptable.[4] Finally, villagers bet for low stakes on 'traditional' games played at specific times, such as during the harvest or at marriage ceremonies. Women often played these games, which attracted little attention from either the state or elite reformers because they were viewed as integral parts of the life of the 'village community', and not as a threat to social order.[5]

GAMBLING AS RECREATION

Organized gambling was managed by men who hoped to make a profit. Some persons earned their livelihood from it, but many organizers were shopkeepers, small landowners, labourers, domestic servants, or men with no fixed occupation. The extent to which the quest for a profit motivated these men depended on whether the gambling was run as a business or whether it served individuals with social connections established previously through kinship, friendship, or work. Many games were open to anyone, others were restricted to persons who could be vouched for by one of the regular players, and some were played by a small number of men who knew each other. On occasion over one hundred persons were present, but ten to fifty was the more common range. When only friends were involved smaller groups were usual. Gambling was practised in rural areas, especially in the low country, as well as in the cities, towns, and larger villages. Women rarely participated, but ethnic, caste, and religious lines were freely crossed.[6] All three major ethnic groups, the Sinhalese, Moors, and Tamils, played together in localities where they were present in the general population. Most gamblers, like most of the population, were Sinhalese, but Moors were probably more involved than their overall numbers warranted, especially as organizers. Houses, shops, sheds, and open spaces in gardens and forests were among the more commonly used places. Many games took place in the middle of the night.

The games played varied; it was usually based predominantly on chance, not skill. The most popular game in the early twentieth century, and probably earlier, was *bebi kapanava*, literally 'cutting the baby'.[7] The gamblers sat down in a circle and placed their stakes on a mat. After the playing cards (which had been introduced to Sri Lanka by the Dutch) were shuffled and cut, one player named any card he liked. The cards were then dealt, face up, to each player. The man to whom the named card was dealt won the amount that had been staked, less the manager's commission (*ton*), which was usually 4 per cent. At the larger gambling places there were three or four groups of men playing this game, with other persons watching the play, moving in and out of the circles between hands. A similar game played with dice instead of cards was also very common. Another game consisted of predicting on which side a tossed coconut shell, sea shell, or bone would land. Cock-fighting was popular in the coastal districts north of Colombo.

Excitement and companionship, rather than any expectation that a fortune would be made, were the chief attractions for most players. Gambling was very popular during holiday seasons and at marriages, and special booths were set up at fairs and religious festivals, which were important recreational occasions. Gaming places were spots where one could temporarily forget the daily struggle for existence and focus intensely on the cards or dice, in the company of people in search of similar diversion. Most men had irregular incomes and were

in debt. Placing bets with extra cash provided both entertainment and the possibility of an immediate windfall.[8]

People who played games of chance lost money. Since the
organizer appropriated 4 per cent of every pool, the gambler
who staked one rupee twenty-five times found himself an
average of one rupee short. Of course, if he was lucky he would
lose less than a rupee or come away a winner, and if unlucky
lose more than a rupee. Although gamblers usually lost money,
there is no evidence that they regarded the services provided by
the organizers as exploitative. In fact, it is probable that only a
minority of the organizers prospered in the long run. The
amounts staked were small, and there were many expenses,
including the salaries of assistants and watchers, bribes for
headmen or the police, rent for the use of land, and the cost
of dice and cards. Unlike the organizers of some other types
of illegal activity, such as cattle theft, managers of gaming
places were rarely able to project a respectable image, and they
were not immune from judicial punishment.[9] Most had modest
social origins, although there were a few exceptions, such as a
monk who was convicted for keeping his temple as a gaming
place.[10]

GOVERNMENT AND ELITE ATTITUDES

Gambling gave rise to resistance because the government and
Sinhalese elites believed that it undermined society and was
contrary to the public good, not because gambling itself
originated as a cultural practice that challenged relations of
power. In the early years of British rule neither the colonial
government nor elites approved of gambling, but they had
little interest in the recreations of ordinary people. This
attitude changed during the nineteenth century, largely as a
result of the adoption in Sri Lanka, by both the state and elites,
of new ideas concerning respectability and social order that
were prevalent in Victorian Britain. Those who wielded power
sought to remake the lives of poor people in their own image,
and impose the values of sobriety, thrift, and economic rationality upon them. In the case of gambling, the chosen
instrument for change was the criminal law.

Governments took little interest in gambling in the eighteenth century. In the Kandyan kingdom, which was annexed by the British in 1815, it was a minor offence, but was punished rarely.[11] In the low country, which was ruled by the Dutch, the criminal law ignored it.[12] The British made no immediate move to suppress the practice. In 1806, ten years after taking control of the low country, they sold the right to operate three gaming houses in Colombo, where unlicensed dens and gambling in public were prohibited.[13] Similar arrangements were later implemented in some of the other larger towns, including Kandy.[14] The gaming rents were justified on the ground that once people were forced to go to specific places to gamble, those who valued their reputation would stay away. But this was no deterrent for men without pretensions to respectability, and in 1832 Colombo residents told a government committee that thieves frequented the gaming houses.[15] The gaming rents never raised much money; in the late 1820s, for instance, they accounted for little over one-tenth of 1 per cent of the state's revenue.[16] They were abolished in 1834 because they were said to give 'a public sanction for habits which are injurious to society'.[17] Public gaming was prohibited in Colombo, but it remained legal in most other localities.

In 1840 the governor, J. A. Stewart MacKenzie, proposed that restrictions on gambling be included in the vagrancy ordinance that was under discussion.[18] The chief justice, Sir Anthony Oliphant, agreed that disorder arose from gambling, but he argued against direct legislation, declaring that 'you may as well attempt to prevent fornication'.[19] Nevertheless, provisions to punish gaming were included in Ordinance 4 of 1841. The scope of this law provides an indication of official attitudes to gambling at this time. The legislation laid out three classes into which individuals could fall: idle and disorderly persons, rogues and vagabonds, and incorrigible rogues.[20] A first conviction for unlawful gaming rendered the offender liable to punishment as a rogue and vagabond; a second conviction was cause to label him an incorrigible rogue. Other behaviour covered by the vagrancy ordinance included the use of abusive language, begging, prostitution, sleeping on private property without permission from the owner, failing to maintain a wife or child, indecent exposure, and loitering with intent to commit a crime. The law also set compulsory closing hours for taverns and made it illegal for tavern keepers to accept credit or any object except money as payment for alcoholic beverages. In other words, it covered an entire class of behaviour that offended the social vision of the British, and which had previously fallen largely outside criminal law.

Two conditions had to be met for gaming to be illegal. First, there had to be 'gaming, playing or betting ... at cock-fighting, or with any table, dice, cards, or other instrument for gaming, at any game or pretended game of chance'. Thus, betting on sporting events other than cock-fighting, or on games of skill, remained legal. This definition excluded forms of gambling favoured by British residents and Sri Lankan elites. Second, the activity had to take place 'in any street, road, highway, or other open and public place, or in any tavern, shop or place for the sale of spirits or liquor, or kept or used for the purpose of common or promiscuous gaming'. As a result, private gambling among friends did not come under the ordinance. The punishment for unlawful gaming was imprisonment for any period of up to one month, or a fine of up to two pounds (twenty rupees after the currency reforms of 1872).[21] Second offenders were liable to imprisonment for up to four months and to corporal punishment not exceeding twenty-five lashes.

The vagrancy ordinance also made provision for the punishment of keepers of gaming places. Persons found guilty under this clause were punished with six months' imprisonment and a fine of five pounds; the court had no discretion to impose a lighter sentence. Second offenders were imprisoned for one year and fined ten pounds.

One other aspect of the law needs mention. It allowed the court to order, at its discretion, the whole or part of any fine paid by a guilty person 'to be paid over, or applied to the use and benefit of the persons who shall first have given information against or been active in the apprehending of such offender, or shall appear otherwise deserving of reward in the matter'. The ordinance thus provided a financial incentive for persons to inform the authorities of illegal gambling, or to initiate prosecutions.

The long history of anti-gambling laws and sentiment in England was not the primary force behind these provisions. This older tradition was fuelled by religious concern, and focused on the moral condition of the individual gambler as well as the social consequences of gambling.[22] It was not strong enough to prevent the British from attempting to profit from licensed gaming houses in the early years of their rule in Sri Lanka. The move in 1841 to make gambling criminal stemmed instead from the nineteenth-century effort to create a disciplined and productive society compatible with modern capitalism. In Britain itself this project encompassed both social-reform movements such as temperance, and new instruments of coercion such as the modern police force.[23] In Sri Lanka, where the British sought to create a useful outpost of the empire, officials perceived gambling as a manifestation of a way of life contrary to the settled, ordered, and prosperous colony they hoped to establish. Gambling encouraged poor people to fritter away what little money they had in an unproductive manner, it took place at obscure places during all hours of the night, it enabled the lower classes to assemble without supervision, and it caused crime and poverty.

It is by seeing the vagrancy ordinance as part of this larger effort to shape society along orderly and respectable lines that the precise definition of unlawful gaming is best understood. It was not gambling itself that was the social evil; both gambling favoured by the respectable classes and private games played by poor people remained legal. There was broad agreement among officials that private gambling should be exempt from official intervention, but it was felt that public places which furnished the lower classes with the means of ruining themselves and their families could not be tolerated.[24] In other words, the suppression of gambling was justified with reference to the public good. Similar arguments underlay the other provisions of the vagrancy ordinance. Beggars, for instance, could be punished only if they were able to work or had other means to support themselves; other beggars were exempt, except when they offended public decency by exposing 'any wounds, deformities, leprosy, or loathsome diseases'.

Officials were not alone in their concern about gambling; elite Sinhalese also believed that it was a serious social evil. Many of these people took advantage of opportunities generated by the nineteenth-century expansion of the plantations to improve their economic and social position; they were traders, contractors, plantation-owners, clerks, lawyers, and notaries.[25] Their very success was dependent upon the adoption of Victorian values of work, respectability, and thrift. Some were Christians, but the Buddhists among them were important lay supporters of the late-nineteenth-century Buddhist revival. Partly prompted by the attacks of Christian missionaries, many Buddhists adopted the tactics of their adversaries in order to defend their religion.[26] In the process they often accepted values and assumptions that lay at the centre of the missionary arguments. Revivalists, for instance, responded to Protestant moralizing about Sinhalese drunkenness and crime with the argument that Buddhist texts had a stronger position against alcohol and violence than the Bible. They also pointed out that drunkenness and crime were common in Christian nations. But the accusation that most Buddhists were ignorant and degraded was not denied; during the temperance movement of 1904 some elite leaders even claimed that the Sinhalese were a 'criminal race'.[27] Revivalists dismissed popular beliefs and emphasized ancient texts, which they interpreted as promoting many of the middle-class values dear to the Victorians. In the words of Charles Batuwantuduwe, a prominent Buddhist, the temperance leadership sought to 'raise moral standards and promote thrift'.[28]

Sinhalese elites viewed gambling within this ideological framework. The Sinhala-educated intelligentsia, who still lived in close proximity to many poor people, were especially concerned. Like British officials, they believed that gambling was a matter for the criminal courts, and they sometimes organized petitions asking the government to suppress it in a particular locality.[29] The Sinhala press also carried many letters condemning gambling. Frustrated writers named the places where gambling was carried out in the hope of embarrassing the authorities into action.[30] A resident of Kindelpitiya argued that the government should take stronger action against gambling because revenue was lost when young men spent their time at gaming places instead of working in the fields.[31] The accusation that headmen and the police were in league with gamblers was a constant theme of this correspondence. One writer, for instance, complained about lawlessness in the village of Vaboda.[32] He described the gambling shed kept by one

Tepanis Silva, and claimed that the devils who frequented it also used obscene language in public, killed cattle, and went to the headman's house to drink illicit arrack. The headman took no action because he made money from the sale of arrack and received a share of the meat.

Although respectable Sinhalese supported the use of the law to suppress gambling, they also made some effort to persuade people to refrain from the practice. Beginning in the 1880s, elites established local religious and educational associations (*samagam*), which were designed to promote the ideals of social harmony and restraint that were the hallmarks of the new Buddhism.[33] Many of these organizations were little more than small debating societies, but others attempted to influence ordinary people. Their primary concern was the promotion of Buddhist doctrine, but some had a broad range of interests. An association at Panadura, which sought to teach young people Buddhism and secular science, listed the prevention of gambling as one of four social welfare activities; the others were the clearance and maintenance of roads, the prevention of false litigation, and the promotion of self-help.[34] Revivalists believed that the lower classes could improve their moral and economic status if they adopted authentic Buddhist practice, which precluded both drinking and gambling.

Sinhalese elites and British officials shared many common attitudes towards gambling. Both believed that it caused crime and poverty, that social disruption during the nineteenth century had contributed to its increase, and that it was an indication of the demeaned character of the common people. Elites, however, placed their disapproval in a distinct historical context. They put the primary blame on cultural Westernization, and sought a return to the culture of an idyllic ancient past, when there was no crime, gambling or unpleasantness. Although they had no desire to bring British rule to an immediate end, they believed that social harmony and unity were possible only with a return to Buddhist values. The British, in contrast, saw the increase in gambling as stemming primarily from social and economic changes, including increased prosperity, which had transformed traditional society. They did not doubt the overall desirability of these changes, but they took the alleged increases in gambling and crime as indications that Sri

Lankans were not yet advanced enough to appreciate fully the colonial order. These differences between elites and officials did not lead to conflict over government policy towards gambling because both groups agreed that the criminal law was the proper way to deal with the immediate problem.

Not all Sinhalese outside the underclass opposed gambling. In the low country many men of influence, including village headmen and small landowners, supported and sometimes organized it. These men, whose wealth was based primarily on local agriculture, were selective in their adoption of the ideology of the Buddhist revival. Gambling was often a part of village culture, and not all notables were ready to jettison it in favour of the new emphasis on thrift and order. The outrage of newspaper correspondents at the connivance of headmen with gamblers reflected not an increase in corruption among headmen but a growing distaste among the upwardly-mobile Sinhalese elites for the earthier side of village life. In the towns, too, gambling was not restricted to labourers and servants; it also took place among persons with some claim to the respect of the underclass. The participants in a private game interrupted at Hambantota at two o'clock one morning included the police sergeant, the chief headman's clerk, and a middle-level headman.[35] These men, however, would probably have condemned gambling among their social inferiors.

In 1871 the British sought to take advantage of the elite desire for social order by establishing 'village tribunals' in some rural areas. These courts, which were presided over by high-status Sri Lankans appointed by the government, were a response to the belief that the disruption of traditional society had led to a decline in respect for authority and an increase in crime.[36] The formal courts themselves were seen as contributing to this process. Sir Hercules Robinson, the governor from 1865 to 1872, declared that European legal procedure had 'failed to meet the first needs of a semi-civilized Oriental peasantry'.[37] The British hoped that the new tribunals, which were designed to reflect indigenous models of justice, would buttress traditional authority in the countryside. They were given jurisdiction over petty theft and assault, malicious damage to property, cattle trespass, and the violation of local irrigation rules. They also enforced rules made by local governments 'for the prevention of gambling and cock-fighting'.[38] In many areas local elites passed rules that simply made gambling an offence, with no reference to the type of game or the place where it was played. The tribunals were empowered to fine offenders a maximum of ten rupees, or, after 1889, twenty rupees. They did not oust the jurisdiction of the formal courts, but they did expand the types of gambling that were subject to punishment.

The passage of the vagrancy ordinance and the village tribunals act did not allay the concern of officials, who continued to identify gambling as an important cause of crime and disorder. They often blamed migrants from the low country for introducing gambling and crime to the Kandyan districts of the interior.[39] Louis Liesching, the district judge at Nuvarakalaviya in 1870, wrote that crimes of greed existed only where civilization had advanced, 'where drinking and gambling prevail'.[40] A. R. Dawson, the assistant government agent for the Kandyan district of Kagalla, had similar views. He noted in 1874 that several gangs of professional gamblers, all from the maritime districts, had been broken up. 'Cattle stealing', he continued, 'had in consequence decreased ... and complaints of thefts of unripe produce are less frequent.'[41] Officials in the low country also associated gambling with crime. C. M. Lushington, assistant government agent at Negombo in 1890, wrote that 'almost every village has its cock-pit, every group of villages has its gambling den, and near to each is a tavern or a place for illicit sale of arrack. Drink leads to gambling, gambling to crime of a more serious nature.'[42] In the eyes of most officials gambling was a serious threat to social peace, and by extension to British authority itself. Charles Liesching, the district judge at Negombo, admitted in 1874 that some persons believed that the law made 'invidious distinctions' between European and 'native' gamblers, but he argued that European gamblers did not turn to crime to make up their losses: 'It is the evils into which gambling drives a race, deficient in moral stamina, which justify exceptional legislation in their case.'[43]

There were few voices of dissent to the dominant view that linked gambling with crime. One of these was W. W. Fisher, Crown counsel for the North-Western Province, who wrote in 1890 that 'during upwards of five years in which I have been

conducting Crown prosecutions my memory does not furnish
me with a single criminal case which has had the remotest connection with gambling, except prosecutions, which are frequent,
for the act itself'.[44] Fisher believed that 'gambling, undesirable
as it may in itself be, has been unjustly gibbeted as a cause of
crime'. He was probably correct. Gambling was a principal
recreation among the majority of men who lacked respectability, including many 'village bullies', thieves, and other un-
savoury characters. Elites and officials were right in assigning it
a central role in popular culture, but they viewed its presence
as a sign of the demeaned character of the common people. The
stereotype linking gambling and crime was probably established by first identifying the underclass as the group from
which most criminals were drawn, and then attributing
crime to those aspects of popular culture, including gambling,
disliked by elites and officials.[45] The numerous declarations
that gambling caused crime contain remarkably few examples
of the alleged relationship, and a survey of homicides between
1896 and 1902 found that only 2 per cent of them could be
traced to gambling disputes.[46]

The prevalence of official and elite views condemning gambling led to new and tougher legislation: Ordinance 19 of 1889.[47]
This law sought to make convictions easier and punishments
harsher. It was one of several measures, beginning with the
establishment of village tribunals, that were taken in the late
nineteenth century to improve the efficiency of the courts and
combat the perceived increase in crime.[48] In 1885 a penal code
and code of criminal procedure were implemented, and these
were followed by other laws designed to simplify judicial procedure and speed up justice. The new gambling legislation, like
these other measures, was justified with reference to the ineffectiveness of the law as it stood. It provoked no political
opposition; the only amendment discussed and passed in the
legislative council exempted rest-houses and proprietary clubs
from its provisions.

Like the vagrancy ordinance, the new statute defined unlawful gaming according to both the type of game and the
place where it was played. The 1889 law singled out 'the act of
betting or playing a game for a stake'. Playing a game of
chance was no longer the essence of the offence; it was the

laying of a stake on a game, whether of chance or skill. Two
exceptions were made. First, 'cock-fighting, whether for a stake
or not, and whether practised publicly or privately', was
labelled unlawful; previously private cock-fighting was legal.
Second, the ordinance exempted billiards, bagatelle, and 'any
game which is also an athletic exercise'.

   To be unlawful, gaming, except for cock-fighting, also had
to be carried out in any one of three categories of places. The
first was 'in or upon any path, street, road, or place to which
the public have access, whether as of right or not'. This
broadened the language of the vagrancy ordinance, which had
covered any 'open or public place'. The second category extended the earlier prohibition of gambling at taverns to cover
distilleries. The third made laying a stake illegal if it took
place at a 'common gaming place', which was defined as 'any
place kept or used for betting or the playing of games for stakes,
and to which the public may have access with or without payment'. The ordinance stated explicitly that such a place needed
to be so used on one occasion only. This category was also
worded more broadly than its equivalent in the vagrancy
ordinance, which had implied that evidence of repeated gaming
was necessary to render the play unlawful.

   In response to long-standing complaints about the difficulty
of gaining convictions, the 1889 legislation included a provision that enabled the prosecution to put the burden of proof on
the defence. If a magistrate, on being satisfied with written
information on oath that there was good reason to believe that
a place was being kept as a common gaming place, issued a
warrant authorizing the police to enter and search the place
in question; and if upon this action any instruments for gaming
were found, or if any persons were seen or heard to escape, or
if the occupants resisted the entry of the police, then the place
was assumed to be a common gaming place. Any person found
there, or found escaping, was presumed, unless proved to the
contrary, to be guilty of unlawful gaming.

   The new law also made provision for harsher punishments.
The maximum penalty for unlawful gaming was set at a fine
not exceeding one hundred rupees, or imprisonment not exceeding six months, or both. Persons who kept or managed a
common gaming place were subject to a fine of up to five

hundred rupees or imprisonment for one year, or both. The maximum fines for both these offences were five times those available under the earlier law.

Attitudes towards gambling changed little after the passage of the 1889 ordinance. There was no substantive change to the law, and officials viewed gambling in much the same way as their predecessors. George Cookson, the assistant government agent at Matara, asserted in 1905 that 'the ordinary Sinhalese is a person almost wholly undisciplined either by education, home training, religion, or the circumstances of his daily life. To this defect must be added a passion for revenge which trivial injuries and even well-merited punishment evoke. The crime of the people springs from these two characteristics, and its growth is fostered by gambling, drink and litigation.'[49] L. F. Knollys, the inspector-general of police from 1892 to 1902, claimed that 'the regular gambling dens' were 'a very real and active sort of evil' because the 'bad characters' who gathered in them planned crimes in order to recoup their losses.[50] H. L. Dowbiggin, who held the same office from 1913 to 1937, declared that 'there is no question but that unlawful gaming and crime go together. Unlawful gaming places attract bad characters, and the fact that the gaming places are not raided has a bad moral effect throughout the district.'[51] He believed that the increasing popularity of volley-ball might reduce the prevalence of gambling in the long run.[52] Elite Sinhalese held similar views. In 1914 Dr C. A. Hewavitarne, a Buddhist leader, declared that 'the energy that goes to waste in gambling and drink and crime would be soon converted into healthier channels of co-operation and activity' if temperance societies set up tea shops and promoted village games.[53]

RESISTANCE TO THE LAW

There is no evidence that legislative changes, increased police activity, or the propaganda of Sinhalese elites reduced the scale of gambling during the British period. On the contrary, the sources give the impression that gambling increased. As the nineteenth century progressed, more people had cash incomes that could support them somewhat above the subsistence level, giving them the means to participate in gambling. The extensive migration of low-country Sinhalese and Moors to Kandyan districts also contributed to the spread of organized gambling, since the practice was more firmly rooted in low-country culture. Many Sinhalese accused of unlawful gaming in the Kanydan region had low-country names.

In 1841, when the vagrancy ordinance was passed, the state had few resources with which to suppress gambling. The judicial system relied to a great extent on private individuals; neither the police nor headmen prosecuted many criminal cases.[54] Nevertheless, prosecutions for gambling were dependent on official action because there were no victims to institute prosecutions and because the organized deployment of several men was usually necessary to gain convictions. Since the police force was small and ineffective in the mid nineteenth century, the law against gaming was little enforced, especially outside the main towns.

The police became more active during the tenure of G. W. R. Campbell, who was inspector-general from 1866 to 1890. The force remained predominantly urban, but it became larger and more effective.[55] Campbell, like most other British officials, believed that gambling led to more serious crimes, and under his direction the police carried out raids regularly and charged gamblers in court.[56] The authorities received their information from a variety of sources: general knowledge, police investigations, petitions, complaints from individuals outraged by gambling, and tip-offs from persons with a grudge against the gamblers. When possible, the police collected evidence before the raid by observing the gaming place for some days and sending informers there to gamble. When convictions were obtained rewards were paid, although it is probable that many of those who co-operated with the police did so for other than financial reasons.

Campbell's policy was followed by his successors, but there are no comprehensive statistics concerning the number of police raids, prosecutions, or convictions. The number of prosecutions is available only from 1893 to 1906. The data for these years, which do not include village tribunal cases, indicate that a substantial proportion of prosecutions, often as many as one-third, were in Colombo, and that in many smaller localities the number of cases varied sharply, presumably according to the enthusiasm of the local police. An average of 316 cases and 1,689 persons were prosecuted each year during this period. Statistics from the 1920s indicate that the level of prosecutions changed little in Colombo, but that there was an increase in rural areas.

Gamblers employed a number of different strategies to avoid punishment. Some were confrontational, but most were not. Perhaps the most common technique was to gamble in places that did not intrude on the consciousness of persons who were likely to object. Many gaming places were out of sight, behind closed doors or in a shed some distance from the nearest road. They attracted members of the underclass from the surrounding area, but the local representatives of the state were either unaware of them or they pretended that this was the case. It was widely believed that gaming-house managers made regular payments to individual policemen and headmen, who in return tried to prevent action against gaming and gave warning in the event of a police raid.[57] Policemen were also paid to give contradictory evidence in court, or to release gamblers before charges were filed against them. In 1876 four policemen, including an inspector, were dismissed from the force after it was revealed that they had freed eight gamblers, each of whom had paid a bribe of ten rupees.[58] Sometimes bribes were unnecessary; village headmen often did not share the elite abhorrence of gambling, particularly in areas where cock-fighting was an established custom.

When the police did arrive at a gaming place, escape was very common. Gamblers often fled out of a back exit maintained specifically for this purpose, and they employed watchers to ensure that sufficient notice was given. Escape was sometimes made easier by limited violence, which was employed mainly to delay the entry of the authorities.

There was a steady trickle of incidents where gamblers offered serious violence in response to police raids. In February 1868, for instance, a party of eighteen policemen left Colombo in closed carts at 10 p.m., hoping to surprise gamblers at the village of Sedavatta, which had an established reputation for lawlessness. But word of the arrival of the police leaked out, and some three hundred villagers attacked the police party and forced it to retreat. This incident eventually led to the establishment of a police station in the village.[59] Another clash occurred in 1873, when the police raiding a gambling site at Yagodamulla, near Minuvangoda in the Western Province, were overpowered by the gamblers.[60] They were stripped of their uniforms, given sarongs (standard Sinhalese dress), and turned over to a headman as burglars. But this resistance proved to be too direct for the gamblers' own good; convictions for unlawful gaming and keeping a gaming house soon followed, and, as at Sedavatta, a police station was established nearby.

In Colombo, where the police presence was heavy, there were no open battles between large numbers of police and gamblers, but there were many cases of individual violence. In 1876, for instance, the body of a police detective was found floating in a well near a 'notorious' gaming place; the police assumed that he had been murdered by gamblers.[61] Twenty years later another policeman, who was trying to observe a well-known gaming place, was attacked, and suffered a broken leg.[62] In neither of these cases was there enough evidence to institute prosecutions.

Violence between gamblers and the police increased in the early twentieth century, mainly because raids were carried out in rural areas where the state had taken little notice of gambling in the nineteenth century. After the reforms of 1906 police stations were gradually established in the countryside, where policing had previously been the responsibility of headmen.[63] In 1907 a man helping the police raid a rural gaming place was struck with an agricultural implement and killed.[64] Two years later, another informant was stabbed to death during a police raid in the countryside, and in 1910 police raiding a gambling spot were attacked with brickbats and had to take refuge in a house, which the gamblers then set on fire.[65] These were not isolated incidents. In 1927 Dowbiggin wrote that 'raiding a large illegal gaming place is perhaps one of the most exciting, and at the same time one of the most dangerous duties which the police have to perform. It is seldom, in such raids, that a Police Officer escapes with no injury at all, especially when the raid is made during the night time.'[66]

Better training and more competent leadership aided the police in the twentieth century. For instance, in 1920 three policemen swam a river and five others approached through the jungle in order to raid a gaming place at the Maha Saman temple festival.[67] Five years later, sixteen policemen travelled by car from Galle to carry out a raid on a riverbank near Gintota, and in 1928 the railway authorities stopped a train to allow a police party to disembark and raid a gaming place on the seashore near Panadura.[68]

Despite the increased effectiveness of the police's efforts to suppress gambling, a number of long-standing and generally-known gaming places were able to operate in the late nineteenth and early twentieth centuries. The most famous establishment was that run by Naino Marikar in Messenger Street, Colombo, from the 1880s to around 1910. Naino served at least one jail term and his house was often under police surveillance, but he stayed in business through a combination of bribes, limited violence, and legal struggles.[69] Other organizers, such as Simeon Singho, who was convicted in 1917, periodically shifted the location of their operations.[70] As late as 1936 the police raided a gaming place in the Central Province that was said to be twenty years old.[71]

RESISTANCE WITHIN THE LAW

The previous section describes the efforts of gamblers to avoid, undermine, or confront the representatives of the state who were supposed to bring them to justice. These tactics had a good deal of success, but the police did carry out raids and arrest gamblers. The struggle to avoid punishment did not stop at this point. On the contrary, the colonial judicial system was an important forum for further battle. Not only did accused persons successfully deny guilt, but they often did so on legal grounds that forced the state to place restrictions on the use of its own power.

The judicial system, which was influenced by the softer side of utilitarianism, was less authoritarian and more autonomous from the executive branch of government than in most other parts of colonial South Asia.[72] The courts, both civil and criminal, were used heavily. Officials and elites did not however attribute the high level of litigation to faith in British justice. Instead, they believed that there was an inordinate number of false accusations. Many officials blamed this 'litigiousness' on the failure of a backward people to appreciate modern institutions, but the specific manner in which the colonial judicial system was introduced, including its use of the English language, provided ordinary people with little opportunity or reason to act according to the principles upon which it was based.[73] Faced with the necessity of dealing with an alien but effective form of power, Sri Lankans treated the colonial courts as morally neutral and manipulated them to their own advantage. They regarded testimony not as true or false, but as effective or ineffective.

In these circumstances it is not surprising that people used the legal process for all sorts of purposes: to further land disputes, intimidate enemies, punish thieves, and gain revenge for wrongs, both real and imagined. They also used it to dispute state attempts to control popular recreations such as drinking and gambling.[74] While relatively wealthy and sophisticated persons were usually better able to make use of the courts than their adversaries, even the underclass had access to informal legal advice, and judicial rulings were unpredictable.

Most gambling cases were tried in police courts, the lowest tier of the formal court system.[75] Many magistrates believed that the testimony of Sri Lankans who brought criminal cases, including the police and headmen, was not reliable. Gamblers took advantage of this suspicion whenever possible. In 1870, for instance, a magistrate dismissed a prosecution after stating that he did not believe a word of the police evidence.[76] At times gamblers used the courts to harass prosecutors. In 1880 a sergeant and three constables arrested six gamblers outside a tavern, and charged them under the clause that forbade gaming in taverns. The magistrate found the men guilty, but the supreme court overturned the convictions because the law made it illegal to game in taverns, but said nothing about tavern premises. Meanwhile, the counter-case filed against the policemen, accusing them of wrongful arrest, was successful. Prison terms were imposed, and, in Campbell's indignant words, 'the Sergeant and Constables were marched off in uniform to the jail amidst a torrent of jeers from the disreputable hangers-on of courts and from the prisoners inside the jail after their arrival there.'[77] The policemen were released two days later, but their humiliation could not be erased.

Appeals to the supreme court played a central role in the judicial struggles over gambling. The procedure was fairly simple: the convicted man drew up a brief statement indicating the grounds of his appeal, and this was sent to the supreme court along with the transcript of the trial and the magistrate's judgment. The appellant normally needed to pay for legal advice to draw up the appeal, and it was advantageous to have legal representation at Colombo when the supreme court heard the case, but appeals were sometimes sustained when the appellant was not represented. Even when the court rejected the legal argument made by the appellant, it could still free him for other reasons. Most supreme court judges were British lawyers without long experience in the colony, and they tended to interpret the law with less concern for the general interests of the colonial government than most officials would have liked. In the late nineteenth and twentieth centuries Sri Lankan lawyers also sat on the supreme court; these men had made their careers within the local legal tradition, which also valued judicial interpretations that followed the letter of the law.

The many victories won on appeal had significance beyond the immediate cases decided because magistrates were unwilling to convict in similar cases for fear that their rulings would be reversed.[78] Supreme court judgments also forced the police to be cautious in their attempts to prosecute gamblers. The prosecution was forced to prove the charge fully, often a difficult task because the law was designed to cover only gaming carried out in specific circumstances. Many gamblers pursued ingenious defences, and gaming-place managers sometimes hired nationally-prominent lawyers. In contrast, in the nineteenth century most prosecutors, whether policemen, headmen, or private individuals, did not have formal legal representation, and were prone to make errors when presenting their case.

Many legal objections to convictions were not specific to gambling, but common to all police court cases. One of the most important was defects in the plaint which formed the basis of the charge. In the nineteenth century the supreme court was usually willing to overturn convictions in cases with vague or incorrect plaints, even when the evidence indicated that the accused was guilty of a crime. The judicial system was based on the defendant's right to provide evidence in his defence, and he was thought unable to do so without a specific charge to be answered.

A case decided in 1883 illustrates how faulty plaints led to acquittals and successful appeals.[79] The plaint charged that the defendants were 'engaged at a game of chance' with a coin in the land called Hathbodia, at Puwakdandawa, kept or used for the purpose of promiscuous gaming. The supreme court noted that 'the ordinance makes it an offence to "game, play or bet" in particular places, and nowhere is it made an offence to be "engaged at a game of chance" '. It also ruled that the description of the place where the prosecution proposed to prove the occurrence of gaming was too vague. Furthermore, the court objected to the allegation that the place in question was 'kept or used for gaming', because

> keeping and using are very different things, and evidence which would support the one might be wholly insufficient to support the other, and an accused party has a right to know definitely what particular description of the place it is that the prosecutor relies on, to bring him within the penal provisions of a law which he is alleged to have violated.

The court concluded that 'upon these several grounds the plaint is conspicuously defective, and cannot support a conviction'.

Prosecutions also failed for a variety of other procedural reasons. Sometimes the magistrate convicted on a charge different from that in the plaint: for instance, when the plaint charged the accused with unlawful gaming, but the evidence showed that he had kept a gaming house.[80] Other errors corrected by the supreme court included sentencing as second offenders when there was only hearsay evidence of an earlier conviction, the filing of the plaint more than one month after the alleged offence, and the use of evidence taken at one trial to convict defendants at another trial.[81] The failure to obtain the necessary certificate from the queen's advocate, which between 1868 and 1885 enabled police courts to try persons accused of keeping a gaming house, also led to acquittals.[82] These appeals had repercussions beyond the individual cases at stake; they ensured that legal forms which favoured defendants were observed in practice.

Before 1889 the prosecution needed to show that the game

was one of chance. Most successful appeals on this ground argued that there was no evidence of the type of gaming that had taken place.[83] Games that required a degree of skill, such as one that was played with marbles, were ruled legal.[84] After 1889, when the law was changed so that the laying of a stake was the crucial element, convictions were upheld in cases where there was betting on games of skill.[85]

The more usual challenge was over the place where the gambling took place. Under the 1841 ordinance it was very difficult to gain a conviction for gaming in an 'open or public place' other than a street or road. The courts consistently overturned attempts to extend the definition to other places. The verandah of a house, an 'open lane', a privately-owned garden, a ditch on the sea beach, and a garden near the road to a plantation were all declared not to be covered by the ordinance.[86] As a result, the framers of the 1889 legislation expanded the definition of places where gaming was illegal to include 'a place to which the public have access, whether as of right or not'. An 1890 supreme court decision held that the new wording covered a much broader range of places, virtually anywhere that the public could physically go, but this ruling was overturned a year later, when it was held that an unenclosed garden that abutted a road was not a public place.[87] In 1903 the supreme court reversed this decision and found that the public did have access to a garden surrounded by roads and houses.[88] This change was confirmed the following year, when an appeal by peasants found gaming on a threshing floor visible from a road was dismissed.[89] This was as far as the court was willing to expand the definition of a public place. It was ruled in a series of later decisions that government property, shops, verandahs of shops or houses, and open spaces on plantations did not fall under the ordinance.[90]

The largest number of legal battles was over the definition of a common gaming place. This was because most gaming was not covered by the other sections of the law, and because the sections on common gaming places were the most ambiguous parts of the 1841 and 1889 legislations.

The courts generally required clear evidence before determining under the vagrancy ordinance that a place was kept for common and promiscuous gaming. Hearsay evidence was not sufficient. In 1847, for instance, the evidence of a witness who stated that he had 'before been informed about four times lately that the first accused was gambling' was held inadmissible.[91] Nor was the fact that there had been an earlier conviction for keeping the place in question as a gaming house sufficient; new evidence had to be obtained showing that it had continued to be so kept.[92] Generally, some evidence of gaming on previous occasions was required; it was insufficient to show that the men gathered were not friends or relatives.[93] The courts did rule, however, that a wide variety of places could serve the purpose of gaming dens: private residences, sheds, and clearings in the forest were all eligible, so long as it could be proved that the place in question was open to the public and had been used for gaming on a previous occasion.[94]

Although the courts usually required fairly strict proof, some borderline cases were won by the prosecution. In 1870 the supreme court stated that an attempt to escape upon the arrival of the police could be used as evidence, as could the fact that the prisoner had in court 'asked questions of the witnesses as to the character which his house bears in the village, to which the answers were that it is reported to be a gambling house'.[95] Two years later the testimony that 'I knew that shed was used for gambling and I have previously complained about it to the police' was accepted as evidence because there had been no cross-examination to show that the witness was speaking from hearsay.[96]

The gaming ordinance of 1889 slightly broadened the working definition of a common gaming place. The main change was that proof of gaming on earlier occasions was not necessary. In 1895 the supreme court reiterated that there had to be clear evidence of public access: 'The real essence of the offence is publicity which attracts idlers of all sorts to various forms of public nuisance.'[97] Friends or acquaintances, the court continued, could play all they liked in a private dwelling.[98] Direct evidence showing gamblers coming and going over a period of time was desirable to establish that there was public access, but indirect evidence such as attempts to escape upon the arrival of the police was also taken into consideration.[99]

Assumptions about Sri Lankan social relations influenced judicial rulings concerning common gaming places in the twentieth century. Some magistrates interpreted the mixed occupational, caste, or ethnic composition of a group of gamblers as evidence that the spot where the gaming took place was open to the public. The supreme court did not entirely reject such reasoning, but was unwilling to give it much weight. In 1920, for instance, the court agreed with a magistrate that the presence of a 'Sanitary Board cooly' in a group made up largely of persons 'of the status of proctors' clerks' was 'peculiar', but it quashed the conviction because there was no other evidence of public access.[100] Similarly, in 1937 the supreme court rejected a magistrate's ruling that the presence of people from different castes and walks of life 'establishes beyond any doubt . . . that anyone could have repaired to this spot and indulged in unlawful gaming'. The higher court cautioned that 'it is dangerous to draw inferences from the fact of different castes or even communities [gambling together]. Friends cut across these lines.'[101]

The presumptive proof clause of the 1889 ordinance, which put the burden of proof on the defence when the police entered with a search warrant, was ineffective during the first ten to fifteen years after its passage because judicial challenges forced the police to follow its complex requirements to the letter. The supreme court felt the clause's provisions had to be adhered to strictly because the legislation was so draconian.[102] It overturned convictions in cases where the warrant had been obtained on vague or second-hand evidence; it was not enough for the police or a private individual simply to testify that gambling was going on in the place concerned.[103] The information provided to obtain the warrant had to be accurate: in 1901 men found gaming in a garden outside a house were acquitted because the warrant had specified that the house itself was being kept as a gaming place.[104] Finally, the failure of the magistrate to read back oral evidence to the deponent before obtaining his signature invalidated the warrant.[105]

Once the police finally mastered the details of the presumptive proof clause, many of the legal defences employed in the nineteenth century were rendered useless. The prosecution no longer had to provide detailed evidence proving the existence of a common gaming place. Instead, the defence had to prove that the gathering had been within the meaning of the law.

Moreover, the prosecution did not need to demonstrate that each defendant had laid a stake. In 1879, in a major victory for gamblers, the supreme court had ruled that being present at a common gaming place was not sufficient for a conviction, and that the general statement of a witness that he saw so-and-so engaged in gaming was not valid evidence.[106] Instead, the witness had to describe the facts that he had observed, and leave it to the court to decide whether or not an offence had been committed. The presumptive proof clause circumvented the need for this detailed evidence, which remained necessary when the police entered the premises without a warrant.[107]

Contrary to the general trend, convictions of managers of gaming places became, in some respects, more difficult in the twentieth century. In 1895, in a decision that stood until the end of the colonial period, the supreme court ruled that the 1889 law was worded so that there had to be evidence of managing the place, not only the gaming.[108] The defendant had taken commissions from a group of men gambling under a mango tree, but there was no evidence that he had any right to the land, or exercised any control over it, and his conviction was overturned.

In the 1890s somewhat less than half the persons charged with unlawful gaming were convicted, and it is probable that the proportion was even smaller during many periods earlier in the century. By 1910 around 90 per cent of prosecutions for gambling succeeded. The higher conviction rate may have been partly brought about by more selectivity about which cases to prosecute, but it nonetheless represents a significant advance in the state's capability, or willingness, to punish unlawful gaming. The broader wording of the 1889 ordinance and increased police efficiency were important changes that contributed to this trend. The penal code and code of criminal procedure, which were implemented in 1885, also made gambling convictions easier because they eliminated many technical grounds for appeal that applied to all criminal cases.[109]

Many gamblers avoided punishment by exploiting a contradiction between two goals of the state: the establishment of the rule of law, and the creation of a disciplined and settled social order. The British believed that law was most just and effective when individual judgments were taken according to legal codes and precedents, without reference to the broader goals of government policy. This ideal view of the colonial legal system, which was contrasted with the capriciousness of judicial rulings under earlier governments, served as an important justification for British rule.[110] In the early nineteenth century the British believed that the rule of law would promote social progress by demonstrating the advantages of predictability and fair play. This hope faded in later decades, when it became clear that Sri Lankans were using the courts to pursue ends that were contrary to official aims. The British saw the legal struggles of gamblers, which made possible the continuation of practices that most officials believed caused crime and poverty, as an indication that an 'advanced' judicial system was inappropriate for Sri Lanka.

The legal reforms of the late nineteenth century, including the codes of 1885 and the gaming ordinance of 1889, reflected this loss of faith. Judicial policy sought to eliminate 'technicalities' and make the courts a more effective instrument of social control. The reform and expansion of the police force, which was undertaken after 1906, further reinforced the authoritarian trend in the administration of law and order. In the long run, the actions of gamblers and other Sri Lankans who manipulated the courts provoked the government to adopt more coercive administrative measures. These changes, however, did not make it impossible for Sri Lankans to use legal means to frustrate state objectives; they only made it more difficult. When officials believed that their authority was under direct threat, as during the anti-Muslim riots of 1915, the rule of law was jettisoned; but under normal circumstances the British were unwilling to abandon it. Gamblers continued to use the courts, a state instrument of control, to defend an aspect of their culture that officials and elites sought to suppress.

CONCLUSIONS

The resistance by gamblers to the attempts by Sinhalese elites and the state to reshape popular culture and create a stable, ordered, and thrifty society was remarkably effective. Public gambling was first made criminal in 1841, and many elites ex-

pressed their strong distaste after around 1860, but at the end
of the colonial period the practice was at least as prevalent as
it had been in the early nineteenth century. Lower-class men
used a variety of ongoing techniques to resist attempts by ruling
groups to suppress gambling. They played in isolated sheds in
the middle of the night, they bribed the police and headmen,
and they often met police raids with violence. Finally, gamblers
employed the rules and language of the judicial system in ways
that turned the criminal courts themselves into sites of resistance.

These events demonstrate that everyday resistance extends
not only to the control of material resources, as demonstrated by
James Scott in *Weapons of the Weak*, but to the definition of
values, ideology, and culture.[111] Neither the government nor
elites sought to extract a greater surplus from the underclass
by suppressing gambling. In fact, they believed that gambling
caused poverty, and that poor people would be better-off for
abandoning it. The struggle over gambling was a conflict over
values. Many men found satisfaction, companionship, and
leisure in gambling, and they believed that this aspect of their
culture was worth preserving. Those who sought to suppress
gambling believed that it was incompatible with the disciplined,
productive, and moral social order that they envisioned for
Sri Lanka.

In the mid nineteenth century most Sri Lankans probably
viewed the law against gambling as one of a number of seemingly pointless regulations, such as restrictions on slash-and-
burn cultivation or safety requirements imposed on carters,
that were designed primarily to enable the police and headmen
to extract bribes. In the late nineteenth and early twentieth
centuries, when elites communicated to ordinary people their
moral and religious objections to gambling, the law may have
gained a vague moral authority that it lacked earlier. The extensive, if brief, success of the temperance movement of 1904
indicates that many men, even in the underclass, acknowledged the cultural superiority of restraint and self-discipline,
at least when it was expressed in Buddhist terms.[112] In the
long run the practical effect of this change was limited to
upwardly-mobile individuals who aspired to respectability.
The underclass was selective in its adoption of the new Buddhist

values. Labourers and peasants sometimes responded to appeals based on cultural pride, but they did not identify closely with the values of thrift and work, which were central to the elite worldview that condemned gambling. Moreover, any moral authority the law may have gained from revivalist propaganda was undermined by the legal distinction between 'public' and 'private' gambling, which had only an instrumental meaning for the underclass. The hostility that met police raids in the early twentieth century indicates that many men continued to subscribe to a collective ethic that sanctioned gambling.

The battles over gambling demonstrate that neither resistance nor domination is autonomous, and that relations of power are complex even when they are not contested openly. Gamblers penetrated and made use of institutions that also served as instruments of domination. The police, for instance, were paid by the government to suppress public gaming, but they were also paid by gamblers to ignore it. The courts were used not only to punish gambling, but to constrain the actions of those who sought to suppress it. The legal profession was also available to both sides. Although gamblers sometimes confronted authority directly, most of the time they tried to evade or deflect it. The most effective way to accomplish this was to work within institutions that were subject to the formal control of dominant groups. Although resistance carried out in this manner was often successful, dominant groups had the option of changing the rules. The techniques used by gamblers for most of the nineteenth century became less effective at the beginning of the twentieth century, when the state improved the efficiency of the police force and passed legislation to make convictions easier to obtain.

There was another sense in which gamblers could not escape domination. In the eyes of the British, successful resistance by gamblers illustrated the benign nature of colonial rule and confirmed the moral superiority of the foreign rulers. It enabled them to portray Sri Lankans as sophisticated enough to take advantage of the judicial system, but not advanced enough to appreciate the principles behind it. A nation at this stage of development was obviously not ready for self-rule.

The existence of gambling served a similar but distinct function for Sinhalese elites. In the late nineteenth and early twentieth centuries they portrayed ordinary people as backward, uneducated, and divorced from their own glorious pre-colonial historical tradition. Resistance by gamblers reinforced this stereotype, which enabled elites to bolster their own position as the only social group capable of using modern methods to restore Sinhalese greatness. Moreover, since elites blamed gambling, drinking, and crime on the disruptive effects of British rule, the condemnation of gambling sometimes took on a nationalist connotation. Opposition to gambling was in this sense part of an ideological worldview associated with resistance to foreign rule.

The differences between the contexts in which elites and the state placed their opposition to gambling had no practical significance; it did not lead to differences over policy. The study of gambling provides a straightforward case of power-holders seeking to impose their own social vision on a reluctant underclass. The state and elites were united in their determination to suppress public gaming, but resistance by gamblers was ongoing, complicated, and effective. Most of it was carried out within structures under the formal control of the ruling classes. Resistance under these conditions did not challenge authority directly, but it did contend the manner in which power was employed.

APPENDIX
Colonial Law Report References

Sri Lankan legal citations follow the English practice, which places the volume number before and the page number after the report's abbreviation. For example, *Serahamay* v. *Rankira* (1904), 8 NLR 40 refers to the case brought by Serahamy against Rankira that was decided by the supreme court in 1904 and published in the eighth volume of the *New Law Reports*, p. 40. Many early reports do not include the names of the parties. In these instances citations use the case number. For example, P. C. Matara no. 8427 (1852), 1 Beling 57 refers to case number 8427 filed in Matara Police Court, which was decided by the supreme court in 1852 and published in the first volume of William Beling's *Handy Book*, p. 57. Unless otherwise noted, all reports were published in Colombo. Full bibliographical details are found in my article 'Sri Lankan Law Reports as an Historical Source', which is to be published in *Sri Lanka Archives*.

ABBREVIATIONS

Beling	*Handy Book of Police Courts, being a digest of the orders of the Supreme Court in Police Court Cases,* 2 vols (1863–9).
Browne	*Browne's Reports of cases decided in the Supreme and Other Courts of Ceylon,* 3 vols (1900–2).
CLJ	*Ceylon Law Journal: embodying reports and notes of cases,* 9 vols (1936–47).
CLR	*The Ceylon Law Reports, being reports of cases decided by the Supreme Court of Ceylon,* 3 vols (1892–7).
CLW	*Ceylon Law Weekly,* 38 vols (1931–48).
CWR	*Ceylon Weekly Reporter,* 8 vols (1915–20).
Fernando	*Decisions of the Supreme Court on appeals from Police Courts and Courts of Request* (Kandy, 1878).
Grenier	*The Appeal Reports from 1872 (1873, 1874), being reports of cases argued and determined in the Supreme Court of Ceylon sitting in appeal,* 3 vols (1872–4).
Leader	*The 'Leader' Law Reports, being reports of current decisions of the Supreme Court of Ceylon,* 6 vols (1907–12).
Lorenz	*The Appeal Reports: being reports of cases argued and determined in the Supreme Court of Ceylon sitting in appeal,* 3 vols (1860–71).
Morgan	*A Digest of the Decisions of the Supreme Court sitting at Colombo, since the promulgation of the charter of 1833,* 2 vols (1857–62).
NLR	*The New Law Reports,* 49 vols (1896–1948).
Notes	*Notes of Cases decided by the Supreme Court of Ceylon,* 6 vols (1914–18).
Ramanathan	*Reports of Important Cases heard and determined by the Supreme Court of Ceylon,* 5 vols (1878–90).
Recorder	*The Ceylon Law Recorder,* 22 vols (1919–48).
SCC	*Supreme Court Circular,* 9 vols (1879–92).
SCR	*Supreme Court Reports,* 3 vols (1892–6).
Vanderstraaten	*The Decisions of the Supreme Court sitting in Appeal, from 1869 to 1871* (1874).
Weerekoon	*The Supreme Court Decisions in Appeal,* 7 vols (1908–12).

NOTES

I would like to thank John Paul, Gyan Prakash, Jonathan Spencer, and especially Doug Haynes for their useful comments on earlier drafts of this essay. Other versions were presented at the Annual Conference on South Asia at Madison, Wisconsin, in November 1988; and at the Recent Research on Sri Lanka conference at Paris in May 1989; I benefited from the discussions on these occasions.

1. For examples, see Lucy Carroll, 'The Temperance Movement in India: Politics and Social Reform', *Modern Asian Studies*, vol. 10 (1976), pp. 417–47; Anand A. Yang, 'Dangerous Castes and Tribes: The Criminal Tribes Act and the Magahiya Doms of Northeast India', in Anand A. Yang (ed.), *Crime and Criminality in British India* (Tucson: 1985), pp. 108–27; Veena Talwar Oldenburg, *The Making of Colonial Lucknow, 1856–77* (Princeton: 1984), pp. 71–2, 96–144; Kenneth Jones, *Arya Dharm: Hindu Consciousness in 19th-Century Punjab* (Berkeley and Los Angeles: 1976), pp. 94–108; David Kopf, *The Brahmo Samaj and the Shaping of the Modern Indian Mind* (Princeton: 1979), pp. 118–28; Charles H. Heimsath, 'The Origin and Enactment of the Indian Age of Consent Bill, 1891', *Journal of Asian Studies*, vol. 21 (1962), pp. 491–504; John D. Rogers, 'Cultural Nationalism and Social Reform: The 1904 Temperance Movement in Sri Lanka', *Indian Economic and Social History Review*, vol. 26 (1989), pp. 319–41.
2. John G. Butcher, 'The Demise of the Revenue Farm System in the Federated Malay States', *Modern Asian Studies*, vol. 17 (1983), pp. 387–412; John G. Butcher, 'An Historical Enigma: A Note on the Anti-Gambling Petition of 1905', *Journal of the Malaysian Branch of the Royal Asiatic Society*, vol. 56 (1983), pp. 1–9.
3. Lotteries were outlawed because they were thought to have 'ruinous effects' on poor persons. Colin Campbell to Lord Stanley, 8 August 1844, Colonial Office Records, Kew, London (hereafter cited as CO) 54/212 (130). For information on lotteries, see *B. R. Adolphus* v. *Sangerelingam Kannen* (1862), 2 Morgan i; *Wijeyenaike Appuhamy* v. *Liesching* (1865), 3 Ramanathan 176; George M. Fowler, *Administration Report for the Western Province 1904* (Colombo), A4. Hereafter all Administration Reports will be cited as *AR*. For an explanation of the references to law reports, see the appendix.
4. H. Woosnam Mills, 'Sport', in Arnold Wright (ed.), *Twentieth Century Impressions of Ceylon* (London: 1907), pp. 255–61.
5. H. Parker, *Ancient Ceylon: An Account of the Aborigines and a Part of the Early Civilisation* (London: 1909), pp. 570–642.
6. Some women assisted in the management of gaming places; see P. C. Navalapitiya no. 16168 (1870), Vanderstraaten 55; H. L. Dowbiggin, *AR of the Inspector-General of Police 1927*, B15. For an account claiming that women gambled at a gaming place in Colombo, see *Lakrivikirana* (Colombo), 13 April 1872.

7. For a description of *bebi kapanava* see Parker, *Ancient Ceylon*, pp. 621–2.

8. For a similar argument regarding the appeal of gambling among the British working-classes, see Ross McKibbin, 'Working-class Gambling in Britain, 1880–1939', *Past and Present*, no. 82 (1979), pp. 160–71.

9. For the almost invulnerable position of the organizers of cattle theft, see John D. Rogers, *Crime, Justice, and Society in Colonial Sri Lanka* (London and Riverdale: 1987), pp. 94–8.

10. P. C. Kandy no. 47012 (1860), 1 Beling 142. Also see P. C. Matara no. 78927 (1877), 5 Ramanathan 277; *Halaldeen* v. *Yothan* (1937), 9 CLW 149.

11. Frederic A. Hayley, *A Treatise on the Laws and Customs of the Sinhalese including the portions still surviving under the name Kandyan Law* (Colombo: 1923), p. 121.

12. *Don Harmanis de Silva* v. *Wedi Tantrige Babappu* (1882), 5 SCC 2.

13. Regulation 14 of 1806.

14. Regulation 6 of 1813; Regulation 6 of 1815; Regulation 4 of 1819; Regulation 14 of 1820.

15. G. K. Pippet, *A History of the Ceylon Police, 1795–1870* (Colombo: 1941), vol. 1, pp. 33, 39.

16. G. C. Mendis (ed.), *The Colebrooke–Cameron Papers: Documents on British Colonial Policy in Ceylon, 1796–1833* (Oxford: 1956), vol. 1, p. 78.

17. William Colebrooke to Viscount Goderich, 31 January 1832, *Colebrooke–Cameron Papers*, pp. 105–6, 266–7.

18. Pippet, *History*, p. 68.

19. Anthony Oliphant to J. A. Stewart MacKenzie, 30 August 1840, quoted in Pippet, *History*, p. 68.

20. These three categories were copied from the English vagrancy ordinance of 1824. See David J. V. Jones, *Crime, Protest, Community, and Police in Nineteenth-Century Britain* (London: 1982), p. 198.

21. In 1872 the official currency changed from the British pound to the Ceylon rupee. For legal purposes all references to sterling were converted at the rate of two shillings for every rupee.

22. John Disney, *The Laws of Gaming, Wagers, Horse-Racing and Gaming-Houses* (London: 1806); Richard Hey, *Three Dissertations: On the Pernicious Effects of Gaming, on Duelling, and on Suicide* (Cambridge: 1812).

23. James Walvin, *Leisure and Society, 1830–1950* (London: 1978), pp. 1–68; John Lowerson and John Myerscough, *Time to Spare in Victorian England* (Hassocks: 1977), pp. 1–17; Robert D. Storch, 'The Problem of Working-class Leisure: Some Roots of Middle-class Reform in the Industrial North, 1825–50, in A. P. Donajgrodzki (ed.), *Social Control in Nineteenth Century Britain* (London: 1977), pp. 138–62; Brian Harrison, *Drink and the Victorians: The Temperance Question in England, 1815–72* (London: 1971); Clive Emsley, *Crime and Society in England, 1750–1900* (London: 1987), pp. 48–77; Jones, *Crime, Protest, Community, and Police*; M. J. D. Roberts, 'Public and Private in Early Nineteenth-Century London: The Vagrant Act of 1822 and its Enforcement', *Social History*, vol. 13 (1988), pp. 273–94.

24. Sir Charles Marshall, *Judgments and other decisions and directions of the*

Supreme Court of the Island of Ceylon, from the promulgation of the New Charter, 1st Oct. 1833 to March 1836 (Colombo: 1839), pp. 208–10; Bertram Bastiampillai, 'Social Administration in North Sri Lanka (Ceylon) in the Mid Nineteenth Century: A Review of the Diverse Duties of a Colonial Provincial Administrator', *Vidyodaya*, vol. 14 (1986), pp. 29–30.

25. For a discussion of Sri Lankan elites, see Michael Roberts, 'Elite Formations and Elites, 1832–1931', in Michael Roberts (ed.), *Collective Identities, Nationalisms, and Protest in Modern Sri Lanka* (Colombo: 1979), pp. 153–213.

26. Kitsiri Malalgoda, *Buddhism in Sinhalese Society, 1750–1900: A Study of Religious Revival and Change* (Berkeley and Los Angeles: 1976); L. A. Wickremeratne, 'Religion, Nationalism, and Social Change in Ceylon, 1865–85', *Journal of the Royal Asiatic Society*, no. 2 (1969), pp. 123–50; Gananath Obeyesekere, 'Personal Identity and Cultural Crisis: The Case of Anagarika Dharmapala of Sri Lanka', in Frank E. Reynolds and Donald Capps (eds), *The Biographical Process: Studies in the History and Psychology of Religion* (The Hague: 1976), pp. 221–52.

27. *Standard* (Colombo), 12 July 1904; *Sarasavi Sandarasa* (Colombo), 24 June 1904.

28. *Independent* (Colombo), 26 January 1905.

29. Marshall, *Judgments*, p. 209; A. C. Dep, *A History of the Ceylon Police, 1866–1913* (Colombo: 1969), vol. 2, p. 45; Petition from Ragama Pattu, 28 February 1890, Department of National Archives, Colombo (hereafter cited as SLNA) 33/2758.

30. This statement is based on a survey of the *Lakrivikirana* between 1865 and 1873. For examples from the English-language press, see *Observer*, 3 August 1854; *Bi-Monthly Examiner* (Colombo), 21 April 1869; *Times of Ceylon* (Colombo), 6 June 1904; *Independent*, 10 August 1904, 19 August 1904, 28 September 1904; *Catholic Messenger* (Colombo), 26 January 1875, 17 August 1875.

31. *Lakrivikirana*, 20 April 1872.

32. Ibid., 5 April 1873.

33. Michael Roberts, 'The Political Antecedents of the Revivalist Elite in the MEP Coalition of 1956', *Ceylon Studies Seminar*, no. 11 (1969–70), pp. 14–26.

34. Ibid., p. 16.

35. Leonard Woolf, *Growing: An Autobiography of the Years 1904–11* (London: 1961), p. 235.

36. Vijaya Samaraweera, 'The "Village Community" and Reform in Colonial Sri Lanka', *Ceylon Journal of Historical and Social Studies*, vol. 8 (1978), pp. 68–75; Rogers, *Crime*, pp. 55–6.

37. Quoted in Vijaya Samaraweera, 'Litigation, Sri Henry Maine's Writings and the Ceylon Village Communities Ordinance of 1871', in L. Prematilleke, K. Indrapala, and J. van Lohuizen-De Leeuw (eds), *Senarat Paranavitana Commemoration Volume* (Leiden: 1978), p. 193.

38. Ordinance 26 of 1871.

39. Rogers, *Crime*, pp. 210–11.

40. Louis Leisching, *AR of the District Judge at Nuvarakalaviya 1870*, p. 247.
41. A. R. Dawson, *AR for Kagalla District 1874*, p. 28.
42. C. M. Lushington, *AR for Negombo District 1890*, B12.
43. Charles Liesching, *AR of the District Judge at Negombo 1874*, p. 51. For other examples of official views, see R. Massie, *AR for Matale District 1872*, p. 62; C. E. D. Pennycuick, *AR of the District Judge at Badulla 1871*, p. 325; D. E. de Saram, *AR of the District Judge at Kurunagala 1871*, p. 319; P. C. Colombo no. 5400 (1873), 2 Grenier 23; P. W. Conolly, *AR of the District Judge at Negombo 1875*, p. 25; Herbert Wace, *AR for Kalutara District 1881*, 19A; F. R. Ellis, *AR for Kalutara District 1883*, 87A; Samuel Haughton, *AR for Negombo District 1886*, 142A.
44. W. W. Fisher, *AR of the Crown Counsel for the North-Western Province 1890*, A9. Also see Edward Elliott, *AR for the Southern Province 1892*, E7.
45. For a similar argument, regarding middle-class analyses of crime in Victorian England, see Emsley, *Crime*, pp. 55–6.
46. J. West Ridgeway, *Administration of the Affairs of Ceylon, 1896 to 1903* (Colombo: 1903), p. 83.
47. Arthur Gordon to Lord Knutsford, 10 January 1890, CO 54/586 (11).
48. Rogers, *Crime*, pp. 56–60.
49. George Cookson, *AR for Matara District 1905*, D44.
50. L. F. Knollys, *AR of the Inspector-General of Police 1892*, B5.
51. Dowbiggin, *AR of the Inspector-General of Police 1920*, B17. For other examples of official views, see P. A. Templer, *AR for the Central Province 1892*, C5; R. W. Ievers, *AR for the Southern Province 1893*, E6; H. L. Crawford, *AR for the North-Western Province 1901*, G9.
52. Dowbiggin, *AR of the Inspector-General of Police 1933*, A20.
53. *Maha Bodhi and the United Buddhist World* (Colombo), January 1914.
54. Rogers, *Crime*, pp. 44–7.
55. Ibid., pp. 48–55.
56. G. W. R. Campbell, *AR of the Inspector-General of Police 1880*, 31B; G. W. R. Campbell, *AR of the Inspector-General of Police 1884*, 53C.
57. Dep, *History*, pp. 316–17; G. Lawson to Hercules Robinson, 25 July 1870, SLNA 6/3442; G. W. R. Campbell to Colonial Secretary, 19 September 1870, SLNA 6/3401; F. H. Campbell, *AR of the District Judge at Tangalla 1874*, 57; E. M. Byrde, *AR for Negombo District 1887*, 59A; Knollys, *AR of the Inspector-General of Police 1892*, B6; *Lakrivikirana*, 5 February 1870, 13 April 1872, 20 April 1872, 22 February 1873, 5 April 1873, 10 May 1873; *Sarasavi Sandarasa*, 28 February 1888.
58. Dep, *History*, pp. 107–8.
59. Ibid., p. 45.
60. *Catholic Messenger*, 17 November 1873, 24 December 1873.
61. Dep, *History*, p. 103.
62. Ibid., p. 358.
63. Rogers, *Crime*, pp. 54–5.
64. Dep, *History*, p. 451.
65. Ibid., pp. 452, 453. For other examples of violence between the police and gamblers during this period, see ibid., pp. 393, 451.

66. Dowbiggin, *AR of the Inspector-General of Police 1927*, B15.

67. Dowbiggin, *AR of the Inspector-General of Police 1920*, B17.

68. Dowbiggin, *AR of the Inspector-General of Police 1925*, B20; Dowbiggin, *AR of the Inspector-General of Police 1928*, B17.

69. K. R. Perera, *suda hatanaya saha kotalavala inspaktartuma gana vannavak* [Gambling and a Eulogy about Inspector Kotalavala] (Colombo: 1893), p. 4; Dep, *History*, pp. 317, 358, 361, 452; *Ludovici v. Nicholas Appu* (1900), 4 NLR 12. The story of Naino's arrest by Inspector Kotalawala entered Sinhalese folklore. In the mid 1980s the incident was acted out at a Colombo theatre, and Sri Lankan television produced a brief account of it. I am indebted to Gamani Gunawardane and Kumari Jayawardena for this information.

70. Dowbiggin, *AR of the Inspector-General of Police 1917*, B8.

71. P. N. Banks, *AR of the Inspector-General of Police 1936*, A20.

72. Vijaya Samaraweera, 'The Ceylon Charter of Justice of 1833: A Benthamite Blueprint for Judicial Reform', *Journal of Imperial and Commonwealth History*, vol. 2 (1974), pp. 263–77; Rogers, *Crime*, pp. 42–7.

73. This interpretation is based on Rogers, *Crime*, pp. 60–77.

74. For examples of judicial conflicts over drinking, see John D. Rogers, 'Drinking, Gambling, and the State in Sri Lanka, 1796–1912', paper presented to the conference on Policing the Empire, Birkbeck College, May 1988.

75. The 'police courts' had no connection with the police force. Before 1868 trials for keeping a gaming place were prosecuted in the district courts because the police courts were unable to impose the punishment required by law. After 1896 the municipal courts, which had powers and procedures similar to the police courts, tried most gambling cases in Colombo and other municipalities.

76. Dep, *History*, pp. 55–6.

77. Ibid., p. 198; *Hassim Doll v. Pedro Appu* (1880), 3 SCC 25. For other examples of counter-cases, see ibid., pp. 45, 317, 361, 398.

78. Persons convicted by village tribunals had to submit appeals to the government agent instead of the supreme court.

79. *Don Thomis Abedera Gunaratna v. Hettihewage Don Davit* (1883), 5 SCC 206. Earlier cases of this type include P. C. Matara no. 8427 (1852), 1 Beling 57; P. C. Matara no. 4216 (1852), 1 Beling 58; P. C. Galle no. 55732 (1866), 2 Beling 104; P. C. Matara no. 53353 (1868), 2 Beling 133; P. C. Avissavella no. 7568 (1868), 2 Beling 135; *Dingiri Banda v. Muttam* (1878), 1 SCC 21.

80. P. C. Colombo no. 14627 (1849), 1 Beling 26; P. C. Chilaw no. 9467 (1873), 2 Grenier 94.

81. P. C. Colombo no. 14627 (1849), 1 Beling 26; P. C. Kalutara no. 48654 (1873), 2 Grenier 50; P. C. Matara no. 78621 (1877), 5 Ramanathan 238; *N. de S. Gooneratne v. Diappu* (1882), 5 SCC 27; P. C. Colombo no. 5498 (1873), 2 Grenier 63; P. C. Matara no. 78621 (1877), 5 Ramanathan 238.

82. P. C. Matara no. 72597 (1874), 3 Grenier 4; *Dunuwille v. Setua* (1875),

Fernando 8; *Don Cornelis* v. *Hendrik Perera* (1875), 4 Ramanathan 227; P. C. Avissavella no. 6087 (1877), 5 Ramanathan 11; *N. de S. Goone-ratne* v. *Diappu* (1882), 5 SCC 27.

83. P. C. Kurunagala no. 5484 (1865), 2 Beling 101; P. C. Balapitiya no. 38109 (1870), Vanderstraaten 40; P. C. Galle no. 88747 (1874), 3 Grenier 39.

84. P. C. Matale no. 690 (1872), 1 Grenier 15; P. C. Jaffna no. 2838 (1877), 5 Ramanathan 83; P. C. Matara 78394 (1877), 5 Ramanathan 206.

85. *Modder* v. *Silva* (1912), 15 NLR 189; *Inspector of Police, Maradana* v. *Stanton* (1924), 26 NLR 214.

86. *Perera* v. *Leveris* (1859), 3 Lorenz 174; P. C. Negombo no. 20229 (1870), Vanderstraaten 41; P. C. Colombo no. 270, 1 Grenier 4; P. C. Matale no. 987 (1872), 1 Grenier 20; P. C. Panadura no. 20085 (1872), 1 Grenier 34; P. C. Matale no. 8224 (1874), 3 Grenier 75; *Hakim* v. *Carolis* (1879), 2 SCC 137; *G. F. Kirtisingha* v. *Don Suwaris Perera* (1888), 8 SCC 131.

87. *Wijemanne* v. *Sauneris* (1890), 9 SCC 172; *Perera* v. *Perera* (1891), 2 CLR 6.

88. *Elstone* v. *Martelis Appu* (1903), 6 NLR 256.

89. *Serahamy* v. *Rankira* (1904), 8 NLR 40. Also see *Nair* v. *Dodanwela* (1925), 6 Recorder 172.

90. *Banda* v. *Marimuttu* (1915), 3 Notes 51; *Burmester* v. *Muttusamy* (1916), 19 NLR 153; *Perera* v. *Singho* (1921), 23 NLR 154; *Sub-Inspector of Police Dandegamuwa* v. *Gan Aratchy* (1922), 1 Times 106; *Weerakoon* v. *Cumara* (1922), 24 NLR 29; *Nair* v. *Israel* (1923), 25 NLR 96.

91. P. C. Galle no. 3617 (1847), 1 Beling 11. Also see P. C. Balapitiya no. 37430 (1869), Vanderstraaten 7; *H. Siman de Soyza* v. *Dedimany Surebiyal Silva* (1881), 4 SCC 38.

92. P. C. Panadura no. 5747 (1864), 2 Beling 72; *Paulo Bastian* v. *Dias* (1879), 2 SCC 77.

93. P. C. Harrispattoo no. 7041 (1865), 2 Beling 93; P. C. Matale no. 8224 (1874), 3 Grenier 75.

94. P. C. Galle no. 73329 (1871), Vanderstraaten 123; P. C. Matale no. 2668 (1873), 2 Grenier 7; P. C. Kandy no. 100268 (1874), 3 Grenier 78; P. C. Jaffna no. 11743 (1877), 5 Ramanathan 12.

95. P. C. Navalapitiya no. 16168 (1870), Vanderstraaten 55.

96. P. C. Galagedara (1872), 1 Grenier 2.

97. *Jayawardana* v. *Don Thomas* (1895), 1 NLR 216.

98. *Ludovici* v. *Nicholas Appu* (1900), 4 NLR 12.

99. *Police Sergeant of Hatton* v. *Sandanam* (1908), 1 Leader 73; *L. O. Modder* v. *A. M. Mohammado Lebbe* (1909), 3 Leader 1.7; *Attorney-General* v. *Assan Ali* (1912), 1 Notes 33; *Dissanayake* v. *Fernando* (1913), 17 NLR 114; *Police Officer Beliatta* v. *Babunappu* (1921), 23 NLR 165; *Manu-kulasuriya* v. *Merasha* (1922), 24 NLR 33; *Nambiar* v. *Wijeywardene* (1924), 27 NLR 30; *Ibrahiam Saibo* v. *Abaren Appu* (1931), 1 CLW 76; *Edwards* v. *Perera* (1935), 4 CLW 60; *S. B. Thoradenya* v. *S. V. M. Ismail* (1939), 4 CLJ 64.

100. *Police Sergeant Tangalla* v. *Porthenis* (1920), 22 NLR 163.
101. *Wittensleger* v. *Appuhamy* (1937), 39 NLR 93. Also see *Weerakoon* v. *Appuhamy* (1921), 23 NLR 5; and *Fernando* v. *D. K. Liyanage* (1939), 4 CLJ 63.
102. For exceptions, see *Meedin* v. *Gauder* (1913), 1 Notes 60; *Kathir* v. *Mohideen* (1918), 5 CWR 155, summarized in S. Rajaratnam, *Digest of Cases Reported... 1914 to 1936* (Colombo: 1936), p. 910.
103. *Keegel* v. *James Appu* (1897), 3 NLR 76; *Nugawela* v. *Sardina* (1898), 3 NLR 121; *Police Sergeant of Hatton* v. *Sandanam* (1908), 1 Leader 73; *Police Sergeant Tangalla* v. *Porthenis* (1920), 22 NLR 163; *Silva* v. *Silva* (1920), 22 NLR 27; *Doole* v. *Fernando* (1923), 2 Times 19.
104. *C. A. Hole* v. *Carolis Silva* (1901), 2 Browne 317. Also see *Rajapakse* v. *Somapala* (1939), 4 CLJ 118.
105. *Parson* v. *Kandiah* (1927), 29 NLR 94; *Sub-Inspector of Police* v. *Jacolis Peiris* (1929), 30 NLR 509; *Bartholomeusz* v. *Mendis* (1930), 32 NLR 333; *Beddewela* v. *Abraham* (1933), 11 Times 57; *Edwards* v. *Perera* (1935), 4 CLW 60.
106. G. W. R. Campbell, *AR of the Inspector-General of Police 1883*, 31C; F. R. Ellis, *AR for Kalutara District 1883*, 87A; *Sinne Tamby* v. *Sinno Appu* (1879), 2 SCC 75; *Paulo Bastian* v. *Dias* (1879), 2 SCC 77; *H. Siman de Soyza* v. *Dedimany Surebiyal Silva* (1881), 4 SCC 38; *Appuhami Korala* v. *Delindurala* (1883), 5 SCC 178.
107. *Don Simon* v. *Sinno Appu* (1893), 2 CLR 193; *Puhaitamby* v. *Karolis* (1893), 2 SCR 62; *Perera* v. *Sadirappu* (1893), 2 SCR 75; *E. C. Seneviratne* v. *Usubu Lebbe Avulu Marikar* (1909), 2 Leader 122; *Banda Aratchi* v. *Siyatu* (1916), 2 CWR 292, summarized in Rajaratnam, *Digest of Cases*, 907; *Nambiar* v. *Wijeywardene* (1924), 27 NLR 30.
108. *The Queen* v. *Dapanadurage Seya* (1895), 1 Weerekoon 21; *Ratwatte* v. *Kadoris* (1909), 12 NLR 245; *Weerakoon* v. *Gabriel Appuhamy* (1909), 3 Leader 2.14; *Hart* v. *Warnasuriya* (1911), 6 Weerekoon 52.
109. Rogers, *Crime*, pp. 56–8.
110. For an excellent discussion of the cultural impact of colonial law in British India, see Nicholas B. Dirks, 'From Little King to Landlord: Property, Law, and the Gift under the Madras Permanent Settlement', *Comparative Studies in Society and History*, vol. 28 (1986), pp. 307–33.
111. James C. Scott, *Weapons of the Weak: Everyday Forms of Peasant Resistance* (New Haven: 1985).
112. Rogers, 'Cultural Nationalism and Social Reform'.

7

Ritual and Resistance: Subversion as a Social Fact

NICHOLAS B. DIRKS

'There is subversion, no end of subversion, only not for us.'[1]

The social history of modern India has developed side by side with anthropology. Often, social history has simply received its fundamental understandings of what constitutes 'society' in India from an anthropology which itself betrays all too clearly the traces of colonial forms of knowledge about India. While social historians of areas outside of South Asia (or other third world areas in anthropologyland) have worked in greater autonomy from anthropology, they have recently turned to anthropology to enable them to understand many aspects of social life which had not been addressed by political or intellectual history, and yet later proved equally intractable to the quantitative methods of early social history. In both cases, social historians have consumed anthropological theories and rubrics too uncritically, little realizing the possibility that interdisciplinary collaboration should leave neither of the constituent disciplines untouched. In this paper I will use the critical perspective of this volume, focusing on everyday forms of resistance, to criticize both anthropological assumptions about ritual, and historical reifications of these assumptions. In taking 'ritual' as my subject, I will also argue that too often the combination of the key terms 'everyday' and 'resistance' leads us to look for new arenas where resistance takes place rather than realizing that there are many old arenas also brimming with resistance. Finally, I seek to suggest that our old theories of either 'resistance' or 'the political' are not all that are at risk in this enterprise, but also the underlying presupposi-

tions of order that undergird and normalize even such potentially radical undertakings as this volume (or this paper).

Ritual is a term that sanctifies and marks off a space and a time
of special significance. Ritual may be part of everyday life, but
it is fundamentally opposed to 'the everyday'. Anthropologists
have typically identified ritual as a moment and an arena in
which meaning is crystallized, in which social experience is
distilled and displayed. As summarized by Geertz, Durkheim
and Robertson-Smith set the terms of anthropological discourse on ritual by emphasizing the manner in which ritual
'reinforce[s] the traditional social ties between individuals
... the social structure of a group is strengthened and perpetuated through the ritualistic or mythic symbolization of the
underlying social values upon which it rests.'[2] Rituals are thus
seen as embodying the essence of culture, 'as dramatizing the
basic myths and visions of reality, the basic values and moral
truths, upon which ... [the] ... world rests'.[3] This is not to
say that anthropologists have always treated ritual as static. In
her first book Ortner (showing Geertz's influence) clarifies that
while she says that rituals 'dramatize basic assumptions of fact
and value in the culture' she in fact is coding a more complex assertion, namely that 'such "fundamental assumptions"
are actually constructed, or reconstructed, and their funda-
mentality re-established, in the course of the rituals themselves'.[4] Nonetheless, as her more current work indicates,[5] this
earlier clarification reflected a particular moment in anthropology when Durkheimian assumptions about meaning and
ritual were being re-evaluated but left basically unchallenged.
Ritual might have been viewed as a process that was profoundly integrated into the complex and shifting social worlds of
anthropological subjects, but ritual was still the principal site
of cultural construction, and culture was fundamentally about
shared meanings and social values.

Interestingly, some years later, when summarizing theoretical developments in anthropology since the sixties, Ortner
noted that ritual had been shifted from centre-stage by new
concerns in anthropology with practice and everyday life.[6] This
new call to practice has been part of a general move away from
traditional subjects such as kinship and ritual, or at least away

from traditional approaches to these subjects. And history, viewed more as process than as chronology, is fundamental to this new concern with practice. The movement towards history and practice is not motivated, as the movement towards anthropology was for a time among historians, with a concern about a paucity of meaning and culture, but rather just the opposite; there has been a sense that studies of meaning had become too aestheticized, too abstracted from the everyday contexts in which meanings are produced, reproduced, and manipulated. Nonetheless, even calls for practice-oriented anthropologies from such theorists as Bourdieu confirm the residual centrality of the cultural: in Bourdieu's theoretical proposals capital is now modified by the adjective symbolic.[7]

In recent years, as social history has become increasingly anthropologized, historians have appropriated ritual as a subject and employed anthropological perspectives on ritual. William Sewell invoked a Geertzian conception of ritual to demonstrate that ritual performances—in his particular story rituals that employed old regime forms in post-revolution contexts—were used to symbolically mark and socially solidify the emerging communities of labour in late-eighteenth and early-nineteenth-century France.[8] More commonly, the names of Turner, Van Gennep, and Gluckman rather than Geertz have been cited when historians have attempted to grasp ritual. Geertz has been used by historians principally for his semiotic theory of culture, not for his critique of functionalist analyses of ritual.[9] Following from these anthropological authors, historians have typically been interested in rituals such as the carnival or the charivari, in rites of inversion or status reversal. Some historians have accepted the functionalist undergirding of anthropological writing about these rituals, concurring at least to some extent that rituals, in Gluckman's terms, 'obviously include a protest against the established order' but 'are intended to preserve and strengthen the established order'.[10] As Natalie Davis puts it, rituals

are ultimately sources of order and stability in a hierarchical society. They can clarify the structure by the process of reversing it. They can provide an expression of, and a safety valve for, conflicts within the system. They can correct and relieve the system when it has become authoritarian. But, so it is argued, they do not question the basic order of the society itself. They can renew the system, but they cannot change it.[11]

From a textual perspective, Stephen Greenblatt has recognized that the anxiety about royal authority induced by Shakespeare in such plays as *Richard II* and *Henry V* serves only in the end to enhance the power of authority; as he says, 'actions that should have the effect of radically undermining authority turn out to be the props of that authority'.[12]

Returning to the carnival, many historians have recognized in it something more than this, seizing on the pre-political elements of class struggle and contestation, concentrating on the unsettling and disorderly aspects of the periodic inversion. However, in so doing they have had to suspend the teleological framing they might perhaps have rather recorded as critics of the social order; rituals rarely became highly politicized, and often did lapse back into the social orders that produced them, whether or not that social order was reinforced or slightly shaken as a result. Subversion was either contained, or transformed into order.

Indeed, in literary studies, which since the translation of Bakhtin's extraordinary book on Rabelais in 1968 has become even more carnivalesque than social history, the relation between periodic disorder and subversion on the one hand and order and containment on the other has been widely debated. Terry Eagleton is one of many critics of Bakhtin who thinks that Bakhtin's celebration of the political potential and meaning of the carnival is misguided:

Indeed carnival is so vivaciously celebrated that the necessary political criticism is almost too obvious to make. Carnival, after all, is a *licensed* affair in every sense, a permissible rupture of hegemony, a contained popular blow-off as disturbing and relatively ineffectual as a revolutionary work of art. As Shakespeare's Olivia remarks, there is no slander in an allowed fool.[13]

Be this as it may, it is in fact striking how frequently violent social clashes apparently coincided with carnival. And while carnival was always licensed, not all that happened in carnival was similarly licensed. Carnival was socially dangerous, semiotically demystifying, and culturally disrespectful, even though it often confirmed authority, renewed social relations, and was rarely either politicized or progressive.[14]

In all these debates the question whether ritual can occasion, or serve as the occasion for, resistance is read in terms of one specific form of ritual and one particular kind of resistance. We hear only about the carnival or the charivari, about rituals that involve reversal and inversion, not about rituals that are about power/authority of both secular and sacred kinds. And we evaluate the politics of ritual only in terms of a discourse on resistance that seeks out contestatory and confrontational up-surges by the lower classes. It is perhaps no accident that Natalie Davis was less affected by these discursive blinkers than many of her contemporaries since her most critical discussion of the carnival concerns the status of women, who could not participate in public and politicized moments of confrontation, consigned as they were to the private, the domestic, and the particular. A concern with gender issues has led some writers to criticize the virile assumptions underlying most writings on resistance.[15]

Meanwhile, the move among anthropologists from symbolic analysis to practice theory has led to increasing focus on both the everyday and the non-ritual. Jean Comaroff, an anthropo-logist who has worked among the Tshidi of southern Africa and who was clearly deeply influenced by the practice theory of Bourdieu, turned to the everyday for a sense of the repressed and oppressed tensions characteristic of a system of violently established and maintained hegemony such as exists in south Africa. She found that, 'while awareness of oppression obviously runs deep, reaction may appear erratic, diffuse, and difficult to characterize. It is here that we must look beyond the conven-tionally explicit domains of "political action" and "con-sciousness"; for, when expressions of dissent are prevented from attaining the level of open discourse, a subtle but systematic breach of authoritative cultural codes might make a statement of protest which, by virtue of being rooted in a shared structural predicament and experience of dispossession, conveys an un-ambiguous message'.[16] But the message *is* ambiguous, and anthropologists are still struggling to open up theoretical and empirical spaces for culturally-constituted counter-hegemonies.

Among historians, a concern with the social has also led to a concern with the everyday, and social historians interested in a

social history of confrontation have redefined their categories of
the political and the confrontational. Alf Ludtke exemplifies this
trend in his writing on workers' movements and protests in
Imperial Germany. As he writes in a recent essay:

My focus will be on the total spectrum of expressions and daily
assertions by individuals as well as by different groups and classes. I
will emphasize not simply the ways in which people tried to raise
demands or resist the demands of others, but also those modes of self-
reliance whereby [in theoretical terms] people reappropriated these
constraints and pressures—the specific, even peculiar, practices whereby individuals handled their anxieties and desires. I wish to transgress and then blur the usual boundaries between political and
private.[17]

Elsewhere Ludtke writes that protests should be 'regarded as
occasional manifestations of a wide complex of structured processes and situations' and that 'research into traces of suppressed needs should not be confined to manifest expressions of
dissatisfaction, opposition, and resistance'.[18] In this turn to the
'everyday', ritual has too often been left out of the picture.
However, ritual is not just a dramatic event, but a vital com-
ponent of everyday experience.[19]

As we increasingly, and from differing perspectives, examine
ordinary life, the fixtures of ordinariness give way to fractures
and we see that struggle is everywhere, even where it is least
dramatic, and least visible.[20] Struggle becomes visible where
previously we could not see it, a trope for a critical vision of
the world. Consensus is no longer assumed unless proven otherwise, but even more unsettling for our social science, rebellion
and resistance can no longer be identified through traditional
indices of the extraordinary. The ordinary and the extraordinary trade places.

   In the study of rural India, anthropology has provided most
of our social scientific terms of reference. And in anthropology
'order' has always been the chief ordering principle of discourse. When anthropology puts particular emphasis on order,
it sanctifies it with the adjective 'ritual'. Ritual is not only
principally about order, it is often the domain in which our
sociological conception of society is properly realized. We have
already noted that anthropologists have often viewed rituals in

terms of religious or cultural meanings. They have interpreted the social significance rituals have either directly in terms of these meanings, or—in what is just a slight transformation of this view—as productive of social solidarity. In this view, social relations are displayed and renewed and the hierarchical forms underlying social relations confirmed and strengthened by ritual.

Perhaps, therefore, it comes as no surprise that a writer like James Scott, who has made an important and eloquent plea for the study of everyday forms of peasant resistance, ignores the possibility that ritual could constitute an important site of resistance.[21] Partly, this reveals his basic economistic emphases; but it is also because he is suspicious of ritual. In a long and rich book he makes only two brief references to rituals of status reversal, and several other references to ritual as something which is constitutive of community. Scott is therefore exemplary of how writers concerned with resistance themselves accept with little modification the Durkheimian foundations of our social scientific conceptions of ritual.

However, Jean Comaroff among others has argued that ritual need not be about order and domination alone. She has found, at least in her work on southern Africa, that

ritual provides an appropriate medium through which the values and structures of a contradictory world may be addressed and manipulated. . . . The widespread syncretistic movements that have accompanied capitalist penetration into the Third World are frequently also subversive bricolages; that is, they are motivated by an opposition to the dominant system. While they have generally lacked the degree of self-consciousness of some religious or aesthetic movements, or of the marginal youth cultures of the modern West, they are nevertheless a purposive attempt to defy the authority of the hegemonic order . . . Such exercises do more than just express revolt, they are also more than mere acts of self-representation. Rather, they are at once both expressive and pragmatic, for they aim to change the real world by inducing transformations in the world of symbol and rite.[22]

It is this mode of situating ritual practice and ideology in a world of hegemony and struggle in which representation itself is one of the most contested resources which I follow in this paper.

But I also seek to go further, as also to start with a more

basic premise. I will not evaluate ritual practice on the basis of whether or not it aims to change the real world, however much it may lack self-consciousness. Rather, I will look at traditional village rituals in India which at face value have the effect of restoring social relations and upholding relations of authority both within the village and between it and the larger political unit of the kingdom or later state. And I will seek to determine if the way in which order and disorder have been narrativized as basic components of ritual practice, is in fact adequate to the multiple foci and forms of disorder as I encountered them. For anthropologists have viewed ritual not only as merely a sociological mechanism for the production of order, but also as a cosmological and symbolic site for the containment of chaos and the regeneration of the world (as we, or they, know it).

Elsewhere I have argued that current anthropological writing on ritual underplays, both at the level of kingdoms or large political units and at the level of village rituals and festivals, the social fact that ritual constitutes a tremendously important arena for the cultural construction of authority and the dramatic display of the social lineaments of power.[23] However, although I presented examples of conflict, I saw them largely as products of the breakdown of authority under colonialism. Here I shall argue that precisely because of the centrality of authority to the ritual process, ritual has always been a crucial site of struggle, involving both claims about authority and struggles against (and within) it. By historicizing the study of ritual, we can see that while rituals provide critical moments for the definition of collectivities and the articulation of rank and power, they often occasion more conflict than consensus, and that each consensus is provisional, as much a social moment of liminality in which all relations of power (and powerlessness) are up for grabs as it is a time for the reconstitution and celebration of a highly political (and thus disorderly) ritual order. Resistance to authority can be seen to occur precisely when and where it is least expected.

The ritual I will focus on is crucial here because although it is only one of several village rituals it is the one that inaugurates all other village rituals, often setting the calendrical and cosmological agenda for the yearly ritual cycle. The Aiyanar festival, called the kutirai etuppu, was critical also in that it vividly reflected and displayed the hierarchical relations within the village, with the village headman, or ampalam, as the ostensive centre of these relations. The priests for this ritual, who also acted as the potters who made the clay horses that were consecrated in the central ritual action, had to obtain permission from the village headman in order to begin making the horses for the festival. The ampalam was the host for the festival which began and ended at his house and his emblems were as importantly involved in the procession as were the clay horses themselves; the ampalam received the first honours, which he then distributed to the other members of the village at the conclusion of the ritual. In short, the ampalam represented the totality of the village in a rite which was seen and said by some to celebrate and regenerate the village itself.

When I was in the field—for me the little kingdom of Pudukkottai, one of the largest of the little kingdoms in the early modern period of the Tamil-speaking region of southern India and later under the British Raj the only Princely State in the Tamil country—it took little time to realize that Aiyanar was a critical deity, and the yearly festival in his honour a crucial festival, in the ritual life of the social formations constituting the focus of my general ethno-historical research. Village elders and headmen would regularly take me to their own Aiyanar shrine as the most important stop on the village tour. They would tell me all about their village festival, how it was famous for miles around, how I would be able to observe and recognize the political centrality of the headman, that I should definitely plan to return to their village on the occasion of the festival. Clearly ritual was important, and clearly this was the social ritual par excellence, at least in the post-independence days of a post-royal kingdom. During the course of my fieldwork, I attended and took extensive notes on about twelve of these festivals in different villages throughout the state. Because of my interest in local social relations and structures of authority, I was drawn into this festival, which became, quite by surprise, a chief focus of my ethnographic research.

There was one festival in particular that I looked forward to attending. The village headman had been an especially rewarding informant, or guide, and spent many hours telling me about the complex details of social organization in his village and his natu, the territorial unit that was coterminous with the settlement zone of his subcaste group (also called natu) of Kallars, the royal caste in Pudukkottai. He was a patriarch of classic proportions. He told me about the Aiyanar festival with the care and comprehension of a radio cricket commentator, and as the festival neared he even visited my house in town on two occasions to submit to further questions and my tape recorder. I was told exactly when the festival would begin, and we agreed that I would arrive soon after dusk, to participate in the final preparations which would culminate in the commencement of the festival around midnight (like many of these rituals, it was to take place through the night). When the festival was still a week away, I expected a formal visit from the headman to invite me as an honoured outside guest, but when he failed to turn up I assumed he was unable to come because he was enmeshed in the myriad preparations for the festival. So on the appointed evening I drove my motorcycle the requisite thirty-five miles across potholed tarmac and dusty bullock cart tracks, only to arrive in a village that was virtually dark, with no visible evidence of any approaching festivities. The village headman looked dismayed and surprised as I rolled up on my Enfield, though less dismayed than me since I heard, as I switched off my engine, the unmistakable hiss of a rapidly deflating tyre, the devastating effect of a large acacia thorn's union with my non-radial Dunlop. The headman told me that the festival had been called off, and that he had hoped I would have guessed this since he had not come with the formal invitation. In any case, he said, he could not have come to tell me that there would be no festival, since this would have been inauspicious, and would have made it even more unlikely than it already was that the festival could take place. But, of course, this admirable foresight had not turned things around; the festival could not be organized, a long-standing factional dispute in the village was not in the end resolved, and the festival became yet another casualty of this dispute. My immediate concern, apart from the fact that my tyre was flat and I was not carrying a spare, was that I had lost a brilliant opportunity to match theory, narrative, and practice, to follow up the story of a festival that I had been tracking industriously over the preceding weeks and months. But as my host instructed his son and assorted relatives to hitch the bullock cart to arrange for my long and bumpy transport back to town, my disappointment yielded to bewilderment. For I learned that the festival on which I had such exquisite detail had not taken place for seven years, and that no one in the village had any genuine expectation that it would take place this year.

Most fieldwork stories are similarly allegorized. We begin with calm self-confidence, our initial assumptions and convictions yet unchecked by the chaotic realities and serendipities of the field. We then find ourselves in some disastrous predicament which, in unsettling us (and sometimes them), enables us to cross the fault line of cultural difference, to familiarize ourselves with the concerns and logics of new social terrains, to achieve new forms of communion with our anthropological subjects, to achieve wisdom. In fact, at the time I was simply seriously annoyed. Yet, I should also note that although I had been aware of the extent to which Aiyanar festivals gave rise to conflict and dispute at the time, it was only then, and increasingly over the years since, that I have realized the extent to which this story illustrates the flip side of my concern with how village rituals reflected and displayed political authority and political relations. I had begun thinking about Aiyanar by using the Aiyanar festival to attack Dumont's notion (which he developed in a number of places but not insignificantly in an important article on the Aiyanar festival in Tamil Nadu) that religion/ritual always encompasses politics/power.[24] Having established this, it was still difficult to come to terms with the fact that Aiyanar festivals were always sites for struggle and contestation; that speech about the festivals reflected concerns about ritual order and auspiciousness that were part of a different ritual order than the ritual event itself; that even when the ritual event did not happen it was as significant as when it did. The non-event of the called-off ritual was not, in fact, a non-event, after all.

During the rest of my fieldwork I learned that many of the other great events of ritual calendars were similar non-events, that Aiyanar festivals did not happen almost as often as they did, and that when they happened they did not always include everyone in the village, or result in the village communal harmony that I had previously assumed, and indeed that this communal harmony was disturbed not only along the so-called traditional lines of caste or faction but along developing class lines as well. I also learned that while at one level the festival was about the re-establishment of control over the disorder of a threatening nature, it was also about the range of possibilities that existed precisely at the moment of maximal contact between order and disorder. But it is now time to backtrack to the festival itself, before we allow it, as it did that night for me, to deconstruct itself.

In Pudukkottai, Aiyanar was often the principal village deity, though there are villages which include Aiyanar temples in which the village deity was said to be a goddess. According to most of my informants, the most significant feature of Aiyanar was his role as the protector. He was more specifically called the protection diety, the protector of boundaries, and the one who protected those who took refuge with him. The kutirai etuppu festival—or the installation of the horses—began a month before the main festival day. The head of the potters (Velars), the community that made the terracotta offerings and often acted as principal priests for Aiyanar, would take a handful of clay (pitiman) from the village tank. The pitiman was placed in a brass plate and handed to the village ampalam, who then returned it to the Velars, along with the ritual dues. The ampalam had to make this gift, signifying his permission for the festival to begin, to entitle the Velars to proceed with the preparation of the offerings. The gift was made in part in the form of puja, as the blessed return of a gift that was first offered to the superior being. The central position of the ampalam was thus enunciated and displayed at the moment of the festival's inauguration.

Throughout the festival itself, though each one varied in details, the role of the ampalam was particularly conspicuous, as important as the deity. The festival began and ended at his house, the central locus of all village gatherings. There the first ritual action of the festival had taken place a month earlier, when the ampalam returned the pitiman to the head of the Velars. Similarly, the first ritual action of the festival day was often the puja performed to the ampalam's family deity, adorned with the emblems which represented and encapsulated the family's heritage. Granted by the Raja, and passed from generation to generation within the family, these emblems now symbolized that this festival was sponsored by the village ampalam, a festival at once personal and public, the private puja of the ampalam's family and the public performance of the entire village.

In Dumont's well-known analysis of this festival he places too much importance both on the opposition between purity and impurity (deducing from diet that Aiyanar is principally modelled on the Brahman, even though in behaviour and legend Aiyanar is far more like the king) and on his contention that Aiyanar's relation to other village deities reflects the subordination of the political to the religious. The kingly aspects of the deity and the critical role of the ampalam are either ignored or accorded only secondary importance. Dumont's failure to provide a fully satisfactory analysis of Aiyanar and his festival is part of his larger refusal to grant that a king can, in certain contexts, encompass and incorporate the divine, the brahmanic, as well as the social and political constituents of caste solidarity and warrior strength. In the village, where the king was represented by the ampalam, the festival at once elevated the ampalam and his political authority, displayed the ampalam's relation to the king, effected an identity between the latter and the village, and produced, through the celebration of a festival on behalf of a god who so dramatically exemplified the royal function, the conditions under which the village could be victorious against the forces of evil.

But this is not the whole story. For it is precisely the political permeability of ritual that makes possible a succession of contested performances, readings, and tellings. In India kingship had been the dominant trope for the political, but far from the only one. As I stated at the beginning, the Aiyanar festival frequently did not happen, or occasioned everything from violent dispute to multiple celebration, as in one village where three separate village festivals took place under the leadership of three rival castes and their factional affiliates.

For example, in the early 1920s in Tiruvappur, a village close to Pudukkottai town and made up mostly of Kallars, weavers, and service castes, the Velars petitioned that they were under no compulsion to give or receive the pitiman from the village headman. With appropriate bureaucratic justification, they insisted that since the headman's inam lands did not specify that he should give the pitiman, there was no other authoritative basis for the claim that pitiman be given only by the headman. The headman in turn petitioned the government that the performance of the festival without his permission, granted through the pitiman, was an infringement of his hereditary right, as proved by the fact that his family had been granted inam lands with the specific injunction to conduct the ordinary pujas and other festivals in the Aiyanar temples of Tiruvappur. Both petitions employed the same colonial logic, giving inams (and the authority of local headmen) a rational–legal basis they had not possessed in pre-colonial times.

For the Diwan's assistant, the Diwan Peishkar, the resolution of the case rested first on the proper interpretation of the significance of the grant of pitiman. His inquiries led him to decide quite correctly that the grant of pitiman signified far more than the intended co-operation of the headmen or Nattars.

> If it signifies mere co-operation without the slightest tinge of authority or idea of special privilege the villagers would not have objected to the continuance of the system. On the other hand, the grant of pitiman is considered to be a grant of permission by the nattars to conduct the kutirai etuppu. Both the nattars and the artisans view it in this light and it is why the former are unwilling to lose the privilege and the latter anxious to discontinue the system.[25]

He then had to decide whether this privilege could be sustained under the bureaucratic terms of service implied by the wording of the inam grant, which was vague enough to accommodate both interpretations put forward in the petition and counter-petition. The Diwan Peishkar investigated customs in other Aiyanar temples to determine precedent only to find that each case differed, hardly the stuff of precedent. To further complicate matters, the Diwan Peishkar felt that he had to determine whether the dispute concerned the hereditary privileges of the headmen as traditional caste headmen or, in a deliberately alienating bureaucratic move, as state functionaries.

The Brahmanical Diwan Peishkar was also troubled by his belief that religion was an individual concern, and that all devotees should be able to commission the Velars to make horses for them without the intervention of the Nattar. Such control over the individual vows of others seemed to him 'revolting to a devotee's sense of honour and reason'. The Diwan Peishkar recommended that the Nattars be allowed to commission the installation of horses on their own behalf, but not on behalf of others. The separation of the individual rights of Nattars from their right to commission horses on behalf of the entire village only made sense, however, in terms of a newly formulated bureaucratic conception of religion, since the individual vows of devotees would have been encompassed by the social fact that the festival, even when contested, was a village festival. The Diwan Peishkar's recommendation struck at the core of the headman's objections, since he saw his privilege as an enactment of his authoritative position in the village temple and indeed in the village at large. But in the invention of an autonomous domain and logic of religion, the underlying social issues were ignored. The struggle between the service and dominant groups was a struggle over authority, and thus had its most visible and important expression in the Aiyanar ritual, which itself resisted bureaucratic appropriation by the new Brahman–British religious sensibility (though it succumbed to the bureaucratic definition of the inam).

As it turned out, the Diwan was less zealous than the Diwan Peishkar to upset the local structure of authoritative relations in Tiruvappur. He recommended that the Nattars continue to be vested with the right to give the pitiman. He did, however, insist that the Nattars had to signify their permission by giving back the pitiman immediately and routinely, thus heading off the mischievous possibility that they might abuse their right, a sacred trust. 'Authority' was defended in name, but was undermined by the attempts of the bureaucratic establishment to make religion an individual and private rather than a social and public affair. Although this did not allay all the concerns of the petitioners, they had at least been able to use the language of government to lodge an important formal complaint.

Tiruvappur had been the scene of many similar disputes at least as early as 1885. At one point the local Paraiyars asserted themselves against the ampalam by refusing to beat drums outside the temple. In another instance, the Velars again resisted the authoritative claims of the Kallar headman, denying his privilege to carry the scythe used for the ritual slaughter and present it to the Velars who actually did the cutting. On one occasion they even refused, in their role as priests, to make pracatam (offerings) from Aiyanar to the ampalam. Again the Diwan upheld the rights of the ampalams, at the same time that he tried to rationalize the exercise of these rights.

Many similar disputes took place, but only a few of them leaked into official view, usually because the disputes were dealt with in summary (and no doubt brutal) fashion by the local dominant groups. So although these files alerted me to a record of contention, it was only in towns close to the court, and also in bigger towns and temples such as those considered by Appadurai and Breckenridge, that ritual was a clearly contentious affair in the historical record.[26] Many of these disputes concerned the distribution of honours and pracatam in temples and locked dominant lineages and their headmen in fervent dispute with each other; otherwise the disputes were usually buried by the dominant group (which had to seek no higher authority). Thus when Appadurai and Breckenridge proposed that ritual in south India involved conflict, they were referring to mainly one form of conflict, that which anthropologists working on India had until then recognized and accepted: factionalism. Indebted though I am to their analysis, I only realized the full range of dispute and contestation through my own combination of ethnographic accidents and historical investigations.

I found many other instances in which ritual turned out to be a core arena for resistance, particularly for groups such as artisans and untouchables who could resist by simply withholding their services. The closest thing to a municipal strike in the history of Pudukkottai town took place in the early 1930s when the untouchables protested the establishment of a municipal crematorium by withholding their ritual funereal services for all their patron groups. The municipality backed down in short order because of the consternation of one high-caste family after another who felt they were dishonouring their dead. Kathleen Gough has vividly documented the breakdown of village ritual in rural Tanjavur where untouchable groups, fired in part by the growth of a local communist movement, increasingly withheld their ritual services from village festivals.[27] Nonetheless, Gough's assertion that village rituals would not recover from the effects of recent change and growing class consciousness has not been sustained by the experience of the last thirty years. In fact, village rituals continue to be important precisely because of their association with conflict.

Although village rituals were clearly sites for struggle between elite groups and their factions over who was in charge,[28] this was only part of the story. Rituals were sites for struggle of all kinds, including—as my earlier story suggests—the struggle between discourse and event. Ritual was a discursive and practical field in which a great deal was at stake and a great deal was up for grabs. But when conflict developed in ritual it always made the ritual a site for appropriation as well as for struggle. The headman of the darkened quiet village appropriated the interpretive function of a ritual that he always knew would not take place, and was embarrassed only when I pressed my curiosity and showed up without the proper invitation. The Brahman administrators of Pudukkottai appropriated the dispute for their own purposes of undermining the religious authority of rural Kallar elites and implementing new colonial standards for the evaluation of religious activity and the establishment of religion within a newly created domain of civil society. Anthropologists have appropriated ritual to advocate the religious dimensions, character, and force of the social, which in the case of Dumont's transformation of Durkheim is located in a world of religiously validated hierarchy. Appadurai and Breckenridge found struggle at the top level of ritual and argued that temples provided political arenas of dispute.[29] These appropriations—like my own—are all examples of the way ritual has become central to the field of power relations in southern India. Further, these appropriations have never fully succeeded in containing the power of ritual, and they are all checked by the profoundly subversive character of traditional ritual practice (at least as I observed, and did not observe, it in southern India). Not only did ritual discourse and ritual practice operate at angles to each other, both discourse and practice were open to a multiplicity of contesting and resisting agencies, even when these agencies were themselves constituted by (or in relation to) the concealed agencies of colonial hegemony.

But I have so far completely ignored one of the most important but also complex sources of agency and action in the Aiyanar festival. I do not mean the lord Aiyanar himself, but rather his incarnation in the form of the *camiyatis*, the people in the village who during the course of the festival were routinely possessed by the lord Aiyanar. Possession was an absolutely critical part of this and other village festivals in the south. Apart from the goat sacrifice and the feast it was the most charged event in village ritual practice. Once again I must retell the festival, which I will do with reference to the Aiyanar festival celebrated in the predominantly Kallar village of Puvaracakuti, in Vallanatu, about eight miles southeast of Pudukkottai town in early July 1982.

The festival began at the house of the ampalam. When I arrived the ampalam was bathing and a number of village folk and members of the ampalam's family were busy decorating the ampalam's house, festooning it with mango and coconut leaves. The Paraiyars who had assembled some distance from the house built small fires to tune their drums. Flowers, coconuts, and other items for the puja were brought to the front porch of the house. There were five red ribbons to tie on the horns of the horses and bulls, five towels for the possessed camiyatis and towels for the service castes such as the dhobi, barber, and Paraiyars. The ampalam came to the front porch after his bath, and worshipped the images of gods and goddesses hung on the interior walls of the porch.

The emblems of the ampalam were brought out from the vacant house next door, called the big house, which was unoccupied because of a quarrel within the ampalam's family between collateral contestants for the position of ampalam. These emblems consisted of a spear, a sword, a cane, and a club. The emblems symbolized the office and authority of the ampalam, and were said to have been presented many generations before by the Raja. Under a small tiled roof mandapam (pavilion) about twenty yards to the west of the ampalam's house, they were placed next to the pattavan, a sword representing an ancestor of the ampalam's family who was worshipped as the family deity. The emblems and the pattavan were shown the flame, camphor was burnt, and coconuts were broken, the three most common elements of any performance of puja. After this, the emblems were carried by other Kallars in the village, and the ampalam was summoned. The first procession of the day was ready to begin.

The emblems were carried by Kallars. The entire procession was led by Paraiyars beating their drums. Though the ampalam was the central character, attention was increasingly focused on the camiyatis, here five Kallars who were to be possessed by the god. Initially chosen for possessing special spiritual powers, they were the hereditary camiyatis who participated in the festival each year. They walked immediately behind the drum-beating Paraiyars. Not yet in full trance, the camiyatis began to show signs of possession as they walked on to the beat of the drums, their bodies sporadically quivering at the touch of Aiyanar, who was shortly to enter into them. The procession walked straight to the small structural temple to Aiyanar. A puja was performed for Aiyanar, and sacred ash was distributed to all those present. The camiyatis then picked up bags of ash and began walking back to the village, accompanied by the Paraiyars. As they walked through the village, the women of each house came towards them and poured water over their feet to cool them. The camiyatis blessed the women with the ash they carried. We walked through the Kallar section of town, via the ampalam's house, to the Velar settlement on the eastern side of the village. There the procession was welcomed by the playing of the mela telam (drum) by the Melakkarars (the pipers) of a nearby temple and by exploding fire crackers. Six terracotta figures, each about four feet high, were lined up on the Velar street—one elephant, three horses, and two bulls—in the final stages of decoration. They had been whitewashed, painted with coloured stripes, and crowned with stalks of flowering paddy and the ribbons from the ampalam's house. The five Kallar camiyatis stood in front of the terracotta figures. A Paraiyar from a nearby village came forward, and carefully dressed the camiyatis in special clothes. The Paraiyar wore a garland made of silver balls, his head was wrapped with a red cloth, his chest was draped with multicoloured strands of cloth, a new towel was tied around his waist, and garlands of bells were wrapped around him. His face was painted with vermilion and

sandal paste. This Paraiyar was called the munnoti, the leader
or the one who went first. In a few minutes he became possessed on his own, to the music of the drums and nadaswaram
played by the Melakkarars. He began to jump wildly when the
incense and camphor smoke were shown to him and he stared
fixedly at the sky. He suddenly leapt into the crowd, snatched
the ampalam's spear, and began to beat the ground with it. He
was jumping and running around and through the crowd, all
the while circumambulating the six figures. The ampalam
then came up to him, garlanded him and smeared sacred ash on
his forehead. After this, the munnoti led the other camiyatis into
states of possession. Someone whispered in my ear that the munnoti was the burning lamp which lights other lamps. Full
possession was achieved when the munnoti held the camphor
up to the camiyatis, one by one.

Now that the camiyatis were fully possessed, the procession
was ready to commence. The Paraiyars went first, followed at
some distance by the Melakkarars, then by the munnoti and the
five camiyatis, then the terracotta offerings, with the elephant
in the lead, followed by the smaller offerings of individual villagers. Behind them walked the ampalam, surrounded by many
of his kinsmen. As the procession moved around the village, on
its way back to the Aiyanar temple, villagers came up to the
camiyatis to be blessed, often asking questions about the
future which the camiyatis answered. When we reached the
temple, the eyes of the terracotta figures were opened with the
blood of a cock, sacrificed by the munnoti (who was then
given the cock). The terracotta animals were then installed in
front of the temple. A grand puja was held to Aiyanar. The
Velar priests offered tamarind rice, broke coconuts, and then
showed the light, after which they offered ash to the worship-
pers. Then the priests left the Aiyanar shrine, shutting its doors.
Aiyanar was said to be vegetarian, and ought not to see the
sacrifice to Karuppar, the fierce black god whose shrine is
always next to Aiyanar.

Moving to Karuppar, the priests performed puja again. The
villagers surged forward en masse to obtain some ash. One
of the priests laid a stone a few yards in front of the Karuppar
temple. The villagers assembled in a circle; finally a goat was
brought forward, and judged proper. The fifth camiyati came

forward bearing a large sword taken from the Karuppar shrine. With one swift slice he cut off the goat's head. As they intently watched the spilling of blood and the final convulsions of the goat's body, the crowd became increasingly excited and jubilant. The carcass of the goat, which had been donated by the ampalam's family, was now handed over to the Velar priests.

A cloth was laid on the ground for the ampalam to sit on. The Velars brought him the huge bowl of tamarind rice and all the pracatam from the puja: flowers, coconuts, and plantains. Sitting there the ampalam distributed the honours, first to the Kallar lineage heads, then to the Valaiyars, and the artisans. Finally, the village elders took up the ampalam's emblems once again, and beckoned to him to lead the procession back to the village. All returned to his house, where the emblems were returned to their accustomed place. This concluded, the village Kallars and Paraiyars were given their pracatam in the village square in front of the ampalam's house, along with sufficient rice and a chicken for a feast of their own.

The final distribution of honours both confirmed the authority of the ampalam and displayed the hierarchical relations of all the caste groups in the village. Or so it seemed. This harmonious village festival began to deconstruct itself when I came to realize shortly after I attended the festival that a rival group of Konars, traditionally herders but now an increasingly powerful agricultural caste, had seceded from the ritual performance and instead held their own kutirai etuppu some weeks later. Thus the appearance of harmony that presented itself so forcefully began to unravel as soon as I began to poke into the affairs of the village. After what I have already argued in this paper, this is hardly surprising. But here I will comment on one important aspect of the festival that I completely ignored in my earlier analysis. From the account it is clearly seen that possession was a central part of the ritual drama. However, what was possession all about, what did it signify?

Most of the literature on possession deals with the nasty kind, when it is the devil rather than the lord who has taken up residence within our mortal coil. And so rather than the exorcist we have its opposite—a man whose skill and power is precisely to induce possession rather than rid us of it. But this too is an extraordinary form of power, and one that has many dangers. It is significant that for this role an untouchable is chosen; while all the regular camiyatis are of the dominant Kallar caste, the one person who makes their possession possible could never be invited into their houses nor be allowed to dine with them. And his power was not completely contained by hierarchy, for there were moments of real fear when he seized the ampalam's spear and began dancing wildly about. The fear of Aiyanar was clearly enhanced by his choice of this unruly Paraiyar as his principal vehicle and agent. When I went to visit him he was completely drunk, and he combined in his person an exaggerated deference and a smouldering bitterness. On the one hand he acted as if he was deeply honoured that I should visit him; his failure to recognize me for a moment or two seemed due more to drink than any difficulty in remembering my presence in the festival through the daze of his own possession. On the other hand, he was the one who told me that there was a rival festival in the village hosted by Konars or shepherds, and as he told me this he almost laughed at the hollow claims of the Kallar headmen who could no longer control an inferior caste group.

Indeed, this was not the only moment of danger, not the only reason why containment was a live issue throughout the festival. Aiyanar was clearly hard to handle, and his agents in possession had to negotiate a delicate balance between play-acting and overacting. I was repeatedly told that the possession was real, that it took many years to learn how to accept the visitation of the lord, that it required the supervision of a man of special powers both to learn and to do, and that after a spell of possession it would take days and sometimes weeks for the possessed person, exhausted and shaken by the experience, to return fully to normal. And I was told that if a camiyati turned out not to be really possessed, simply play-acting, they would ridicule him and exclude him completely from the festival and its proceedings.

After all, the festival was critical for the well-being of the village, and if Aiyanar was misrepresented by an impostor, then the festival might fail, and certainly the advice handed down by the lord to the anxious and enquiring villagers would be spurious. But there were also times when possession could prove too much; the camiyati was called the vessel, and when this vessel could not contain the concentrated power of the lord, it might crack. In such instances the camiyati would not recover from possession, would stay deranged and disturbed, and then there would be need of an exorcist.

It is possible to account for all of this with a traditional view of ritual. Van Gennep was keenly aware of the danger and disorder that was part of ritual, and built this into his explanation of liminality and ritual transformation.[30] But his theory has a tendency to contain danger too readily, too automatically, and to assume that disorder is epiphenomenal. I would propose here that possession was yet another aspect in which ritual practice was genuinely dangerous and always already subversive. Part of the subversiveness had to do with what we have already considered, the constant possibility of conflict, fission, paralysis, and hermeneutic if not agonistic explosion. But the subversiveness had also to do with the politics of representation and misrepresentation inherent in both the role of the headman and that of the camiyatis.

First, the festival was a powerful spectacle precisely because of the role of the possessed camiyatis. The festival seemed to me at times, particularly since I attended many different festivals in different villages, like theatre. Victor Turner has already commented on this correlation, using the term 'ritual drama', by which he meant that ritual could be analysed as if it was an unfolding drama with the participants as actors who engaged in the unseen forces of life through the vicarious agencies of ritualistic enactment.[31] But if what I witnessed was theatre to the participants, it was very different from what has come to be accepted as theatre in the West. Stephen Greenblatt has noted that 'the theatre elicits from us complicity rather than belief'.[32] But in rural southern India there were elements of both complicity and belief; there were roles and masquerades that depended on far more than skilful artifice and conceit. This was 'theatre lived' not 'theatre played', as Greenblatt observed when citing an ethnographic example.[33] But even this opposition does not capture the power of this ritual experience. For there was the possibility that something could go wrong, and this provided an urgency and unpredictability to the drama that renders a theatrical metaphor too dramatic and possibly sacrilegious. One of the inescapable implications of the cami-yati's predicament—the risk that possession could be in-authentic—was that all agency and all representation in the ritual was at risk as well. Identity was most fragile at the moment of its transformation and multiple reference. And the risk that the possessed might be faking it no doubt raised the possibility that the headman, whose authority and connections with the king were both celebrated and renewed in the festival, might also be faking it. After all, everyone knew (though at the time I did not) that the headman claimed a sovereignty over the entire village that was not granted by the rival shepherds. Thus, participation in the festival was highly politicized. Indeed, even the role of the lord was thus politi-cized: on whose side was which god? But it was the com-pelling, contestable, and dangerous components of the ritual drama that also raised the stakes. The spectators did not simply gaze, they vied with each other to participate more actively and more centrally in the festival, to interlocute the camiyatis, to see the cutting of the goat, and to collect and consume the prasada—the transubstantiated return—of the lord. They also vied with one another to celebrate, to control, and to interpret the ritual.

I have given just a few illustrations to suggest what I might mean by the subversive nature of ritual practice and discourse. I will close with one last observation. Each ritual event is patterned activity to be sure, but it is also invented anew as it happens. When I witnessed one festival, there was frequent confusion about what was to be done. At one point a participant in the festival leaned over to me, realizing that I had seen many similar festivals, and asked me what I thought they should do next. At the time I thought that I was already intruding too much on the authenticity of the ritual event and that to offer an opinion would be to go across the fragile threshold of legitimate participation implied in the oxymoronic motto of anthropology: participant observation. But I was wrong, for the authenticity of the event was inscribed in its performance, not in some time and custom sanctioned version of the ritual. And the authenticity of the Aiyanar festival was in particular inscribed in its uncertainty and its contestability, even when it didn't actually take place.

NOTES

1. Greenblatt's transformation of Kafka. See S. Greenblatt, *Shakespearean Negotiations* (Berkeley: University of California Press, 1988). I am grateful to my colleagues in history and anthropology at the University of Michigan for their comments in seminars when I delivered this paper. I am also particularly indebted to Val Daniel, Geoff Eley, Steven Mullaney, Gyan Prakash, and Sherry Ortner.

2. C. Geertz, *The Interpretation of Cultures* (New York: Basic Books, 1973), p. 142.

3. Sherry Ortner, *Sherpas Through Their Rituals* (Cambridge: Cambridge University Press, 1978), p. 1.

4. Ibid., p. 2.

5. Sherry Ortner, *High Religion* (Princeton: Princeton University Press, 1989).

6. Sherry Ortner, 'Theory in Anthropology since the Sixties', *Comparative Studies in Society and History*, 26: 1.

7. See Pierre Bourdieu, *Outline of a Theory of Practice*, trans. Richard Nice (Cambridge: Cambridge University Press, 1982).

8. See William Sewell, *Work and Revolution in France* (Cambridge: Cambridge University Press, 1980).

9. Stuart Clark, 'French Historians and Early Modern Popular Culture', *Past and Present*, no. 100, 1985; Hans Medick, 'Missionaries in the Row Boat? Ethnological Ways of Knowing as a Challenge to Social History', *Comparative Studies in Society and History*, 29: 1, 1987.

10. Max Gluckman, *Custom and Conflict in Africa* (Oxford: Blackwell, 1965).

11. Natalie Davis, *Society and Culture in Early Modern France* (Palo Alto: Stanford University Press, 1965).

12. J. Dollimore and A. Sinfield, *Political Shakespeare* (Manchester: Manchester University Press, 1985).

13. T. Eagleton, *Walter Benjamin: Towards a Revolutionary Criticism* (London: Verso, 1981).

14. P. Stallybrass and A. White, *The Politics and Poetics of Transgression* (Ithaca: Cornell University Press, 1986).

15. R. O'Hanlon, 'Recovering the Subject: Subaltern Studies and Histories of Resistance in Colonial South Asia', *Modern Asian Studies*, 22: 1, 1988.

16. J. Comaroff, *Body of Power, Spirit of Resistance* (Chicago: University of Chicago Press, 1985).

17. A. Ludtke, 'Organisational Order or Eigensinn? Workers' Privacy and Workers' Politics in Imperial Germany', in Sean Wilentz (ed.), *Rites*

of Power: Symbolism, Ritual and Politics since the Middle Ages (Philadelphia: University of Pennsylvania Press, 1985).

18. A. Ludtke, 'Everyday Life: The Articulation of Needs and "Proletarian Consciousness"—Some Remarks on Concepts', unpublished Mss., n.d.

19. See F. Hall, T. Jefferson and B. Roberts (eds), *Resistance through Rituals* (London: Hutchinson, 1976); D. Hebdige, *Subculture: The Meaning of Style* (New York: Methuen, 1979).

20. See M. de Certeau, *The Practice of Everyday Life* (Berkeley: University of California Press, 1984).

21. James Scott, *Weapons of the Weak* (New Haven: Yale University Press, 1985).

22. J. Comaroff, 1985.

23. N. Dirks, *The Hollow Crown: Ethnohistory of an Indian Kingdom* (Cambridge: Cambridge University Press, 1987).

24. L. Dumont, 'A Structural Definition of a Folk Deity', *Contributions to Indian Sociology*, 3: 75–87, 1959.

25. R.D. no. 1587 of 1923, dt. 30-3-25, Puddukottai Record Office.

26. A. Appadurai and C. Breckenridge, 'The South Indian Temple: Authority, Honour and Redistribution', *Contributions to Indian Sociology*, n.s., 10(2): 187–211, 1976.

27. K. Gough, 'The Social Structure of a Tanjore Village', in McKim Marriott (ed.), *Village India* (Chicago: University of Chicago Press, 1955).

28. See N. Dirks, 1987.

29. A. Appadurai and C. Breckenridge, 1976.

30. A. Van Gennep, *The Rites of Passage* (Chicago: University of Chicago Press, 1960).

31. V. Turner, *The Ritual Process* (Chicago: Aldine, 1969).

32. See S. Greenblatt, 1988.

33. Ibid.

8

From Avoidance to Confrontation? A Contestatory History of Merchant-State Relations in Surat 1600–1924

DOUGLAS HAYNES

'The people are cattle and the king is the keeper of the cattle compound,' declared a merchant in the western Indian city of Surat while addressing nearly two thousand fellow businessmen in 1918.[1] For the high-caste Hindu and Jain merchants who composed this now anonymous speaker's audience, the metaphor of the mute and helpless cow reliant upon a strong but benevolent master must have been a powerful one, one which symbolized their own sense of dependence upon the British rulers of India. But surprisingly this adage had not been offered at some ritual of obeisance to the colonizers. Instead the businessmen had gathered to initiate resistance to a new income tax law that threatened to double their tax payments and force them to divulge detailed information about how they conducted business. At this meeting the merchants resolved to refuse to fill out their tax forms or to pay their taxes until the measure was rescinded, even if this meant risking arrest and imprisonment. They also expressed a solidarity with traders of Bombay and Ahmedabad who had already passed similar resolutions a few days earlier. Yet they considered all these actions to be consistent with an attitude of deference to the colonial rulers and loyalty to the Empire.

Episodes such as the income tax movement of 1918 have never been at the centre of South Asian historiography. The study of resistance on the subcontinent has instead focused largely on the development of nationalist challenges to colonial rule and, more recently, on the struggles and insurgencies of 'subaltern' groups, particularly peasants.[2] Recent writing on the politics of Indian mercantile communities, by contrast, has concentrated on the contributions that traders, bankers, and industrialists have made to the formation and functioning of precolonial, colonial and postcolonial state structures.[3] Much of this new scholarship portrays merchant–ruler relations as relatively stable, unthreatened by the actions of ruling groups who depended on the financial resources and local connections the merchants controlled. With the exception of the research done on those moments when businessmen associated with the nationalist movement during the twentieth century, therefore, this is generally a history with resistance largely left out. The continuous efforts of businessmen to contend and frustrate efforts of state systems to intrude into the mercantile sphere of life during a variety of periods have yet to be made part of the contemporary reassessment.

This essay attempts to construct a contestatory history of merchant relations with rulers—a history with resistance put back in. It examines the political actions of high-caste Hindu and Jain merchants in a single urban centre, the city of Surat in western India, from the seventeenth century up to the first Gandhian campaign, the Non-Co-operation Movement of 1920 to 1924. The struggles of merchants, I argue, are central to an understanding of the character of the social and political order in Surat throughout this whole period. Through their resistances, local businessmen perpetuated their places of wealth, respectability and social control in Surat. They also contributed mightily to the shape of the state itself, at times even helping to effect major transitions in power.

By examining the character of their struggles during three centuries, I will explore the processes by which merchants adapted their means of protest to changes in the larger political system of which they were part. I take here as a starting point a model developed by Michael Adas to characterize changes in the resistances of peasants in Southeast Asia over a similarly long period of time. In his article Adas brings to light the importance of various forms of *avoidance protest*, such as the flight of peasants from their villages, withdrawal into religious sectarianism, and shifts from one patron to another. Such techniques of resistance, he suggests, were especially relevant in precolonial societies where the states were characterized by poor networks of communication, a limited capacity for coercion and constant conflict within the ruling group. In the colonial empires, by contrast, the development of centralized bureaucracies with vastly enhanced military powers and superior networks of communication frustrated the use of avoidance strategies and drove peasants increasingly to consider more dramatic, violent and confrontational means of resisting state demands.[4] The revolutionary and nationalist struggles of the twentieth century were a manifestation of the peasants' need to develop more effective means of coping with an increasingly inflexible state.[5] Rather than seek alternative patrons in moments of resistance, peasants seemed to have increasingly sought radical alternatives whose purpose was to destroy colonialism.

I find Adas's model very useful in many respects. It focuses on forms of resistance that have often been ignored; it calls on us to pay attention to the ways in which state structures influence the shape of peasant struggles. But as might be expected, important modifications are required if the model is to be applied to the resistances of merchants in Surat. Traders and bankers in the city were privileged figures in local society as well as persons who consistently tried to develop special relationships with members of the ruling group. Their preoccupations with maintaining social order and upholding elite notions of personal and familial dignity militated against the eventual adoption of aggressive, potentially violent, and revolutionary methods of resistance. Thus even as the colonial state became more intrusive in its intention and more repressive in its capabilities, the merchants generally eschewed forms of political action that might have endangered their commerce and their position of local dominance. Strategically, the merchants favoured 'avoidance techniques', including the closing of shops, the withdrawal of services to rulers, attempts to link themselves with alternative patrons, and even flight from the city. Symbolically, they rarely offered a direct challenge to the dominant ideology of the state. To paraphrase James Scott, their resistances generally constituted 'contests within hegemony', that is, struggles whose claims to justice were grounded in the dominant group's principles and moral categories.[6] As in the protest against the income tax in 1918, merchants often lodged their struggles in an idiom of *deference* and subordination. Rarely did businessmen seek in their resistance a more abstract 'liberation' by which they would dismantle the state, free themselves from the demands of their political overlords, and forge a consciousness completely independent of the ruling hegemony.

Thus, though changes that do follow the pattern described by Adas took place in the character of the larger polity, the merchants of Surat really did not make a transition from 'avoidance' to 'confrontation'. Instead, we see them making continuous adaptations to the development of the modern state, exploiting new openings which colonialism unintentionally provided for the restitution of their concerns, adapting the idiom of their protest to the changing ideology and structure of British rule, but never abandoning their low-profile, risk-averse methods of making their resistance felt. Through continued use of avoidance and other forms of non-confrontational protest, the merchants contended and reshaped their relations with the state while blocking the potential of more serious changes to the social order from below. Viewed from this perspective, the Non-Co-operation Movement of 1920–2 was not the culmination of progressively more aggressive resistances, but a temporary response to a particularly acute local crisis, one that restored less dramatic mechanisms the businessmen had previously possessed for defending their social integrity and their local place of privilege. For the merchants, the movement also served to forge political relations of subordination with a new set of important power-wielders, the leaders of the Indian National Congress.

THE MERCHANTS OF SURAT

The pre-eminent theme in history-writing on Surat has been its 'decline' as a commercial city. In the seventeenth century, the city was India's leading international port, a vibrant entrepôt containing a diverse set of mercantile groupings, both indigenous and foreign, and an overall population of two to four hundred thousand people. By the early twentieth century, the city had become a satellite of Bombay, had lost its cosmopolitan character, and had declined in population to slightly more than one hundred thousand persons. Yet, despite this seemingly major shift in its overall fortunes, Surat retained its significance as a centre of commerce and small-scale industry. The city also remained the home of a prosperous, if no longer fabulously rich, set of high-caste Hindu and Jain business families, largely from Bania or Brahman backgrounds. Continuing to exercise a dominant position in this community by virtue of its wealth, involvement in religious giving, and connections to the imperial rulers, was a small elite of especially prominent sheths (commercial magnates). The larger community of 'Brahman-Banias' included several thousand other families with varying degrees of wealth and prestige, families who generally lived lives of some comfort and status, especially in comparison to the poorer and more subordinate groups of petty traders, artisans, and labourers. These continuities in economic practice and social structure enable the historian of protest to partially set aside the relationship between resistance and socio-economic change, and focus on the adjustments of merchants to the changing character of the state.

Throughout these three centuries, the concerns of the Hindu–Jain businessmen tended to cluster around sustaining the ability of their family firms to reproduce themselves both economically and socially from one generation to another. Success in this effort depended largely upon the maintenance of the family *abru*. Even more than its English equivalent 'credit', the word abru suggested both the reliability of the family business firm in trade and its social reputation. The conflation of these two meanings in a single word was hardly a coincidence. In high-caste society, status and creditworthiness were inextricably related. A firm's ability to mobilize capital and to carry on transactions without actual exchanges of cash was based in part upon the family's general respectability.[7] At the same time, familial prestige was dependent upon the firm's perceived reputation for honouring its business commitments.

The determinants of abru, of course, were hardly constant. Nevertheless, there were some central elements in its composition that persisted over time. In terms of business dealings, these included the maintenance of secrecy in commercial dealings, the honouring of all financial commitments, and, for the banker, the ability to offer security to depositors. Socially, business families established their reputations through adherence to an austere set of community behaviour standards: restraint and frugality in personal lifestyle, observance of ahimsa (non-harm to living creatures), control over the sexuality of female family members, abstention from public conflicts, avoidance of polluting contacts with low-caste persons, and engagement in religious patronage to Vaishnava or Jain deities. The sustenance of abru in both of its interrelated senses depended highly on protecting the merchant domain from penetration by social inferiors or by the political overlords of the city.[8]

Throughout the period studied here, the merchants of Surat lived in state systems dominated by ruling groups from outside their community. In part because they had never been successful in developing an armed capacity, in part because mercantile values disapproved of the formal exercise of political power and the use of military might, Surati traders and bankers never attempted to assert rulership over their city directly. Instead, they abdicated this role to tiny groups of alien conquerors: the nobles of the Mughal Empire during the seventeenth and early eighteenth centuries; independent Mughal princes, Maratha warlords, and the officers of the East India Company during the latter half of the eighteenth century; the civil servants of the British Raj during the nineteenth and early twentieth centuries; and the leaders of the Congress Party after World War I.

Merchant relations with these political overlords have always been ambivalent. Concern with the preservation of wealth and family status, with the extension of trade, and with the sustenance of religious values consistently propelled mercantile figures to seek out alliances with the powerful extra-local authorities who controlled the port, enforced law and order, and collected revenues from the countryside. Association with the ruling group could also lead to the acquisition of honours and considerable material advantages. The rulers in turn often depended upon wealthy and prominent local figures in preserving the local peace, in financing the public administration, and even in collecting revenue from the countryside. All the major states in Surat's history have been built around partnerships of mutual interest between the mercantile community and members of the ruling group.

But these merchant–ruler alliances were also characterized by considerable uncertainty. Surat's overlords were drawn from groups whose foci of cultural identification lay outside the city and whose notions of prerogatives and obligations as rulers operated in tension with local norms. Traders could never be sure that their governors would respect their concern with maintaining family credit and prestige. There always existed the danger that the ruling group, motivated by external impulses and cultural imperatives, would seriously enter into merchant-controlled spheres of life and endanger the traders' abru and business practices. Resistance by merchants to these attempts played a major role in shaping the form of state–locality relations.

RESISTANCE AND THE PRECOLONIAL STATE

The Mughal Period

As Adas himself has suggested, the Mughal polity was a 'contest state'.[9] The Empire was characterized by a wide number of competing power centres, both in the imperial capital itself and in farflung district headquarters. The noblemen of this empire —the mansabdars—constantly contested each other at a variety of levels, though such competition may have been particularly acute in Surat because of the tremendous resources that poured through the city. Moreover, while each official was delegated a formal position in the local Mughal bureaucracy, the area of jurisidiction each enjoyed in practice was poorly delineated, and overlapping claims to wealth and power intensified internal conflict. Due to the imperfect control exerted by the empire over its officers, the actions of individual nobles tended to affect the lives of local residents of Surat more than the policies of the centre. The Emperor could, however, intervene in local disputes as a response to pleas from any contending party.

Mughal rule presented special insecurities for Hindu and Jain merchants. The perpetuation of family livelihoods, the sustenance of business credit, and the maintenance of social order depended upon the state's ability and willingness to provide protection. But it was often those best able to provide that protection—the agents of the Mughal government—who constituted the greatest source of political danger to the community. Officials of the Empire regarded the exaction of money, jewels, and other valuable items from the trading population as a legitimate prerogative of rulership. For bankers, repeated seizures of property could both cause immediate material damage and pose a danger to their reputations as individuals who honoured their commercial obligations and who kept deposits secure. When inspired by militant Islamicizing impulses, the actions of the noblemen could also threaten Hindu and Jain religious sensibilities.

The merchants, however, were often able to deflect these pressures by acquiring allies within the nobility and by playing members of the ruling group against each other. In their battles for power and influence, the mansabdars themselves always needed to gain the support of moneyed and influential local persons. Local sheths could supply the funds necessary for the expansion of a nobleman's household and armies and for the provision of services and gifts that might determine his advancement in the imperial hierarchy. Even the emperor himself relied heavily on finance from prominent Gujarati capitalists. Thus, even at times when they were threatened by the actions of a particular mansabdar, wealthy magnates were often able to find other noble-patrons who would provide protective services. A number of local businessmen built up longstanding ties with powerful Mughal sponsors.[10] Traders with particularly close bonds to influential mansabdars could escape arbitrary exactions, gain exemptions from most forms of taxes, and acquire protection from sudden invasions of their households.

Such merchant–mansabdar relations were generally grounded in an idiom of social deference. Merchants communicated their supplication to the Mughals by payment of tribute, by attendance in local and imperial courts, and by other forms of symbolic expression. It would be mistaken to view such deferential behaviour simply as a pose calculated to fool members of the governing elite. Such an interpretation would assume that merchants had less commitment to the patron–client bond than their rulers and that they could conceive of their relations to the state outside deferential terms. It is more profitable to see deference as a cultural adaptation to the rule of outsiders by which merchants were able to convert relations characterized by inequalities in power and by conflicting cultural concerns into moral relations based upon mutual expectation. The businessmen continuously offered to their rulers acknowledgement of their subordinate status but at the same time held the ruling elite accountable to a set of obligations to its client-subjects inherent in its own avowed norms.[11]

The development of such deferential ties never completely eliminated the danger of assaults by the ruling group on merchant life; local businessmen still regularly found a need to engage in a range of defensive behaviours that served to check demands and initiatives from above. But even as they participated in actions of social protest, the merchants were rarely willing to abandon the ethical leverage that deferential relationships with their powerful political patrons gave them. In fact, techniques of denial and avoidance often allowed businessmen to invoke their own position of clientage as a special reason that the ruling group should hear their pleas for justice.

The merchants' means of defending their interests fell into two main categories. First, there were what James Scott has called 'everyday' techniques of resistance, that is, small-scale, individual steps to obstruct the nobility, such as the non-payment or incomplete payment of taxes, false compliance with state regulations, evasive speech, the maintenance of tight controls over information about family resources and business practice, and even migration on an individual basis to some other trading centre where more satisfactory protective services were available from some other patron.[12] Concealment appears to have been a particularly important defence mechanism. The Banias of Gujarat possessed a special reputation for evasiveness in their speech and action. They often hid their wealth and lived in spartan households with minimal furnishings, thus making it impossible for outsiders to estimate the size of their seizable or taxable assets. Seventeenth-century English travellers in fact attributed the simplicity of the merchant lifestyle not to Hindu and Jain traditions of non-possession and self-abnegation but to fear of Mughal seizures;[13] it might be more correct to say that these traditions and the efforts to evade Mughal pressures reinforced one another. Such day-to-day methods of blocking the mansabdars' efforts to extract greater resources from the community were widespread in local society, and seem to have been grounded in a folk culture that regarded these measures as legitimate means of protecting the mercantile domain. Cumulatively these behaviours placed serious constraints on what members of the ruling group actually could accomplish in extracting resources from the business community. But these actions never offered a symbolic challenge to the nobility. In Gramscian terms, we may think of them as being informed by a 'contradictory consciousness'— a fragmentary outlook that implicitly denied important demands made by the overlords and that may have even provided the merchants with a sense of identity and solidarity in resistance but which nonetheless did not constitute a fully articulated challenge to the state. Through such forms of struggle, a merchant family could hope to maintain its low profile and to sustain protective relationships it had built up through deferential behaviour. Unfortunately, since much of this resistance was clandestine, it is difficult to find sufficient evidence to allow a more thorough exploration.

Less common, but better documented, were incidents of collective protest. Collective action was undertaken only as a last resort, usually when the rulers overstepped the bounds of 'everyday' oppression and exploitation, and entered into areas of socio-economic life the merchant community considered its own preserve. Such protests always averted direct confrontations with the ruling group as a whole. Surati merchants recognized perhaps that they lacked the armed capacity to establish and protect their own city-states, and they did not want to risk unleashing forces from deeper within urban society that might endanger commercial continuity and their position of social pre-eminence. More effective in achieving these limited goals than confrontational protest were strategies of avoidance, including threats to leave the city and actual mass migration. In Mughal times, such acts were entirely consistent with the larger posture of deference that commercial magnates had adopted through other aspects of their symbolic behaviour. Through such acts of denial, the merchants attempted to induce members of the nobility to hear their claims to justice and intervene on their behalf.

In 1616, for instance, the merchants acted collectively against the judge of the customs house, who, in his eagerness to increase revenue collections, had used violence against a community leader. According to East India Company records, local Banias organized a major protest against the judge that involved the entire community leaving Surat temporarily:

> the whole multitude assembled shut up their shops and (*as their custom*), after a general complaint to the Governor, left the city, pretending to go to the Court for justice, but with much fair usage and fairer promises were fetched back by Abram Chan [the governor of Surat], who joining with them informed his master [the emperor Jahangir] of many insolencies committed by this peevish Customer, which, with your Lordship's complaint, is generally observed to be the cause of his expulsion [italics mine].[14]

If the Company account is to be trusted, the methods employed by the merchants in this case—the shutting down of commerce, the threat of leaving the city, and appeals to the emperor or some other powerful nobleman—were already well-established means of seeking justice at the time of the event. Apparently, the governor regarded the merchants' actions as legitimate forms of self-expression rather than as acts of defiance against the Empire that needed to be suppressed. His willingness to back the business community was critical to its eventual victory. The individual officer was removed, but the larger structure of Mughal rule had never been challenged.[15]

Though other episodes of similar behaviour exist,[16] the most interesting example occurred in 1669. In that year, probably as a response to edicts from the emperor Aurangzeb calling for the zealous promotion of Islam, a qazi (Muslim judge) of Surat tried to convert several leading Hindu merchants to his religion, exacted huge sums of money from the community upon the threat of destroying Hindu and Jain temples, and even circumcised one Hindu clerk (who committed suicide in response). The merchants of the city, angered by these assaults on their religion and social dignity, began to consider leaving town in protest. At one point, five representatives of the community even went to ask Gerald Aungier, chief of the East India Company in Surat, whether the English could provide the merchants protection if they were to flee to Bombay. Aungier 'saw a great advantage might accrue' to the new settlement to the south, but decided that the Company simply could not risk antagonizing Aurangzeb. He advised the merchants to 'convey themselves at present to Ahmadavad [a major city in northern Gujarat] and from thence make their generall humble requests to the King, who would certainly ease their present burthen in some degree'. Soon thereafter, the leading organization of the merchants in the city, the Mahajan, resolved that all the traders should shut down their shops and leave the city. Eight thousand departed for Bharuch, about forty miles to the north, promising that they would 'go to the king for justice'.

The qazi, in a rage, asked the Governor of the city to stop this act of flight. The Governor, however, took the side of the Banias, saying 'they are Kings subjects and may travell in his country where they please'. In Surat, all business ground to a complete halt. According to English Factory Records:

In the interim, the people of Surat suffered great want, for the Bannians having bound themselves under severe penalties not to open any of their shops without order from their Mahager of Generall Councill, there was not any provisions to bee got; the tanksell [mint] and customhouse shut, no mony to bee procured, soe much as for house expences, much less for trade, which was wholy at a stand; and so it will be until their returne.[17]

Soon the situation had become so serious that the continuity of the city's trade was in question. Bankers and other wealthy traders considered 'calling in their stocks and (according to the custome of the country) burying the greatest part under ground'. These measures undoubtedly produced extreme discomfort for the mansabdars who depended upon local traders for their supplies and upon the local shroffs for the continued supply of finance.

In Bharuch, under the safe protection of local officials, the merchants sent several memorials to Aurangzeb, 'using all probable means to justify' themselves to the king. There they were also courted extensively by the Governor of Ahmedabad who asked them to settle permanently in his city. Finally, after nearly two months, a letter came from the court, reprimanding the qazi, and, in the words of the English documents, guaranteeing the merchants 'their safety and more freedome in their religion'. The merchants returned to Surat and resumed their commerce 'to the great satisfaction of the Governor, officers, and all the inhabitants of the town [presumably with the exception of the qazi]'.[18]

Unfortunately there is no record of the content of the traders' letters to the Emperor. Nevertheless, it is possible to construct something of the idiom of this protest from the merchants' own behaviour. The businessmen seem to have regarded the emperor as a special patron, a figure who could dispense a personal justice, even if such an action would directly contradict his avowed policy of furthering Islam. The merchants no doubt followed Aungier's advice that they make their request in their 'generall humble' terms, an approach that possibly involved the presentation of at least some token of tribute. The merchants also sought out and received offers of support from other potential noble-patrons in Surat, Bharuch and Ahmedabad. They clearly recognized within their struggle the crucial importance of attaining powerful protectors and accepted their subordination to these overlords while pleading for justice. Their protest was aimed at reconstituting the terms of their political dependence, at providing firm bounds on the actions of specific members of the ruling group, but not at replacing the Mughal political order.

Such examples suggest that the merchants already possessed well-established means of expressing their resistances long before the advent of constitutional democracy. The episodes also suggest that use of avoidance tactics could be extremely effective in limiting threats to the merchants' collective integrity posed by Mughal noblemen. If the business community could forge a solidarity within itself, and if it could gain the support of powerful persons within the ruling group, then the chances of success were quite good.

In part, the efficacy of seventeenth-century avoidance protest stemmed from the plethora of potential alternative patrons present within the contest state and on the ability of the Emperor himself to step in when his local officials seriously offended merchant sensibilities. In part the success of the merchants stemmed from the fact that the form of their actions possessed a certain legitimacy within the worldview of the Mughals. In contrast to armed revolts and violent uprisings, which challenged the aura of military expansion so critical to the authority of the emperor,[19] acts such as the closing of shops, collective exit from the city, and appeals for personal justice to the emperior or a nobleman did not constitute a symbolic affront to the ruling group as a whole. Apparently much of the Mughal nobility interpreted migration of a group from its place of residence as evidence of the failure on the part of the individual officer to meet the needs of his subjects, not as an assault on the Empire. Collective flight highlighted the oppressive behaviour of the specific mansabdar to his superiors, often inducing the superior to intervene. Protest rooted in an idiom of denial and personal deference thus could be quite useful in reshaping merchant–ruler relations on a more satisfactory ground.

The Early Eighteenth Century

Tactics which proved so successful in the seventeenth century, however, were far less fruitful during the early eighteenth century, when the imperial position of the Mughal polity had weakened. From very early in the century it had become clear that the imperial centre could not prevent Maratha warriors from making advances into the Gujarati countryside, nor exert any control over the competition for power between mansabdars within the city. Local nobles continued to seek the legitimation of their statuses in the Mughal capital, and spent large sums of money to obtain imperial sanads. Increasingly, however, the Emperor merely sanctioned positions obtained entirely through local struggles.

It is doubtful that Mughal nobles in Surat regarded the growing autonomy of their position entirely in a favourable light. Increasingly they were cut off from their most important external source of funds, their land grants (jagirs), due to unsettled conditions in the interior. Moreover, the Marathas, through heavy military pressure on the city, had obtained rights to a quarter of the customs revenue of the port. Since the emperor was now completely unable to check the conflict between members of the nobility, individual mansabdars needed to maintain larger armies just to preserve any local authority. In order to sustain their soldiers and maintain the lifestyle expected of them, the mansabdars now placed increasing pressure on the local trading population. Ashin Das Gupta has demonstrated convincingly that shifts in power from one nobleman to another did not ease the demands placed on the merchants; the growing inflexibility of the political order was more a product of the larger structural situation than of the personalities of individual rulers.[20]

The changed political environment thus heightened the insecurity inherent in the merchants' position. Not only were businessmen subjected to increasing oppression; they now could no longer take recourse to the emperor for justice with any hope of success. Some Muslim merchants responded to the weakening of Mughal power and to their own growing needs for protection by establishing personal armies. But most merchants, particularly Hindu traders, became more vulnerable than ever to the actions of local potentates.

Despite the inflexibility of the political order, Surat's merchants adopted more confrontational means of making their grievances felt only very slowly. An excellent but little known article by Das Gupta demonstrates the efforts of merchants to check a particularly rapacious governor during the late 1720s and early 1730s through the stoppage of commerce, threats to leave the city, and other tactics of denial. Only when these methods had failed did local businessmen back an armed coup engineered by a rival mansabdar and members of several of the European companies.[21] This coup clearly was more than an attempt to redress a particular grievance; it was an effort to alter significantly the local shape of power. The trading community in this case felt compelled to step outside the idiom of supplication to the local governor and to actively seek the governor's replacement.

This episode warns us against any simple attempt to stereotype the merchants as inherently non-violent. Surat's businessmen resorted to armed action only when the situation had become desperate and only after they had used strategies of avoidance and petition repeatedly and unsuccessfully. And even in the midst of the armed revolt, the purpose of the businessmen was to install a new Mughal prince in the governorship, not to seize power for themselves. They recognized that they did not possess the military capability or the political authority needed to establish and sustain a merchant city-state. They simply sought to ease their own oppression through the support of a new candidate for local power. Moreover, they continued to work within a Mughal idiom, seeking sanction for their candidate for the governorship from Delhi. Unfortunately for the merchants, the new governor faced the same fiscal dilemmas as his predecessor, and again fell heavily upon the community to meet his expenses. The absence of a more satisfactory set of sponsors with a resource base outside the city meant that collective action was doomed largely to reproduce not only the merchants' continued subordination but a set of conditions they deemed extremely oppressive.

The great change of the late eighteenth century was the rise of just such a set of potential sponsors: the servants of the East India Company. By mid century, the English had ceased to be merely participants in the trade of the city; they had become a western Indian power. The growing prosperity of Bombay, which was under the control of the Company, now provided the English with a secure base and significant resources to launch themselves into local politics. Then, in 1759, came the 'Castle Revolution', when, with the help of at least some of the city's traders, the Company took control over the Surat castle, leaving the Governor, Mia Achan, in charge of the city administration. The Company reserved to itself the right to appoint Mia Achan's successors.

To many of the city's merchants the British as patrons were far superior to any member of the Mughal aristocracy. The nobility during this period continued to make heavy demands on local residents, establishing hundreds of new duties on trade. In addition, the civil administration had proved incapable of maintaining law and order, failing in the last decades of the century to prevent a series of attacks by lower-class Muslims against prosperous traders and bankers. The officers of the Company, by contrast, depended for their incomes less on squeezing the merchants than on trading with them, and thus tended to employ their power to ensure the continuity of commerce. Both indigenous and European traders desired to eliminate personal exactions, town duties, barriers to the flow of currency, and other obstacles to a freer trade. The self-conception of the Englishmen as defenders of merchant rights against the injustices of the Nawab and British rhetoric decrying local instability and espousing the obstructions placed on commerce may have struck a responsive chord among some local men involved in business endeavour.[22]

While recent work by Michelgugliemo Torri warns against any attempt to suggest that the Banias *as a whole* supported British ascendancy,[23] a number of important businessmen did align themselves with the Company on an individual basis. Beginning in the 1740s, a few Surati sheths asked for and received the status of 'protected merchants'. When the English gained control over the castle, their numbers grew. Lakshmi Subramanian has demonstrated that the city's bankers provided the English with the capital necessary to finance both trade and military expansion throughout the later eighteenth century.[24] The bonds between merchant and English officer were often cemented symbolically as well through tribute and exchange of gifts.[25] Some merchants obtained English protection through migration to Bombay, an act that may have been in part a form of personal resistance. Through such steps, taken often on an individual basis, the trading community began to shift its political allegiances and to construct an 'Anglo-Bania order' that would eventually transform itself into colonial rule.

Merchants particularly sought out the protective services of the Company in moments of community action, when traders perceived a collective threat to their position stemming from the Mughal nobility. The most dramatic and best documented of these actions occurred in 1795.[26] Significantly the issue involved on this occasion was the inability of the Nawab to protect the businessmen against violence from the city's underclass. On 6 August, in response to the imprisonment of a crier at a local mosque, a large number of Muslim artisans, labourers, and petty traders attacked the neighbourhoods of high-caste residents, looting shops and houses, tearing account books of bankers, destroying temples and damaging images of Hindu gods, and, in one household, stripping female members of their clothes and seizing their jewellery. After the riots, the business community continued to fear for its safety and the honour of its women. Bankers worried about damage to their credit, as they stated in a petition to the English:

The entire belief that property is perfectly secure in the house of a shroff forms what is called his credit [undoubtedly, a translation of abru], which more than actual money is the instrument of his dealing and the greater source of his profits. Those who come to trade in this city either bring their bills on the shroffs or lodge the produce of their goods with them during their stay from many parts of India . . . for all these sums deposited, no receipts are given, the books of the shroffs and the opinion of their faith and substance are the total dependence of the people who deal with them. From this it will be felt how much their credit depends on the belief of the effectual protection by the Government they love [i.e. that of the Company].[27]

The document went on to argue that even the credit of up-country traders dealing in cotton was at risk, since they carried the bills of exchange of Surati shroffs. In short, a wide range of the merchants' core preoccupations was threatened by the insurgency of the Muslim underclasses.

In petitions they wrote to the East India Company, the leaders of the community made clear that they believed much of the blame for the riots lay with the Mughal nobility's failure to provide protection. Community headmen were particularly upset that the local administration had refused to issue them a written guarantee of the future safety of the merchants and their property. The petitioners even considered one leading Mughal nobleman to have been personally involved in instigating the Muslim crowd.

The merchants adopted a two-pronged approach in dealing with the crisis. First, they employed a series of defensive strategies similar to ones used in previous protests. Immediately after the riots, they resolved to shut their shops and refuse to carry on their businesses until they had received assurances of protection from the Nawab. The Mahajan issued strictures to all shopkeepers, warning them to keep their businesses closed. Industrial production ground to a complete halt, food was unavailable, and finance could not be obtained anywhere in the town. At one point, the merchants even threatened to leave the city altogether. If their security was not guaranteed, community leaders complained, 'we who wholly depend on it [protection] for our maintenance must in course follow [in flight], although reluctantly, from our houses and property being here and from the natural attachment we have to our birth place and to the sanctity of the holy river Tapi.'[28]

At the same time, the traders pleaded with the English to provide protection, most dramatically in a rather lengthy petition written about a week after the riots. In this document, they claimed to be 'unarmed and unguarded', 'relying wholly for safety on the protection of the English flag'. They reviewed the history of the English in Surat, contending that the Company had attained control of the castle in 1759 'at the request and advice of the inhabitants for the general good and quiet of the place [Surat]', and that, at the time, the British had promised to provide the merchants with protection in return for their support. They went on to state:

Your petitioners as the principal trading inhabitants of this city have ever considered themselves as under the special protection of the company, referring themselves to the English chief for the time being even in ordinary occasions amongst themselves relative either to money disputes or to businesses of their caste and religion, but particularly applying to him in cases of grievance, or apprehension either committed by the Mogul Governor, or any of his numerous officers who all sanction their actions with his name, and whose oppression would soon dispeople the town unless awed and checked by the authority of the English chief as governour of the Mogul's castle which alone gives him a general right of protection to all the inhabitants.[29]

Thus, by asserting that the position of the English was based upon a sort of historically established social contract, by appealing to the self-image of Englishmen as guarantors of the life and property of Indians against Mughal despots, and by evoking the symbolism of the flag, the magnates hoped to persuade the Bombay government to provide better protection and possibly to assume direct control over the city. Through their pleas, the petitioners translated their concerns with abru, with the maintenance of social order, and with their religious practice—the central concerns of their cultural order—into the terms of the Englishmen's professed values, and then attempted to compel the Company's servants to hold to these principles. Taken as a whole, the tone of the petition was openly deferential but implicitly demanding. In evoking their sense of dependence on the Company, the merchants staked out a claim to expanded patronage in a period of crisis. But in this process of pleading for English support against the governor's policies, they also symbolically transferred some of their loyalty from the Nawab to the British and constructed their own moral subordination to the Company.

These appeals actually had considerable effect. The English responded by assuring the merchants that 'no exertion in our power shall be wanting for protection of their persons and property in common with the rest of the inhabitants who since the acquisition of the Castle have been deemed virtually under protection of the Company'. The Surat Council soon issued a report criticizing the Nawab for failing to act effectively and recommending that a military unit of the Company be established in the city. While the Bombay Government initially rejected this suggestion on the grounds of expense, it did pressure the governor to be more vigorous in his protective role.[30] Then, only five years later, the Company totally eliminated the formal political power of the Nawab's successor. The inability of the Mughal administration to preserve local law and order served as the most important justification for this step. It was the duty of the Company, Lord Wellesley, Governor-General of India, argued at the time, 'to protect the persons and properties of the inhabitants of that city [Surat]' and to furnish 'a just, wise, and efficient administration'.[31]

The political goals of the merchants in 1795 were quite radical in comparison to those of 1669. They challenged the authority of the old Mughal nobility, which had proven itself unable or unwilling to meet their concerns, and to strengthen their alliances with the English. At times, their petitions seemed almost to call directly for the assumption of British rule. The means they adopted to accomplish their ends, however, were hardly novel. They sought to establish political leverage largely by engaging in their traditional techniques of denial; they appealed for justice to a set of potential patrons in the language of those patrons; they exploited tensions between competitors for power in the city in order to defend themselves against dangers to their abru from above and below. The greater effectiveness of the 1795 actions as opposed to those of 1732 was largely due to the close links that the merchants had built up with the English through trade and banking, and to the improved ability of the Company to take action.

Ultimately, the community's resistance contributed to the development of the power and authority of a new set of alien rulers who again could not be counted on to act consistently in the merchants' interest. The protestors in this instance, however, sought not political 'freedom' but the re-establishment of relatively stable relations of clientage. By placing pressure on a powerful set of political overlords, they acted to preserve their personal safety, the continuity of their commerce, their credit, and their own social dominance in the city at a time when all these were seriously endangered by the action of Muslim subalterns.

Thus businessmen in the precolonial period repeatedly took recourse to collective actions of avoidance in order to check threats to their community. The goals of such action were not consistently restorative in a political sense. Though the actors in the seventeenth-century examples cited above attempted to gain redress of their grievances through established procedures of seeking justice within Mughal rule, those of 1732 tried eventually to overthrow the local governor, and those of 1795 seemingly sought to replace Mughal sovereignty with that of Company rule. Yet in each case, the traders hoped to gain the patronage of a warrior group that possessed access to armed force rather than to establish their own autonomous power. In each case, they appealed to these overlords in an idiom that they hoped the overlords would find compelling. By paying deference to the rulers (or potential rulers) and by evoking the values and self-conception of the ruling group, the merchants sought to establish entitlement to protective services. But they also subordinated themselves formally to these figures, constructing the hegemony of imperial rule in the very process of resisting state efforts to control their lives.

PROTEST AND THE COLONIAL STATE

The Nineteenth Century

The advent of the colonial era by no means spelled a sudden transformation in the character of the state. The need of the new rulers for finance from indigenous bankers, their dependence upon powerful mediating figures in the effort to maintain local stability, limitations in their knowledge and understanding of the peoples over whom they now ruled, continued difficulties in communication until the establishment of the telegraph and railways, and constant worries about the potential for rebellion, all meant that the imposition of colonial control was a gradual, hesitant process. Nevertheless, with time, the consolidation of the British Raj did make possible the slow supersession of the 'contest' state by a form of government based, at least at its highest levels, in a bureaucratic model of political authority. During the first decades after the replacement of the Nawab's administration, the East India Company tightened its control over its representatives in western India, gradually converting them from swashbuckling entrepreneurs into comfortable civil servants receiving regular and substantial salaries from above. Better pay, improvements in communication, and the establishment of clearer chains of command now made possible a firmer integration of the local officer into an administration headquartered in Calcutta. Among the handful of British civil servants actually present in Surat, the lines of authority and the areas of jurisdiction were drawn rigorously, with all local administrators formally subordinate to the Collector. Accompanying these changes was the emergence of a new professional ethos emphasizing the importance of committed service to the Raj, and denigrating conspicuous consumption, the use of office for the acquisition of personal fortune, or the development of potentially compromising personal relationships with the Indians. The success of this integrative process can no doubt be exaggerated. Underneath the officials of the Indian Civil Service was a larger body of poorly paid native administrators whose conception of office had not undergone a similar transformation. But for the merchants, 'plunder' and other behaviours by individual members of the ruling group were becoming less a source of political insecurity than policies issuing from the provincial and central governments. These changes had a profound effect on the form of mercantile resistance, gradually closing some channels of protest while opening others in an often unconscious manner.

For much of the first half of the nineteenth century, the merchants felt little need for collective action. State demands on the community were probably lighter than at any other time in the city's history. Motivated by a desire to foster 'free trade' throughout its dominion, the East India Company eliminated most of the duties on commerce imposed by eighteenth century rulers. It also deliberately refrained from imposing new forms of direct taxation.[32] Heavy British levies on the country-side during this time were undoubtedly responsible for pro-ducing a major decline in the prosperity of Surat's business classes, but these imperial policies stimulated little collective response from the traders and bankers. Merchant protest had never been a means of advancing just any interest of the com-munity; it had instead primarily been a way of blocking state attempts to penetrate the inner domains of mercantile life.

Around the middle of the century, however, the colonial agenda for Indian cities became increasingly ambitious. On the one hand, urban centres began to assume a more central place in the revenue structure of the Raj. On the other, civil servants began to consider the application of English munici-pal ideals to Indian towns. They urged the adoption of land surveys and of bylaws to control unsanitary practices and regulate the use of 'public' space. They formulated plans to improve urban health, the flow of commerce, police services and education in an effort to meet Victorian standards of civic responsibility. They thought of providing cities with roads and bridges, public parks and water fountains, clock towers and drainage systems, libraries and schools. All of these schemes cost money, and since the Government of India was generally un-willing to strain its own budget, it increasingly sought funds from local sources. In most cities, the imperial administration set up municipalities composed of government officials and 'leading citizens' to develop urban services and to tax the local populace.

In Surat, most residents regarded the British agenda of 'improvement' as an imposition that threatened their control over crucial areas of their lives. There was at first little indi-genous interest in acquiring most of the services British civil servants felt that the city needed. Surat's property-owners were rarely ready to pay for services that benefited neighbourhoods other than their own. Sanitary schemes won little acceptance anywhere in the town; since few Suratis subscribed to the germ theory of disease causation, there was no felt need for cleaner sources of water, drainage works or disinfection projects. At the same time there was considerable resentment of the means the municipality used in promoting urban health. The local body passed a whole series of bylaws regulating construction, unsanitary conditions, 'offensive and dangerous trades', and the use of land—laws which in theory required observance by everyone. A city survey fixed urban land rights, suddenly defining large areas of the city as 'public space' not to be utilized for private purposes. The municipality flirted dangerously with placing restrictions on caste feasts and with exterminating stray cattle and dogs. During epidemics, it sought direct access to the homes and persons of the merchants, entering the houses of members of the community with sweepers of untouchable caste background to carry out disinfection efforts, and, in the case of the plague of 1896–7, compelling some residents to relocate to temporary camps outside the city until the danger had passed. District Collector T. C. Hope, president of the Surat Municipality during a period of especially extensive reform between 1867 and 1871, would remark of his local experiences in promoting 'reform': 'municipal government can never be a popular government in the sense that it is liked by the people because the very *raison d'être* of the Municipality is a perpetual war with those problems which are normal with the mass of the population, and are either followed or looked on with favour by too many of the upper classes.'[33] Many local merchants might have agreed that a silent 'war' was indeed going on, one in which they had to be constantly vigilant in efforts to guard their domain.

The most broadly resented imperial initiatives were new taxes. The municipality raised new cesses to pay for the costs of urban services; the provincial government sought new revenues to expand its resource base. The colonial administration, moreover, hoped to replace town duties—the traditional form of taxation—with more direct taxes such as income taxes, water rates, house taxes and licence taxes, feeling that the former constituted an obstruction to the full development of commerce. Surat's traders and other high-caste residents clearly viewed direct taxation as an unwanted intrusion. Direct levies could prove especially damaging to a merchant's *abru* since such cesses involved entry into local households and shops to determine property values as well as detailed assessments of income, wealth, and business practice that could become public. The apportionment of taxation, moreover, did not take into account the status of the taxpayer. Undoubtedly the colonial preoccupation with 'improvement' involved systematic penetration into a domain previously occupied and controlled by the trading community.[34]

At first glance, it would also appear that the merchants had lost their most effective means of resisting this colonial agenda. Nineteenth-century shifts in the character of the state incapacitated some older collective forms of registering protest. Once bureaucratic principles of government had hardened, for instance, traders could rarely hope to reverse major policies of the imperial administration by appeal to the rivals of local civil servants. State policy issued increasingly from the province or the centre, leaving individual officers with little authority to overturn the most objectionable measures. Changes in state structure also made migration futile as a tactic of resistance. If traders were to leave town in protest against some measure, they would very likely have found the same or similar regulations in effect in their new location.

The difficulties of collective resistance through avoidance also became greater because the British increasingly viewed such tactics as the closing of shops and the temporary non-observance of state regulations as deliberate attacks on their authority. In this outlook, they were generally mistaken, since traders took such steps, as during the seventeenth century, to highlight their own appeals to the rulers' personal sense of justice, not to question the legitimacy of Empire. When such action violated the sanctity of 'the rule of law', that is, when the merchants withheld their compliance with some new regulation until their objections had been heard, civil administrators quickly jumped to the conclusion that the protest was a sign of a possible insurrection to come and began to prepare themselves to use force to quash the movement. Use of violence by the state could in turn lead to acts of counter-violence by artisans and petty traders resentful of this interference with established procedures for registering dissent, acts that could threaten local trade and the privileged place of merchants and bankers in the city.

In 1860, for instance, local merchants organized opposition to a new income tax by deciding to close their shops and refuse to pay their taxes; the government quickly broke up the effort by charging protesting crowds with mounted police and imprisoning many key participants.[35] In 1878, collective resistance took an even more serious turn, this time in response to a new licence tax on all commercial establishments in the Bombay Presidency. For western Indian traders, the new measure combined the two worst features of colonial taxation: higher levies and detailed forms requiring the provision of much information about business practice. Surat's movement against the measure at first took a peaceful form. Leadership issued largely from a handful of English-educated professionals, who ran a campaign against the tax in the local press, and from the headmen of the merchant community, including the Nagarsheth (the leader of the Jains) and the sheth of the Mahajan. On the 27th of February, these two magnates issued a public notice asking the citizens of Surat to attend a meeting in order to draft a petition to the British government. The notice objected to the new measure in the language of constitutional justice, complaining that the provincial administration had passed this law without consulting the local population. It also argued that the regulation unfairly discriminated against businessmen since wealthy professionals would be exempt from the new taxation. Finally, it suggested that the current economic circumstances made the traders unable to pay: 'in this time of acute inflation, we poor merchants . . . are brought under this heavy burden by the government in its wisdom.' The purposes of the meeting, the two sheths argued, would be to inform the government of 'the sufferings and sentiments' of the people of Surat.[36]

The traders soon added strategies of denial that included violations of colonial law, patterning their protest after a similar movement that had taken place in Surat in 1844. When the government began a house to house enquiry to prepare the licence tax forms, the traders refused to co-operate, antagonized in part by the extreme zealousness of the Indian officials collecting the information. On 1 April, prominent sheths and representatives from almost 'every class and caste' resolved that all business should cease and that community sanctions should be employed against those who violated these orders. The merchants made a special effort to prevent European officers from obtaining supplies in the bazaar; a few citizens even began to withdraw monies from government savings banks and to cash in government currency notes. The intent of the movement was primarily to highlight the businessmen's pleas for justice before individual British officers, and to induce local officials to suspend the act temporarily while forwarding the citizenry's objections to the provincial and imperial administrations. It is not clear whether the merchants ever explicitly demanded the permanent cancellation of the measure.

British civil servants, however, tended to interpret the merchants' behaviour as a challenge to the state. The district magistrate, E. C. K. Olivant, simply did not have the authority to suspend a measure sent down from above, nor did he have any inclination to do so. Rather than view the protest as a legitimate procedure for attaining justice, he regarded the whole affair as an attempt to 'coerce' him to revoke the measure. He informed the protestors—to quote his later report to the Bombay government—that 'I should [i.e. I will] rigourously punish the first breach of the peace or any criminal offences, that I should hold the chief people responsible, who had brought about the closing of the shops, and that I would not put off the operations of the new Act for a single hour in consequence of their demonstration.'[37] He called upon the most prominent magnates to order all the merchants to reopen their shops. When it became clear that this effort had failed, he decided to import grain into the city via rail and then had sheds erected in the city square to sell grain to those with no remaining stocks in their homes. A unit of sepoys was also made ready.

The opening of the government grain shops, which broke the hold merchants had imposed over the supply of essential commodities to the city, appears to have been the immediate precipitant of the ensuing riot. Seemingly, what now motivated the larger crowd was less resentment against the licence tax than anger that traditionally accepted means of expressing dissent were being undermined by the government. Artisans, labourers and petty traders from the outlying neighbourhoods of the city —most of whom would not have been affected directly by the licence tax at all—attacked the goods yard at the railway station armed with bamboo sticks in efforts to bring the importation of grain to a halt. When this attempt had been repulsed, the crowd travelled on through the city, forcing the nearby Gulam Baba Mills to close down and later assaulting an English police officer. Soldiers arrived to rescue the European only to be met by a hail of stones and brickbats. The sepoys then fired at the rioters, killing two and wounding several others. A handful of 'agitators' believed to be responsible for the protest were soon arrested, including one prominent lawyer who was dragged off in public disgrace, handcuffed together with a low-caste Dubla. A few dozen participants in the 'mob' drawn from the lower-classes were also charged with creating disturbances.

As the government determinedly resorted to repressive action in suppressing the protest, and as a rising of subaltern groups began to take shape in response, the merchants were caught in an increasingly awkward position. If they were to abandon the collective action, not only would they give up their most powerful means of expressing dissatisfaction, they could lose their standing in local society as well. But violence would threaten local order and bring into question the businessmen's ties of clientage with British officials. For some time, the leading merchants tried to stay on both sides of the fence. Before civil administrators, they continued to maintain their posture of deference. On 3 April, when the Collector called the traders' leaders to his office, many left ready to reopen their shops. But that night, with the Collector absent, they resolved to 'stand firmly by the compact which all classes had been induced to enter into'. The next day, according to one British official, the 'leading merchants held aloof, or made professions of assistance but did nothing and urgently pressed that the enactment in question remain a dead letter'. Finally, after the riots and the police firing, high-caste traders and bankers abandoned their support of the movement, which then soon collapsed. The protest had taken directions they had not intended originally, and was increasingly threatening their position in local society.[38]

This episode illustrates particularly well the dilemma of merchant collective action during the late nineteenth century. Traders entered into protest not to challenge British rule, but to contest particular government policies. They remained willing to couch their appeals for justice in the terms of colonial norms. But since British officers were ready to interpret such steps as the closing of shops and the withdrawal of services to the administration as signs of subversive activity, traders clearly risked harming their protective relationships by following traditional patterns of resistance. Moreover, once frustrations spread deeper into local society, the danger of discontent taking a more militant direction grew, bringing both the continuity of commerce and of merchant dominance in local society into danger. These conditions created a serious ambivalence within the community about the continued viability of collective acts of denial as means of conveying dissent.

But did this mean the merchants were now faced with a choice between quiescence and violent confrontation? Had, as Adas's model might suggest, the changing character of the state under colonialism neutralized most indigenous defence mechanisms short of violent opposition? The answer is clearly that it had not. Businessmen still retained a number of means for defending their interests that stopped short of direct confrontation. British rule in fact had closed some older channels the merchants had possessed for making their voices felt but it had opened other channels, sometimes unintentionally.

First of all, merchants were not without influence in the late-nineteenth-century colonial order. A small number of especially prominent magnates and their publicists successfully established themselves as critical collaborators of the British. Through involvement in public philanthropy, imperial ritual, municipal affairs, and other activities considered meritorious by Victorian values, these notables built up symbolic as well as material ties with the civil servants who occupied the highest rungs of the local civil administration. District Collectors regularly consulted these individuals on most matters of importance. A few of the magnates even won titles for their service to government and their dedication to Empire. Such individuals may have been reluctant to associate themselves with public movements against municipal or imperial policy, but they could use their position behind the scenes to blunt the impact of reform for the trading community. On the municipality, for instance, councillors were often successful in blocking measures of improve-

ment either by raising objections in meetings, by raising legal
technicalities and referring regulations back to committees, or
even by failing to attend meetings. They could also affect the
the ultimate form of local regulations initially proposed by
high-ranking British officers. An excellent example was the
house tax, whose schedule was skewed regressively so that
substantial merchants and other prosperous city-dwellers
actually paid a significantly smaller proportion of their property values than poorer householders. Councillors who became honorary magistrates often let off violators of bylaws
without punishment and reduced house assessments for their
friends, caste-fellows and kinspeople. Civil administrators found
such behaviour frustrating. But since they were usually unable
to prove any legal violation and since they were dependent on
the support of these same individuals in maintaining local
order, they often grudgingly accepted what they regarded as
footdragging and petty 'corruption'.[39]

Residents of the city also ignored or complied incompletely
with many regulations on the books. Surati traders violated bylaws extensively; they regularly kept their tax payments in
arrears, a behaviour that plagued municipal finances throughout the late nineteenth century. In most cases, such steps were
uncoordinated efforts taken by individual families, but collectively they could nonetheless assume very serious proportions.
On each occasion when the municipality instituted direct taxes
—the cesspool tax in the 1870, the water rate in the late 1890s,
and the sanitary cess in the early 1900s—it found itself facing
widespread, semi-organized boycotts of the new levies.[40] When
the local body required the citizens to acquire land-titles in a
survey of the city taken in 1867—a measure which fixed property rights and defined vast areas of the city as public space—
large numbers of householders simply refused to pay for their
titles. Nearly ten years later, the city survey was still not complete, despite the fact that no formal protest had ever really
taken shape.[41]

Such everyday resistance may have only rarely forced
municipal councillors or colonial administrators to rescind
objectionable policies that had already been formally adopted.
But these efforts did have a real impact on how thoroughgoing
the enforcement of regulations actually could be and on the

willingness of policymakers to push through further measures in the future. British administrators worried that the adoption of more ambitious bylaws and taxation measures would only increase the opportunities for native officials to take bribes from citizens anxious to skirt regulations, would cause councillors sincerely committed to the enforcement of municipal law to lose their social standing, and would require the establishment of an expensive bureaucracy to enforce the rules.[42] As a consequence, the programme of urban 'improvement', so ambitious in theory, was seriously diluted in practice. In many cases, the inertia produced by fears of local resistance could be overcome only when civil administrators considered a crisis situation to exist.

Finally, and most publicly, the businessmen could take recourse to legal and constitutional procedures to check reforming efforts. Often this involved a decision by the traders to associate with English-educated publicists capable of employing the idiom of the colonial rulers. One common tactic was to flood the municipality with petitions objecting to bylaws or new taxation measures, petitions which the local body and the provincial administration were legally bound to consider before implementing any measure. The most dramatic and effective case of this sort occurred from 1889 to 1895, after the municipality had decided to institute a house tax in Surat in order to pay for an expensive new waterworks system. When the idea of the new tax was broached, the residents at first filed hundreds of objections to the measure. After meeting its responsibility to consider each of these objections one by one, the council then decided to go ahead with the planned taxation. Local citizens then responded with two separate petition campaigns in the city organized by 'committees' 'representing' the inhabitants of the various wards of the city. On one occasion, 10,000 signatures were collected on a memorial that was then sent to the provincial government.

These petitions raised dozens of reasons why the new measure should be rejected. They pointed out the declining condition of the city and the poverty of its ratepayers, the conflict of the tax regulations with 'all principles of economy and justice', the likelihood that the measures might alienate the population from British rule, the absence of 'facts and figures' to prove the need

for the new waterworks, and the 'selfish interests' of the com-
missioners who had sanctioned the measure. Most importantly,
they stressed the opposition of 'the people' to the house tax. One
petition denounced those who supported the bill for trying 'to
dishonour the principle of British rule by disregarding *Vox
Populi*'. But even after these petitions had been dismissed, the
protesters were not done; they filed more than 17,000 complaints in local courts, forcing the municipality to allocate
Rs. 10,000 to defend the tax.[43] In short, the opponents of the
house tax contended the legitimacy of the measure by calling
upon constitutional standards of justice and by employing
channels that the Raj itself had provided for expressing grievance. More than four years went by before the house tax took
effect. Frederick Lely, district collector during the house tax
movement, would later remark: 'My six years' experience of the
Surat Municipality was a continuous battle with a small set of
men whose one conception of public duty was to block everything progressive by some verbal impediment in the law.'[44]

Though Lely's implication that the agitation had a narrow
social base was clearly mistaken, his statement did point clearly
to the ability of such merchant resistance virtually to stymie
government efforts through rhetoric rooted in the rulers' own
normative system. He and other administrators may not have
given up their short-term commitment to either the waterworks or the house tax as a result of this struggle. They did,
however, become extremely reluctant to pursue further measures of reform. Soon after the house tax movement, the municipality abandoned a scheme to build an expensive new
drainage system in the city that would have required further
new taxes. For nearly five decades, the hugely increased volume
of waste waters produced by the new waterworks simply seeped
into the urban soil, creating conditions far more unhealthy than
had ever existed before.

None of these varied merchant efforts really involved an explicit challenge to British rule, whatever the civil servants of the
Raj might have thought. Indeed businessmen often participated
in constitutional struggle in a spirit of deference and loyalty to
the colonial rulers. As in precolonial times, the merchants
spoke the language of their overlords in order to evoke principles of justice embedded in that language; they appealed to

civil administrators to honour the most dearly held values of British culture. Such appeals placed members of the ruling group, who claimed that their legal and constitutional code represented the epitome of civilizations, in an awkward position. The British often felt compelled to listen to petitions, to consider appeals in what they believed to be a spirit of 'fair play', and usually to raise their own counter-objections to Indian rhetoric in the same discourse of civic politics. The principle of constitutional dissent gave merchants of Surat and their English-educated publicists a wedge with which to drive home their own preoccupations and to make their voices felt without completely damaging their reputation for loyalty.

Thus, while local businessmen may have lost their most dramatic traditional means of expressing resistance, they still had not been reduced to powerlessness. Adjusting the idiom of their protest, they found a means of slowing the pace of colonial reform without unleashing a resistance from below that could have threatened their local position of wealth, influence and status. One might say that British colonialism in India never developed the inflexibility suggested in Adas's portrayal of colonial states in Southeast Asia, and that this left room for the continued possibility of contestation within the ruling hegemony; but one must acknowledge at the same time that much of the flexibility of the Raj and its agenda of 'progress' was actually induced by the merchant struggles.

World War I and Gandhian Protest

World War I provided an abrupt shock to the relations that had developed between the trading community and the colonial regime through the nineteenth century, forcing the merchants to consider anew the viability of strategies involving collective forms of avoidance protest. The war created a crisis in the city that ruined some traders and brought many other firms to the brink of dissolution. Giving first priority to the exigencies of the war effort, the Government of India adopted a whole series of measures—import and export restrictions, price controls, and regulations on adulteration in goods such as cotton—that represented an unprecedented interference by government into commercial practice and merchant custom.[45] On top of new commercial controls came new taxation. Faced with extreme fiscal difficulties, the provincial government both raised the level of the overall income taxation and added a 'super tax' in the higher brackets. The income taxes collected in the Presidency as a whole increased nearly ten times over between 1915 and 1921.[46] But as odious to Surat's traders as the amount of taxation were the new tax forms, which were far more detailed than anything they had been required to submit before. The merchants, whose credit as businessmen was dependent on maintaining the secrecy of their dealings, felt threatened by having to divulge a wide range of facts about their incomes and assets, and to convert their account books, based on the Hindu year, to the Christian calendar. In Surat, spokesmen for the merchant community complained that the measure 'hurts us not only economically, it also damages our reputations'.[47]

Since civil servants gave first priority to wartime exigencies, they often gave little thought to the objections of local businessmen. The movement against the income tax mentioned in the opening paragraph of this essay is instructive. Following the previous merchant protest in the city, the traders combined avoidance strategies with deferential appeals to imperial authorities. In late August 1918, a gathering of nearly two thousand traders, headed by the Mahajan Sheth, the Nagarsheth, and Sardar Ishwardas Jagjivandas Store (a government title holder and prominent figure in the *Mahajan*), met in the city to decide on how to approach the government. Throughout the meeting, speakers stressed their loyalty: 'We are loyal subjects of the government', stated Store, 'the government is our mabap (father and mother).' 'We will carry on our action loyally, just as a hungry and thirsty child asks its parents [for food and drink]', he added. The meeting dissociated itself with the emerging Home Rule movement, and a youth who tried to inject a more radical tone into the proceedings was stopped from speaking. The traders decided to refuse to fill out their forms or to pay their taxes, and they formed a committee to present their grievances to the government.[48] Obviously, they were hoping to draw upon well-established community procedures for calling attention to their dissatisfactions.

Despite the overall tone of the meeting, the Bombay govern-

ment was not about to consider the no-tax movement as anything but unlawful and seditious. It threatened to prosecute
Store and a few of the movement's other leaders. Store, unable
to break his close personal ties with leading officials, quickly
capitulated, leaving the merchants leaderless and embittered.
The failure of the income tax protest left the traders uncertain
about the value of traditional protest strategies and disgruntled
with their headmen.[49]

This sense of crisis was also furthered by municipal policies
and the increasing inadequacy of everyday defence mechanisms
in checking these policies. During the war the Bombay government tightened its hold over municipalities in the Presidency in
an effort to ensure that the local bodies would continue to be
instruments of 'progress' as it granted Indians greater formal
powers of self-government. Just before the war, Bombay had
increased the number of elected (as opposed to nominated)
councillors in Surat to twenty of the total number of thirty, and
granted the council the privilege of choosing its own President.
But soon thereafter, worried that the increased powers would
lead to 'factionalism', 'corruption', fiscal chaos and a decline of
public services, the provincial government announced that it
would appoint a Municipal Commissioner to run the municipal
administration and enforce local bylaws. Under the direction
of the new commissioner, H. Denning, the municipal bureaucracy, freed from the need to be responsive to the elected councillors or to local sentiments, entered areas of urban life that had
never before been part of its purview.

Earlier, in 1913, the municipality, under heavy pressure from
Bombay, had passed a new set of bylaws designed to improve
sanitary conditions in the city. These rules regulated such
diverse matters of merchant and artisan practice as the storage
of tar and resin, the disposal of household waste, and the
construction of new buildings. They required universal birth
and death registration; they barred the holding of caste feasts
on city streets for more than two hours. Especially odious to
local traders were the rules on housing construction, which obli-
gated builders of new structures to reserve half of their property
as open space, and which controlled the height and extension of
ventilation a building might have. These procedures affected
both large landholders, who generally tried to squeeze as much

profit from their property as possible, and poorer city-dwellers,
who often needed to use all of their tiny holdings for their houses
or their shops.[50] Residents tried to block the adoption of the
bylaws through established grievance procedures, filing hundreds of objections to the municipality. One challenged new
drainage restrictions, arguing that 'the right to discharge the
overflow of their privies into the streets is a long established
right of all citizens'. Another charged that the new building
regulations 'would work hardship and encourage corruption'.
Most of these objections, however, proved futile.[51]

In the past, passage of a bylaw in the council had by no
means meant its implementation in practice. Municipal committees and honorary magistrates had often turned a blind eye
to the enforcement of the regulations, perhaps as favours to
kinsmen and friends or in return for small payments. But the
Municipal Commissioner was intent on enforcing the letter of
the law, not caring whether he was popular or not. Cases in
municipal courts went up by three times in his first year, fines
assessed for violations almost four times, and the amount realized in fines almost five times. After 1916, these violations
dropped off, since, in the words of the District Collector, 'the
public are beginning to realize that the regulations are meant to
be observed.'[52] Owners of property were still attempting 'by
every subterfuge to evade the operation of the laws',[53] but the
Municipal Commissioner felt that he had made real strides
toward defeating such efforts.

In short, then, the crisis of the war issued not only from new
administrative regulations but also from measures which
tended to weaken both the residents' everyday defensive mechanisms and organized protests involving avoidance tactics. Nor
did the Home Rule movement, which developed in the city
after 1916, offer much support. Surat's Home Rule League
focused largely on constitutional issues, and failed to take up
any significant merchant concern. Part of the problem also
lay in the Home Rulers' own acceptance of the notion of
'progress' and their determination to prove that they were as
committed to modernization as the British rulers. When they
captured the municipal council in 1918, they proceeded to
adopt perhaps one of the most ambitious schemes of reform
ever undertaken by the municipality, a law instituting uni-

versal and compulsory education in Surat for children under 12. The city's merchants resented suddenly being required to send their children to school and to support the education of large numbers of low- and middle-caste children through an additional cess on their direct tax bill.[54]

It was in this context of increasing desperation and ineffectiveness on the part of the merchants that the followers of Mahatma Gandhi rose to political significance in the city. The Gandhians offered a strategy for coping with the aggressive advance of the state that did not involve violent confrontation. The appeal of Gandhian protest lay less in the issues around which it was fought—the Rowlatt Act, and the Punjab and the Khilafat wrongs, all matters far removed from mercantile preoccupations—but in the idiom of resistance and the methodology of protest. From the merchant perspective, Gandhian resistance meshed with and extended indigenous cultural principles and traditions of expressing dissent.[55]

Gandhi himself was very conscious of the connections between precolonial modes of resistance and the strategies he and the Congress leadership devised for opposing the Raj. Just months before the adoption of the Non-Co-operation resolution by the Congress in 1920, he wrote: 'withdrawing co-operation from a government which breaks its promises is a course followed from immemorial times. The history of our country provides instance after instance of subjects oppressed by a king leaving the kingdom . . . when they find things unbearable.'[56] He referred to the hartal (closing of shops) as 'our ancient Indian institution for expressing national sorrow . . . It is a means, more powerful than monster meetings, of expressing national opinion.'[57] But Gandhi also made innovations in the tactics of avoidance that rendered these more viable methods of bringing pressure on the twentieth-century state. Encouraging collective flight was certainly not a major part of his approach during Non-co-operation.[58] Instead, he encouraged a whole host of other actions involving the withdrawal both of critical services and symbolic support.

The tactics of avoidance were certainly central to Gandhian resistance in Surat. The Rowlatt Satyagraha in April 1919 involved the closing of shops and the taking of vows not to obey the unjust laws. In December defiance of the peace celebra-

tions called for shop closings and refusal to take part in obser-
vances commemorating British victory in the European war.
The Non-Co-operation campaign of 1920–2 itself centred on
a series of abstemious acts: resignation of titles, the suspension of
legal practice, withdrawal from government schools, and the
boycott of elections. Local merchants shut their shops on dozens
of occasions between 1919 and 1924. The traders refused to
observe the visits of imperial dignitaries, which had always been
a major opportunity for them to display their loyalty to the Raj.
For Surat the most significant collective actions of defiance
associated with these years came after the Bombay administration suspended the local municipality, which had refused all
government supervision and finance and had handed over
Rs. 40,000 from local funds to the national schools. In response
to the suspension of the local body, the Gandhians organized a
massive campaign for the non-payment of municipal taxes,
effectively paralysing the administration of the local body for
several years. Thus, acts of denial remained critical to local
resistance, but they clearly were no longer couched in an idiom
of deference. Instead, the Gandhians now employed avoidance
protest to challenge colonialism directly and to promote the
ascendancy of the Congress.[59]

The Gandhians' strategies appealed to the high-caste Hindu
and Jain community for a number of reasons. First, the new
leadership developed a powerful new language for encouraging protest, one rooted in the vocabulary of Gujarati religiosity,
which emphasized the virtue of acts of abstinence and self-
control. Involvement in protest was an act of renunciation
(tyag), of self-suffering, and of penance (tapascharya). Going to
jail was an action of sacrifice for the nation (deshyagna). Wearing homespun cloth was an expression of one's dharma (literally, sacred duty) to the nation. The Gandhians also drew upon
the idiom of honour and self-respect, suggesting for instance
that it was a matter of abru for merchants to donate money to
the National Education Society. Such language created a
psychic link between mercantile ethics and the morality of
opposing the British government. Rhetoric stressing the self-
lessness of resistance essentially confirmed the merchants' sense
of the moral rightness of their actions, and contributed to a
growing feeling of ethical ascendancy vis-à-vis the British. This

appeal played a critical role in shattering the hegemony of colonial rule.[60]

But the Gandhians also promoted social order as they stimulated action. The followers of Gandhi, most prominently Dayalji Desai, regularly preached the importance of ahimsa (non-violence) and the control of personal emotions in any form of resistance. When minor episodes of violence broke out during the Rowlatt Satyagraha, Congress leaders arrived quickly on the scene to warn protesters that this behaviour was not consonant with the teachings of Gandhi.[61] The Mahatma's willingness to withdraw support for political action once violence had developed certainly gave some assurance to the merchants that the movement was unlikely to take a direction that would endanger their position.

Finally, the Congress served as a powerful source of extra-local alliance for the merchants in their protest. All through this essay, we have seen that the traders were unlikely to take bold actions without the support of powerful aspirants to political authority. Traditional patterns of collective avoidance, essentially effective when it had been possible to appeal to the Emperor against his officials in the seventeenth century or to the English East India Company against Mughal governors during the late eighteenth century, had become increasingly futile during the nineteenth century, when the British Raj converted itself from a contest state to a polity based more upon bureaucratic principles. The failure of actions such as the income tax agitations of 1860, the licence tax movement of 1878, and the income tax protests of 1918, had proved the difficulty of redressing merchant grievances through forms of protest that the British were likely to regard as challenges to their authority. The nationwide scale of the Non-Co-operation movement, however, meant that protest in Surat could not be so easily isolated and suppressed. Traders entered collective protest more confidently, knowing that they had the backing of a larger movement and a well-developed organization. While now expressed in an idiom of national self-determination, this behaviour was consistent with a well-established strategy of latching on to alternative centres of power in the effort to defend merchant society against the actions of imperial over-lords.

However, historians must be careful not to attribute too close a convergence between the purposes of Congress leaders and local merchants. In fact, the business community always maintained a certain distance from the national organization even as it participated in the larger movement. In modes of resistance that involved little danger to their families or their livelihoods, Surati traders generally manifested high degrees of involvement. But when support of non-co-operation necessitated the adoption of a high-profile posture that might place the well-being of their families at risk, the businessmen were more wary. The Gandhians, for instance, were unsuccessful in generating a permanent pool of activists from among mercantile families, and had to resort to the countryside to find recruits for picketing cloth and liquor shops. Only one or two businessmen underwent imprisonment during Non-Co-operation. No final merging of the nationalists and the merchants took place; instead there was an alliance of two sets of individuals with somewhat distinct interests, one seeking political power and the end of colonialism, the other the re-establishment of a certain equilibrium in its relations with the ruling elite.[62]

In the end, local businessmen were too dependent on the colonial order to cut themselves off from it completely. Local bankers received their credit from imperial banks; exporters required the co-operation of port authorities; businessmen needed licences and the use of railway wagons; merchants dealing in local manufactures required electricity to be provided to their artisan-clients by public utility companies. The need for basic literate skills had become essential to doing business throughout the city, so mercantile families could hardly afford to keep their children out of the government-funded schools. When it became apparent that the nationalists possessed no immediate mechanism for seizing power, members of the business community became ever more reluctant to undertake public acts of resistance. Once the imminence of swaraj seemed to recede, high-caste Suratis slowly withdrew themselves from an active support for Congress politics, bringing the movement to a halt by 1924.

From a nationalist perspective, it is hard to argue that Non-Co-operation had achieved much success. The Congress failed to gain redress of the Punjab and Khilafat 'wrongs', and it failed to win swaraj (independence) within one year. From the perspective of Surat's merchants, however, the movement had achieved a number of considerable victories. By the end of 1922, the position of commissioner had been eliminated, municipal administration was in a shambles, most bylaws could no longer be enforced, and the Universal and Compulsory Primary Education Act had become inoperative. Many house-holders had escaped paying their direct taxes to the local body for one year or more. Residents could completely ignore some government regulations; other laws now could be enforced only in an uneven fashion. In short, the whole process of engineering 'progress' through legislation reached a complete though tem-porary impasse. Much of the paralysis of government policy can be attributed to the merchant resistance carried out under the umbrella of the Congress.

From a nationalist outlook, the end of the Non-Co-operation movement also seems to have been the beginning of a new period of apathy in Indian political life. From a merchant point of view, however, it may have merely marked the renewed viability of non-confrontational defensive measures. Indeed, by the late 1920s, the everyday resistance of local traders and artisans would be frustrating reforming efforts undertaken by a new municipal council led by M. K. Dixit, one of the chief leaders of the Non-Co-operation movement. Nationalist and merchant objectives, which had intersected briefly during the early twenties, now diverged significantly.

In effect, Surat's merchants had struck a new balance with the colonial rulers, one that enabled them to sustain the con-tinuity of their business firms and retain their places of pro-minence in local society. This ability to recreate relatively stable merchant–ruler relations owes much to the tactics of denial employed in the period of open collective resistance. Violence might have made any long-term accommodation between the colonizers and the colonized difficult. But after Non-Co-operation, it was possible for the merchants to continue to func-tion and to maintain their local dominance despite the reassertion of British power.

At the same time, the merchants were slowly beginning to contribute to the construction of a new political order, which one might call the Congress–Bania order. Through their involvement in Non-Co-operation, the traders had begun to bolster the legitimacy of a new nationalist elite that would, over the course of the next three decades, come to assume power. In every stage of the Congress's rise to power in Surat, business support was critical. Conspiratorial theories which view the Congress as a mere instrument of business interests, however, simply fail to capture the complexity of the relationship that was developing. To a great extent, merchants and capitalists were recreating the subordinate position they had always retained in their alliances with political overlords. Under the Congress, they would again find themselves subject to the domination of a ruling elite whose norms did not jibe neatly with their own. Leading figures in the party often did hold sincere allegiances to socialism, the redistribution of wealth, and the development of a planned economy. Businessmen had to face licensing, pricing, import–export controls, and taxation measures that were far more extensive than any regulations they had to deal with during the colonial period. But as in the colonial era, they continued to use everyday methods of defending their interests, including incomplete reporting and false compliance with regulations, the maintenance of secrecy in their business and property dealings, and the cultivation of friends in high places. And, as also in colonial times, they continued to resort to the language of constitutionalism and the principles of representative government in frustrating and checking the agenda of a ruling elite committed to a concept of progress at odds with their own central preoccupations.

CONCLUSION

No less than the Indian peasants, who have been the subject of extensive research in recent years, high-caste merchants of Surat possessed strong traditions of defending themselves against attempts by ruling groups to penetrate local society and to extract resources from it. Merchant resistance seriously affected the shape of political relations in the city from Mughal times into the twentieth century. While the wealth and social networks controlled by the businessmen often made them desired clients of local aspirants to power, this fact never ensured that relationships with political overlords would be stable and unthreatening. Struggle had important effects on the state and its policies. Merchant efforts regularly served to check intrusive agendas of individual officials or the entire ruling group. In periods of political transition, such as that immediately before the British rise to power or during the phase of Congress ascendancy, merchant protest could even be instrumental in hastening the shift in political control from one ruling group to another.

Yet in most periods, the merchants avoided direct confrontations with their rulers. Simply conceptualized, local business-men possessed two levels of techniques for protecting their concerns, both of which stopped short of violence and con-frontation: (1) 'Everyday' resistance, the ongoing subtle, often loosely co-ordinated, efforts of individual trading and banking families to short-circuit imperial initiatives; and (2) the more dramatic forms of organized protest, which usually involved the collective denial of services to the political overlords and other acts of 'non-co-operation' in order to force the ruler to reconsi-der his actions or policies. But the tactics of the businessmen were hardly static; Surati merchants were constantly adding and devising new weapons of non-confrontational resistance to their arsenal as the late colonial state closed certain avenues for expressing opposition and opened others.

To a great extent, the resistances of merchants in Surat took place within a hegemony associated with rule by external political overlords. The dependence of local traders and bankers on alliances with more powerful political leaders meant that the business community would formulate its principles of justice at least partially through reference to the value system and lan-guage of its sponsors. The merchants of Surat continuously called upon their ruler-patrons to honour principles implicit in the ruling groups' own ideology; they attempted to cultivate relationships of deference with imperial officials that might give them some sort of moral leverage over the administrators' actions. When one ruling group replaced another, or as the value system of the ruling group changed, the merchants gradu-ally adjusted their idiom of making claims to justice. During the three hundred years examined in this essay, there was little movement toward increasingly confrontational modes of resistance over time; such a shift would have endangered the relationships merchants were constantly trying to establish with their rulers as well as the businessmen's place in their own society. There was, however, change in the vocabulary and grammar of redressing grievances as merchants accommodated themselves to the colonial order and finally to the modern nation-state. In the precolonial polity and even in early British times, businessmen evoked an ideal of a moral and personal ruler who would intervene against his own officials when his subjects were oppressed. The making of political claims based upon a bond of clientage to the political overlords was very attractive to the Suratis even as late as the early twentieth century, but it often proved ineffective in a state based in theory upon 'rational', bureaucratic principle. Increasingly important to the pursuit of political justice as the merchants perceived it was the language of constitutional politics where supposedly impersonal values—'public opinion', 'the public good', 'progress', 'custom' and 'the law'—held sway.

Viewed in light of the long-term history of merchant protest in Surat, the Gandhian movements of 1919–24 appear not as an awakening of an apathetic and apolitical merchant population, but as a shrewd response of a politically astute community subjected momentarily to conditions of special stress. By associating themselves with Congress movements, the merchants were able to revitalize their resistance to particularly offensive colonial policies. The followers of Mahatma Gandhi offered to local businessmen an effective method of checking the advance of the state that was consonant with their pre-existing social and cultural preoccupations but did not provoke the administration into fully employing its repressive capabilities or unleash serious unrest from below.

No doubt, participation in Gandhian politics required the merchant to step outside the imperial hegemony and to associate with a radical movement that challenged the British Raj. Yet to see Gandhian movements as marking a permanent shift away from non-confrontational strategies of dissent would be mistaken. As in their earlier expressions of social protest, the primary purpose of businessmen in entering Non-Co-operation was not to accomplish 'liberation' but to check intrusions into their own domain by the state and re-establish merchant-ruler relations on a safer footing. Once the immediate wartime and post-war crisis had eased, Surati businessmen backed away from nationalist agitations, eager to re-establish their position within a revived though somewhat tamer colonial order. Between 1924 and 1929, and later between 1932 and 1947, they carried on their struggles through the far less dramatic techniques of everyday and constitutional resistance. They contested state demands without challenging the state symbolically, often again working within the language of social deference and an idiom of justice that they had appropriated from their now increasingly Indian rulers. And, when the Congress itself assumed power, they would again find themselves in their old and curious position of being part of the state but at the same time constantly resisting that state's demands. Thus, though Non-Co-operation was a logical development in the politics of Surati businessmen, it by no means marked some final ending point in the history of mercantile resistance. Instead, it was a temporary, dramatic means of expressing dissent that reinvigorated older, less confrontational mechanisms of self-defence that the businessmen would continue to employ right into the post-independence era.

The study of merchants in Surat demonstrates that any history of the political behaviour of South Asian businessmen must take into account the role of struggle and dissent. But the reverse proposition may also be true: any greater history of resistance in South Asia might do well to pay attention to the resistances of businessmen and landed groups. The analysis of elite forms of struggle may actually be critical to an understanding of the fate of resistances among subaltern groups. In Surat, merchants acted in 1795 to prevent attacks upon their local place of credit and social dominance from below. In 1878, they withdrew their support from the licence tax protests after incidents of violence had occurred, essentially bringing to a halt collective actions in which petty traders and artisans were assuming an increasingly critical role. After World War I, they gave their support to a movement that gave top priority to assuring that social protest would not move in a violent and uncontrolled direction. In short, the strategies of resistance engaged in by Surati merchants were also strategies of containing and controlling underclass movements. As Ramachandra Guha has argued, understanding the structure of social domination is critical to explaining the socio-cultural idiom in which protest is expressed.[63] The struggles of peasants, artisans, and labourers cannot be examined in isolation from the resistances of the elite groups above them.

In another sense, the position of merchants may be more analogous to that of peasant groupings than historians have realized. True, Surat's businessmen have always possessed far more leverage within the subcontinent's various polities than ordinary figures living in the countryside; they also enjoyed a position of privilege and wealth that made them especially reluctant to confront the state. But Indian peasants have historically shared with these merchants limited access to military power and a vulnerability to landed and ruling groups with value systems differing from their own, factors which I have argued were critical in influencing the adoption of avoidance and denial as protest. Much sociological and historical theory may exaggerate the tendency of peasants to adopt confrontational, liberation-oriented forms of struggle under modern circumstances; it may also not acknowledge sufficiently the extent to which peasants who do participate in revolutionary movements may in effect be latching themselves on to a set of ruler-patrons who offer them more satisfactory terms of dependence rather than seeking 'liberation' as we are prone to conceive it.

While this perspective may be less exciting and less psychically satisfying than models which portray a dramatic shift toward more radical, revolutionary forms of social protest over time, it may be more realistic for many areas of the world. A long-term model for non-revolutionary societies may need to take into account the continuous contesting of political relations between rulers and privileged groups on the one hand, and between elites and subalterns on the other, that take place in 'everyday' life. It may need to examine how subordinate groups often pursue justice through contests within cultural hegemony rather than through direct challenges to domination. It may also need to analyse how the underclasses accommodate themselves culturally to changes in the character and the ideology of the state. Finally, it may have to admit that structures of power and structures of inequality are often reproduced and reinvented—rather than undermined—through resistance. No doubt the study of merchants in Surat is too much of a special case to provide a firm basis for an alternative model of long-term change and continuity that could apply to resistances of subaltern groups in India and elsewhere in the previously colonized world. But hopefully it does raise questions that could prove useful in any attempt to explore the relationship between popular struggles of precolonial and early colonial times and those of the twentieth century.[64]

NOTES

Gyan Prakash, Ramachandra Guha, Howard Spodek, Michael Adas, Chris Bayly, Eugene Irschick, and David Hardiman all made valuable comments on earlier versions of this essay. The essay was originally conceived of as a companion piece to an article 'From Tribute to Philanthropy', *Journal of Asian Studies*, XCVI (1987), pp. 339–60.

1. *Gujarat Mitra*, 1 Sept. 1918, p. 11.
2. See particularly the six volumes of the *Subaltern Studies* series edited by Ranajit Guha.
3. On the Mughal period, see, for instance, Karen Leonard, 'The "Great Firm" Theory of the Mughal Empire', *Comparative Studies in Society and History*, XXI (1979), pp. 151–67; Michael Pearson, *Merchants and Rulers in Gujarat: The Response to the Portuguese during the Sixteenth Century* (Berkeley and Los Angeles: University of California Press, 1976). An important article on the successor states is Phillip Calkins, 'The Formation of a Regionally Oriented Ruling Group in Bengal, 1700–1740', *Journal of Asian Studies*, XXIX (1970), pp. 151–67. On the development of colonialism, important studies include C. A. Bayly, *Rulers, Townsmen and Bazaars: North Indian Society in the Age of British Expansion* (Cambridge: Cambridge University Press, 1983); Lakshmi Subramanian, 'Capital and Crowd in a Declining Asian Port', *Modern Asian Studies*, XIX (1985), pp. 205–37; and David Washbrook, 'Progress and Problems: South Asian Economic and Social History, c. 1720–1860', *Modern Asian Studies*, XXII (1988), pp. 75–6. Finally, for the Indian National Congress, see several essays in Bipan Chandra, *Nationalism and Colonialism in Modern India* (New Delhi: Orient Longman, 1979); Sumit Sarkar, 'The Logic of Gandhian Nationalism: Civil Disobedience and the Gandhi–Irwin Pact, 1930–1', *Indian Historical Review*, III (1976), pp. 114–46; A. D. D. Gordon, *Businessmen and Politics: Rising Nationalism and a Modernising Economy in Bombay, 1918–33* (New Delhi: Manohar, 1978); Claude Markovitz, *Indian Business and Nationalist Politics, 1931–9: The Indigenous Capitalist Class and the Rise of the Congress Party* (Cambridge:

Cambridge University Press, 1985). The examination of relations between businessmen and the Congress has a much longer history—for the most part associated with the Marxist tradition—that predates the more recent work cited above.

4. Michael Adas, 'From Avoidance to Confrontation: Peasant Protest in Precolonial and Colonial Southeast Asia', *Comparative Studies in Society and History*, XXIII (1981), pp. 217–47.

5. Adas certainly recognizes the continued presence of tactics of avoidance in the midst of modern struggles, but the emphasis in his article cited above is clearly on the transition to more confrontational forms. This is less true in some other writing, such as 'Bandits, Monks, and Pretender Kings: Patterns of Peasant Resistance and Protest in Colonial Burma, 1826–1941', in Robert P. Weller and Scott E. Guggenheim (eds), *Power and Protest in the Countryside: Studies of Rural Unrest in Asia, Europe, and Latin America* (Durham: Duke Press, 1982).

6. See James Scott, *Weapons of the Weak: Everyday Forms of Peasant Resistance* (New Haven: Yale University Press, 1985), pp. 335–40.

7. See Haynes, 'From Tribute to Philanthropy'. This analysis is influenced by the work of C. A. Bayly, particularly 'Old-Style Merchants and Risk', unpublished paper for the Workshop on Risk and Uncertainty in South Asia, University of Pennsylvania, 1977.

8. For a deeper treatment of merchant economy, society and culture in Surat during these three centuries, see Haynes, *Rhetoric and Ritual in Colonial India: The Shaping of a Public Culture in Surat City* (forthcoming from the University of California Press in the USA, and Oxford University Press in India).

9. See Adas, 'From Avoidance to Confrontation', pp. 219–25.

10. See Michael Pearson, *Merchants and Rulers in Gujarat: The Response to the Portuguese in the Sixteenth Century* (Berkeley: University of California Press, 1976), pp. 126–32; Haynes, 'From Tribute to Philanthropy'.

11. This understanding of deference has been influenced by, and is a response to, such work as James Scott, *Weapons of the Weak*; Howard Newby, 'The Deferential Dialectic', *Comparative Studies in Society and History*, XVII (1975), pp. 139–64; Patrick Joyce, *Work, Society and Politics: The Culture of the Factory in Late Victorian England* (New Brunswick: Rutgers University Press, 1980), chap. III; I do depart here from Scott's view of deference as a self-conscious strategy calculated to deceive dominant groups.

12. Scott, *Weapons of the Weak*; James Scott and Benedict Kerkvliet (eds), 'Everyday Forms of Peasant Resistance in Southeast Asia', special issue in *The Journal of Peasant Studies*, XIII (1986); and especially Michael Adas, 'From Footdragging to Flight: The Evasive History of Peasant Avoidance Protest in South and Southeast Asia', pp. 64–86.

13. Ovington, *A Voyage to Surat*, p. 187.

14. See William Foster (ed.), *Letters Received by the East India Company from its Servants in the East, 1602–17* (London: Sampson, Low, Marston and Company, 1900), p. 320, recounted in Michael Pearson, *Merchants and Rulers in Gujarat*, p. 122.

15. Ibid.
16. One interesting account is found in *The Travels of Abbe Carre in India and the Near East, 1672 to 1674* (London: Hakluyt Society, 1947), Hakluyt Society Publication, ser. 2, XCV, pp. 147–8.
17. William Foster (ed.), *The English Factories in India, 1668–9* (Oxford: Clarendon Press, 1927), p. 192.
18. Ibid., pp. 190–2, 197–8, 205.
19. Michael N. Pearson, 'Shivaji and the Decline of the Mughal Empire', *The Journal of Asian Studies*, XXXV (1976), pp. 221–36.
20. Ashin Das Gupta, 'Trade and Politics in Eighteenth Century India', in D. S. Richards (ed.), *Islam and the Trade of Asia* (Philadelphia: University of Pennsylvania Press, 1970); Das Gupta, *Indian Merchants and the Decline of Surat, c. 1700–50* (Weisbaden: Franz Steiner Verlag, 1979).
21. 'Crisis at Surat', *Bengal Past and Present*, LXXXVI (1967), pp. 148–62.
22. This argument is made at a more general level in Washbrook, 'Progress and Problems'.
23. 'Surat during the Second Half of the Eighteenth Century: What Kind of Social Order?—A Rejoinder to Lakshmi Subramanian', *Modern Asian Studies*, XXI (1987), pp. 679–710. Torri very convincingly points out both that there was no single monolithic approach of the Banias to the British and that prominent Muslims as well as Hindus were among those aligning themselves with the Company.
24. Lakshmi Subramanian, 'Capital and Crowd in a Declining Asian Port'. Subramanian is responsible for developing the concept of the 'Anglo-Bania order' which I have employed here.
25. Haynes, 'From Tribute to Philanthropy'.
26. This episode is described and analysed at length in Subramanian, 'Capital and Crowd', and Torri, 'Surat during the Second Half of the Eighteenth Century'. The main source for these articles and the treatment that follows is Maharashtra State Archives (hereafter cited as B.A. [Bombay Archives]), Surat Factory Diary, XXXII (1795).
27. Surat Factory Diary, XXXII (1795), pp. 381–2.
28. Ibid., p. 381.
29. Ibid., pp. 378–9.
30. Subramanian, 'Capital and Crowd', p. 236.
31. Pamela Nightingale, *Trade and Empire in Western India, 1784–1806* (Cambridge: Cambridge University Press, 1970), p. 171.
32. In 1808, the Company briefly considered raising a house tax in Surat, but dismissed the idea after conducting an investigation into how the local population might respond. 'Among the Hindus', reported the investigating officer, 'the operation of a tax upon their houses acts in their conceptions with the force almost of a personal intrusion, from which their religious prejudices shrink, and among the Mahommedans, their being confounded with other castes is an alarm no less serious to their pride.' B.A., Revenue Diary, LXI (1808), pp. 849–51.
33. *Surat Municipal Record*, 1868–1914; the quote comes from *Surat Municipal Record*, 1916–17, p. 223.

288   *Douglas Haynes*

34. 'Revenue Commissioner of Surat to Bombay Government, 22 February 1808', in B.A., Revenue Diary, CLI (1808), pp. 848–51; Government of India, *Indian Taxation Enquiry Committee* (Madras, 1926); *Surat Municipal Record*, 1872, p. 20; 1894, p. 97; 1895–6, pp. 9–17; 1902–3, pp. 77–83; *Gujarat Mitra*, 2 May 1898, p. 2. For an especially strong case of resistance to the imposition of direct taxation in Banaras, see Richard Heitler, 'The Varanasi House Tax Hartal of 1810–11', *Indian Economic and Social History Review*, IX (1972), pp. 239–57.

35. Bombay State, *Source Material of the History of the Indian Freedom Movement in Bombay*, vol. I (Bombay, 1957), pp. 19–22.

36. Ibid., p. 33.

37. Ibid., p. 35.

38. Ibid., pp. 29–49.

39. B.A., G.D. 1893, XCII, comp. 600, p. 86; G.D. 1895, CV, comp. 1041, pp. 126–7; G.D. 1909, LXVII, comp. 110, pt II, p. 555; for British recognition of this situation, see J. K. Spence to Secretary to Government, G.D., April 1899, in B.A., G.D. 1901, comp. 347, p. 80.

40. *Surat Municipal Record*, 1872, p. 20; 1894, p. 97; 1895–6, pp. 9–17; 1902–3, pp. 77–83; *Gujarat Mitra*, 2 May 1898, p. 2.

41. *Surat Municipal Record*, 1877, p. 69.

42. 'Letter from J. K. Spence to Secretary to Government, G.D. April 1899', in B.A., G.D. 1901, vol. VII, comp. 347, pp. 79–80.

43. For papers relating to the housetax battle, see B.A., G.D. 1892, LCVII, comp. 600; G.D. 1893, LCII, comp. 600; G.D. 1895, CI, comp. 1041; *Surat Municipal Record*, 1895–6, pp. 9–17.

44. 'Remarks on the Draft of the Bombay District Municipal Act, 1899 by F. S. P. Lely, 6th April 1899', in B.A., G.D., VII, comp. 347, p. 33.

45. 'Collector's Report, 1913–14', in B.A., R.D. 1915, comp. 511, pt VI, pp. 10–11; 'Collector's Report, 1916–17', in B.A., R.D. 1918, comp. 511, pt IV, p. 11; *Gujarat Mitra*, 12 March 1916, p. 11; 19 March 1916, p. 6; 14 Oct. 1917, p. 5; 23 June 1918, p. 16.5; *Times of India*, 30 April, p. 8.

46. *Businessmen and Politics*, p. 22.

47. *Gujarat Mitra*, 1 Sept. 1918, p. 11.

48. Ibid., pp. 5–6, 11.

49. Ibid., 22 Dec. 1918, pp. 5–6, 11.

50. See B.A., G.D. 1914, comp. 1379; G.D. 1916, comp. 862, pp. 57–8; G.D. 1915, comp. 72 and various administrative reports of the Surat Municipality.

51. 'Collector, Surat to Commissioner, Northern Division, 12 May 1913', in B.A., G.D. 1914, comp. 1379, p. 13. Also other papers in files referred to in note 45, below.

52. *Surat Municipal Record*, 1916–17, pp. 46–7; 'Collector of Surat, 4 Aug. 1916', in G.D. 1917, comp. 653, p. 106.

53. Ibid., p. 33.

54. *Surat Municipal Record*, 1918–19, p. 140; *Bombay Chronicle*, 22 July 1920, p. 13; *Surat Municipal Record*, 1919–20, p. 8; *Gujarat Mitra*, 10 July 1921, p. 7.

55. See, for instance, Howard Spodek, 'On the Origins of Gandhi's Political Methodology: The Heritage of Kathiawad and Gujarat', *Journal of Asian Studies*, XXX (1971), pp. 361–72; and of course Lloyd and Susanne Rudolph, 'The Traditional Roots of Charisma: Gandhi', in *The Modernity of Tradition: Political Development in India* (Chicago: University of Chicago Press, 1967).

56. *The Collected Works of Mahatma Gandhi* (Ahmedabad: Navjivan Press, 1965), vol. XVIII, p. 29.

57. Ibid., vol. XV, p. 278.

58. It did become an important strategy for some Gujarati peasants during the Civil Disobedience Movement of 1930–2. See David Hardiman, *Peasant Nationalists of Gujarat: Kheda District 1917–34* (Delhi: Oxford University Press, 1981).

59. See Haynes, *Rhetoric and Ritual in Colonial India*, chapter X.

60. Ibid.

61. *Gujarat Mitra*, 13 April 1919, pp. 5–12.

62. Haynes, *Rhetoric and Ritual in Colonial India*, chapter XI.

63. Ramachandra Guha, 'Forestry and Social Protest in Kumaun', in Ranajit Guha (ed.), *Subaltern Studies IV: Writings on South Asian History and Society* (Delhi: Oxford University Press, 1985), pp. 54–100.

64. This essay has been influenced in different ways that could not be directly explicated in the text by C. A. Bayly, 'Indigenous Social Formations and the "World System": North India since *c.* 1700', unpublished paper written for the Conference on South Asia and the World Capitalist System, Medford, Mass., Dec. 1986; and Eugene Irschick, 'Gandhian Non-Violent Protest: Rituals of Avoidance or Rituals of Confrontation?', *Economic and Political Weekly*, XXI (1986), pp. 1276–85.

9

South Asian Resistance in Comparative Perspective

MICHAEL ADAS

Given the time period when the study of protest and resistance in Third World societies first became a serious and sustained enterprise for social scientists with varying area studies orientations, it was inevitable that peasants and revolutions would dominate much of their research and scholarship. Depending upon perspective and political persuasion, the trauma or triumph of the Chinese revolution focused attention on hitherto largely neglected agrarian groups and their potential for violent, confrontational protest. Victorious and failed 'peoples' wars' in Latin America and South East Asia, and above all the protracted struggle of the peasant-based liberation movements in Vietnam, further intensified scholarly absorption with peasant issues. They also fixed in the academic mind, and in the popular imagination, a reified and romanticized image of the peasantry, downtrodden and exploited but conscious of its predicament and ready to strike back directly and violently at its oppressors whenever opportunities arose. Though there were important exceptions, the study of the conditions of the rural underclasses in a variety of Third World settings with an eye to identifying the causes that led to movements of overt protest, neglected elite groups and broader socio-economic contests or reduced them to caricatures that obscured key forms of material and symbolic interaction between elite groups and cultivators as well as between different social strata within the 'peasantry' itself.

   In this intellectual climate, there appeared to be little place for the findings of South Asian specialists who had devoted their careers to unravelling the complexities of one of the world's largest and most diverse concentrations of peasants. The decidedly non-revolutionary path that the peoples of South Asia had taken to independence and the mistaken but remarkably durable view of Gandhi, who accounted for much of what those who were not area specialists knew about India, as a leader of 'passive'—hence non-confrontational—resistance, rendered India of little interest to those in search of peasants in revolution. Non-Indianists dismissed the South Asian peasantry as atypical; the more thoughtful among social scientists specializing in area studies regarded it as a troubling exception to the defiant and confrontational peasant norm. Stereotypes of the South Asian village and its caste-ridden inhabitants, which generations of paternalistic British administrators and the writings of Karl Marx had done so much to establish as stagnant, inert, passive and apolitical,[1] appeared to confirm the impression that evidence drawn from South Asian examples would do little to advance our understanding of the 'real' peasant.

It is not surprising then that the South Asian peasantry was passed over by scholars in search of case examples for works on patterns of peasant protest and revolution. India is not mentioned in Eric Wolf's 1969 study of the major 'peasant wars' of the twentieth century, which remains one of the best examples of the comparative protest genre.[2] The main antagonists in the 'moral economy' debate had little to say about South Asia,[3] though some of those who have tested their arguments have made use of South Asian examples and illustrations.[4] Despite a listing of references to government reports from post-independence India, Jeffery Paige's broadly-based paradigm with case studies on 'social movements and agrarian agriculture in the underdeveloped world' makes almost no use of Indian evidence.[5] Paige's neglect of India is all the more telling because he is concerned with uncovering patterns in a wide variety of agrarian protest actions, not just revolutions, and he is one of the few scholars in this period to have given serious attention to the theoretical implications of the composition and responses of elite groups and systems of elite dominance in different settings.

Comparativists and generalists, working on peasant protest in the 1960s and 1970s, who did bother to mention the peasants of South Asia usually characterized them in ways that simply reinforced the image of the passive, docile and intensely conservative cultivators, an image that had much to do with their neglect by non-Indianist area specialists. In the 'prelude' to his study of *The Rebels*[6] in the post–Second World War era, for example, Brian Crozier implicitly justifies his neglect of India with the remark: 'Millions in India are passive in conditions that would indeed be intolerable if suddenly imposed on people used to greater comfort and a higher intake of calories.' Claude Welch, Jr., whose use of the Telengana rebellions in the late 1940s marked a major departure from the comparativist scholars' neglect or dismissal of examples of Indian protest, did much to amplify the suggestions made by Crozier regarding the atypicality of the Indian rural classes in a world that appeared to be coming apart due to disruptions caused by recurring peasant risings. After noting that Indian peasants 'have not been *totally* passive' (italics mine) and citing the 'Mutiny', the Moplah rising and the Santhal disturbances to prove it,[7] Welch goes on to argue that the Telengana conflict was notable because it ran counter to the prevailing Indian trend of acquiescence in the face of poverty and exploitation. Predictably, Welch sees caste and karma as the keys to the Indian peasants' passivity:

... for most of its history, rural Telengana appears to have slumbered, its residents accepting what outsiders often perceived as injustices as the product of fate. Better, it seemed, to conform to present inequalities in the hope the next incarnation of one's soul would be less toilsome. The belief in karma justified conformity to one's situation, despite its vicissitudes, as part of the cosmic order.[8]

Apparently unaware that his underlying assumptions about the hegemonic functions of Hindu ideology were at variance with the work of many specialists who had done research on low-caste groups,[9] Welch goes on to argue that 'caste customs and regulations ... maintained a compartmentalized and essentially homeostatic society and crippled any attempts at joint action.'[10]

Given the widespread acceptance of these explanations for the supposedly atypical absence of resistance on the part of Indian peasants, it is little wonder that in his pioneering comparative study of the impact of differing agrarian systems in the *Social Origins of Dictatorship and Democracy*, Barrington Moore, Jr. returns again and again to issues relating to the 'apparent' or 'supposed' political docility of the Indian peasantry. As his hedging modifiers suggest, Moore questions the reliability of this stereotype and argues that 'There *is* revolutionary potential among the Indian peasants.' Moore also builds a much more sophisticated argument for the hegemonic functions of the caste system than the rather cursory dismissal of his work by South Asian specialists would lead one to expect, an argument that incorporates, with much caution, the karma/acceptance of misery connection that so many authors take for granted. But as Moore points out, his inclusion of India among his cases of social upheaval was prompted by the exceptional nature of the course of development in the subcontinent. India provides him with a negative case, where the peasantry displays little of the rebelliousness that movements and regimes in other areas must harness or quell. Moore sees the Indian peasantry, past and present, as stasis-prone, inefficient, self-repressive and ultimately co-opted by Gandhi's non-violent and non-revolutionary approach to decolonization. He remarks on the low level of violent resistance on the part of the Indian peasantry, despite their 'appalling misery', and concludes that 'evidence of [the peasantry's] submissiveness' and 'willing acceptance of personal degradation' is 'overwhelming'. Moore finds the record of peasant risings in India 'unimpressive' when compared to China.[11] If a budding student of peasant protest were not already predisposed to do so, Moore's view of the South Asian peasantry as self-repressed, myopic, fatalistic and easily co-opted would most likely prod him or her to move on to other areas where peasant behaviour exhibited the resistance and rebellion that were widely (usually implicitly) accepted as the norm.

Admittedly, the near exclusion of South Asianists from the growth industry of peasant protest studies in the 1960s and 1970s was to some extent self-inflicted. In their writings and innumerable conference and seminar papers, South Asian specialists stressed the complexity and uniqueness of the type of society and culture system that had developed in the subcontinent. Most argued, ironically mirroring the assumptions of comparativists like Moore and Welch, that caste was the key variable behind a pattern of social organization and ritual performance that had no counterpart elsewhere. Both implicitly and explicitly, the comparability of Indian case examples to those drawn from areas beyond the South Asian cultural zone was questioned or its very possibility denied. At the same time, comparativists like Barrington Moore, Jr., who dared to venture into the Indianists' terrain, were almost invariably dismissed for their failure to appreciate the subtleties and inner workings of the caste-based Indian social order. With few exceptions, perhaps most notably Burton Stein who made extensive and imaginative use of the work of African anthropologists on segmentary societies in his own work on patterns of state and society building in South India,[12] South Asianists took little note of the analytical approaches developed by scholars working in other areas. References to Van Gennep, Turner or Lévi-Strauss, much less Braudel, Foucault or Geertz, are rare in their publications. Though these authors were presumably read by South Asianists, most assumed that the noncaste case evidence of scholars working in other culture areas was not comparable and their theoretical insights not applicable given the unique characteristics of South Asian social systems.

Beginning with the presupposition of South Asia's exceptionalism, a number of approaches developed either to account for the low level of social protest in the subcontinent or to explore the implications of its highly developed systems of social control for modes of human social organization more generally. One of the boldest of the latter was explored in the work of Louis Dumont and his disciples.[13] Though Dumont saw Indian caste organization as the most extreme and ritually-burdened of systems of human social division, he used it to advance comparative analysis by arguing that the rationalization and acceptance of hierarchy, which it had carried to the extreme, was in fact the norm in human social history. By contrast, the idealization of equality and the premium placed on mobility in Western societies in recent centuries was a new and aberrant development. Dumont's discussion of the structure and workings of the caste hierarchy not only offered an explanation of the high degree of social control he believed to be characteristic of

South Asian peoples, it implicitly accounted for the low level of protest among long subjugated and exploited groups like the untouchables and tribal peoples who were being incorporated into the caste order.

Another way of accounting for the apparently low level of social conflict in South Asia was pioneered by a succession of studies exploring the dynamics of caste factions and their on-going contests for control over resources and local influence.[14] Though practitioners of this approach did not themselves relate their findings to the issues of the level and modes of peasant protest in South Asia, their emphasis on vertical rather than horizontal cleavages and social struggle between patron–client (jajman–kamin) systems, rather than class strata, suggested that social divisions were no less pronounced in rural India than in other peasant societies; they simply took different forms. The emphasis on factional contest over class conflict was in turn incorporated into the writings of some of the most pro-minent members of the 'Cambridge school' of South Asian historians.[15] Opportunism and rivalries between caste factions dominated by local notables are seen as the keys both to the consolidation of British power in the subcontinent and to the emergence of nationalist political alternatives. The Gandhian non-violence stressed by Moore and others recedes in impor-tance as an explanation for the alleged passivity of the Indian peasantry. Though again explicit links to the literature of social protest are rarely made, the dynamics of the local power struc-ture takes precedence and the frustrations and aspirations of the cultivating classes are channelled into inter-factional contests for social pre-eminence and political advantage.

A very different approach to the history of social protest in South Asia was pioneered by historians like S. B. Chaudhuri, who rejected the view that Indian peasants rarely rose up in rebellion. In two works, which surveyed incidents of con-frontational or violent resistance to colonial rule in the nine-teenth century,[16] Chaudhuri sought (again implicitly) to establish a place for Indianists in the rebellious peasant main-stream of area studies. After a hiatus of over two decades, Chaudhuri's efforts to demonstrate the high degree of class consciousness and active protest on the part of the South Asian peasantry were taken up in the vastly more sophisticated and more thoroughly researched studies of the group of social scientists identified with the *Subaltern Studies* series. Contributions to the volumes published thus far focus on case studies, as well as on theoretical overviews, involving incidents of confrontational, usually violent, protest in South Asia.[17] Much of the work of the subalternists raises important questions about the predominant view of the passive South Asian peasant.[18] But in countering one myth, the subalternists are in danger of creating another, that violence and confrontation were the dominant modes of response by exploited subordinate groups in South Asia. The relative paucity of the cases of confrontational protest, much less rebellion, that have so far been uncovered, the often small numbers of participants involved and the limited duration of the incidents studied, caution against the adoption of this view. As Gyan Prakash has argued,[19] the subaltern approach also isolates moments of confrontational or violent resistance from the more fundamental, ongoing struggles of subordinate groups to limit, indeed contest, the demands of dominant groups for deference and resources. The view underlying this argument that social systems are not equilibria that are periodically broken by violent assaults, but arenas in which different social groups continually vie for control over status, power and material goods, has been advanced by a number of scholars working on patterns of protest and elite response in recent years.[20]

It would be unfortunate if the confrontational approach to social dynamics in South Asia were embraced by specialists working on the history of the subcontinent at the very point when those studying protest in other areas are beginning to challenge the highly romanticized notion of the rebellious peasant. As the essays in this volume amply demonstrate, for a variety of reasons South Asianists have much to contribute to the very different approaches to protest and resistance that have been developed in recent decades, approaches that give serious attention to systems of social control and modes of contesting power and dominance beyond dramatic and rare instances of overt challenges or violent outbursts.

The avoidance or everyday resistance approach to peasant responses to elite domination owes much to studies of slave societies and those based on enserfed labour. In the early 1970s, the revisionist studies of scholars like Eugene Genovese and Gerald Mullin provided essential correctives to the earlier work of Herbert Aptheker, who had (much like Chaudhuri had done for Indian peasants) attempted to construct a tradition of slave revolution from scattered and slender evidence of risings spread over several centuries.[21] Instead of violent resistance, which, Genovese and Mullin stressed, had occurred but was invariably met with brutal repression, a whole range of non-confrontational slave responses including false deference, cheating, pilfering, and sloth, intentional clumsiness, arson, vandalism, and flight were shown to be the predominant modes of dealing with harsh and restrictive systems of labour control. The findings of scholars working on slave societies corresponded to those of earlier and contemporary studies on serf systems in western Europe and Russia. Rather than openly challenging the lord of the manor or the owner of the estate, serfs preferred to buffer the effects of their demands and gradually erode their exercise of control by smaller, everyday tactics of denial of deference and resources. In times of crisis, serfs, like slaves, preferred flight to violent confrontations, which generally proved as futile and as costly in lives as slave rebellions.[22] Research on modes of protest that did not involve direct confrontation was also prompted by the works of E. J. Hobsbawm on millenarian movements of withdrawal and banditry as a form of rural protest.[23]

Serious attention to alternatives to violent, confrontational protest has been a rather recent development in studies focused on African and Asian societies. Thus far, two related but organizationally and historically quite different configurations of response have been the focus of research and discussion. Anthropologists and political scientists working in contemporary societies have explored the forms of 'everyday resistance'—from mockery and sarcasm to pilfering and arson—that subordinate groups employ to combat the hegemonic claims of landholding or political elites and to counter what are viewed as exploitative demands for taxes or a share of the crop. The work of James Scott in particular has identified a whole range of these protective and retributive measures that raise important questions about the effectiveness of systems of social control and the degree to which underclass groups adhere

to the hegemonic ideologies that are intended to justify them.[24]
For scholars dealing with past situations, for which source
materials on everyday forms of resistance are at best meagre,
other, less ephemeral, modes of response, which have been
characterized as 'avoidance protest', have been the focus of
attention. Flight to sparsely settled frontier areas or the domains
of rival patrons, banditry, formal petitions, 'sit-ins' before the
residences of state officials, as well as clandestine retributive
acts involving crop and implement destruction or arson and
'witchcraft', have been the focus of an increasing number of
works in the past decade or so.[25] These modes of defence and
protest are far more dramatic and dangerous than everyday
acts of defiance and retribution and much more disruptive,
even dangerous, for the social systems in which they occur.

Though everyday resistance received little notice from social
scientists working on South Asia in the first decades after independence, modes of avoidance protest were treated in a
number of early works, most notably and extensively in Irfan
Habib's path-breaking study of the Indian peasantry under
Mughal rule.[26] A heightened interest in patterns of social
interaction and political organization at the local and regional
level, in part inspired by the work of the Cambridge school, led
in the late 1970s to important discoveries of the widespread
resort to collusion between village notables and rural officials
in the falsification of records, underreporting, and concealment
as modes of resistance to the revenue demands of the British
colonizers.[27] Works on agrarian conditions in different areas
and on grass-roots support for nationalist organizations also
dealt with incidents of peasant flight, banditry or clandestine
reprisal.[28] In each of the instances cited, the study of peasant
defences and non-violent modes of resistance to elite demands
and techniques of political mobilization yielded valuable insights into the systems of social stratification and subordination
that gave rise to these peasant responses.

As these examples suggest, important work has been done
in recent years on non-confrontational protest in South Asia.
But almost all the research and thinking on avoidance responses has been case specific, little concerned with the bearing
of the events in question on broader theoretical problems relating to subordination and resistance, and oblivious to work on

these patterns in other geographical areas. Like work done in other areas, studies of non-confrontational protest in South Asia have been focused almost exclusively upon contests between peasant groups of different social strata or between cultivators and the agents of the precolonial and colonial state.[29]

The nature of previous work on everyday resistance and avoidance protest in both South Asia and elsewhere underscores some of the most significant contributions of the essays in the present volume. These studies of everyday and avoidance resistance expand our approaches to these phenomena in numerous ways. Most obviously, they extend the scope of our investigations in many directions beyond the peasant groups which were the main concern of these who first explored non-confrontational forms of resistance.[30] Some of the essays explore hitherto neglected forms of everyday resistance and modes of avoidance response among non-peasant social groups, including women (O'Hanlon, Oldenburg), merchants (Haynes), and urban workers (Chandavarkar). It is noteworthy, I think, that half of the contributions to the collection are devoted to resistance and protest in urban settings. The essays that deal with everyday resistance or more extensive forms of protest in more familiar rural settings add new dimensions to our approach to issues in this sphere: Dirks emphasizes the importance of ritual rivalries in factional and inter-village contests; Prakash stresses the importance of ancestral myths and legends in defining subordinate and superordinate status; and Rogers shows the ways in which a pastime like gambling can become a vehicle for resistance by townsmen and rural cultivators to hegemonic ideas and the extension of state control. The studies of Haynes and Prakash reach into the precolonial past, painstakingly reconstructing, from sparse and difficult source materials, long-standing techniques employed by subordinate groups to contest the demands of dominant elites.

In encompassing new groups, extended time periods, and the ritual and ideological dimensions of everyday resistance and avoidance protest, the collection as a whole greatly expands the research agenda for all who are working on ongoing and non-confrontational responses of subordinate groups to their subjugation and exploitation. For South Asianists, it signals a shift which is clearly apparent in recent monographs on South

Asian history and anthropology: the extensive and fruitful application of theories and analytical approaches formulated by scholars working in other geographical areas. Though caution needs to be exercised in appropriating too readily paradigms or concepts worked out in response to very different social and cultural contexts, many of the studies in the present volume suggest that the isolation of South Asianists has given way to a heightened awareness of, and receptivity to, work in other areas. Coming at a time when we are beginning to realize the importance of cross-cultural and comparative analysis, these trends may well give South Asianists a central role in the testing and formulation of ideas relating to protest in its more typical non-confrontational guise. Not only are the sources available to the South Asianist on these patterns among the richest and best preserved on any non-Western area, but the study of everyday or avoidance protest necessarily places emphasis on symbolic and physical systems of social control and rituals of dominance and deference, which are found in South Asia in a variety, complexity and abundance unmatched by any other area. The realization that rebellions and revolutions are rare occurrences calls into question the assumptions that South Asia is atypical or unique. From a perspective which views resistance and protest as ongoing, constantly reworked, predominantly non-violent, and preferably non-confrontational components of evolving social systems, South Asian examples may well tell us a great deal about what the norm is.

Of the many ideas and insights contained in the essays in *Contesting Power*, several have a special bearing on the ways in which we approach the study of everyday resistance and avoidance protest. The often limited returns accruing to groups who resort to the modes of everyday resistance or avoidance protest discussed in these studies caution against another sort of romanticization, against overstating the extent to which these responses can ameliorate the plight of the exploited and permit them to punish their oppressors. Though the Bhuinyas may receive satisfaction from their bards' retelling of the mythical tales that chronicle the origins of their subjugations, they remain nonetheless the despised and unclean drudge labourers of high-caste groups. The 'matinée shows' of courtesans of Lucknow may mock and invert 'accepted' gender roles and

sexual practices, but the women who find some escape in these
entertainments continue to be commoditized and used by their
clients. Tarabai Shinde, who dared publish a tract protesting
the degradation of Hindu widows, lived the rest of her life in
isolation, the butt of children's taunts and the censorious remarks of the self-appointed defenders of 'polite' society. As
these examples indicate, the efficacy of everyday resistance and
avoidance protest ought not to be overestimated. Though they
may win temporary respite from oppressive demands or give
those who resort to them a sense of being able to strike back at
their exploiters, however feebly, in the long term they serve to
perpetuate the systems of domination in which they are employed. They make the insufferable endurable, and channel
into subterfuge and symbolic reprisal indignation and hostility
that might otherwise be directed toward modes of protest
which have the potential to force fundamental transformations
in the relationships between subordinate and superordinate
groups.

Taken together, the essays demonstrate that ongoing contests
for power, material resources and deference occur at all social
levels and sectors. They are as fundamental to gender relationships as to the interaction between different caste and class
groups. As Gyan Prakash stresses (pp. 145–74), counter-myths
and modes of resistance are integral parts of hegemonic ideologies and systems of social control. They arise and evolve with
systems of domination, which are not imposed wholecloth from
above, but constructed piecemeal through interaction over long
periods of time—interaction involving demands and testing,
claims and concessions on the part of both subordinate and
superordinate groups. This ongoing process of negotiating the
terms and recasting the rhetoric of domination and subordination is best illustrated by Douglas Haynes's survey of the
responses of the merchants of Surat over several centuries to a
succession of political overlords, regional officials and nationalist challengers to the British colonizers.[31] Haynes's studies,
as well as the essay by Nicholas Dirks, also suggest that techniques of everyday resistance and avoidance defence are not
the exclusive preserve of oppressed groups on the lowest rung of
the social ladder. They can be employed by local notables and
well-to-do townspeople to protest the excessive demands of the

state or regional administrative officials, or to gain the upper hand in the factional struggles and inter-village and peer group rivalries that are dominant forces in local political life.

As virtually all the contributions to the volume remind us, subordinate groups play an active role in the construction and continuing reformulation of the systems of social control, rituals of deference, and hegemonic ideologies that do so much to define the conditions under which they live. Modes of resistance and (usually covert) defiance and counter-ideologies are inherent parts of that process of construction and reformulation. In this sense, the widely-employed approach to Gramsci's admittedly amorphous notion of hegemony distorts the realities of dominance and subordination. Social control is always contested; deference is always hedged; there are always myths and proverbs, legends and moral convictions, that challenge the validity of ideologies of dominance.

From this perspective, violent protest can be seen not as an abrupt or episodic outburst of social conflict, but the result of the breakdown of the ongoing negotiations; the failure of the defensive and everyday retributive mechanisms developed by subordinate groups to contain the demands or respond to the excesses of the dominant. Revolutions occur in the relatively rare situations when these breakdowns are so severe and widespread that they undermine the very systems in which they occur. Metaphorically, they shatter the arenas in which the defences and modes of response have been devised to buffer the persistent contests between different social groups. Rebellion then is on the far end of a continuum of responses to oppression and exploitation that extends from everyday reactions like grumbling, work slowdowns, and cursing the overseer behind his back to more organized and disruptive measures such as flight and banditry. All are embedded in ongoing and mutable systems of domination and subordination that shape gestures of deference and modes of defiance, estimates of fair play, and myths explaining the origins of injustice.

NOTES

1. Marx's classic, and often quoted, formulation can be found in Marx and Engels, *On Colonialism* (Moscow: n.d.), pp. 36–7.
2. Nor is it mentioned, except in passing, in works like John Walton's, *Reluctant Rebels* (New York: 1984) or Gerard Chaliand's, *Revolution in the Third World* (New York: 1977).
3. Excluding Burma, one of James Scott's main cases, which historically lies outside the South Asian cultural zone. See Scott, *The Moral Economy of the Peasant* (New Haven: 1976) and Samuel Popkin, *The Rational Peasant: The Political Economy of Rural Society in Vietnam* (Berkeley: 1979).
4. See, for example, Paul R. Greenough, 'Indulgence and Abundance as Asian Peasant Values: A Bengali Case in Point', *Journal of Asian Studies*, 42/4 (1983), pp. 831–50; Arjun Appadurai, 'How Moral is South Asia's Economy—A Review Article', *JAS*, 43/3 (1984), pp. 481–98, and the studies reviewed therein, and Michael Adas, 'The Moral Economy and Peasant Responses to Commercialization in South Asia', *Proceedings of the Pennsylvania South Asia Seminar* (Philadelphia: 1987).
5. *Agrarian Revolution* (London: 1975).
6. Boston: 1960, p. 9.
7. *Anatomy of a Rebellion* (Albany, New York: 1980), p. 11.
8. Ibid., pp. 52–3.
9. See, for example, Kathleen Gough, 'Brahmin Kinship in a Tamil Village', *American Anthropologist*, 58/4 (1956), pp. 826–53; Gerald Berreman, 'The Brahminical View of Caste', *Contributions to Indian Sociology*, n.s., 5/1 (1971), pp. 16–23; and especially Joan Mencher, 'The Caste System Upside Down, or the Not-So-Mysterious East', *Current Anthropology*, 15/4 (1974), pp. 469–93. For case evidence that indicates that some of the ideas assumed by Welch to have been enlisted in the service of social control did permeate to the lowest castes, see Michael Moffat, *An Untouchable Community in South Asia* (Princeton: 1979).
10. Welch, *Anatomy*, p. 56.
11. *Social Origins of Dictatorship and Democracy: Lord and Peasant in the Making of the Modern World* (Boston: 1966), esp. pp. 334–40, 369, 379, 382–5.
12. See, for example, 'The Segmentary State in South Indian History', in Richard G. Fox (ed.), *Realm and Region in Traditional India* (Durham, North Carolina: 1977); and his seminal work, *Peasant State and Society in Medieval South India* (Delhi: 1980).
13. See especially Dumont, *Homo Hierarchicus: The Caste System and Its Implications* (London: 1970).
14. Two of the classics of this genre are Oscar Lewis, *Village Life in Northern India* (New York: 1965) and André Beteille, *Caste, Class, and Power: Changing Patterns of Stratification in a Tanjore Village* (Berkeley: 1971).
15. This process is particularly apparent in the earlier of the detailed regional studies by the proponents of this approach. See, for example, David Washbrook, *The Emergence of Provincial Politics: The Madras*

Presidency, 1870–1920 (Cambridge: 1976); and Christopher J. Baker, *The Politics of South India, 1920–1937* (Cambridge: 1976).

16. *Civil Disturbances during the British Rule in India* (Calcutta: 1955); and *Civil Rebellion in the Indian Mutinies, 1857–9* (Calcutta: 1957).

17. The series editor Ranajit Guha has, of course, in his own contributions and larger work on *Elementary Aspects of Peasant Insurgency in Colonial India* (Delhi: 1983), done much to set the agenda for the school as a whole.

18. However, the fact that many of Guha's case examples and his contributions to the series are drawn from incidents of conflict occurring in hill and forest or non-tribal areas, where the institutions and rituals of the caste hierarchy were weak or marginal, might be interpreted by the advocates of the passive South Asian peasant school as confirming some of their central arguments.

19. 'Empowered Resistance and Contested Power in South Asia: The State of Its Historiography', unpublished essay, pp. 3–6.

20. For a highly theoretical statement of this approach, see Charles Tilly, *From Mobilization to Revolution* (Reading, Mass: 1978). See also his application to specific French examples in 'Routine Conflicts and Peasant Rebellions in Seventeenth-Century France', in Robert P. Weller and Scott Guggenheim (eds), *Power and Protest in the Countryside* (Durham, N.C.: 1982) and *The Contentious French* (Glencoe, Illinois: 1988). For Asian examples, see Adas and Scott, discussed below.

21. Aptheker's perspective was argued in *American Negro Slave Revolts* (New York: 1943). For Genovese, see *Roll, Jordan, Roll* (New York: 1972), esp. book four; and Mullin, *Flight and Rebellion: Slave Resistance in Eighteenth-Century Virginia* (Oxford: 1972). For a superb recent work that represents a continuation of this corrective approach to the rebellious slave myth, see Michael Craton, *Testing the Chains: Resistance to Slavery in the British West Indies* (Ithaca, New York: 1982).

22. See, for example, Jerome Blum, *Lord and Peasant in Russia* (Princeton: 1961), esp. chapter fourteen; and Rodney Hilton, *Bond Men Made Free* (New York: 1973).

23. *Social Bandits and Primitive Rebels* (London: 1959) and *Bandits* (New York: 1969).

24. See especially *Weapons of the Weak* (New Haven, Conn.: 1985). For further examples drawn from contemporary Southeast Asia, see the contributions by Turton, White, Fegan and Kerkvliet in Scott and Kerkvliet (eds), *Everyday Forms of Peasant Resistance in South-east Asia* (London: 1986). For African examples of many of these patterns, see Allen Isaacman, Stephen Michael, et al., 'Cotton is the Mother of Poverty', *International Journal of African Studies*, 13/4 (1980).

25. For Asian examples see Michael Adas, 'From Avoidance to Confrontation: Peasant Protest in Precolonial and Colonial Southeast Asia', *Comparative Studies in Society and History*, 23/2 (1981); and 'From Foot-dragging to Flight: The Evasive History of Peasant Avoidance Protest in South and South-east Asia', in Scott and Kerkvliet, *Everyday Forms of Peasant Resistance*, pp. 64–86. For case studies from Africa, see Allen

Isaacman, *The Tradition of Resistance in Mozambique* (Berkeley: 1976) and Donald Crummey (ed.), *Banditry, Rebellion and Social Protest in Africa* (London: 1986).

26. *The Agrarian System of Mughal India* (Bombay: 1963). These patterns are also treated in Ravinder Kumar, 'The Rise of the Rich Peasants in Western India', in D. A. Low (ed.), *Soundings in South Asian History* (Berkeley: 1968), and Blair Kling, *The Blue Mutiny: The Indigo Disturbances in Bengal, 1859–62* (Philadelphia: 1966).

27. The work of Clive Dewey has been particularly important with regard to these avoidance measures. See, for example, '*Patwari* and *Chaukidar*: Subordinate Officials and the Reliability of India's Agricultural Statistics', in Clive Dewey and A. G. Hopkins (eds), *The Imperial Impact in Africa and South Asia* (London: 1979). See also P. Robb, 'Hierarchy and Resources: Peasant Stratification in Late-Nineteenth-Century Bihar', *Modern Asian Studies*, 13 (1979); and C. Baker, 'Tamilnad Estates in the Twentieth Century', *Indian Social and Economic History Review*, 13 (1976).

28. See, for example, David Hardiman, 'The Crisis of the Lesser Patidars: Peasant Agitations in Kheda District, Gujarat, 1917–34', in D. A. Low (ed.), *Congress and the Raj* (London: 1977); and Steven Henningham, 'Agrarian Relations in North Bihar', *Indian Economic and Social History Review*, 14 (1979).

29. In the past few years Africanists have given increasing attention to the key roles played by women, especially the so-called market women, in political agitation in the colonial period. In some instances, their activities represented interesting variants of non-violent resistance. See, for example, Judith van Allen, 'Aba Riots or the Igbo "Women's War"? ', in Nancy Hafkin and Edna Bay (eds), *Women in Africa: Studies in Social and Economic Change* (Stanford: 1976).

30. It is notable that most of those who have developed these patterns thus far have done so as a consequence of findings made while researching and writing on agrarian rebellions.

31. These themes are treated even more fully in his *Rhetoric and Ritual in Colonial India* (forthcoming from the University of California Press in the USA, and Oxford University Press in India).

Index

Adas, Michael, vii, 9, 12, 240–2, 267
Aiyanar (deity in South India), 224, 232, 234
Aiyanar festival, 220–2; non-occurrence of, 222–4, 225; possession of *camiyatis* during, 230–6; as site of contestation and conflict, 223–4, 225–8, 233, 235–7
Appadurai, Arjun, 228, 229
Arnold, David, 8
asceticism, as a form of resistance, 46–9
avoidance protest, vii, 5, 9, 34, 49, 240–1, 296–9, 301; among courtesans of Lucknow, 34–5, 49; Gandhi's use of, 275–6; among merchants of Surat, 242–3, 248–52, 253, 256–7, 258, 263–7, 275–6, 284
Awadh, kingdom of, 27, 28, 29, 30, 33, 49, 52, 56–7

Beauvoir, Simone de, 147
Bhuinyas: their history, 145–9; and *kamiauti*, 145, 161–2; marriages among, 145, 160–2; oral traditions of, 16–17, 19, 145–6, 149–68, 169–70, 299, 300; their outcaste status, 149, 157–60, 165
Bombay Mill-Owners' Association, 116, 126, 132, 134
Bombay Textile Labour Union, 131
Bourdieu, Pierre, 215, 217
Breckenridge, Carol, 228, 229
Buddhist revivalism (in Sri Lanka): its influence on attitudes towards gambling, 182–5

Cambridge 'school' of historians, 24, 295, 298
Campbell, G. W. R., 190–1, 194
capitalism, in India, 15–16; *see also* mill-owners
Caroll, Lucy, 66, 75

caste: as a ground of contestation, 6, 157–60, 165, 169; and the classical Hindu theory, 158; its importance in representations of India, 5, 291, 292–3; ranking, 17, 158–9; and 'sanskritization', 72, 149
chaudharayans: in courtesan establishments, 31, 32, 38–9
Chaudhuri, S. B., 295, 297
colonial legal system: as site of resistance, 4, 17, 19, 176, 194–201, 269–70; and women, 66–8; *see also* Hindu law
colonialism: its agenda for urban reform, 18, 19, 28, 261–3, 269; its construction of Hindu 'tradition', 72, 75, 76–8; its efforts to control gambling, 17, 18, 176, 179–82; its efforts to control labour, 132–4; its efforts to control prostitution, 28, 29, 33; its role in constructing gender relations, 14, 19, 65–7, 72–9, 80–1; its use of repression, 132–3, 265–6, 267
Comaroff, Jean, 217, 219
communists, in Bombay, 132–4
courtesans (of Lucknow), 3, 13, 23–60, 300; history of, 26, 27–8, 30–2, 52; homosexuality among, 24, 45–6, 53–5; lifestyle of, 13, 17, 30–1, 46–9, 51–2; *nakhre* of, 28, 43–5, 52, 53–5; recruitment of, 32–8; resistance to colonial controls by, 28; use of *burqa* among, 42–3

Dange, S. A., 102
Das Gupta, Ashin, 253
Davis, Natalie, 215–16, 217
deference: its importance in merchant–state relations, 239, 242, 246–7, 251–2, 257, 259, 270, 283
Desai, Dayalji, 277
Deshmukh, Gopal Hari, 66

merchants: under colonial rule,
259–71; determinants of their
social reputations, 243–4, 255–6;
effects of World War I upon,
271–4; resistance of, 4, 18, 19,
239–40, 247–52, 253, 256–9, 264–7,
268–71, 272, 273–4, 280–1, 301;
under Mughal rule, 245–52; ties to
political overlords, 244–5, 246–7,
254–6, 258, 267–8, 279–80
mill-owners, 15, 109–10; conflicts and
divisions among, 118, 126; their
methods of controlling and disciplining labour, 125–30, 133, 134,
137; *see also* labour; rationalization
Miller, Joseph C., 151, 173
Mirza Hadi Ruswa, 32–3
Mitchell, Timothy, 1
Moore, Barrington, 5, 293
Mughal nobility: during the seventeenth century, 244, 245–52;
during the eighteenth century,
252–9
Mullin, Gerald, 297

non-Brahman politics, 71, 89; and
conceptions of gender, 74, 79, 92;
and widow remarriage, 69, 71–2,
84–5
Non-Co-operation movement
(1920–2), 242, 275, 276–80,
282–3

O'Hanlon, Rosalind, 9
O'Malley, L. S. S., 154
oral traditions: and caste hierarchy,
146–9, 153, 158–60; clichés and
plots, 151–3, 160–2; as performances, 155, 164–5; as resistance,
16–17, 146–8, 153, 159–60, 163–6,
169–70; and the warrior figure,
161–3; versions of, 153–7, 167–8
Orientalism, 6
Ortner, Sherry, 214–15

Paige, Jeffery, 291
Pandit, Vishnushastri, 66, 67

Paraiyars, 227, 230–3
peasantry: and everyday forms of
resistance, 111, 135–6
Phule, Jotirao, 84–5, 89, 102
police: in colonial Sri Lanka, 190–4
popular culture, 16–18, 168–9
Prakash, Gyan, 76, 296
Prarthana Samaj, 82
production relations, 15–16, 137; *see
also* labour; rationalization

Ranade, M. G., 66, 82
rationalization, 109–10, 111–18, 124,
135; resistance to, 4, 15, 110,
118–23; its consequences for
textile workers, 115–16, 117–18
ritual: its role in constituting authority
relations, 229; role-reversals in,
16, 217; as site of resistance, 219,
220, 226, 228–30, 235; traditional
anthropological approaches to,
214–20; *see also* Aiyanar festival
Rowlatt satyagraha, 275, 277
Roy, Rammohan, 66
Roy, S. C., 155

Said, Edward, 72
Saklatwala, S. D., 119, 123
Saraswati, Pandita Ramabai, 68
Sarkar, Sumit, 8
sati, 69, 74
Satyashodak Samaj, 89
Scott, James, vii, 1, 2, 9–11, 12,
50–1, 53, 135, 136, 202, 219, 241,
247, 297
Shinde, Tarabai, 14, 19, 68–9, 79,
89–103, 301; attack on male
representations of women, 94–6,
97–101; critique of male politics
under colonialism, 98–100; critique
of male sexuality, 96–7; inversion
of male representations, 101–2
Steele, Arthur, 65
Stein, Burton, 294
Stones, Fred, 116, 120–1, 122–3
Stri-purusha-tulana, 64, 92–103; its
reception in Maharashtra, 102
strikes, *see* labour